Presidents Creating the Presidency

Presidents Creating the Presidency

DEEDS DONE IN WORDS

Karlyn Kohrs Campbell and Kathleen Hall Jamieson

The University of Chicago Press * Chicago and London

KARLYN KOHRS CAMPBELL is professor of communication studies at the University of Minnesota. KATHLEEN HALL JAMIESON is the Elizabeth Ware Packard Professor of Communication at the Annenberg School for Communication and Walter and Leonore Annenberg Director of the Annenberg Public Policy Center at the University of Pennsylvania.

The University of Chicago Press, Chicago 60637
The University of Chicago Press, Ltd., London
© 1990, 2008 by The University of Chicago
All rights reserved. Published 2008
Printed in the United States of America

17 16 15 14 13 12 11 10 09 08   2 3 4 5

ISBN-13: 978-0-226-09220-1 (cloth)
ISBN-13: 978-0-226-09221-8 (paper)
ISBN-10: 0-226-09220-8 (cloth)
ISBN-10: 0-226-09221-6 (paper)

Library of Congress Cataloging-in-Publication Data

Campbell, Karlyn Kohrs.
    Presidents creating the presidency : deeds done in words / Karlyn Kohrs Campbell and Kathleen Hall Jamieson.
        p. cm.
    Includes bibliographical references and index.
    ISBN-13: 978-0-226-09220-1 (cloth : alk. paper)
    ISBN-10: 0-226-09220-8 (cloth : alk. paper)
    ISBN-13: 978-0-226-09221-8 (pbk. : alk. paper)
    ISBN-10: 0-226-09221-6 (pbk. : alk. paper)
    1. Rhetoric—Political aspects—United States. 2. Political oratory—United States. 3. Presidents—United States—Language. I. Jamieson, Kathleen Hall. II. Title.
    PN239.P64C36 2008
    808'.066352—dc22

                                                    2007031668

To the women who should have been president;
To the women who tried to be president;
To the women who will be president.

Contents

Preface

We have been thinking together about genre since 1976, when we co-organized a conference on the topic. That seminar produced our first collaborative work on what we at the time described as "constellations." This book had its origins in the happy times we shared while writing our textbook, *Interplay of Influence*, now in its sixth edition, and this book's ancestor, *Deeds Done in Words*. Much of what we have written here emerged from our mutual interest in the role played by types of rhetoric in creating and sustaining long-lived institutions such as the Roman Catholic papacy, the British monarchy, and the U.S. presidency.

We have many debts. The first is to each other. Unlike many coauthors, we have never been on a faculty together. We cherish the shared spaces we have found in places as disparate as a convent in St. Louis and offices at the East-West Center in Hawaii and at the universities we have at various times called home. In the years before the Internet, our late-night calls all but ensured that those invested in Ma Bell would do well.

We are indebted as well to our students and to our colleagues at the University of Minnesota and the University of Pennsylvania. We appreciate the support of these institutions and, in particular, of ambassadors Walter and Leonore Annenberg and the Annenberg Foundation. We offer special thanks to Jeffrey Tulis of the University of Texas and David Zarefsky of Northwestern University for their detailed comments on earlier drafts of this manuscript. We are grateful to our editor, John Tryneski, for his good humor and wise counsel. Miriam White, Josh Gesell, and Jeff Gottfried served ably as our footnote checkers. Jeff played a particularly important role.

Chapter 2 is a revision of an essay originally published in *Presidential Studies Quarterly* 15 (1985): 394–411; chapter 3 is a revision of an essay originally published in the *Quarterly Journal of Speech* 68 (1982): 146–57. We thank them for permission to reprint this material.

The influence of Paul Newell Campbell persists, although he is now with us only in spirit.

These and many others have made this a better book; any errors of fact, logic, and proportion are our own.

ONE

Introduction: The Rhetorical Presidency

The assumption that the U.S. government as it exists today was present in embryonic form when the Constitution was ratified is an easy one, but false. When Benjamin Franklin told the delegates at the end of the Constitutional Convention that he was now convinced that the sun depicted on the back of George Washington's chair was rising, not setting, he was reflecting real doubts that he and the other framers had felt about the future of the political experiment on which the nation was embarking. Because the Constitutional Convention essentially upended the Articles of Confederation, under which the country had functioned to that point, it was the founders' second attempt to institutionalize the concepts underlying democracy.

What they created followed no prior blueprint; rather, it was a unique amalgam of innovations extracted from experience in colonial and state governments, British precedents, and the conceptions of theorists who had written about the nature of governance. In his 1797 inaugural address, John Adams characterized the Constitution "as the result of good heads prompted by good hearts, as an experiment better adapted to the genius, character, situation, and relations of this nation and country than any which had ever been proposed or suggested."[1] One aspect of this anomalous and unprecedented institution that enabled it to survive is the subject of this book.

Through foresight and serendipity, the founders created a structure ordered by general and interlocking functions in which much was unspecified and, hence, could be negotiated through interaction among the three branches of government; that is, through processes infused with rhetoric. As a consequence, what came into existence was a complex set of interrelated institutions capable of maintaining themselves and at the same time flexible enough to incorporate the changes required by circumstance.

The U.S. Constitution nowhere refers to "the presidency," only to the president or to the executive as one of the three branches of government. What we now understand as the presidency has come into being as a result of the actions of all our presidents, a process in which rhetorical practices have been of particular importance. As it now exists, the presidency is an amalgam of roles and practices shaped by what presidents have done. At any given moment, an awareness of these roles and capacities shapes the practices of the incumbent.

From our perspective, the institutions of our government constitute an experiment in rhetorical adaptation in which the initiatives of any one branch can be modified and refined by the reactions of the others, and in which the flaws or idiosyncrasies of any one branch at any given time can be accommodated by action in the others. The moments that signal expansion and contraction of the executive are often marked by rhetoric. One early instance in which the power of the presidency was expanded by rhetorical assertion occurred the first time a vice president ascended to the presidency. John Tyler was notified that William Henry Harrison had died when he received a message addressed to "John Tyler, Vice-President of the United States."[2] The Constitution does not say that the vice president becomes the president upon being sworn in after the death of the president. Article 2, section 1 says only that if the office becomes vacant, "the Powers and Duties ... shall devolve on the Vice President." When Tyler's inaugural address was published, it was under his title as president. Similarly, he signed his papers "John Tyler, President of the United States."[3] In effect, he assumed the office as well as the powers and duties of the presidency by asserting that they were his.

Accordingly, it is vital to study the presidency from its beginnings in order to identify the assertion of powers and the rationalization of those powers that occurs retrospectively. Washington's avoidance of monarchical practices set precedents followed by his successors. Andrew Jackson substantially enlarged the executive veto power by asserting that, unlike members of Congress, he represented the whole people, and by urging that all three branches should assess the constitutionality of policies. Subsequently, Jackson's protégé, James Polk, who was Speaker of the House throughout much of Jackson's presidency, provided in his fourth and last annual message a detailed rationale for the executive veto as a part of the complex system of checks and balances of our system of government.[4]

Although the assertion of presidential prerogatives relies on the rhetorical practices of each president's predecessors, executive power has grown in fits and starts, consolidated as it is appropriated by successors and accepted by the other branches of government or, conversely, curtailed by the Supreme Court and Congress. When, for example,

Harry Truman assumed the right to take over the steel mills in early 1952, he asserted his right to do so in a speech to the nation, among other places. When the Court ruled in *Youngstown Steel v. Sawyer* that the president had overstepped his constitutional authority, that moment, too, was marked rhetorically. In the most important of the opinions offered by the majority, Justice Robert H. Jackson noted that because Congress had considered granting Truman this power and decided to withhold it, the president's claim was constitutionally unjustified.

Presidential war powers were first used carefully by James Madison in the War of 1812, a war that aroused considerable dissent. These powers were expanded by Polk in the Mexican War, but they were ultimately curtailed by the appropriating power of Congress, which was also a factor in ending the war in Vietnam in 1974.[5] Abraham Lincoln's expanded uses of the powers of the commander in chief of the armed forces to fight the Civil War now are referenced as precedents by George W. Bush.

Throughout its history, as these examples illustrate, the U.S. government has been a delicately interdependent system, and governance has been a dance among the three branches choreographed in broad movements by the Constitution. In Federalist no. 49, James Madison wrote that "the several departments being perfectly co-ordinate by the terms of their common commission, neither of them, it is evident, can pretend to an exclusive or superior right of settling the boundaries between their respective powers."[6]

The Constitution spells out the powers of the three branches of government. The legislative branch is established in article 1, section 1: "All legislative Powers herein granted shall be vested in a Congress of the United States, which shall consist of a Senate and House of Representatives." Article 2, section 1 establishes the executive branch: "The executive Power shall be vested in a President of the United States of America." The same article prescribes that "[b]efore he enter on the Execution of his Office, he shall take the following Oath or Affirmation—'I do solemnly swear (or affirm) that I will faithfully execute the Office of the President of the United States, and will to the best of my Ability, preserve, protect and defend the Constitution of the United States.'" Article 2, section 2 declares that "[t]he President shall be the Commander in Chief of the Army and Navy of the United States, and of the Militia of the several States, when called into the actual Service of the United States." The power "[t]o declare War," however, resides with Congress.[7] Article 2, section 3 says that the president "shall take Care that the Laws be faithfully executed." Article 3, section 1 establishes the judicial branch: "The judicial Power of the United States shall be vested in one supreme Court, and in such inferior Courts as the Congress may from time to time ordain and establish."

What these provisions mean in practice has been decided on a case-by-case basis in the push and pull of rhetoric by and among those speaking for the three branches of government. When a right was asserted by one branch and that assertion was permitted to stand, it gradually came to be assumed, and as such had the capacity to be a starting premise in subsequent contests between the branches.

The first strong assertion of the power of the Court, for example, came in *Marbury v. Madison*[8] in 1803, when Chief Justice John Marshall wrote, "[I]t is emphatically the province and duty of the judicial department to say what the law is." What Marshall was affirming was not the primacy of judicial interpretation, but the right of the judiciary to come to independent conclusions about the law and the Constitution. In the contest between Court and president, an early instance of presidential assertion occurred when Andrew Jackson refused to enforce the Supreme Court's ruling in the Cherokee Nation case.[9]

That the rhetorical types through which this interacting system works have emerged in usage and through give-and-take between the three branches is easily illustrated. George Washington, for example, interpreted that section of the Constitution ordinarily read as mandating the State of the Union message as requiring an inaugural address.[10] In response to early State of the Union messages, Congress issued obsequious speeches in reply, imitating British parliamentary responses to the Speech from the Throne; these were soon dropped, however, as inconsistent with democratic government.[11] Custom, not the Constitution, determines that State of the Union addresses are delivered at the opening session of Congress; changing conceptions of the presidential role have made their delivery sometimes written, sometimes oral. Washington's proclamation of neutrality, despite a treaty that pledged the nation to support France against England, was an opening move in the interaction among the branches that redefined presidential war powers. Only through congressional debate between a president's accusers and defenders, modified by presidential self-defense rhetoric and influenced by Supreme Court opinions, has Congress reached a temporary consensus about what constitutes an impeachable offense by a president. Only through enunciation in proclamations and accompanying remarks has some agreement emerged about the appropriate timing and justifications for presidential pardons. In and through the exercise

of the veto, presidents have come to assert an executive role in the legislative process. As presidents have come to address the citizenry more
frequently, intensifying the need for a transition allowing the public to
see their former leaders as ordinary citizens, the farewell address in the
final days of a presidency has become customary, although it originated
with George Washington. The effect of earlier presidential rhetoric on
the discourse of subsequent presidents is illustrated by presidential war
rhetoric, in which the lines of argument available and the timing of its
appearance, although not the essential form, have been strongly influenced by precedents.

The Constitution permits varying levels of discretionary power in
rhetorical action and provides for varying degrees of rhetorical effect.
A presidential pardon may be issued without consultation; its effect is
immediate and not subject to any form of appeal or review. The initiatives described in a State of the Union address may evoke legislative action from Congress, or the executive's proposals may languish. A veto
message invites reconsideration; it may end a legislative initiative or, if
sufficient legislative resolve exists, lead to reassertion of the legislative
will. As an illustration of this process, recall that Congress can attach
conditions to executive implementation of a specific policy, as it did
during the administration of Herbert Hoover. Or the Court can declare
a legislative veto unconstitutional, as it did during the administration
of Jimmy Carter; a president and Congress can then negotiate informal
agreements that perform a similar function, as they did early in the first
Bush administration in a compromise permitting continued humanitarian aid to the Nicaraguan Contras. Presidents can claim the right to
ignore provisions in legislation they have just signed; when they make
this move in what we call the de facto item veto (see chapter 8), Congress can consider and may enact legislation to give itself standing to
have this process of exception taking reviewed in court. In other words,
the Constitution offers presidents a wide range of powers while giving
other branches powers that circumscribe them.

The Constitution allows similar rhetorical latitude to the other
branches. As illustrated dramatically in *Marbury v. Madison,* the Supreme Court creates itself and defines its powers through its opinions.
It is a venue in which executive and legislative powers are negotiated in
suits before the Court. In turn, through advice and consent on appoint-
ments and through legislation, the limits of its powers are continually
renegotiated with the president and Congress. Similarly, Congress asserts its powers and justifies them rhetorically, and the president and

the Court respond to its initiatives, now extending and now decreasing what it is permitted to do. As we note frequently, there has been a highly visible, ongoing struggle for power between the executive and legislative branches, with now the president, now Congress, achieving dominance.

Our focus in this book is on one partner in this political fencing match: the presidency. Many books have been written about the U.S. presidency; many more will be written. The allure of the presidency is its influence on domestic and foreign affairs. Presidential rhetoric is one source of executive power, enhanced in the modern presidency by the ability of presidents to speak when, where, and on whatever topic they choose and to reach a national audience through coverage by the electronic media.

This book is about presidential rhetoric. Specifically, it is about the kinds of rhetoric that have come to typify the presidency from the nation's beginnings to the present. In what follows, we look at the presidency as it has emerged through the rhetorical practices of our presidents.

No book could examine all presidential discourse. Because we are attempting to explore the link between rhetoric and the presidency, we examine presidential discourse from our nation's inception to the present, particularly those forms that are grounded in constitutional provisions, entailed in fulfilling the constitutional responsibilities of the executive, or now accepted as customary. Others may wish to explore this link in other forms of presidential discourse, but we have limited our concerns to those rhetorical genres that most clearly illustrate the tie between rhetorical action and the maintenance and development of the presidency. Put differently, the genres analyzed in subsequent chapters are those we see as the structural supports for the edifice of the presidency. Through them, presidents perform functions that are useful, and sometimes essential, to maintaining the powers of the executive.

Because our focus is on the presidency, we are interested in public, not private, discourse. As a result, we ignore private negotiations, presidential correspondence, and communication with White House staff and the members of the cabinet. Because we are interested in the presidency, we limit ourselves to types of discourse that have existed from the beginning, have long histories, or in the case of the two genres we add in this revised and expanded study, the national eulogy and the de facto item veto, whose features seem to us to be uniquely suited to expand presidential power. In general, we view presidents as having carved out genres that mark beginnings and endings, preserve the executive powers of the presidency, adapt it to changing conditions, and promote policy initiatives and respond to them. Most of the rhetorical types we examine were initiated by George Washington. James Madison issued the first speech requesting a declaration of war; John Tyler first responded to a formal accusation that he had violated the oath of office; Andrew Jackson issued the first signing statement that constituted a de facto item veto; Andrew Johnson first responded to articles of impeachment passed by the House of Representatives.[12]

We begin with the assumption that, when articulated by the president, each type becomes special. Only a president can issue a presidential inaugural and, in the process, become "the president"; only a president can issue a pardon and, in so doing, absolve a malefactor of a federal crime; only a president can state objections to a piece of legislation and thereby invite its reconsideration by Congress. The identity of the presidents as spokespersons, fulfilling constitutional roles and exercising their executive power, gives this discourse a distinctive character. In turn, the identity and character of the presidency arise out of such discourse. Moreover, we view the emergence of identifiable genres across time as creating a coherent sense of the presidency that transcends the idiosyncratic use of any one of these genres by any single president. As they recur through time, these forms of rhetorical action become ritualistic; their enactment becomes part of the process through which presidents play their role as the symbolic, as well as the real, head of state.

Presidents address many audiences, but "the people" are always listening. Skillful presidents not only adapt to their audiences, but also engage in transforming those who hear them into the audiences they desire. Presidents have envisioned the public in many different ways, and they have shaped addresses in order to give the people a particular identity.[13] Frequently that identity is a familiar one: presidents often describe the people as peace loving, generous, and democratic. But in some cases, their rhetoric involves dramatic redefinitions.

In his second inaugural address, near the end of the long, difficult, and divisive Civil War, Lincoln saw all Americans as governed by a just God who favored neither side, a perspective that shattered the clichéd assumption that God is always on "our" side. The speech succeeded for the immediate audience to the extent that its members embraced Lincoln's conception of all Americans as sinners being punished by the war for their complicity in creating and sustaining the institution of slavery. Only after constituting the people in such terms could Lincoln call for reconciliation, for attempts "to bind up the nation's wounds." Although disguised as descriptions, such definitions attempt to refashion the way citizens see themselves. Lincoln's speech left a profound legacy because subsequent generations of Americans—both historians and the general public—came to see the Civil War through Lincoln's eyes.[14]

The rhetorical roles of the presidency, as well as the policy implications of presidential language, are evident in such processes. In the words of Murray Edelman, "political language *is* political reality."[15] Indeed, the centrality of rhetoric to presidential power has often been noted. For Fred Greenstein, effective presidential leadership is tied to effective communication.[16] David Zarefsky argues that "from the time that political conflict became a fact of life, presidents needed more power and resources than the Constitution offers, and they found in rhetoric the means at least to narrow if not close the gap."[17]

If an audience conceives itself as caring for others, particularly those less fortunate, and as dedicated to the notion that when individuals cannot care for themselves, the state ought to, then it will favor the kinds of programs championed by Franklin Roosevelt and Lyndon Johnson. By contrast, if the audience sees itself as committed primarily to free enterprise and personal responsibility, it will oppose much of the New Deal and the War on Poverty and favor the Reagan agenda of "getting government off the backs of the people."

In this book we examine the roles that presidents have invited Americans to assume, the people they have asked us to be. When we say that presidents constitute the people, we mean that all presidents have the opportunity to persuade us to conceive of ourselves in ways compatible with their views of government and the world. At the same time, presidents invite us to see them, the presidency, the country, and the country's role in specific ways.

We are concerned here with the rhetoric of a state—of a polis—and, as Aristotle tells us, different systems of government generate different types of discourse.[18] Public discourse reflects the philosophical presuppositions, as well as the structure, of the state in which it is found. In succeeding chapters, for example, we discuss epideictic, or ceremonial, discourse, a form of rhetoric common to all humankind, but we describe its special embodiment in the presidential inaugural address and the national eulogy. We also talk about deliberative, or policy-related, rhetoric, but in the distinctive forms in which it appears in presidential State of the Union addresses, veto messages, and de facto item vetoes.

We refer to the apologia, whose touchstone is Plato's description of Socrates' apologia at his trial, but which takes a special form in the presidential rhetoric of self-defense. In other words, we are concerned with types of presidential discourse that are akin to traditional rhetorical forms, but are given a peculiar shape and character by the presidency and the system of which it is a part.

Our focus is on public communication addressed to citizens or their representatives. Presidents cannot limit their influence to those with whom they can communicate directly and personally. The office entails a public rhetorical role. Public communication is the medium through which the national fabric is woven. The private communication of presidents—to staff, to the cabinet, and to members of Congress—is of considerable interest in understanding the workings of the executive branch and the styles and personalities of individual presidents. Voters, however, do not form their impressions of presidents from private conversations unless, as in the case of Richard Nixon, they become public. Thus, we ignore all private communication, including that between presidents and other world leaders. Similarly, except in the rare instances in which former or future presidents discuss the nature of the office, we limit our analysis to the rhetoric of its occupants.

GENERIC FRAMEWORK

What is unique about our approach is the generic framework we have adopted, which we believe has a special plausibility when applied to presidential rhetoric. Ordinary citizens, journalists, scholars, and politicians routinely refer to presidential speeches as inaugurals, State of the Union addresses, veto messages, war rhetoric, and farewell addresses, for example. Those labels suggest an implicit understanding that each type of speech is somehow distinct, with identifiable features and functions. In this book we argue that the discourses so labeled can be viewed as genres defined by their pragmatic ends and typified by their substantive, stylistic, and strategic similarities.

In two instances, the labels we attach are not in common use. As a result, our embrace of the labels "national eulogy" and "de facto item veto" places a special burden on us to justify the value in seeing the discourses we bundle under these names as generically distinctive. We also assume the obligation to argue that these characterizations offer a more useful way of seeing the elements we identify than alternative designations others have applied.

In the chapters that follow, we explore the characteristics that prompt us to approach presidential discourse as, for example, inaugurals or State of the Union addresses. Substantive, stylistic, and strategic characteristics, however, are not the only elements in this discourse that can be considered. One might also categorize and analyze presidential rhetoric according to its intended audience—Congress, the people, the opposition party, other countries—or according to the leadership style it reflects.[19] But we use the categories we do because, for our purposes, they seem to be the most illuminating. And that is our goal—to find the critical framework that is most enlightening for our purposes. Generic criticism is peculiarly suited to exploring the relationship between rhetorical action and the development and maintenance of the presidency because, as we show, rhetorical form follows institutional function. Indeed, as Adena Rosmarin has argued, "The genre is the critic's heuristic tool," a way of analyzing discourse that is tested by the insights it provides.[20]

In 1978, in the introduction to *Form and Genre: Shaping Rhetorical Action*, we suggested that "a genre is composed of a constellation of recognizable forms bound together by an internal dynamic." We also argued that "[g]eneric exemplars have an internal consistency" and contain elements that imply other elements,[21] and that the elements in a genre "exist in a reciprocal, dynamic relationship" (20). To advance our case, we turned to the papal encyclical, which "presupposes truths of natural law known by God's vicar on earth who interprets and explicates the law":

> This premise dictates a deductively structured document which employs a formal and authoritative tone that is consistent with dogmatic statement. It also entails the use of absolutistic, categorical vocabulary. Encyclicals assume print form because the sort of doctrinal matters addressed require a careful, prepared, precise form of communicating God's will. . . . Each of these elements implies the others. The rhetoric of dogma, for example, cannot be structured inductively without undermining the dogmatic tone and the sense of authority pivotal to the document. One might even argue that the concept of papal authority on certain doctrinal matters entails the form of address which is the encyclical. (21)

One of the insights we gain from this approach is that the structure of some discourses is generically constrained. In the inaugural, for example, presidents must first be invested with the office by the oath taking before they can speak to unify the people. In a national eulogy, presidents must assume the role of national priest before they can assign meaning to the tragic events with which the country is struggling. Presidents must also lead the nation in mourning the deaths before telling the nation how executive action will ensure that the tragedy will not recur. In the farewell, the transition to the role of citizen occurs at the end of the address, not the beginning. Key differences set one genre off from another. The veto is built on reason giving; the de facto item veto is built on an assertion of executive prerogatives.

At that time, we also suggested that the constellations on which we focused were ways of seeing elements in the discourse and their interaction. In a sense beyond the tautological, the regularities we observed were "perceived patterns" (25). Whereas, through convention or instruction, audiences might attach a label such as eulogy to an address, and might legitimately perceive or seek out elements in it consistent with that label, a critic might focus on different elements in the same rhetoric and offer insight into it from that perspective as well.

We do not wish to understate the importance of conventional labels, such as inaugural or farewell address. By affixing such labels, at a minimum, we identify the touchstones against which we assess instances of rhetorical action. Label a piece of presidential discourse a farewell, and Washington's final instructions from the presidency and the summative statement by Dwight Eisenhower come into play. These past addresses can reveal former choices and rhetorical potential and, if they are exemplars of acknowledged excellence, help us to see whether—and if so, why—a subsequent address has fallen short. Knowing what we expect of a farewell makes it possible to see Lyndon Johnson's all but compulsive efforts to turn occasion after occasion in his final months in office into bursts of leave-taking, and George H. W. Bush's parallel efforts to avoid such remarks, as the struggles of a president repudiated by the electorate to summon the resources either to insist that he was leaving a legacy or to make sense of the electorate's rejection of his reelection effort. The contrast between the addresses of Washington and Eisenhower and the rhetoric of Johnson and Bush invites the conclusion that a repudiated president makes the transition to the role of citizen from a more problematic rhetorical position than one who has served out two terms or set down the office while still popular enough to secure reelection. Washington, Eisenhower, and Reagan lay down the presidency; Johnson, Carter, and Bush cannot make the transition to the role of citizen with the same grace and with the assumption that the electorate will nod gratefully as they summarize their legacies and offer advice to future generations. In the rhetoric of repudiated presidents is the unspoken assumption that the advice they wish to offer is this: acknowledge that you have elected the weaker candidate and apologize for rejecting my legacy. They do not go willingly into that goodbye.

What gives coherence to the elements we identify in each genre is the sustaining function that they jointly perform. The connective tissue is performance of the role of president in a situationally appropriate fashion. Within the presidency there are several available roles that presuppose that presidential power. Central among them is the role of national priest, a notion persuasively advanced by Robert Bellah and whose rhetorical incarnations were marked out by Roderick Hart in *The Political Pulpit*.[22] The president takes on a priestly role in the inaugural by representing the nation before God and praying for the nation, especially in the case of an ascendant vice president whose inaugural speech must vacate the office by appropriately memorializing the dead president before he can assume that office himself. Another example is the national eulogy, in which the president leads the nation in a commemorative service before setting forth the actions the government and the country will take to ensure that there is no recurrence of the tragedy that is the subject of his rhetoric. Finally, in the farewell, the president draws on the moral leadership inherent in the role of priest to offer the country advice designed to ensure that it will survive into the future.

As national priest, the president is the custodian of national values, values that are at play in every genre we explore, values embodied in the Constitution but extended beyond it to encompass what we have learned as a nation and memorialized in past presidential discourse. In the inaugural, the president rehearses national values to establish that they will inform this administration, simultaneously unifying the nation around them; this process is repeated in the inaugural segments of ascendant vice presidential speeches. The national eulogy arises because national values have been attacked; those who have died incarnate them and become symbols of the nation. In pardoning, the president has a special role: to recognize those circumstances in which justice must be tempered by mercy. Pardons are justified as acts of healing the body politic at critical moments, such as when a president's actions have led to his resignation or when those who fled the draft during a divisive war need to be reintegrated into the citizenry in order to put that war behind us. Pardoning is a priestly role because these decisions are moral, not legal.

As Bill Clinton's case illustrates, when the president's ability to assume the priestly role can be challenged because he seemingly has failed to live up to his oath of office, he defends himself against impeachment by deploying those same shared values and by arguing that he retains the priestly capacity despite the supposed transgressions. Clinton's example tells us about the link to the priestly role in impeachment; in effect, he was impeached for failing to maintain his role as custodian of national values. Those who argued for his impeachment stressed that his sexual encounters with Monica Lewinsky occurred in, or in the shadow of, the sacred space of the Oval Office. His defenders argued that however deplorable these transgressions might have been, they were not an exercise of presidential authority, which means that you can impeach Clinton the man, but not Clinton the president.

In farewell addresses, presidents assume a priestly role like that of Moses in the book of Deuteronomy as the custodian of values who is able to speak about them from a distinct vantage point. At moments when the presidential role causes controversy, the farewell, as illustrated by Truman's speech, helps the country make sense of the presidency, an understanding echoed in George W. Bush's repeated assertions that, as president, he is the decider. Eisenhower's role as custodian of national values let him talk about the military-industrial complex in unique terms.

The president must be able to speak for the nation—beyond its partisan divisions. The Constitution assigns the president the distinctive role of assessing the state of the nation and the special authority to set priorities—to recommend necessary and expedient legislation. In vetoing, the president speaks for the Constitution and for what is arguably best for the nation.

When military action is initiated, the presidency becomes a role described in article 2, section 2 of the Constitution as "Commander in Chief of the Army and Navy of the United States and of the Militia of the several States, when called into the actual Service of the United States." That investiture occurs under two conditions: (1) when Congress enacts a declaration of war or passes a resolution authorizing military action, such as the Gulf of Tonkin Resolution or the congressional authorization of the 1991 Gulf War, and (2) when the president mobilizes the nation to respond to attack or invasion, illustrated by the investiture of Lincoln during the Civil War and that of Franklin Roosevelt in response to the Japanese attack on Pearl Harbor. The role of commander in chief has been enlarged significantly through executive assertion of that role, as in the invasion of Grenada, justified by the threat posed to U.S. nationals in a speech by Ronald Reagan, and the invasion of Panama, justified in a speech by George H. W. Bush. Currently, as Garry Wills has noted, commander in chief "has become a synonym for 'president,'"[23] a significant expansion of executive power.

Generic criticism has long been widely accepted, yet this critical perspective has proved to be surprisingly easy to misunderstand.[24] "Genre," of course, means "a kind, a sort, a species, a category," and in this book we are concerned with types or categories of presidential rhetoric. That a concept of genre is necessary to any critical consideration of any object, process, or event can easily be demonstrated: if one tries to think about a poem or a political speech without using any terms that refer to kind or relationship to other items, one's thoughts quickly grind to an unpleasant halt. To deal with anything at all without classifying or typing it, without remarking on its similarities or dissimilarities to other like or unlike things, is simply not possible.

On one level, then, all criticism is generic criticism,[25] because even if one magically stumbled on, say, a group of sounds (note that one cannot say "musical sounds" or "linguistic sounds" because those kinds of sounds are genres) that bore no relationship to any other group of sounds, one would immediately have to imagine a category, a genre, into which the newly found sound group could be placed. The first question one would face is simply this: What is a group of sounds of this kind like? If one could say only that these sounds were unlike anything else, the critical effort would die aborning. In its broadest and most general sense, then, genre is a classifying term.

A problem arises, however, as soon as one moves beyond this level to claim that a group of plays is properly regarded as tragedies or presidential addresses as farewells. The problem cannot be better stated than it was by Paul Hernadi: "How can I define tragedy (or any other genre) before I know on which works to base the definition, yet how can I know on which works to base the definition until I have defined tragedy?"[26] The answer is that one cannot "know" in a simple, final sense. No matter what generic scheme one uses to approach, say, presidential addresses, there will always be other ways to approach them. And that is perhaps the first thing generic critics can know. They can know that the critical categories they are using are only one set among many, which is to say, the critic can know that generic classification of literary or rhetorical works "has very little in common with the botanist's or the zoologist's unequivocal classification of species."[27]

The next question is, of course, if we are using a system of critical categorization that is but one among many, how can we claim truth of any sort for our efforts? Our answer is that the truth found in these pages is the same kind of truth with which critics have dealt for centuries. If the use of a particular genre or group of genres proves illuminating, or offers insights otherwise unavailable, then it is true by definition.[28] But it is never the only truth, and it is always a tentative truth, because the critical argument holds only until a better argument is made.[29]

In other words, as a tool in critical analysis, genre has a second, pragmatic meaning. Although generic analysis emphasizes similarities, generic critics are not interested in any and every similarity. Rather, they are interested in those similarities that make works rhetorically absorbing and consequential. In 1776, George Campbell defined rhetoric pragmatically as "that art or talent by which discourse is adapted to its end."[30] Consistent with that conception, a critical use of genre operates pragmatically to consider ends—that is, the functions or purposes of discourse—and means—the strategies of language and argument through which such rhetorical ends can be achieved. In short, generic analysis studies the links between function and form.

A generic perspective applied to the major types of presidential discourse emphasizes continuity within change and treats recurrence as evidence that symbolic institutional needs are at least as powerful as the force of events in shaping the rhetoric of any historical period. Some of these genres have undergone change as their exercise redefined institutional boundaries. Others have remained relatively stable from the time of George Washington to the present, as illustrated by the fundamental continuity of the inaugural. We note the increasing institutionalization of the farewell, a type of presidential discourse that began with Washington and Jackson, and we trace the similarities through time in presidential strategies of self-defense. While taking into account the special circumstances affecting each case, we observe the recurrent patterns in the speeches of those who ascended to the presidency upon the death or resignation of their predecessors.

Our perspective biases us toward continuity and reduces the significance of any single piece of discourse or message. In this revised and expanded study, we have deliberately emphasized rhetorical action as a process in which generic functions are fulfilled over some period in a series of discourses, as illustrated by the public statements of George W. Bush following the events of September 11, 2001, which culminated in a speech in the National Cathedral, followed by an address to Congress that built on the prior discourse to enunciate policy initiatives. Similarly, although inaugural addresses are distinct speeches, they emerge out of a presidential candidate's original announcement, nomination acceptance address, and campaign speeches, a process illustrated clearly in the discursive development of John F. Kennedy as candidate and campaigner into President Kennedy as he inaugurated his administration.

We are interested in characteristics that transcend individual responses to conditions at a particular moment. As a result, we focus on individual addresses only insofar as they are paradigmatic instances of the type we are analyzing or because their deviation from the norm tests the generic perspective we have taken and so requires special comment. Our treatments of such masterpieces as Washington's farewell, Jackson's bank veto, Lincoln's inaugurals, and Lyndon Johnson's speech on ascending to the presidency have as their purpose not the explication of these speeches as such, but rather an understanding of a type of discourse. As masterpieces, these exemplars both illustrate and transcend their genres. Conversely, we examine Jimmy Carter's unsatisfying farewell and Gerald Ford's unsatisfactory remarks accompanying his pardon of Richard Nixon in order to show that performing given institutional functions necessitates the use of particular means.

SPEECHWRITERS

Certain questions are routinely asked of critics of presidential discourse. How can one speak of presidential discourse when, particularly in recent times, such discourse is crafted by speechwriters? How can one know what presidents were trying to accomplish as they chose from among the available means of persuasion? Finally, how can presidential rhetoric be evaluated? In what follows, we address each of these questions briefly.

Since the earliest recorded history, the need to act rhetorically has generated ghostwriters.[31] In the ancient Greek city-states, logographers, such as Antiphon and Isocrates, penned speeches for others to deliver, particularly for citizens who had to act as their own lawyers in the courts.

For a variety of reasons, the U.S. presidency has been no exception to these long-standing precedents. From the outset, ghostwriters have played a significant role in generating and revising presidential discourse. George Washington had a variety of collaborators, including Alexander Hamilton, James Madison, John Jay, and his secretary, David

Humphreys.[32] Hamilton, for example, wrote a draft of Washington's famous farewell, then edited Washington's revised version.[33] Ghostwriters enabled Andrew Jackson to convert "his vigorous but illiterate thoughts into respectable prose."[34] Jackson's important Nullification Proclamation of December 10, 1832, was written by Secretary of State Edward Livingston and bears both their signatures.[35] Secretary of State Martin Van Buren assisted Jackson in preparing the Maysville Road veto message; Amos Kendall, Andrew Jackson Donelson, and Roger B. Taney helped him to prepare the 1832 bank veto message.[36]

Even the most eloquent presidents have been assisted by others. William Seward advised Lincoln on his first inaugural and made a key contribution to its conclusion.[37] Raymond Moley drafted Franklin Roosevelt's first inaugural, and Louis Howe added its most memorable line, "The only thing we have to fear is fear itself."[38] Woodrow Wilson's "neutrality of thought" proclamation of August 10, 1914, was originally drafted by Robert Lansing, a counselor to the Department of State and later secretary of state.[39] Theodore Sorenson's key role in creating the rhetoric of John F. Kennedy is well known, but less well known is John Kenneth Galbraith's invention of one of the memorable antitheses of his inaugural address, "Let us never negotiate out of fear, but let us never fear to negotiate."[40] In other words, ghostwriting has been part and parcel of the presidency throughout its history.

Presidents turn to ghostwriters for a number of reasons. First, presidents need to cast their ideas in careful phrases to avoid misinterpretation, a need that invites critical collaboration. In some instances, they need to transcend their stylistic limitations, as Washington and Jackson, among others, recognized.[41] Finally, on many occasions, presidents wish to incarnate their ideas in words that will move their audiences deeply and live through time, goals that require extraordinary rhetorical acumen. Because the processes through which presidents come to the White House do not ensure that its occupants will have highly developed rhetorical skills, presidents turn to ghostwriters for assistance. In addition, because of the demands of the office, which have increased greatly through our history, presidents may not have the time to compose works to meet rhetorical requirements. These tendencies, present from the outset, have been strengthened by the complexity of the issues faced by modern presidents and by the increased rhetorical demands created by the development of the electronic news media.[42]

Apart from this discussion, we refer to presidential ghostwriting only in passing. As a survey of research on the presidency demonstrates, virtually all presidents have had collaborators in creating their rhetoric. Admittedly, ghostwriting practices have varied, and on occasion, those practices have affected presidential effectiveness. For example, Jimmy Carter's combination of texts from two or more speechwriters had an unfortunate effect on the coherence of his prose.[43] When such practice affects a text that we examine in detail, we note it. Our research, however, suggests that ghostwriting is a given of presidential rhetoric.

A second reason not to focus on the issue of authorship is that, despite the pervasive use of ghostwriters, the institutional constraints of the presidency and of the symbolic functions performed by particular genres have been powerful enough in nearly all cases to negate the stylistic idiosyncrasies of individual presidents.[44] That is illustrated, for instance, in the veto messages of Andrew Johnson discussed in chapter 7. When confronting a deviant example of a genre, however, we consider ghostwriting as a possible explanation.

A third reason we do not investigate ghostwriting is that this study is not an exploration of the psyches of individual presidents. We do not move from discourse to biography, but from discourse to perceptions of the presidency as an institution. Admittedly, such perceptions are filtered through the words of speechwriters, but the perception of the institution as created by the words is our concern, not the characters and personalities of individual presidents.[45]

In that regard, we shall treat the presidency as an aggregate of people, as a corporate entity. From that perspective, an administration encompasses more than a single person, the president. In that sense, the presidency is a syndicate generating the actions associated with the head of state, including those deeds done in words. And whoever the author(s) of those words may be, once uttered, the president takes authorial responsibility for them; the words become an integral part of that presidency. Admittedly, in some instances, the use of various speechwriters has created presidencies that present different faces on different occasions. The Richard Nixon who emerged from the pen of Patrick Buchanan, for example, was different from the Nixon who spoke in the words of Raymond Price or William Safire.[46] Despite such variations, however, a definable rhetorical presidency emerged from the discourse of Richard Nixon, and the same is true of the Franklin Roosevelt who emerged from his "brain trust," the Gerald Ford who sometimes made contradictory statements on succeeding days,[47] and the Jimmy Carter who attempted to stitch together in a single speech the disparate views of Zbigniew Brzezinski and Cyrus Vance.[48] As a result, we proceed on the assumption that the discourse claimed by a president constitutes that presidency as a rhetorical entity and that the discourse claimed by the presidents in aggregate is a basis for drawing conclusions about the institution of the presidency, its rhetorical and political development, and the symbolic functions fulfilled by those who occupy it.

EVALUATING PUBLIC DISCOURSE

Critical evaluation, even from a generic perspective, is complicated because, ultimately, no one can read a speaker's mind to know what was intended in a given message. Even the speaker's own recollections, when available, may deceive. But a grasp of the situation confronting a speaker and knowledge of past responses by those in comparable situations can tell us what that speaker realistically hoped to accomplish. The mandates of the Constitution also guide readings of State of the Union and veto messages. From an amalgam of constitutional and situational resources and constraints, combined with knowledge of traditional responses, one can discover not only what speakers accomplished, but also what they should have been trying to accomplish. Hindsight, of course, is a useful guide because in all the instances we analyze, we know whether or not the speaker benefited from the choices made in a specific situation.

In most instances we can and will document our judgments of presidential speeches with evidence from outside sources, including journalistic commentary, polls, the assessments of historians, and continuing references to concepts or doctrines developed in presidential discourse. In other words, we often use generic analysis to explain generally acknowledged successes or failures.

External measures of effects, however, are an inadequate basis for evaluation. It is extremely difficult to link rhetorical acts and effects causally. An unforeseen event may drastically alter reactions to presidential discourse, creating a climate that distorts response. Rejection by a hostile audience, or adulation from the "party press" or a partisan columnist, means little. Speeches that were highly applauded at the moment of delivery may be reassessed quite differently over time, and sentiments rejected in their time may later be seen as prescient. Moreover, what was once highly effective may be reevaluated when subsequent disclosures reveal relevant facts that were omitted or misrepresented.

A generic perspective warrants two kinds of evaluation. First, it empowers a critic to ask how well an individual work is adapted to achieve its ends, a concern analogous to considering the performance rules for kinds of linguistic acts, such as issuing a command or asking a question. For instance, a generic approach to the presidential inaugural establishes a baseline that enables a critic to explain why Jimmy Carter's 1977 inaugural address was so pedestrian.[49] In addition, a generic perspective facilitates the identification of outstanding examples of a given type, messages that not only fulfill generic functions, but do so in innovative and memorable ways, ways that render them unique rhetorical acts with the power to initiate generic change and to facilitate institutional flexibility. For instance, a generic perspective reveals that Abraham Lincoln's 1861 inaugural both fulfills and transcends formulary functions to respond to the immediate crisis and, as a rhetorical masterpiece, to make an enduring statement about the national union.

When coupled with an institutional focus, generic analysis permits still another level of evaluation. The link between generic and institutional analyses elucidates the ways in which rhetoric can foster institutional goals and enables us to evaluate how well presidents have used rhetoric to sustain the presidency and to adapt it to changing circumstances. Throughout the chapters that follow, we shall use these three levels of analysis and evaluation as we endeavor to demonstrate that the questions generated by a generic perspective and an institutional focus are both compatible and illuminating.

As we shall attempt to show, the aesthetic judgments of presidential discourse that we offer are not simply matters of taste. With an understanding of what is required by the Constitution or implied in executive powers, and with knowledge of speeches whose character has been defined by tradition, it is possible to identify the rhetorical functions of each type of presidential discourse and to determine the strategic moves needed to fulfill, as well as those that impede, those functions. As a result, one can judge whether or not a given rhetorical act performed its functions, and in some instances, by comparing it with other like acts, one can assess how a given work transcended the customary and the clichéd to achieve those ends in an affecting and enduring way.

In one sense, then, generic critics have an advantage. Having studied all instances of a given type, they know what a president could have done because they know the options exercised by other presidents on similar occasions. Informed by such comparisons, they are well equipped to ask whether a given speaker chose the best from among the available means of persuasion.

"There is but one national voice in the country and that is the voice of the President," wrote Woodrow Wilson.[50] In what follows, we explore the ways in which institutional functions guide and circumscribe the rhetorical choices of presidents who have asked, with Lyndon Johnson, "How does a public leader find just the right words or the right way to say no more and no less than he [sic][51] means to say bearing in mind that anything he says may topple governments and may involve the lives of innocent men?"[52]

INNOVATIONS

This book builds on our earlier study of presidential rhetoric, *Deeds Done in Words*,[53] but our approach has changed structurally and conceptually since the publication of that book in 1990. The structural changes include two additional chapters that analyze genres that have emerged in the modern period. The national eulogy has arisen because we live in an age in which attempted or successful presidential assassinations, terrorist attacks, and national disasters are seen by the public via dramatic television footage that heightens our shared experiences of danger, death, and destruction, experiences that evoke a strong need for healing and comfort by the nation's leader. Accordingly, we analyze presidential responses on such occasions and the ways in which these national eulogies strengthen or erode the power of the presidents who issue them.

The second genre, which we call the de facto item veto, has emerged as a recurring form in the presidency of George W. Bush. The practice of attaching a statement, while signing legislation passed by Congress, that reinterprets or modifies the legislation has a history that stretches back to actions by James Monroe and Andrew Jackson, and it has been used intermittently by presidents since that time. During the current Bush administration, however, it has become a substitute for the veto message and an important assertion of presidential power based on the concept of the "unitary executive branch." Accordingly, it merits special attention.

These structural changes are related to conceptual changes. Most important of these is a shift from treating generic exemplars primarily as individual speeches to thinking of genres as rhetorical acts that extend over time, and of generic functions as performed in many forms and venues that extend across a variety of speeches, radio addresses, press conferences, interviews, and the like. As our earlier study emphasized, rhetorical genres perform certain functions, but those functions can be incorporated into a variety of discourses. Elements of farewell addresses have typically emerged in more than one speech; proclamations of pardon are often accompanied by speeches, remarks at press conferences, and interviews that explain and interpret what has been done. National eulogies often begin with immediate remarks after a disaster, continue with more extended remarks to the nation, come to fruition in a major speech, and then become a point of reference in addresses to Congress that build on them as a basis for legislation. In other words, we now approach these genres as functions that are not necessarily performed or completed in individual speeches.

Conceptually, this approach relies on thinking of the rhetorical act, rather than the speech or the address. All rhetorical action occurs in relation to history and context; these individual pieces of rhetoric occur in time, and their timing affects their reception because it links what is said now to prior statements by the president, to ongoing events, even to speeches by earlier presidents. Whoever speaks has a public biography that influences the meaning of what is spoken and how it is interpreted and understood, and whether those who hear it believe that the speaker is committed to what is asserted and proposed.[54]

Seeing discourse in terms of rhetorical acts is something critics routinely do when examining the rhetoric employed to pass legislation. Legislative issues, of course, have a history that influences what can be said about them and what is heard by the public and by lawmakers, as illustrated vividly by the Clinton administration's efforts toward health care reform. When it attempted such reform, the discourse proposing changes resonated with such past arguments as those about socialized medicine, the privacy of patients, the independence of physicians, the costs of medical care and who should pay, and the responsibility of state governments for the health of their citizens. The context in which speech emerges is also important. In the case of the Clinton administration, health care reform was made less likely by decisions to address other issues, such as gays in the military, before or while preparing health care reform legislation, which distracted the public and politicians from health care policy. The political context also affects discourse. In this case, Republicans, a majority in the Senate, framed the Clinton proposals as incredibly complicated, bureaucratic, and costly, requiring those speaking for the administration to respond to a multitude of objections.

In a similar vein, we can see inaugural rhetoric, and with it the process of inviting investiture, beginning as early as the victory speech delivered by the candidate once the votes are in and the decision clear. The bargaining process by which a president threatens a veto becomes part of the veto genre. The strategic leaks of parts of the State of the Union address and trial balloons testing its possible content are, in this interpretive frame, part and parcel of that genre.

In other words, our decision to treat genres as extending beyond a single speech reflects this larger, more complex rhetorical reality. To accommodate this change in perspective, we have added sections in some chapters asking how one might view the genre beyond the individual speeches that were the focus of the earlier work.

Our earlier study of rhetorical hybrids is relevant to this changed perspective.[55] As we illustrate in the chapter on the speeches of ascendant vice presidents, and again in the chapter on national eulogies, eulogistic responses to an event can appear in initial comments, expand in a radio address, and culminate in a major televised address to the nation. These eulogistic comments often lay the foundation for deliberation—by educating us on how we should respond to a terrorist act—and for a shift in the president's persona from that of priest in our civil religion, who comforts us at such moments, to that of legislator, who asks Congress to enact laws to respond to the threat, and that of commander in chief, who mobilizes the nation for war. Similarly, as discussed in chapter 3, the symbolic burial of the late president with eulogistic discourse must precede the rhetoric of investiture that invites us to accept a successor as our president. That rhetoric, in turn, may lead directly to deliberative discourse inviting us to memorialize the dead president by enacting legislation that he proposed or that reflects causes for which he fought. Similarly, war rhetoric has expanded from presidential requests for a declaration of war into a series of rhetorical acts that lay the foundation for it, whether in a commencement address that defends preemptive military action, in speeches in many cities that include vivid, dramatic narratives that arouse us to an anger that justifies putting our sons and daughters in harm's way, in national addresses that develop a view of war as endless, a "war on terror," or in speeches to the United Nations General Assembly urging the passage of resolutions that are overheard by the U.S. public.

We have also placed more emphasis in our analyses on a very ancient concept: timing. Early Greek theorists emphasized the importance of *kairos*, timing, and *to prepon*, doing what is appropriate, to develop the critical standard that a skillful speaker is one who is able to say the right thing at the propitious moment. In *Julius Caesar*, Shakespeare expressed that idea metaphorically: "There is a tide in the affairs of men which taken at the flood, leads on to fortune."[56] Again and again in our analyses, we have come to recognize the critical role of timing, as when speaking eloquently at the right moment resurrects a failing presidency or when poor timing makes it impossible for a rhetorical act to fulfill its purpose. Events out of the control of the president call for certain kinds of rhetorical action. In the face of invasion, words must be chosen carefully. We must be made to recognize the real and growing danger, but we must also be mobilized to fight back and reassured that if we do so, victory will be ours. Farewells can be issued successful only in the twilight of a presidency. The opportunity to issue a farewell is related to events: Carter's sense of failure over the Iranian hostage crisis drained him of the confidence to issue a farewell that proclaimed his substantial accomplishments in other areas. George H. W. Bush failed to be reelected, and the right moment for a farewell address to the nation never seemed to emerge for him.

In another conceptual shift, we have paid greater attention to the ways in which the presidential use of discourse enhances executive power and alters the balance of shared powers among the three branches of government. In other words, we take note of presidential efforts to envelop some of the powers of the other branches and of resistance to such efforts by Congress and the Supreme Court. At the core of our understanding of the relationship between presidential discourse and presidential power are two notions: first, that presidential uses of rhetoric can expand the share of power that the executive controls, and second, that presidential uses of rhetoric can increase presidential capital and with it the president's capacity to lead. When that capacity is expanded, so, too, is the president's disposition to claim more of the power that resides at the intersections of the branches. But even in the absence of the eloquent use of rhetoric that expands presidential capital, there are occasions when the presidential reach is more likely to go unchallenged by the other branches. These occasions also create openings for rhetorical assertion of executive prerogatives.

Historians of the courts and the presidency tell us that "judges are most likely to defer to the executive (a) on matters of foreign policy, (b) in times of war and national emergency, (c) when Congress has remained silent, and (d) when the president himself has taken decisive action."[57] In our revised chapter on war rhetoric and in our new chapter on the de facto item veto, we explore the ways in which presidents have used rhetoric to expand and justify their exercise of power.[58]

We start from a premise articulated by presidential scholar Richard Neustadt, who observes that the Constitution did not structure a clean or clear separation of powers among the branches, but instead created "a government of separated institutions *sharing* powers" [emphasis in original].[59] The same notion was expressed by Justice Jackson in the majority opinion in *Youngstown v. Sawyer*,[60] in which he wrote that the Constitution "enjoins upon its branches separateness but interdependence, autonomy but reciprocity."

Presidents use the authority given them in the Constitution as one way to increase their share of power. Across the country's more than two centuries of existence, presidential power has increased at the expense of the courts and Congress, a shift in equilibrium facilitated by activist presidents employing artful rhetoric and by an electoral system that encourages candidates to suggest that as president they will have more power to effect change than the Constitution, literally read and strictly applied, would suggest.

Of course, the Constitution explicitly provides the executive with an array of rhetorical opportunities. The president can call Congress into special session, make recommendations that are necessary and expedient, act as commander in chief, veto legislation, and pardon. Some presidents grasp these grants of authority and deploy them in ways that increase presidential power. Others shy away from the exercise of discretionary powers and use those that are mandated only tentatively. Increasingly in modern times, however, presidents have exploited and enlarged their powers, in part through the use of rhetoric.

The presidents who use these powers tend to be activist presidents or presidents governing in times of perceived crisis. So, for example, although article 2, section 3 grants the president authority "on extraordinary Occasions [to] convene both Houses," this is not a power presidents regularly exercise. When used, the act is rhetorical. By calling a special session of Congress, the president defines the situation as "extraordinary." Franklin Roosevelt, for example, communicated both the urgency of the country's economic situation and that he was determined to act quickly on the promises made in his election campaign when he called Congress into special session and received quick passage of his banking legislation in March 1933. Indeed, threatening to call a special session can propel congressional action. "The threat of a special session has been used by a resolute president to bring a sitting but dilatory Congress back under his legislative leadership," writes Wilfred E. Binkley. "Thus President Wilson warned his first Congress, which was planning to postpone action on the Federal Reserve Bank to a later session, that if they adjourned without action on the bill, he would promptly convene Congress in special session. The threat produced the desired effect."[61]

One of the reasons for our new focus on rhetorical means of exerting control of shared powers is that the importance of executive discourse has increased. Woodrow Wilson could recall times in "our history when presidential messages were utterly without practical significance, perfunctory documents which few persons except the editors of newspapers took the trouble to read."[62] Recall that it was Wilson who overturned more than a century of precedent to deliver the State of the Union address in person to the assembled Congress. In 2005, by contrast, according to presidential scholar Andrew Rudalevige,

> The annual State of the Union address has become a pivotal event, its presentation of presidential priorities parsed by and then parceled out to legislators. The president's initiatives almost invariably receive congressional attention and agenda space, especially in periods of unified government or in times of crisis. Overall, presidents get at least a committee hearing on nine of every ten bills they push and serious consideration of over 80 percent of their most important proposals, a real advantage given the huge number of pending items and limited time available each legislative session.[63]

Changing circumstances have also affected the meaning of the authority granted to the president in the Constitution. So, for example, in their award-winning book on the executive branch, Joel Aberbach and Mark Peterson note, "The most potent explicit presidential power from the contemporary vantage point, that of commander in chief of the armed forces, did not have quite the same connotation when it was granted in a nation lacking a standing army and not widely expected to be a major military power."[64] Faced with civil war, Lincoln claimed and rhetorically justified a previously unanticipated presidential power: suspending the right to a writ of habeas corpus despite a clear constitutional bar to such action. Similarly, George W. Bush has used his role as commander in chief in the war on terror to justify many of the exceptions he has asserted in signing statements that constitute de facto item vetoes.

Some of the powers presidents now assume upon inauguration are of rather recent vintage. Presidents have sidestepped the role given Congress in treaty making "by negotiating international executive agreements that have the force of a treaty but do not require Senate approval."[65] Congressional declarations of war are so infrequent that Congress appears to have ceded that authority to the president by default. The advent of regular use of the signing statement as a de facto item veto creates a genre in which the president can sign an act while taking exception to some of its provisions, an option unmentioned in the Constitution.

In this book, as in our earlier one, our work is a study of the executive branch as an institution, a study of the role of rhetoric in that institution, and a study of the ways in which the rhetorical actions of presidents increase or decrease their powers as individuals and, of even more importance, affect the powers available to their successors. In the chapter on the de facto item veto, for example, we trace the exercise of that power from its use in the early 1800s through the steps by which it came into more frequent use by modern presidents, to its legal analysis and justification during the Clinton administration, and its exercise as a substitute for the veto in the administration of George W. Bush. Throughout this book, we demonstrate the ways in which presidential use of rhetoric alters the presidency.

This book not only has two new chapters, but also has a new organizational structure. We begin with chapters on rhetorical acts that are exercised by the president alone and involve investiture, first as the president in inaugural addresses, then as a vice president who, because of death or resignation, ascends to the presidency, and then as national priest in our civil religion in national eulogies. We end that grouping with the rhetoric of pardoning, a presidential power that is unilateral and virtually unlimited but significantly affects presidential leadership and legacy, as illustrated particularly by the controversial pardons of Gerald Ford, George H. W. Bush, and Bill Clinton.

The next group of chapters focuses on rhetoric that involves interaction between the executive and Congress in State of the Union addresses, veto messages, signing statements that constitute de facto item vetoes, and war rhetoric. We group these genres together in order to focus attention on shared powers and on increases in executive power facilitated in part by presidential use of rhetoric.

The final group of chapters examines the rhetoric of divestiture. We first examine the interaction that occurs in congressional threats of impeachment, presidential efforts to forestall impeachment, and the three cases in which articles of impeachment have been passed by the House of Representatives. In the case of impeachment, the presidential voice is muted; others must speak in accusation and defense. Andrew Johnson and Bill Clinton survived trials in the Senate; Richard Nixon resigned to avoid removal. Finally, we turn to farewell addresses, in which presidents seek to shape their legacy and, through warnings, to influence the future. These rhetorical acts, too, are moments of divestiture, when presidents begin to leave the executive role in order to rejoin the audiences they address in the proud role of citizen.

We begin with inaugurals and end with farewells because these are the moments when those we have elected become presidents and the moments when we see presidents using the liminal period between the election of a successor and the upcoming inauguration to speak from their experience to the future—moments of personal divestiture.

In the years since our earlier study, the presidency has changed, as has presidential use of rhetoric. In the coming chapters, we build on our earlier work to chronicle those changes in the nine genres we originally treated: inaugural addresses, investiture of ascendant vice presidents, pardons, veto messages, State of the Union addresses, war rhetoric, efforts to forestall impeachment, impeachment rhetoric, and farewells. We also argue that insight can be gained by seeing two new forms, the national eulogy and the de facto item veto, through a generic perspective. In the concluding chapter, we ask what value is added to our understanding of genres and the presidency by configuring the genres in the new order used in this book. At the same time, we ask what we have learned by expanding our concept of presidential genres in the three ways central to this book: adding the notion that presidents have increased their share of interbranch powers through rhetoric, seeing the genres as rhetorical acts, and focusing on the ways in which generic rhetorical acts build on or sacrifice rhetorical capital through the use or misuse of timing.

Inaugural Addresses

The presidential inaugural address is a discourse whose significance all recognize, but few praise. Arthur Schlesinger, Jr., for example, acknowledges that during inaugural addresses, "the nation listens for a moment as one people to the words of the man they have chosen for the highest office in the land," but he finds little merit in those words:

> Even in the field of political oratory, the inaugural address is an inferior art form. It is rarely an occasion for original thought or stimulating reflection. The platitude quotient tends to be high, the rhetoric stately and self-serving, the ritual obsessive, and the surprises few.[1]

Conceivably, inaugural addresses mirror the alleged mediocrity of U.S. presidents. In our view, however, inaugurals are maligned because their symbolic function is misunderstood. As we shall show, they are an essential element in a ritual of transition in which the covenant between the citizenry and their leaders is renewed. Conventional wisdom and ordinary language treat inaugural addresses as a class. Likewise, critics have taken them to be a distinct rhetorical type, but generalizing about them has been difficult. Despite their apparent dissimilarities, we shall approach these addresses as a genre, illuminating their common symbolic functions and identifying the qualities that make them distinct. In that process, we shall account for the recurrent and the variable in these speeches, describe the unique functions of the presidential inaugural, and seek to explain the power of those inaugural addresses widely regarded as eloquent.

Presidential inaugurals are a subspecies of the kind of discourse that Aristotle called epideictic, a form of rhetoric that praises or blames on ceremonial occasions, invites the audience to evaluate the speaker's performance, recalls the past and speculates about the future while focusing on the present, employs a noble, dignified literary style, and amplifies or rehearses admitted facts.[2] In a work on rhetoric in the Catholic Church, John O'Malley notes that epideictic rhetoric presents speakers with a unique problem of invention: a problem in discovering and developing appropriate lines of argument. Unlike forensic (courtroom) or deliberative (legislative) speeches that deal "with more immediate and pressing issues" for which "classical theory proposed *topoi* or commonplaces, . . . [t]he occasional or ceremonial nature of epideictic often deprived it of obviously immediate issues."[3] As a result, *memoria*, or recollection of a shared past, becomes an exceptionally important resource for epideictic speeches. O'Malley also calls attention to the distinctively contemplative character of this genre. He comments that "epideictic wants as far as possible to present us with works and deeds, . . . not for metaphysical analysis but quite literally for viewing. . . . 'to look,' to 'view,' to 'gaze upon,' and to 'contemplate.'"[4] Harry Caplan adds that in epideictic discourse a speaker tries, by means of artistry, "to impress his ideas upon [the audience], without action as a goal."[5] And as Edwin Black notes, "The words that are spoken at ceremonial transitions work to fix and consign an event, to articulate a common interpretation of it, so to fashion a public memory of it that it can hardly thereafter be remembered in any other way."[6]

If these criteria are applied, presidential inaugurals are epideictic rhetoric because they are delivered on ceremonial occasions, link past and future in present contemplation, affirm or praise the shared principles that will guide the incoming administration, ask the audience to "gaze upon" traditional values, employ elegant, literary language, and rely on "heightening of effect" by amplification and reaffirmation of what is already known and believed.

The special character of presidential inaugural addresses is defined by these general epideictic features and by the nature of the inauguration ceremony. Inauguration is a rite of passage, a ritual of transition in which a newly elected president is invested with the office of the presidency.[7] As a celebration of democratic change and continuity, the inauguration is a singular moment at which the president has a platform from which to demonstrate a capacity for leadership, an appreciation of the nation's values, a sensitivity to key issues facing the nation, and an ability to mobilize and unify the citizenry in support of a new administration. The ceremony and its timing create an opportunity for the president to speak in ways that amass rhetorical capital and sustain the honeymoon period of a new presidency.

The general qualities of epideictic rhetoric, modified by the nature of presidential investiture, generate four interrelated elements that define the essential presidential inaugural address and differentiate it from other types of epideictic rhetoric.[8] The presidential inaugural (1) unifies the audience by reconstituting its members as "the people," who can witness and ratify the ceremony; (2) rehearses communal values drawn from the past; (3) sets forth the political principles that will guide the new administration; and (4) demonstrates through enactment that the president appreciates the requirements and limitations of executive functions. In addition, each of these ends must be achieved through means appropriate to epideictic address; that is, while urging contemplation rather than action, focusing on the present while incorporating the past and future, and praising the institution of the presidency and the values and form of the government of which it is a part, all processes through which the covenant between the president and the people is renewed.

One indication of the power of these characteristics is that they persist despite differences in the nature of the times in which inaugurals are delivered, the varying rhetorical dispositions of presidents, and the opportunities offered by media that have expanded the immediate audience. They were present when Calvin Coolidge delivered the first inaugural heard on radio in 1925, as well when Harry Truman delivered the first on television in 1949, and in 1993 when Bill Clinton's first inaugural appeared on the Internet.

The inaugural can be seen as a rhetorical act whose themes emerge in an extended series of speeches, beginning with the candidate's acceptance of the nomination by the party and declaration of victory in the election.[9] The early speeches in this series define the newly elected president and make sense of the election. On election night in 1992, for example, former Arkansas governor Bill Clinton told his assembled supporters and the eavesdropping audience on national and international television, "My fellow Americans, on this day, with high hopes and brave hearts, in massive numbers, the American people have voted to make a new beginning." What did Clinton's election mean? "This election is a clarion call for our country to face the challenges of the end of the cold war and the beginning of the next century, to restore growth to our country and opportunity to our people, to empower our own people so that they can take more responsibility for their own lives, to face problems too long ignored, from AIDS to the environment to the conversion of our economy from a defense to a domestic giant."[10] The same thoughts were recast in the language of challenge in Clinton's first inaugural:

To renew America, we must meet challenges abroad as well as at home. There is no longer a clear division between what is foreign and what is domestic. The world economy, the world environment, the world AIDS crisis, the world arms race: they affect us all. Today, as an older order passes, the new world is more free but less stable. Communism's collapse has called forth old animosities and new dangers.[11]

Viewed in this larger perspective and taking into account the effect of mediated coverage, certain elements of the inaugural can be seen to recur.

CONSTITUTING "THE PEOPLE"

The first of these elements is unification of the audience.[12] Before the citizenry or their representatives can witness and ratify an ascent to power, the audience, divided by a hard-fought presidential election campaign, must be unified and reconstituted as "the people." John Adams illustrated the reconstituting power of historical reenactment when he rehearsed the founding of the nation in 1797:

> In this dangerous crisis [under the Articles of Confederation] the people of America were not abandoned by their usual good sense, presence of mind, resolution, or integrity. Measures were pursued to concern a plan to form a more perfect union.[13]

Thomas Jefferson's inaugural sought to create a single people out of partisan division: "We have called by different names brethren of the same principles. We are all republicans. We are all federalists" (8).[14] More recently, in 1961, after a close election and a divisive campaign, John F. Kennedy began, "We observe today not a victory of party, but a celebration of freedom" (165). As one would expect, explicit appeals for unity are most common in addresses that follow divisive campaigns or contested electoral outcomes.[15] In his first inaugural, Bill Clinton spoke of democracy as "[a]n idea ennobled by the faith that our Nation can summon from its myriad diversity the deepest measure of unity."[16]

Surprisingly, George W. Bush's inaugural address in 2001 failed to acknowledge that his election had been contested, that he became president when a decision by the Supreme Court ended the contest, or that his opponent, Al Gore, had received over 500,000 more votes than he. He merely said, "And I thank Vice President Gore for a contest conducted with spirit and ended with grace."[17] He made no attempt to reach out to those who had voted for his opponent. Arguably, his investiture as president of all the people did not occur until he spoke at the National Cathedral following the September 11 attacks on the World Trade Center and the Pentagon[18] (a speech discussed in chapter 4, on national eulogies). Bush's call for unity in his inaugural took a different form: "Our unity, our union, is the serious work of leaders and citizens in every generation. And this is my solemn pledge: I will work to build a single nation of justice and opportunity."[19]

Partisan politicking is not the only source of division. Occasionally a major crisis or a war creates disharmony that must be set aside if the president is to govern all the people. In 1901, acknowledging the continuing disunity created by the Civil War, William McKinley declared, "We are reunited. Sectionalism has disappeared. Division on public questions can no longer be traced by the war maps of 1861" (110). In 1917, in the face of U.S. entry into World War I, Woodrow Wilson affirmed the importance of unity: "It is imperative that we should stand together. We are being forged into a new unity amidst the fires that now blaze throughout the world" (127). In 1989, George H. W. Bush said, "The final lesson of Vietnam is that no great nation can long afford to be sundered by a memory."[20]

Once the audience has been united and reconstituted as the people, it can perform its role in the inaugural ceremony. Inaugural addresses themselves attest to the witnessing role of the people. In 1889, for example, Benjamin Harrison said,

> There is no constitutional or legal requirement that the president shall take the oath of office in the presence of the people, but there is so manifest an appropriateness in the public induction to office of the chief executive of the nation that from the beginning of the Government the people, to whose service the official oath consecrates the officer, have been called to witness the solemn ceremonial. (94)

Similar statements appear in many other inaugurals. John Quincy Adams said, "I appear, my fellow citizens, in your presence and in that of heaven to bind myself" (29). "In the presence of this vast assemblage of my countrymen," said Grover Cleveland, "I am about to supplement and seal by the oath which I have taken the manifestation of the will of a great and free people" (91). "I, too, am a witness," noted Eisenhower, "today testifying in your name to the principles and purposes to which we, as a people, are pledged" (162). Lincoln and McKinley made similar comments (72, 103).

Without the presence of the people, the rite of presidential investiture cannot be completed. The people ratify the president's formal ascent to power by acknowledging the oath taking, witnessing the enactment of the presidential role, and accepting the principles laid down to guide an administration. Benjamin Harrison recognized the interdependence of the president and the people in his inaugural:

> The oath taken in the presence of the people becomes a mutual covenant. . . . My promise is spoken; yours unspoken, but not the less real and solemn. The people of every State have here their representatives. Surely I do not misinterpret the spirit of the occasion when I assume that the whole body of the people covenant with me and with each other today to support and defend the Constitution of the Union of the States, to yield willing obedience to all the laws and each to every other citizen his equal civil and political rights. (94)

Some inaugurals have articulated the notion that the president becomes "the president" through delivering the inaugural address. In other words, the inaugural itself is part of the investiture, a conclusion reinforced when presidents acknowledge it. William Henry Harrison, for example, closes his inaugural address by saying, "Fellow-citizens, being fully invested with that high office to which the partiality of my countrymen has called me, I now take an affectionate leave of you." [21]

Great inaugurals reenact the original process by which the people and their leaders "form a more perfect union." [22] In recreating this mutual covenant, great inaugurals both reconstitute the audience as "the people" and constitute the citizenry as a people in some new way: as those entrusted with the success or failure of the democratic experiment (Washington's first), as members of a perpetual Union (Lincoln's first), as a people whose spiritual strength can overcome material difficulties (Franklin Roosevelt's first), as a people willing to sacrifice for an ideal (Kennedy's), as members of an international community (Wilson's second), or as a people able to transcend political differences (Washington's first, Jefferson's first). In 1865, for instance, Lincoln reconstituted the people as limited by the purposes of the Almighty as he urged the audience to consider God's view of the conflict between North and South: "Both read the same Bible and pray to the same God, and each invokes His aid against the other. . . . The prayers of both could not be answered. Those of neither have been answered fully. The Almighty has His own purposes" (77).[23] In 1913, in his first inaugural, Wilson reconstituted the citizenry as a people capable of reckoning the costs of industrial development: "We have been proud of our industrial achievement, but we have not hitherto stopped thoughtfully enough to count the human cost. . . . We have come now to the sober second thought" (123–24). In 1961, in the middle of the cold war, Kennedy's inaugural went beyond a call for sacrifice to speak of "a call to bear the burden of a long twilight struggle, year in, and year out" (166), a call that suggested *Götterdäm-merung* and denied easy victory or inevitable triumph.[24] Notably, the great inaugurals dramatically illustrate the processes of change within a continuous tradition, including the ways in which the resources of epideictic ritual are yoked to political renewal.

Ceremonially, the inaugural address itself is an adjunct to or an extension of the oath of office, a relationship demonstrated dramatically in the shortest inaugural address, Washington's second. After describing himself as "called upon by the voice of my country" to "this distinguished honor," Washington intensified the constitutional oath with a second pledge:

> Previous to the execution of any official act of the President, the Constitution requires an oath of office. This oath I am now about to take, and in your presence: That if it shall be found during my administration of the Government I have in any instance violated willingly or knowingly the injunctions thereof, I may (besides incurring constitutional punishment) be subject to the upbraidings of all who are now witnesses of the present solemn ceremony. (3)

Although it consists entirely of an avowal of his personal commitment to the constitutional oath, this inaugural also recognized the witnessing role of the audience in the rite of investiture.

That an inaugural address is an extension of the oath of office is certified by many of these speeches. Cleveland, for example, referred to his speech as a supplement to the oath of office (91). Lyndon Johnson said, "The oath I have taken before you and before God is not mine alone, but ours together" (167). One of the more eloquent inaugurals derived its power in part from its construction as an extension of the oath of office and as an invitation to participate in a mutual covenant. In 1961, Kennedy phrased each assertion or promise he articulated as a pledge jointly made by leader and people. His litany of mutual pledges culminated in the following claim: "In your hands, my fellow citizens, more than mine, will rest the final success or failure of our course." Finally, he explicitly invited audience participation by asking, "Will you join in that historic effort?" (166). By casting his speech as an extension of the oath of office and by inviting the audience to join him in these avowals, Kennedy underscored the ritualistic nature of the occasion.

The force of Lincoln's first inaugural, discussed in more detail below, also derived in part from his call for audience participation. In 1881, James Garfield made an appeal that echoed the famous words of Lincoln's first inaugural:

> My countrymen, we do not now differ in our judgment concerning the controversies of past generations, and fifty years hence our children will not be divided in their opinions concerning our controversies. They will surely bless their fathers and their fathers' God that the Union was preserved, that slavery was overthrown, and that both races were made equal before the law. We may hasten or we may retard, but we can not prevent, the final reconciliation. Is it not possible for us now to make a truce with time by anticipating and accepting its inevitable verdict? (88)

REHEARSING NATIONAL VALUES

The next task the new president faces is that of reaffirming traditional values. Because each of the elements forming a presidential inaugural ought to facilitate the president's task of unifying the audience as the people, the traditional values rehearsed by the president need to be selected and framed in ways that unify the audience. Thus, for example, following a campaign replete with charges that he was an atheist, Jefferson's speech assured former adversaries that he recognized the power of the deity by "acknowledging and adoring an overruling Providence, . . . that Infinite Power which rules the destinies of the universe" (9–10). Similarly, the founders were eulogized in early inaugurals, but such encomia disappeared as the Civil War approached. Because William Lloyd Garrison and other abolitionists had widely publicized the founders' slaveholding, public veneration of those founders would ally a president with those who favored slavery and invite the enmity of its opponents.[25] Martin Van Buren's exceptional reference in 1837 to Washington and the other founders can be explained by his continuing need to reassure Southerners about what had been the central issue of the campaign: whether he was secretly an abolitionist.[26] The point to be noted is that when an appeal that was once a unifying recollection of past heroes interferes with the process of reconstituting the audience as a unified people, it is abandoned.

In order to be invested, presidents must demonstrate their qualifications for office by venerating the past and showing that the traditions of the presidency will continue unbroken with them. They must affirm that they will transmit the institution intact to their successors. Consequently, the language of conservation, preservation, maintenance, and renewal pervades these speeches. What we conserve and renew is often sanctified as our "creed," our "faith," or our "sacred trust." Cleveland's statement in 1885 is illustrative:

> On this auspicious occasion we may well renew the pledge of our devotion to the Constitution, which, launched by the founders of the republic and consecrated by their prayers and patriotic devotion, has for almost a century borne the hopes and aspirations of a great people through prosperity and peace and through the shock of foreign conflicts and the perils of domestic strife and vicissitudes. (91)

Presidential invocation of the principles, policies, and presidencies of the past suggests that, in the inaugural address, *memoria,* or shared recollection, is a key source of *inventio,* the development of lines of argument. The final appeal in Lincoln's first inaugural to "the mystic chords of memory" illustrates the symbolic force of a shared past. Coolidge put it more simply: "We can not continue these brilliant successes in the future, unless we continue to learn from the past" (133). Such use of the past is also consistent with the ritualistic process of representing beginnings, origins, and universal relationships. "Today we do more than celebrate America. We rededicate ourselves to the very idea of America," noted Clinton in his first inaugural, "an idea born in revolution and renewed through two centuries of challenge."[27] Eight years later, George W. Bush noted, "We have a place, all of us, in a long story, a story we continue, but whose end we will not see. It is the story of a new world that became a friend and liberator of the old, a story of a slaveholding society that became a servant of freedom, the story of a power that went into the world to protect but not possess, to defend but not to conquer."[28]

The past is conserved by honoring past presidents. Washington was praised by John and John Quincy Adams, Thomas Jefferson, Zachary

Taylor, and Martin Van Buren; James Monroe and Andrew Jackson referred to their illustrious predecessors; Abraham Lincoln spoke of the distinguished citizens who had administered the executive branch.

The past is also conserved by reaffirming the wisdom of past policies and practices. Grover Cleveland, for example, praised policies of Washington, Jefferson, and Monroe (92). William McKinley praised the policy, "wisely inaugurated by Washington," of "keeping ourselves free from entanglement, either as allies or foes" (106). And in his first inaugural, George W. Bush noted that Jefferson would know the themes of this day: "our Nation's grand story of courage and its simple dream of dignity."[29] In 1809, in the nation's sixth inaugural, Madison said, "Unwilling to depart from examples of the most revered authority, I avail myself of the occasion now presented to express the profound impression made on me by the call of my country" (14). Eight years later, Monroe said,

> In commencing the duties of the chief executive office it has been the practice of the distinguished men who have gone before me to explain the principles which would govern them in their respective Administrations. In following their venerated example.... (18)

Over time, earlier presidential inaugurals have frequently been quoted, especially those of Washington, Jefferson, Lincoln, and Franklin Roosevelt. This process of rhetorical introversion illuminates some remarkable coincidences. Warren G. Harding and Jimmy Carter, for example, both quoted the same verse from Micah. Franklin Roosevelt and Carter each quoted a former teacher. Franklin Roosevelt and Kennedy both had a rendezvous with destiny. Reagan paraphrased Jefferson, Nixon paraphrased Kennedy, Kennedy echoed Lincoln, Polk rephrased Jackson, and Reagan echoed Kennedy. In other words, presidents recognize, capitalize on, and are constrained by the inaugurals of their predecessors, which, taken together, form a tradition.

The past is also used analogically to affirm that as we overcame difficulties in the past, so will we now; the venerated past assures us that the nation has a future. Thus, in 1933, in the face of severe economic problems, Franklin Roosevelt told his audience, "Compared with the perils which our forefathers conquered because they believed and were not afraid, we have still much to be thankful for" (145). In 1941, with another crisis looming, he reminded his audience of the difficult tasks that confronted Washington and Lincoln (151).

In the world of inaugural addresses, we have inherited our character as a people; accordingly, veneration of the past not only unifies the audience but also warrants present and future action, as recurring references to avoiding "entangling alliances" have illustrated. A more recent example is found in the 1981 inaugural, in which Reagan paraphrased a statement Jefferson made in 1801:[30] "Sometimes it is said that man can not be trusted with the government of himself. Can he, then, be trusted with the government of others?" (8). Reagan said, "Well, if no one among us is capable of governing himself, then who among us has the capacity to govern someone else?" (180).

In his second inaugural, Clinton linked the values he pledged to support to another national event:

> Thirty-four years ago, the man whose life we celebrate today spoke to us down there, at the other end of this Mall, in words that moved the conscience of a nation. Like a prophet of old, he told of his dream that one day America would rise up and treat all its citizens as equals before the law and in the heart. Martin Luther King's dream was the American dream. His quest is our quest: the ceaseless striving to live out our true creed. Our history has been built on such dreams and labors. And by our dreams and labors, we will redeem the promise of America in the 21st century.[31]

The link between values and commitments is also clear in George W. Bush's second inaugural:

> America's vital interests and our deepest beliefs are now one. From the day of our founding, we have proclaimed that every man and woman on this Earth has rights and dignity and matchless value, because they bear the image of the Maker of heaven and Earth. Across the generations, we have proclaimed the imperative of self-government, because no one is fit to be a master and no one deserves to be a slave. Advancing these ideals is the mission that created our Nation. It is the honorable achievement of our fathers. Now, it is the urgent requirement of our Nation's security and the calling of our time.[32]

ADMINISTRATIVE PHILOSOPHY

The third job of each president is to set forth the principles that will guide the new administration. The incoming president must go beyond the rehearsal of traditional values and veneration of the past to enunciate a political philosophy. Because rhetorical scholars have focused on the specific political principles laid down in individual inaugurals, they have often failed to note that, although these principles vary from inaugural to inaugural, all inaugurals not only lay down political principles, but also present and develop such principles in predictable ways.

In many inaugurals, presidents indicate that they feel obliged to set forth the principles that will govern their tenures in office. Jefferson's 1801 inaugural explicitly acknowledged this obligation:

> About to enter, my fellow-citizens, on the exercise of duties which comprehend everything dear and valuable to you, it is proper you should understand what I deem the essential principles of our Government, and consequently those which ought to shape its Administration. (9)

We know of the generic constraints under which presidents and presidents-elect believe they operate in part because they acknowledge them. In his inaugural, for example, William Henry Harrison announced that "in obedience to a custom coeval with our Government and what I believe to be your expectations I proceed to present to you a summary of the principles which will govern me in the discharge of the duties which I shall be called upon to perform."[33]

We also hear generic constraints voiced by the writers who draft the speeches. As Clinton's speechwriter Michael Waldman wrote, "In crafting an inaugural address, the major question to be asked is: what is the condition of the country, what is the situation, that is to be confronted by the address? . . . In other words, what is the pivot? And in what direction does the new President want to push?"[34]

In keeping with the epideictic character of inaugurals, however, specific policies are proposed for contemplation, not for action. Policy proposals embedded in inaugurals are not an end in themselves, but illustrations of the political philosophy of the speaker. This contemplative, expository function differentiates inaugurals from State of the Union addresses, in which such proposals are presented for congressional action.

So, for instance, in a relatively detailed statement of his political views, James Polk discussed "our revenue laws and the levy of taxes," but this discussion illustrated the political axiom that "no more money shall be collected than the necessities of an economical administration shall require" (57). Similarly, he aired his position on the national debt to illustrate the principle that "melancholy is the condition of that people whose government can be sustained only by a system which periodically transfers large amounts from the labor of the many to the coffers of the few. Such a system is incompatible with the ends for which our Republican Government was instituted" (56–57).

Because William Howard Taft conceived the inaugural address as a vehicle for articulating relatively specific policy, his speech provides a rigorous test of the claim that inaugurals deal with principles rather than practices. He stated that "[t]he office of an inaugural address is to give a summary outline of the main policies of the new administration, so far as they can be anticipated" (115). His tedious list of recommendations, however, was not a call for specific, immediate action, but evidence of continuity and of loyalty to the Constitution. He said, for example, "I have had the honor to be one of the advisers of my distinguished predecessor, and as such, to hold up his hands in the reforms he has initiated.... To render such reforms lasting, however, ... further legislative and executive action are needed" (115). Such reforms ("the suppression of the lawlessness and abuses of power of the great combinations of capital invested in railroads and in industrial enterprises carrying on interstate commerce") were defined as means of maintaining the democratic character of the government. Again, they became illustrations of the broad principles that he would follow.[35]

In his first inaugural, Clinton set forth the priorities of his administration: "We must do what no generation has done before. We must invest more in our own people, in their jobs, in their future, and at the same time cut our massive debt. And we must do so in a world in which we must compete for every opportunity."[36]

In George W. Bush's second inaugural, the link between values and policy is announced clearly: "America's belief in human dignity will guide our policies. Yet rights must be more than the grudging concessions of dictators. They are secured by free dissent and the participation of the governed. In the long run, there is no justice without freedom and there can be no human rights without human liberty."[37]

Just as recollection of the past and rehearsal of traditional values need to be noncontroversial and unifying, recommitment to constitutional principles must unify by assuring those who did not vote for a candidate that the president will, nonetheless, scrupulously protect their rights. The same needs to unify the audience and to speak in the epideictic present also influence the language in which presidents articulate the principles that will govern their administrations.

ENACTING THE PRESIDENTIAL ROLE

The rite of investiture demands that presidents do more than unite the people, rehearse traditional values, and enunciate a political philosophy. Their fourth task is to enact the presidential role, and in so doing, to demonstrate an appreciation of the requirements and limitations of the executive in our system of government. To complete and ratify the president's ascent to power, the inaugural address must demonstrate rhetorically that this person can lead the nation within the constitutionally established limits of executive power and can perform the public, symbolic role of president of all the people. As president, the speaker appropriates the country's history and assumes the right to say what that history means; as president, the speaker asserts that some principles are more salient than others at that moment; as president, the speaker constitutes the audience as the people; and as president, the speaker asks the people to join in a mutual covenant to commit themselves to the political philosophy enunciated in the address.

If an inaugural address is to be part of a rite of investiture, then presidents must speak in the public role of president. An inaugural would not fulfill this function if the address pressed forward the personality or personal history of the incoming president.[38] When evidence is drawn from a president's personal past, it must reveal something about the presidency or about the people or the nation. Personal narrative is inappropriate in a rhetorical genre designed for the formal display of the president as president. The functions of personal material in an inaugural are clearly different from the functions of like material in campaign oratory, in which a high level of self-disclosure and self-aggrandizement is both expected and appropriate. The character of the self-references also distinguishes the inaugural address from other presidential rhetoric.[39]

A dramatic example of inappropriate personal material appeared in the final paragraph of Ulysses S. Grant's second inaugural:

> Throughout the war, and from my candidacy for my present office in 1868 to the close of the last Presidential campaign, I have been the object of abuse and slander scarcely ever equalled in political history, which to-day I feel that I can afford to disregard in view of your verdict, which I gratefully accept as my vindication. (81)

This statement speaks of Grant the person, not of the presidency or of Grant the president. In so doing, it calls into question Grant's ability to fulfill the symbolic role of president of all the people.

In a later inaugural, Carter's use of a statement by a former teacher illustrates a potential pitfall in using personal material. Immediately after thanking Gerald Ford for all he had done to heal the division in the nation, Carter began his speech by saying,

> In this outward and physical ceremony, we attest once again to the inner and spiritual strength of our Nation. As my high school teacher, Miss Julia Coleman, used to say, "We must adjust to changing times and still hold to unchanging principles." (178)

As we have argued, the first duty of a president in an inaugural is to reconstitute the audience as the people. Carter was attempting to forge a national community out of his listeners. Only certain people have the standing to do that, however, and Julia Coleman, however able she may have been as a high school teacher, was not one of them. Later in the inaugural, if Carter had made her the voice of the people expressing a timeless truth, Coleman's aphorism might have been appropriate. Later, despite Coleman's lack of authority, her adage might have been apt had it been an unusual, penetrating, immediately intelligible, vivid statement of the relationship between change and continuity. Even such a claim is questionable, however. In Carter's statement, we have the rhetorical equivalent of what would have occurred had Kennedy begun the second paragraph of his speech, "To paraphrase George St. John, my old headmaster, 'Ask not what your country can do for you. . . .'"[40]

Franklin Roosevelt's first inaugural dramatically asserted presidential leadership and the special importance of executive action at a moment of economic crisis. He spoke of "a leadership of frankness and vigor," and told his audience, "I am convinced that you will again give the support to leadership in these critical days" (145); "This Nation asks for action, and action now"; and "With this pledge taken, I assume unhesitatingly the leadership of this great army of our people" (146). Roosevelt, however, was aware that he was pressing the limits of executive power:

> It is to be hoped that the normal balance of executive and legislative authority may be wholly adequate to meet the unprecedented task before us. But it may be that an unprecedented demand and need for undelayed action may call for temporary departure from that normal balance of public procedure. I am prepared under my constitutional duty to recommend the measures that a stricken nation . . . may require. . . . I shall ask Congress for the one remaining

instrument to meet the crisis—broad Executive power to wage a war against the emergency, as great as the power that would be given to me if we were in fact invaded by a foreign foe. (147)

What is crucial here is that Roosevelt portrayed his leadership as constitutional. Special powers would be conferred by Congress, and those powers would be analogous to the extraordinary powers exercised by previous presidents in similarly extreme circumstances.[41]

An abiding fear of the misuse of executive power pervades our national history. Washington's opponents accused him of wanting to be king; Jackson was called King Andrew, and Van Buren, King Martin; Theodore Roosevelt was attacked in cartoons captioned "Theodore Roosevelt for ever and ever"; Lincoln's abolition of habeas corpus and Franklin Roosevelt's use of executive power, as well as his pursuit of third and fourth terms, were damned as monarchical or, worse, as despotic.[42] The American Revolution was fought, the Declaration of Independence reminds the citizenry, in response to "repeated injuries and usurpations, all having in direct object the establishment of an absolute Tyranny over these States." To allay fears of incipient tyranny, incoming presidents must assure the people that they do not covet power for its own sake and that they recognize and respect constitutional limits on executive authority.

There is a paradox in the demand that presidents demonstrate rhetorically a capacity for effective leadership while carefully acknowledging constitutional limitations. To the extent that they promise strong leadership, they risk being seen as incipient tyrants. By contrast, should they emphasize the limits on executive power, they risk being seen as inept or enfeebled leaders. Eloquent presidents have walked this tightrope with agility, as Lincoln did in his first inaugural when he responded to the fear that he would use executive power to abolish slavery: "I have no purpose, directly or indirectly, to interfere with the institution of slavery in the States where it exists" (72). He attested that this was a consistent position for him by citing statements from his campaign speeches and a plank from the Republican Party platform, material that he characterized as "the most conclusive evidence of which the case is susceptible" (72). On the other hand, responding to abolitionist revulsion against the fugitive slave laws, he quoted article 4 of the Constitution and averred that those laws were merely an extension of that article, a part of the Constitution that he would shortly swear to uphold.

In recognizing the limits on presidential power, inaugurals not only affirm the balance of power and locate executive initiatives in the mandate of the people, but also offer evidence of humility. The new president humbly acknowledges deficiencies, humbly accepts the burdens of office, and humbly invokes God's blessings. The precedent for evincing humility was set in the first inaugural by Washington:

> The magnitude and difficulty of the trust to which the voice of my country called me, being sufficient to awaken in the wisest and most experienced of her citizens a distrustful scrutiny into his qualifications, could not but overwhelm with despondence one who ought to be peculiarly conscious of his own deficiencies. (1)[43]

Washington's attitude was echoed in Carter's less felicitous comment in 1977: "Your strength can compensate for my weakness, and your wisdom can help to minimize my mistakes" (178). Clinton also recognized his own limits in his first inaugural when he said, "To that work I now turn with all the authority of my office. I ask the Congress to join with me. But no President, no Congress, no Government can undertake this mission alone. My fellow Americans, you, too, must play your part in our renewal."[44]

As part of the process of acknowledging the limits of executive power, inaugurals typically place the president and the nation under God. These references to God are not perfunctory: by calling on God, presidents subordinate themselves to a higher power. The God of inaugurals is a personal God who is actively involved in affairs of state, an "Almighty Being whose power regulates the destiny of nations," in the words of Madison (15); a God "who led our fathers," according to Jefferson (13); a God who protects us, according to Monroe (28); a God revealed in our history, according to Cleveland (93); and a God who punishes us, in the words of Lincoln: "He gives to both North and South this terrible war as the woe due to those by whom the offense came" (77).

Presidents enact the presidential role by placing themselves and the nation in God's hands. We should note, however, that it is only after they are fully invested with the office that presidents have claimed the authority to place the nation "under God." For this reason, perhaps, prayers or prayerlike statements have usually occurred near or at the end of inaugurals. This could explain why Eisenhower called the prayer he delivered before his first inaugural "a private prayer." Although he had taken the oath of office, he was not yet fully invested as president, and until he had performed further rhetorical acts of acceptance, he sensed that he lacked the authority to represent the nation before God. This placement of prayers or prayerlike statements is a subtle reminder that the inaugural address is an integral part of the rite of investiture.

In some inaugurals, presidents also explicitly reiterate that whether they like them or not, they will abide by the laws. "On all leading questions agitating the public mind I will always express my views to Congress and urge them according to my judgment, and when I think it advisable will exercise the constitutional privilege of interposing a veto to defeat measures which I oppose; but all laws will be faithfully executed, whether they meet my approval or not," noted Grant in his first inaugural.[45]

EPIDEICTIC RHETORIC

Finally, the four elements described above must be adapted to the character of epideictic rhetoric because the special "timelessness" of epideictic discourse is the key to fusing the elements that symbolically constitute the presidential inaugural. The time of epideictic rhetoric, including inaugurals, is the eternal present, the mythic time that Mircea Eliade calls *illud tempus*, time out of time: "Every ritual has the character of happening now, at this very moment. The time of the event that the ritual commemorates or re-enacts is made present, 're-presented' so to speak, however far back it may have been in ordinary reckoning."[46] This time out of time allows one to experience a universe of eternal relationships—in the case of inauguration, the relationship between the ruler and the ruled—and it has the potential to be reenacted, made present once again, at any moment. This special sense of the present is central to the generic character of the inaugural because the address is about an institution and a form of government fashioned to transcend any given historical moment. The timelessness of an inaugural affirms and ensures the continuity of the constitutional system and the immortality of the presidency as an institution, and timelessness is reflected in its contemplative tone and by the absence of calls to specific and immediate action.

Inaugurals transcend the historical present by reconstituting an existing community, rehearsing the past, affirming traditional values, and articulating timely and timeless principles that will govern the administration of the incoming president. The quality of epideictic timelessness to which inaugurals aspire was captured by Franklin Roosevelt in his 1941 address: "To us there has come a time, in the midst of swift happenings, to pause for a moment and take stock—to recall what our place in history has been, and to rediscover what we are and what we may be" (151). In his second inaugural, George W. Bush placed his presidency in the context of U.S. history: "At this second gathering, our duties are defined not by the words I use but by the history we have seen together. For a half a century, America defended our own freedom by standing watch on distant borders. After the shipwreck of communism came years of relative quiet, years of repose, years of sabbatical, and then there came a day of fire." [47]

Great inaugurals achieve timelessness. They articulate a perspective that transcends the situation that produced them, and for this reason they retain their rhetorical force. For instance, although Lincoln's first inaugural addressed a nation poised on the brink of civil war, Lincoln's message speaks to all situations in which the rights of constituent units are seen to clash with the powers of a central body. Similarly, the eloquent conclusion of Lincoln's second inaugural remains applicable to the wounds the nation suffered in the conflict over the war in Vietnam. Although Franklin Roosevelt's first inaugural assured his hearers that they, as a people under his leadership, could surmount the economic crisis of their time, it also assures audiences through time that Americans can surmount all material problems. Kennedy's inaugural reflected the history of the cold war, but it also expressed the resoluteness required under any circumstances to sustain a struggle against a menacing ideology. Finally, George Washington's inaugural not only spoke to the immediate crisis, but also articulated what Arthur Schlesinger calls "a great strand that binds [the inaugurals] together": [48] "The preservation of the sacred fire of liberty and the destiny of the republican model of government are justly considered, perhaps, as deeply, as finally, staked on the experiment intrusted to the hands of the American people" (2).

Inaugurals bespeak their locus in the eternal present in a high style that heightens experience, invites contemplation, and speaks to the people through time. The language of great inaugurals captures complex, resonant ideas in memorable phrases. Americans still recall Jefferson's "peace, commerce, and honest friendship with all nations, entangling alliances with none" (9). They continue to quote the conclusion of Lincoln's second inaugural:

> With malice toward none, with charity for all, with firmness in the right as God gives us to see the right, let us strive to finish the work we are in, to bind up

the nation's wounds, to care for him who shall have borne the battle and for his widow and his orphan, to do all which may achieve and cherish a just and lasting peace among ourselves and with all nations. (77)[49]

Franklin Roosevelt's "So, first of all, let me assert my firm belief that the only thing we have to fear is fear itself" (145) and John F. Kennedy's "And so, my fellow Americans, ask not what your country can do for you: Ask what you can do for your country" (166) also remain memorable. Such phrases illustrate special rhetorical skill in reinvigorating traditional values; in them, familiar ideas become fresh and take on new meaning.

Stylistically and structurally, great presidential inaugurals are suited to contemplation. Through the use of parallelism, for example, Kennedy revived our traditional commitment to the defense of freedom: "We shall pay any price, bear any burden, meet any hardship, support any friend, oppose any foe, in order to assure the survival and success of liberty" (165). His memorable antithesis, "Let us never negotiate out of fear. But let us never fear to negotiate" (166), was a vivid restatement of our modern tradition of relationship to foreign nations. Kennedy's more famous antithesis quoted above asked citizens to contemplate a redefinition of who they were as a people, a redefinition based on sacrifice. Through the use of assonance, Kennedy underscored the nuclear peril when he spoke of "the steady spread of the deadly atom" (166). By arresting attention, such literary devices invite listeners and readers to ponder these ideas, ideas less suited to contemplation when stated in more mundane language.[50]

The preceding analysis treats presidential inaugurals as one kind of epideictic, or ceremonial, rhetoric. That perspective can create the impression that these speeches are merely ritualistic, meaning that they are insignificant because their content is limited to *memoria*, the shared past. But inaugurals in which presidents have reconstituted the people in new terms and have selectively reaffirmed and reinvigorated those communal values consistent with the philosophy and tone of the incoming administration suggest ways in which a ritualistic occasion may be directed toward other ends. In other words, praise and blame, the key strategies in ceremonial discourse, can be used ideologically to lay the groundwork for policy initiatives.

What usually distinguishes ceremonial address from policy advocacy is deliberation, the argumentative form associated with justifying new policy. Deliberative argument pivots on the issue of expediency; specifically, which policy is best able to address identified problems, which policy will produce more beneficial than harmful consequences, and which is most practical, given available resources.

LINCOLN'S FIRST INAUGURAL

Lincoln's first inaugural address is significant not only as a masterpiece of epideictic discourse, but also as a vehicle for considering the ways in which epideictic rhetoric is related to policy deliberation. In that unusual address, Lincoln integrated key elements of the two genres. Specifically, in the service of epideictic ends (unifying the nation and reaffirming cherished communal values), Lincoln adopted deliberative means (arguments regarding expediency). He asked the audience to contemplate whether or not the policy of secession, already adopted by seven states, was the best means to resolve sectional disputes, and he attempted to allay the fears of Southern slaveholders about interference in their domestic affairs. Lincoln's speech displays epideictic contemplation as a precursor to deliberative decision.[51]

The early parts of the speech are consistent with the inaugural traditions that we have identified. Lincoln began by noting the ceremonial character of the occasion, "a custom as old as the Government itself," and acknowledging the people's role in the ritual of investiture: "I appear before you to address you briefly and to take in your presence the oath prescribed by the Constitution" (72). Although Lincoln's speech differs from other inaugurals because he spoke in a situation of crisis, he reaffirmed the Constitution, including those sections supporting the fugitive slave law, and the limits of executive power. Lincoln also followed precedent in swearing a personal oath: "I take the official oath to-day with no mental reservations and with no purpose to construe the Constitution or laws by any hypercritical rules" (73).

What followed set forth the philosophy and tone of the upcoming administration; in this instance, because there was "substantial division," the focus was on secession. If considered apart from historical precedent, these paragraphs might appear divisively specific. However, when the arguments made here are compared with those laid out a few months earlier in the final annual message of Lincoln's predecessor, James Buchanan, they emerge in a different light. Buchanan had strong Southern sympathies, and although Buchanan and Lincoln held differing views of the president's constitutional right to act to hold the Union together, particularly in the absence of congressional enactments, they agreed that secession was unconstitutional, and their arguments for that conclusion were remarkably similar.[52] As a result, this section of the speech can fairly be construed as a general statement of administrative philosophy and tone that was consistent with an attempt to unify the auditors into a people. In other words, although affected by the unusual historical circumstances, the first half of the speech fulfills traditional expectations for an inaugural address.

The speech becomes exceptional as an inaugural and as epideictic discourse in the paragraphs following Lincoln's question, "To those, however, who really love the Union may I not speak?" (74). These paragraphs present a series of questions designed to induce the audience to think deeply about secession, the reasons for it, and the consequences it would bring. Lincoln asked, "Would it not be wise to ascertain precisely why we do it? Will you hazard so desperate a step? . . . Will . . . you risk the commission of so fearful a mistake?" (74).

The questions were the opening sally in an effort to provoke contemplation of secession as a policy, but although they were rhetorical questions, they were not adequate to this task. They had to be buttressed by reasoning laid out to show that conclusions previously reached might be erroneous. Lincoln established a basic premise: "All profess to be content in the Union if all constitutional rights can be maintained" (74). He developed his argument by maintaining that, as yet, no constitutional rights of slaveholders had been denied, and he challenged his auditors, "Think, if you can, of a single instance in which a plainly written provision of the Constitution has ever been denied" (74). That was a perilous challenge, dependent entirely on widespread agreement that no violations had occurred. As a result, he quickly noted areas of ambiguity:

> No foresight can anticipate nor any document of reasonable length contain express provisions for all possible questions. Shall fugitives from labor be surrendered by national or by State authority? The Constitution does not expressly say. May Congress prohibit slavery in the Territories? The Constitution does not expressly say. Must Congress protect slavery in the Territories? The Constitution does not expressly say. (74)

These areas of ambiguity, he contended, were the issues that divided the nation, and he did not pretend that their resolution would be easy. At that moment, they appeared irreconcilable: "If the minority will not acquiesce, the majority must, or the Government must cease. There is no other alternative, for continuing the Government is acquiescence on one side or the other" (74). He immediately added that, despite such a

standoff, secession was no solution: "If a minority in such case will se-
cede rather than acquiesce, they make a precedent which in turn will
divide and ruin them" (74). He developed this claim by asserting what
he presumed would be a universally accepted principle, that in human
affairs "unanimity is impossible" (75). As a result, he argued, one must
choose between majority rule on the one hand and some form of anarchy or despotism on the other.

What must majority rule decide? He narrowed the current dispute
to conflict over the rightness of slavery and whether or not it should be
extended. Given the intensity of the disagreement, he argued that the
fugitive slave laws and the laws suppressing the foreign slave trade "are
each as well enforced, perhaps, as any law can ever be in a community
where the moral sense of the people imperfectly supports the law itself"
(75). Conflicts over these issues, he argued, would only worsen following separation. He posed a series of rhetorical questions, the answers to
each of which suggested why differences would only intensify following division, asking, for instance, "Can aliens make treaties easier than
friends can make laws?" (75).

Lincoln reminded the audience of legal avenues of redress, such as
amending the Constitution, but proposed nothing, although he indicated that he would not oppose an amendment making the right to hold
slaves in those states where slavery already existed "express and irre-
vocable" (76). His earlier appeal to have "patient confidence in the ultimate justice of the people" was buttressed by rhetorical questions, such
as "Is there any better or equal hope in the world?" and by a reminder of
executive limitations: "This same people have wisely given their public
servants but little power for mischief" (76).

Although he relied heavily on deliberative arguments in the second
half of the speech, the contemplative, epideictic purpose of the entire
address was evident in its conclusion, when Lincoln said, "My countrymen, one and all, think calmly and well upon this subject. Nothing valu-
able can be lost by taking time" (76).

Lincoln's first inaugural subtly invites contemplation of the contrast
between the present haste of the secessionists and the timeless truths
their hasty action could destroy. On the one hand, there is the "eternal
truth and justice" of the Almighty and "perpetual Union," while on the
other hand, there are those who would "hurry ... you in hot haste to
a step which you would never take deliberately" (76). For Lincoln, secession was "precipitate action." In this interplay between the present
moment and timeless truths, even an administration that was wicked,

as the South feared that his would be, could not "seriously injure the Government in the short space of four years" (76).

Lincoln offered his audience two frames through which to view this moment. One, constructed by those who would act impetuously, began with the nation's founding but would end with "destruction of the Union." The second, characterized by contemplation and thoughtful consideration, began at the nation's founding but was endless, presupposing that the Union was perpetual and, hence, beyond the ability of a few to destroy. Lincoln's repeated urging of contemplation invited the audience to adopt the second frame. Both frames were introduced with the inaugural's opening statement, in which Lincoln noted that he stood before the audience "in compliance with a custom as old as government itself" (72). The first ended when Lincoln posited the possibility of "destruction of the Union" (73). The second ended with this affirmation:

> I hold that in contemplation of universal law and of the Constitution the Union of these States is perpetual. Perpetuity is implied, if not expressed, in the fundamental laws of all national governments. It is safe to assert that no government proper ever had a provision in its organic law for its own termination. (73)

Contemplation and perpetuity were repeatedly linked. "Descending from these general principles," he said, "we find the proposition that in legal contemplation the Union is perpetual confirmed by the history of the Union itself" (73).

At the core of the speech is an implied question about the continued life of the Union and the principles for which it was founded. Will secessionists destroy the vital element of perpetuity, making mortal and time-bound what should be perpetual and timeless?

It was in this context that Lincoln melded past, present, and future into the timelessly memorable contemplation of his peroration:

> The mystic chords of memory [the timeless past], stretching from every battlefield and patriot grave [the founding of the nation] to every living heart and hearthstone all over this broad land [the present], will yet swell the chorus of the Union, when again touched, as surely they will be [a confident positing of the future], by the better angels of our nature. (76)

Here is Lincoln's final invitation to contemplation, an exhortation to set aside the hurried, passion-strained tensions of the moment in favor of the perpetual, timeless Union that is greater than any of them.

Lincoln's speech is a masterpiece because it extends the symbolic function of epideictic discourse to include the contemplation that precedes action, because its inducements to contemplation are fused with invitations to participate in the processes by which the speaker reached his conclusions, and because the concerns of the moment are linked to eternal questions. As such, the discourse enacts a respect for thoughtful deliberation by the citizenry, which is the essence of a democratic system, even at the moment of its most intense division and crisis.

CONCLUSION

Our analysis of the U.S. presidential inaugural address suggests the processes by which a distinct genre of epideictic rhetoric comes into being. Its broadest outlines are set by the general characteristics of epideictic discourse. A specific kind of ceremony and occasion refines the genre further. In this case, the presidential inaugural is part of a rite of passage, of investiture, a ritual at a singular moment in the democratic process that establishes a special relationship between speaker and audience. The U.S. presidential investiture requires a mutual covenant between president and people, a rehearsal of fundamental political values, an enunciation of political principles, and the enactment of the presidential persona. The conventions of this rhetorical type emerge because presidents are familiar with the tradition and tend to study past inaugurals before formulating their own.

Presidential inaugurals vary, but that variation itself illuminates the U.S. presidential inaugural as a genre. Circumstances vary, as do the personalities of the presidents, but the variation among inaugurals is predictable.

Inaugural addresses vary substantively because presidents choose to rehearse aspects of national tradition that are consistent with the party or political philosophy they represent. Such selective emphasis is illustrated in Franklin Roosevelt's second inaugural address:

> Instinctively we recognize a deeper need—the need to find through government the instrument of our united purpose to solve for the individual the ever-rising problems of a complex civilization. ... In this we Americans were discovering no wholly new truth; we were writing a new chapter in our book of self-government. ... The essential democracy of our Nation and the safety of our people depend not upon the absence of power, but upon lodging it with those whom the people can change or continue at stated intervals through

an honest and free system of elections. . . . [W]e have made the exercise of all power more democratic; for we have begun to bring private autocratic powers into their proper subordination to the people's government. (148)

Later in the speech, he added, "Today we reconsecrate our country to long-cherished ideals in a suddenly changed civilization" (150). Similarly, in 1981, Ronald Reagan chose to emphasize certain facets of the system in order to affirm values consistent with his conservative political philosophy: "Our government has no power except that granted it by the people. It is time to check and reverse the growth of government which shows signs of having grown beyond the consent of the governed" (181).

A major variation occurs in inaugurals delivered by incumbent presidents. Because a covenant already exists between a reelected president and the people, the need to reconstitute the community is less urgent. Because the country is familiar with a sitting president's political philosophy, the need to preview administrative philosophy and tone is also muted. Reelected presidents tend to recommit themselves to principles articulated in their previous inaugurals or to highlight only those principles relevant to the agenda for their coming terms. In this respect, subsequent inaugurals by the same president tend to be extensions, not replications, of earlier inaugurals.

The inaugural addresses themselves articulate the reason for this generic variation. Lincoln, for instance, did so, although he was president in the midst of the most serious of crises:

At this second appearing to take the oath of the Presidential office there is less occasion for an extended address than there was at the first. Then a statement somewhat in detail of the course to be pursued seemed fitting and proper. Now, at the expiration of four years, during which public declarations have been constantly called forth on every point and phase of the great contest which still absorbs the attention and engrosses the energies of the nation, little that is new could be presented. (77)

Similarly, in 1805, Jefferson reported that his conscience told him he had lived up to the principles he had espoused four years earlier (11). In 1821, Monroe noted, "If the person thus elected has served the preceding term, an opportunity is afforded him to review its principal occurrences and to give the explanation respecting them as in his judgment may be useful to his constituents" (23).

Some presidents have used a subsequent inaugural to review the trials and successes of their earlier terms, and in so doing, they have rehearsed the immediate past, a move rarely made in first inaugurals. When subsequent inaugurals develop specific policies, these are usually described as continuations of policies initiated in the previous term, continuations presumably endorsed by the president's reelection.

Special conditions faced by some presidents have caused some subsequent inaugurals to resemble first inaugurals. For example, in 1917, confronting challenges quite different from those that existed in 1913, Wilson said, "This is not the time for retrospect. It is time rather to speak our thoughts and purposes concerning the present and the immediate future" (126). In the face of the events of World War I, he told his audience,

> We are provincials no longer. The tragic events of the thirty months of vital turmoil through which we have just passed have made us citizens of the world. There can be no turning back. Our own fortunes as a nation are involved whether we would have it so or not. (127)

The war prompted Wilson to constitute the people in a new way, as citizens of the world.

Similarly, the events leading to World War II affected Franklin Roosevelt's inaugural address in 1941: "In this day the task of the people is to save the Nation and its institutions from disruptions from without" (151). That statement of the task diverged sharply from the principles he emphasized in 1933 and 1937.

Variation in inaugural addresses is evidence of an identifiable cluster of elements that form the essential inaugural act. Each apparent variation is an emphasis on or a development of one or more of the key elements we have described. Washington's second inaugural address underscored the role of the audience as witnesses and the address as an extension of the oath of office. Jefferson's first address was a call to unity through the enunciation of political principles. Lincoln's first inaugural was a dramatic appeal to the audience to participate in reaffirming the mutual covenant between the president and the people; his second was an exploration of what it means to say that this nation is "under God." Theodore Roosevelt explored the meaning of our "sacred trust" as it applies to a people with an international role. Franklin Roosevelt's first address explored the nature of executive leadership and the limits of executive power, whereas his second constituted the audience as a caring people. Wilson's first inaugural explored the meaning of U.S. industrial development. Finally, Kennedy's address exploited the possibilities of the noble, dignified, literary language characteristic of the epideictic to such an extent that his address is sometimes attacked for stylistic excess.[53]

From a generic perspective, then, a presidential inaugural reconstitutes the people as an audience that can witness the rite of investiture, rehearses communal values from the past, sets forth the political principles that will guide the new administration, and demonstrates that the president can enact the presidential persona appropriately. Still more generally, the presidential inaugural address is an epideictic ritual that is formal, unifying, abstract, and eloquent. At the core of this ritual lies epideictic timelessness—the fusion of the past and future of the nation in an eternal present in which we reaffirm what Franklin Roosevelt called "our covenant with ourselves" (148), a covenant between the executive and the nation that is the essence of democratic government.

Institutionally, the inaugural address performs two key functions. In and through it, each president is invested with the office, and at a moment of transition, the continuity of the institution of the presidency and of the system of government of which it is a part is affirmed.

Finally, the inaugural address is the first of the rhetorical genres which, taken together, constitute a major part of the presidency as an institution and of individual presidencies.

THREE

Special Inaugural Addresses: The Speeches of Ascendant Vice Presidents

On nine occasions in U.S. history, a vice president has ascended to the presidency. In eight of those cases, the elevation occurred because of the death of a president; in one case, an appointed vice president became president owing to the resignation, in the face of impeachment, of his predecessor. In eight instances, the new president felt impelled to speak, to seek from Congress and the people the investiture that is central to the inaugural address, as described in chapter 2. These speeches, and the absence of a speech by the laconic Calvin Coolidge, allow us to test the claims made in that chapter about the symbolic act performed in an inaugural address and about the function of this initial encounter between the new president and the citizenry.

An "inaugurating" address is dramatically altered under the conditions created by the death of a president. Although speeches made on such occasions include the traditional elements already described, they often differ from other inaugurals in eulogizing the deceased president, in affirming that that president's policies or general principles will shape the actions of the new administration, and in incorporating a level of legislative detail inappropriate to the standard inaugural.

The death of any person creates the need for a unique form of symbolic response: the eulogy. In Western culture, at least, a eulogy acknowledges the death, transforms the relationship between the living and the dead from present to past tense, eases the mourners' terror at confronting their own mortality, consoles them by arguing that the deceased lives on, and reknits the fabric of the community.

The death of a president makes the need for a eulogy even more urgent. The community is threatened because it has lost its leader; the citizenry needs reassurance that communal institutions will survive. The threat to the stability of the nation is magnified when the president is assassinated, an act suggesting the possibility of a deliberate effort to undermine the duly elected government.

Moreover, the Kennedy assassination was a major televisual event. As reported by the Museum of Broadcast Communications,

On Friday 22 November 1963, news bulletins reporting rifle shots during the president's motorcade in Dallas, Texas, broke into normal programming. Soon the three networks preempted their regular schedules and all commercial advertising for a wrenching marathon that would conclude only after the president's burial at Arlington National Cemetery on Monday 25 November.... At 5:59 P.M. Friday, the president's body is returned to Andrews Air Force Base.... When the casket is lowered from the plane, glimpses of Jacqueline Kennedy appear on screen, her dress and stockings still visibly bloodstained. With the new First Lady, Lady Bird Johnson, by his side, LBJ makes a brief statement before the cameras. "We have suffered a loss that cannot be weighed," he intones flatly. "I will do my best. That is all I can do. I ask for your help—and God's." ... Later that same afternoon, in stark counterpoint to the ongoing chaos, thousands of mourners line up to file pass the president's flag draped coffin in the Capitol rotunda.

Monday, 25 November ... bears witness to an extraordinary political-religious spectacle: the ceremonial transfer of the president's coffin by caisson from the Capitol rotunda to St. Matthews Cathedral, ... and on across the Potomac River for burial at Arlington National Cemetery.... No sooner do commentators remind viewers that this day marks the president's son's third birthday, then outside the church, as the caisson passes by, little John F. Kennedy, Jr. salutes. ... Awed by the regal solemnity, network commentators are quiet and restrained, allowing the medium of the moving image to record a series of eloquent sounds: drums and bagpipes, hoofbeats, the cadenced steps of the honor guard, and, at the burial at Arlington, the final sour note of a bugle playing "Taps." ... As if hypnotized, many Americans watch for hour upon hour at a stretch in an unprecedented immersion in deep involvement spectatorship.[1]

"LET US CONTINUE"

Lyndon Johnson's televised speech to a joint session of Congress on November 27—his initial speech as president—exemplifies a highly effective response to the complex demands of such an extraordinary occasion: an ascendant vice presidential speech that is also a national eulogy (see chapter 4).[2]

The assassination of President Kennedy created needs that could be met only in public discourse by his successor. To be successful, this discourse would have to eulogize Kennedy and begin the process of national healing, engage the audience in the act of rhetorically investing Johnson with the office of the presidency, and outline the legislative agenda of the new administration. In other words, it would combine the elements of a eulogy with the investing and previewing functions of an inaugural address.

Before Johnson could tell the audience where he would lead it, the office of the presidency had to be vacated rhetorically and its former occupant laid to rest in a eulogy. Once Congress, the immediate audience, and the nation, the mediated audience, had accepted Johnson as president, a role he played while delivering the eulogy, he could engage them in the act of rhetorical investiture, confident that he would not be spurned. Only then could Johnson articulate the philosophy to which he, Kennedy, and the nation had been, were, and would be committed. In other words, the structure of the speech—the ordering of generic elements—was mandated by the situation.

Put differently, the death of President Kennedy created communal needs that had to be met with both a eulogy for the dead president and a national eulogy that would bring comfort to a nation traumatized by the assassination (a genre discussed at length in chapter 4). In addition, the nature of the presidency created institutional needs that had to be met in an act of investiture, and the unique situation of Vice President Lyndon Johnson created personal needs that could be met only by indicating the future course his administration would follow.

The situation also dictated the theme of Johnson's speech, expressed most clearly in his statement, "Today, in this moment of new resolve, I would say to all my fellow Americans, let us continue" (9). This theme reflected and was reinforced by the structure of the speech. It reflected the questions the speech would answer: What was the meaning of the Kennedy presidency? What was Johnson's commitment to it? Where would that commitment take us?

The eulogy acknowledged President Kennedy's death (he "has been struck down") and its traumatic character ("by the foulest deed of our time"), then established that Kennedy endured ("He lives on in the mind and memories of mankind"). The call to continue Kennedy's programs affirmed Kennedy's immortality in collective commemorative action ("No memorial oration or eulogy could more eloquently honor President Kennedy's memory than the earliest possible passage of the civil rights bill for which he fought so long"). Johnson's pledge to carry on Kennedy's programs bound the eulogy to the investiture, while his call to enact those programs in commemoration of the slain leader linked the eulogy, the investiture, and a preview of Johnson's legislative priorities. Once the theme, "let us continue," was set in place, the legislative preview could become an element in the eulogy. By calling for legislative action as a memorial, Johnson reunited the national and political community in a common purpose and affirmed that, in such action, the community could transcend the death of President Kennedy.

The theme of continuity was also central to investiture, an act formally conferring the authority and symbols of high office. It was only after citing Kennedy's inaugural appeal, "Let us begin," that Johnson declared, "Let us continue." What was begun by Kennedy would be continued by Johnson. The shift invited the audience to invest Johnson with the presidential role. Before risking that shift, Johnson rehearsed the dreams that he, the country, and Kennedy shared, creating a tension between those dreams and their realization, which would be resolved in legislative advocacy: "And now the ideas and the ideals which he so nobly represented must and will be translated into effective action." Such a translation would give Kennedy's death meaning and memorialize him. Johnson reminded the audience that he was uniquely qualified to translate Kennedy's ideas into action: "For thirty-two years Capitol Hill has been my home." Then, in an echo of Kennedy's inaugural assertion, "We shall ... bear any burden," Johnson enlisted the help of Congress and the citizenry: "I cannot bear this burden alone." The echoes of Kennedy's inaugural helped to invest Johnson with the presidency; rhetorically, Johnson was already bearing Kennedy's burden. Johnson's use of Kennedy's inaugural also invited the audience to transfer to him the power it had previously vested in Kennedy. By permitting Johnson to shoulder Kennedy's burden and by agreeing to share that burden, Congress and the nation legitimized Johnson's ascent to the presidency.

The need to legitimize oneself as the president is the by-product of an electoral system in which a president and vice president of the same party are elected together, a system committed to the idea of orderly succession. (This system came into existence with ratification of the Twelfth Amendment to the Constitution on September 25, 1804.) Voting simultaneously for the presidential and the vice presidential candidates is so much a part of the electoral process that voters consider the qualifications of the vice presidential candidate, who would replace the president in case of death or severe disability, only when such qualifications become the focal point of a campaign, as they did in 1968, when Spiro Agnew was sharply contrasted with Edmund Muskie, and in 1976, 1984, 1988, and 2000, when the Robert Dole–Walter Mondale, the George Bush–Geraldine Ferraro, the Lloyd Bentsen–Dan Quayle, and the Richard Cheney–Joseph Lieberman debates highlighted the differences between the vice presidential candidates of the major parties.

The institutional demands of our system can be contrasted with those in a monarchy in which succession is determined biologically, not by popular election; citizens do not invest a new monarch with the right of succession, although they indirectly ratify the succession, through representatives, at the coronation. By contrast, the papacy is an institution in which a new election is mandated when the position is vacated, and the position remains vacant until a successor has been elected. The election itself confers the powers of the office on the new pope, although it is followed by a rite of investiture. Thus, the process by which power passes places rhetorical constraints on institutional leaders.

Having legitimized himself as Kennedy's successor and, hence, as the president, Johnson could turn to policy. Here the speech employed strategies more common to the campaign speech, State of the Union address, or inaugural. In memory of Kennedy, Johnson called for passage of the civil rights bill, Kennedy's tax bill, the foreign aid bill, the pending education bill, and the remaining appropriations bills. The need for action was mandated by Kennedy's death: "The ideas ... must ... be translated into effective action." Policy proposals became a natural extension of the earlier commitment to memorialize Kennedy. Congressional action would ensure that the communal memory of the late president lived on: "John Kennedy's death commands what his life conveyed—that America must move forward." Here Johnson also performed an important eulogistic function by reuniting the community "in new fellowship, making us one people in our hour of sorrow." If this new fellowship occurred and was solemnized in the enactment of civil rights legislation, it would give Kennedy's life new meaning: "So let us here highly resolve that John Fitzgerald Kennedy did not live—or die—in vain."

This statement, at the conclusion of the speech, was the second echo of Lincoln's address at Gettysburg. Earlier, in the middle of the speech, Johnson said, "Let all the world know and none misunderstand that I rededicate this Government to the unswerving support of the United Nations, to the honorable and determined execution of our commitments." This passage followed the rite of rhetorical investiture. Earlier, Johnson had used the pronoun "we." Now that he was invested as president, he could rededicate the country in the first person singular. In both echoes of the Gettysburg Address, Johnson assumed the role of Lincoln—of president. Lincoln dedicated "this ground"; Johnson rededicated. Lincoln said that "the world will little note nor long remember what we say here." By contrast, Johnson asked the world to note what he said, for his words were the rededication that had to come before the actions proposed in the final section of the speech. Lincoln committed his audience to the cause for which the soldiers died; Johnson committed his audience to the cause for which Kennedy lived and died. Just as the honored dead at Gettysburg would not have died in vain if the audience renewed its efforts for the Union, so Kennedy's death would not have been in vain if it produced the legislation for which he had fought.

If the speech were to satisfy the human, communal, and institutional needs created by Kennedy's death, it had to perform three functions: Johnson had to eulogize Kennedy, legitimize himself as president, and unify the community in carrying forward the dead president's policies in his memory. In this triad, the eulogy was dominant. Kennedy's death created the need for the speech. If it was to blend these three functions, then Kennedy, not Johnson, had to be its focus. Hence, Johnson infused the speech with Kennedy's name, Kennedy's words, and Kennedy's policies, and he specifically subordinated himself to Kennedy when he said that "the greatest leader of our time has been struck down."[3]

The need to eulogize Kennedy and to set forth a legislative agenda created a tension that Johnson had to resolve without diminishing the deceased. If Kennedy had been an effective president, why was there so much unfinished business to enact? Johnson surmounted this question by quoting from Kennedy's inaugural, reaffirming that "our national work would not be finished in the first thousand days, nor in the life of this administration nor even perhaps in our lifetime on this planet." Inclusion of this passage transformed the unfinished agenda into a tribute to Kennedy's realistic appraisal of the nature of government rather than an indictment of the effectiveness of his administration.

The need to eulogize Kennedy, to legitimize himself, and, as part of both these functions, to set forth policy created another problem for Johnson. Would his advocacy of specific legislation detract from the eulogy and imply an unbecoming eagerness to assume the reins of administration? Johnson overcame this difficulty by making his advocacy an extension of the eulogy and a way of healing the wounds caused by the assassination: "No words are sad enough to express our sense of loss. No words are strong enough to express our determination to continue the forward thrust of America that he began." If his eulogy was inadequate, it was because no speech could do Kennedy justice; only legislative action would suffice.

In Lyndon Johnson's speech, a single generic form, the eulogy, predominated. Incorporated into Johnson's eulogy was an inaugural, including standard appeals for investiture, but here the inaugural extended its memorializing of the deceased into an appeal to enact Kennedy's legislative agenda. The integration of these forms was a strategic response to the complex demands of the situation, and the order of these elements was fixed by the order in which the communal needs of the audience and the institutional needs of the presidency had to be met.

OTHER VICE PRESIDENTS RESPOND TO DEATH

When a president dies in office, the vice president must deliver a eulogistic statement or court charges of being insensitive to the demands of the office and the needs of the audience. Some recognition of the transfer of power is also required. These two elements can by themselves form a coherent, satisfying message. Whether the discourse will indicate legislative priorities depends on the relationship between the president and the vice president (Thomas Jefferson, of a different party, would not have been expected to commit himself to the policies of John Adams, had Adams died in office), the state of the country (a country at war with a foreign power differs from one at peace in ways reflected in Harry Truman's initial speech), the credibility of the newly invested president (some vice presidents are unknown to the electorate; others are major figures in their own right), and the new president's comfort with the policies already in place. In other words, the death of the country's leader creates human needs that must be addressed regardless of the specific situation in which the successor and the country find themselves; the institutional process by which power is transferred creates expectations that the successor must satisfy regardless of the specifics of the situation. The death of a president and the processes of institutional succession, however, do not necessarily mean that the successor will promise to be committed to the policies of the dead president.

In a time of turmoil or transition, a successor might wish to pause before averring commitment to a predecessor's policies. If those policies were controversial, unpopular, or in a state of flux, then committing the country to them could divide the community that needs to be unified by the eulogy and its attendant elements. This was the situation facing Andrew Johnson. The rapidly changing circumstances, Lincoln's unpopularity among some segments of the country, and Johnson's own fitful history in the vice presidency explain the absence of a legislative forecast in his public statement after Lincoln's assassination. Andrew Johnson explicitly rejected such a preview:

> As to an indication of any policy which may be pursued by me in the adminis-
> tration of the Government, I have to say that that must be left for development
> as the Administration progresses. The message or declaration must be made by
> the acts as they transpire. The only assurance that I can now give of the future
> is reference to the past. The course which I have taken in the past in connection
> with this rebellion must be regarded as a guaranty of the future.[4]

In such circumstances a policy preview cannot be an extension of the eulogy, and because eulogizing is the dominant function to be fulfilled, discussion of policies should be omitted.

Nevertheless, Andrew Johnson's speech, the first presidential speech responding to the death of a president other than by natural causes, was anomalous and highly inappropriate. The opening sentence of the address, "I must be permitted to say that I have been almost over-whelmed by the announcement of the sad event which has so recently occurred,"[5] was preoccupied with Andrew Johnson, not Abraham Lincoln. In what would have been an invitation to investiture in other addresses, Johnson ineptly expressed humility: "I feel incompetent to perform duties so important and responsible as those which have been unexpectedly thrown upon me."[6] He recognized the need to suggest the legislative direction the new administration would follow, but explicitly rejected that option, saying, "that must be left for development as the Administration progresses." He pledged continuity, but with his own past, not Lincoln's. He ended with an appeal for investiture: "I want your encouragement and countenance. . . . I feel in making this request that it will be heartily responded to by you and all other patriots and lovers of a free people."[7] These anomalies can be explained, at least in part, by Johnson's documented insensitivity as a speaker, illustrated by his disoriented vice presidential inaugural, allegedly delivered while he was intoxicated,[8] as well as his histrionic defenses as Congress moved toward impeachment proceedings.[9]

By contrast, Truman's speech after the death of Franklin Roosevelt, which resembles Lyndon Johnson's speech after the death of John F. Kennedy, was appropriate and rhetorically adept. Speaking to a joint session of Congress, Truman began by acknowledging Roosevelt's death, but added, "At a time like this, words are inadequate." Truman acknowledged that no one could fill the void left by Roosevelt, but, he affirmed, "We must carry on."[10] Then, in a statement of investiture, Truman called on all Americans "to help me keep our nation united in defense of those ideals which have been so eloquently proclaimed by Franklin Roosevelt" and assured his audience that he would "support and defend those ideals."[11] After a generalized rehearsal of the ideals, Truman pledged, "In the memory of those who have made the supreme sacrifice—in the memory of our fallen President—we shall not fail!"[12] Then, after a discussion of hope and peace, Truman affirmed that he required the help of Congress and divine guidance to complete the tasks ahead.

Although the eulogy need not always be as elaborate as those delivered by Lyndon Johnson and Harry Truman in circumstances that called for what we describe in chapter 4 as a national eulogy, an acknowledgment of the death of one's predecessor is essential. The brevity of the eulogistic section of John Tyler's 1841 address reflected a situation in which his predecessor died before defining his presidency. Tyler acknowledged "the deeply regretted death" of his predecessor, William Henry Harrison, but he did not see his administration as a continuation of Harrison's (although they were elected on the same ticket—"Tippecanoe and Tyler Too"—their views on key issues differed). Instead, he delivered a speech that closely approximated the inaugural addresses of elected presidents. In it he articulated "the principles which will govern me in the course of my administration."[13] Millard Fillmore's 1851 speech was similar, in part because of Zachary Taylor's short five-month tenure in office. In a special message to "fellow-citizens of the Senate and House of Representatives," he acknowledged that "a great man [President Taylor] has fallen among us, and a whole country is called to an occasion of unexpected, deep, and general mourning." In an invitation to investiture, Fillmore appealed to Congress "to aid me, under the trying circumstances which surround me, in the discharge of the duties from which . . . I dare not shrink." He closed with a faint indication of legislative priorities: "I shall most readily concur in whatever measures the wisdom of the two houses may suggest as befitting this deeply melancholy occasion."[14]

Just as Harrison's brief tenure shaped Tyler's address, the ideological implications of William McKinley's assassination shaped Theodore Roosevelt's response.[15] The unique circumstances of this assassination were reflected in the speech's eulogistic section and in its treatment of legislative concerns. In this address, the eulogy included a defense of McKinley's character: "The blow was not aimed at tyranny or wealth. It was aimed at one of the strongest champions the wage-worker ever had."[16] Having detailed "the Judas-like infamy" of this act, Roosevelt asserted that "we feel the blow not as struck at him, but as struck at the Nation."[17] With that as a transition, Roosevelt could not comfortably invite investiture. Instead, he had to discuss the nation's response to the assassin's assault, so he turned to an attack on anarchism, which was designed to expose the falsity of the claim that anarchists were concerned for the working people. McKinley's conduct "as a gallant soldier," his concern for "the welfare of others," "his kindliness of nature," and his background as a "wage-earner" were all praised as a means of discrediting the claim of his assassin, Leon Czolgosz, that McKinley was "an enemy of the good working people." The attack on anarchism and the defense of McKinley's character were a natural extension of the eulogy. From this defense and attack, legislative recommendations naturally emerged: anarchists should be kept out of this country; the federal courts should be given jurisdiction over those who attempt to kill the president; anarchy, like piracy, should be made an offense against the law of nations.

The circumstances of the assassination also affected Roosevelt's references to the continuity of the presidency: "The blow was aimed not at this President but at all Presidents; at every symbol of government."[18] After reviewing popular reaction to the assassin's act, however, he reassured the audience: "No man will ever be restrained from becoming President by any fear as to his personal safety."[19]

Theodore Roosevelt's message also constitutes a special case because it was a lengthy written document, not a speech. This change in mode of delivery made it difficult for Roosevelt to include an explicit acknowledgment of investiture.[20] Oral discourse can invite investiture from an immediate audience, enabling the president to proceed immediately from the investiture to a description of the policies that will be pursued under the new administration. In a written address, it would be presumptuous to invite the audience to invest the president with the office and then, without waiting for its assent, to usurp it, in effect, by detailing future policies. Thus, a written message either will contain no explicit legislative agenda, as in the case of Fillmore, or will assume investiture and detail specific policies, as in the case of Theodore Roosevelt.

A peculiar set of circumstances led Calvin Coolidge to produce no discourse clearly identifiable as an ascendant vice president's speech. Because Congress was not in session when Warren G. Harding died unexpectedly from apoplexy, following a bout of pneumonia, and because there was neither any precedent for an ascendant vice president to speak to the nation nor any means of reaching a national audience in the infancy of radio, there was no way for Coolidge to assemble the people empowered to invest him symbolically with the office. Accordingly, upon receiving the news of Harding's death on August 3, 1923, while vacationing, he issued a proclamation from Plymouth, Vermont, mourning the death, pledging to continue Harding's policies, asking the cooperation of Harding's associates, and calling on the help of God.[21] Because he had not yet taken the oath of office, it would have been inappropriate for him to seek investiture.

Even after his swearing in, Coolidge put off making a speech previewing his own presidency. Initially, he delayed it on the grounds that it would be inappropriate to do so until Harding was buried, and after the burial, on the pretext that he should not articulate specific plans to any audience other than Congress. Hence, he would not outline his legislative agenda until he delivered his first annual message when Congress reconvened. He declined an invitation to address a service memorializing Harding in September on the grounds that he would "feel free to consider invitations to make speeches on matters of interest and concern to the country" after he had "communicated his views on important questions to Congress when it assembled in December."[22] That annual message began with a short eulogy that memorialized Harding through a commitment to the general principles of good government that Harding was said to represent:

> Since the close of the last Congress the Nation has lost President Harding. The world knew his kindness and his humanity, his greatness and his character. He has left his mark upon history. He has made justice more certain and peace more secure. The surpassing tribute paid to his memory as he was borne across the continent to rest at last at home revealed the place he held in the hearts of the American people. But this is not the occasion for extended reference to the man or his work. In this presence, among those who knew and loved him, that is unnecessary. But we who were associated with him could not resume together the functions of our office without pausing for a moment, and in his memory reconsecrating ourselves to the service of our country. He is gone. We remain. It is our duty, under the inspiration of his example, to take up the burdens he was

permitted to lay down, and to develop and support the wise principles of government which he represented.[23]

Only after delivering this annual message did he deliver an extended eulogy for Harding on December 10.

Practical political considerations and the absence of an appropriate audience affected Coolidge's behavior. Harding died at the end of his third year in office. Presumably, he and Coolidge would have been their party's candidates in the 1924 election. Coolidge required time to determine whether to run, and if he did, on which of Harding's policies he wished to campaign. The *New York Times* accurately identified the central function of Coolidge's first annual message when it headlined its coverage of that speech, "See the Message as Party Platform."[24] Coolidge's behavior is in sharp contrast to that of Lyndon Johnson, but there were two key differences in the situations they faced. Unlike Coolidge, Johnson could and did assemble a national audience because Congress was in session at the time of the assassination and national electronic media were available. In addition, Johnson was confident that his authority and credibility would be enhanced if he were seen as a continuation of his predecessor, which was unclear in Coolidge's case.[25] As a result, circumstances worked to enable and encourage Johnson to speak, whereas the situation Coolidge faced worked to inhibit, even to prevent, him from speaking.

In summary, speeches by vice presidents who become president upon the death of their predecessors reflect the circumstances surrounding their assumption of office. When successful, the speeches encompass those events in a symbolic context establishing that the presidency has survived the trauma. The length and content of the eulogistic portion of the speech, the existence of appeals to investiture, and the presence and nature of legislative concerns are all influenced by the circumstances that occasion the speech.

FORD RESPONDS TO NIXON'S RESIGNATION

On August 9, 1974, Gerald Ford faced an unprecedented rhetorical situation. The elected vice president, Spiro Agnew, had pleaded no contest to a felony charge and resigned. After three articles of impeachment had been passed by the House Committee on the Judiciary, the elected president, Richard Nixon, had also resigned, turning the office over to Ford, the first appointed vice president in the nation's history.

The actions of Agnew and Nixon had challenged fundamental principles once assumed to be held by every occupant of the White House. What resulted was a speech by Ford that differed in some important ways from both quadrennial inaugurals and the speeches of other ascendant vice presidents.[26]

Unlike other ascendant vice presidents, Ford began not by eulogizing his predecessor, but rather by praising the system that enabled the country to vacate the office peacefully. Nor could Ford's speech propose legislative actions as a memorial to his predecessor, given the circumstances under which Nixon left office.

Because he had not been elected to the vice presidency, Ford's primary task was to secure investiture from a public that had played no direct role in his ascent to the presidency. Complicating Ford's position was that the person who had appointed him to the vice presidency had been publicly discredited. For an audience traumatized by the resignation of the elected vice president, then by the resignation of the elected president, Gerald Ford's assumption of the presidency created an ideal test of claims about the symbolic functions of presidential inaugurals. The test is intensified because Ford explicitly denied that he was delivering such a speech: "Not an inaugural address, not a fireside chat, not a campaign speech—just a little straight talk among friends." Nevertheless, his speech established that the office had been vacated, constituted the audience as the people, rehearsed basic constitutional principles, invited investiture, and previewed Ford's approach to the presidency.

The speech began with an affirmation of the fundamental continuity of the presidency that also constituted the audience as "the people": "The oath that I have taken is the same oath that was taken by George Washington and by every President under the Constitution." After acknowledging the unusual nature of the occasion, Ford covenanted with his audience: "Therefore, I feel it is my first duty to make an unprecedented compact with my countrymen." He asked the people to invest him with the office that he had assumed: "I am acutely aware that you have not elected me as your President by your ballots, and so I ask you to confirm me as your President with your prayers." After giving the people another opportunity to ratify their compact with their prayers at the end of the speech, he made it an extension of the oath of office by "reaffirm[ing]" the "promise" he had made on December 6 when he assumed the vice presidency: "to uphold the Constitution, to do what is right as God gives me to see the right, and to do the very best I can for America."

Despite the unusual circumstances of his ascent, Ford offered evidence of his own legitimacy. In place of the popular support that constitutes the mandate of an elected president, he argued, in effect, that impartial, duly constituted surrogates of the electorate had certified his qualifications for the office:

> Those who nominated and confirmed me as Vice President were my friends and are my friends. They were of both parties, elected by all the people and acting under the Constitution in their name. It is only fitting then that I should pledge to them and to you that I will be President of all the people.

To make the point that he had not assumed the presidency under circumstances that could foster distrust, Ford noted that he had not campaigned for the presidency or for the vice presidency and that he had "not subscribed to any partisan platform" or "gained office by any secret promises."[27] In other words, he denied that he was driven to seek the office by ambition or that he had attained it at the price of a secret deal with Richard Nixon. He emphasized his need for the popular support that he could not claim through election when he remarked, near the conclusion of the speech, that he had experienced "the good will of countless Americans I have encountered in forty States." Such statements were also an appeal for unity, a mainstay of presidential inaugurals.

Just as inaugurals promise that the president will conserve basic institutional values, Ford's speech reaffirmed fundamental principles, invoking the authority of a founder and former president: "Thomas Jefferson said the people are the only sure reliance for the preservation of our liberty."

Although the legislative forecast was less explicit in Ford's speech than in most inaugurals, he nonetheless moved quickly to take the reins of government by asking for the right to appear before Congress to share his views "on the priority business of the Nation." The very act of asking for the right to appear affirmed the central role of Congress in governance. As Congress had played a central role in the impeachment process, that affirmation was important.

Because Nixon had resigned in disgrace after the Watergate scandals, Ford did not eulogize his predecessor; however, late in the speech, in what were his most memorable lines, he put to rest the experience of Watergate: "My fellow Americans, our long national nightmare is over. Our Constitution works; our great Republic is a Government of laws and not of men. Here the people rule."

Throughout the speech, Ford reiterated the theme that the presidency had survived intact despite Richard Nixon's activities. He reminded the audience, for example, that although the circumstances were "extraordinary," the oath that he had sworn was the same one taken by Washington and every president "under the Constitution." He promised continuity by pledging an "uninterrupted" search for peace and by assuring his listeners that America "will remain strong and united" and that "its strength will remain dedicated to the safety and sanity of the entire family of man." He affirmed that the bond of "truth" that "holds government together" was "unbroken." He also implied that the business of the government was uninterrupted.

Ford's appeal for unity was reinforced by an allusion to Lincoln's second inaugural and an analogy to the divisions created by the Civil War. Ford borrowed Lincoln's language when he said, "As we bind up the internal wounds of Watergate, more poisonous than those of foreign wars, let us restore the golden rule to our political process." This language suggested that the divisions created by Watergate were equivalent to those created by the Civil War and required special efforts and energy to overcome. This appeal emphasized Ford's plea to the audience to pray for Nixon and to apply God's mercy ("God ordains not only righteousness but love, not only justice but mercy") to this situation.

Ford's plea for mercy was part of his tragic view of the presidency. He described an office whose occupants are prone to fail when he said, "I can only guess at those burdens [of the White House], although I have witnessed at close hand the tragedies that befell three Presidents and the lesser trials of others." This statement recontextualized the presidency of Richard Nixon by implying that failure in the White House was almost inevitable. At the same time, it increased the audience's desire to identify with Ford, pray for Ford, and support Ford because he, too, might face demands that, without unusual public support and divine guidance, would be insurmountable. The same notion recurred in Ford's request that God bless and comfort Nixon's wife and daughters, "whose love and loyalty will forever be a shining legacy to all who bear the lonely burdens of the White House." These were the burdens that Ford had said he could "only guess at," yet their existence invited sympathy for him and for his predecessor. At the same time, this statement reassured those who remained champions of the previous president that his presidency had indeed left "a shining legacy," although the channels of inheritance—through Nixon's "wonderful wife and daughters"—were indirect.

Like other inaugurals, Ford's short speech enacted the covenanting process in and through his words. This invitation to joint oath taking is characteristic of inaugurals. What is celebrated as eloquence in Kennedy's inaugural—the repeated and elegantly phrased invitations to mutual pledge making—is essential to the rite of investiture. By inviting audience participation, inaugurals affirm that the people must covenant with presidents if they are to assume the office. The public's willingness to invest Ford with the office of the presidency was crucial; his speech was satisfying precisely because it successfully invited the audience to participate in making a compact. So, although this speech was not a great inaugural, it was a fitting inaugural for this moment. By artfully reaffirming the centrality of the people and the Constitution, the speech validated Ford's central and most memorable claim: that the long national nightmare was over. The people embraced that claim, and embraced Ford as their president, because through his speech, they had participated in ending the nightmare.

CONCLUSION

Unlike that of the inaugurals of elected presidents, the rhetoric of ascendant vice presidents responds in a direct and detailed way to the particulars of transition. On the one hand, such speeches must respond to the specifics of the occasion; on the other, they must transcend the exigencies of the moment to speak about eternal truths and appeal to eternal values. Whereas the inaugurals of elected presidents exist in the eternal present, these messages begin in the actual present and face the challenge of transcending the specific situation to speak memorably, not simply about that situation, but about the presidency, the people, and their compact.

Like the inaugurals of elected presidents, the speeches of ascendant vice presidents perform functions that are vital for the preservation of the presidency as an institution. They are a part of special rituals of transition that are especially demanding because they occur in periods of confusion and crisis. In such periods, they are vital reaffirmations of the continuity of the institution and of the community. In addition, because the speeches of ascendant vice presidents ordinarily combine elements normally identified with the eulogy and the inaugural address, they are unusually clear instances of the principle that rhetorical form follows rhetorical function.

FOUR

National Eulogies

In this chapter, we liken Pericles' funeral oration and Lincoln's Gettysburg Address to, and differentiate them from, Ronald Reagan's speeches after the explosion of the space shuttle *Challenger*, Bill Clinton's statements after the bombing of the Alfred P. Murrah Federal Building in Oklahoma City, George W. Bush's addresses at the National Cathedral and before Congress following the terrorist attacks of September 11, 2001, and his rhetorical acts following the destruction brought about by Hurricane Katrina. We argue that one can productively see these recent forms of epideictic discourse as national eulogies, a genre in which the president assumes a priestly role to make sense of a catastrophe and transform it from evidence of destruction into a symbol of national resilience. In the case of the September 11 terrorist attacks, Bush also forecasts that the nation will respond decisively in a way that demonstrates the national spirit and protects the nation's citizens and their values, which reinforces the notion that the nation is strong and enduring.

Presidents eulogize many individuals, including their deceased predecessors; for example, Clinton paid tribute to former president Nixon at the time of his death, and George W. Bush did the same for former presidents Reagan and Ford. The deaths that give rise to national eulogies, however, differ from those deaths in important ways. The national eulogy emerges only when someone must make sense of a catastrophic event that unexpectedly kills U.S. civilians while also assaulting a national symbol. Such events include the assassination of John F. Kennedy, treated in chapter 3 on the inaugurals of ascendant vice presidents, as well as the events that gave rise to the rhetorical acts mentioned in the previous paragraph.

To illustrate the institutional functions of the national eulogy, we explore five rhetorical acts. The first two deal with similar situations: the destruction of space shuttles. Comparison of these two events helps to underscore the power of television to create the need for a national eulogy. They are also instances in which the address does not require a pledge to find and prosecute (as in the case of the Oklahoma City bombing) or destroy (as in the case of September 11) those responsible for the deaths. Instead, in each case, an investigation of causes is initiated.

The next two examples are successful responses to terrorist attacks: the destruction of the Murrah Federal Building in Oklahoma City and the September 11 attacks on the World Trade Center towers and the Pentagon. Each demonstrates the utility in seeing the national eulogy as a rhetorical act. Finally, we examine a failed national eulogy. In the wake of Hurricane Katrina, George W. Bush delivered a series of statements that undercut his capacity to do what this genre required. We argue that the inadequate response of the federal agency under his control made it difficult for him to assume the priestly role of empathic comforter that is instrumental in delivering a national eulogy. In this instance, the concept of the rhetorical act helps to explain why the words Bush ultimately delivered could not perform the functions required by the dramatic television coverage of death and devastation in New Orleans.

To understand why the national eulogy is a comparatively recent presidential genre, we begin by contrasting these five tragedies with two earlier catastrophes in the nation's history: the Chicago Fire of 1871 and the San Francisco earthquake of 1906.

The Great Chicago Fire of April 9, 1871, came and went without either public presidential rhetoric or any controversy over its absence. The government leader who responded to the tragedy at the municipal level was Philip Sheridan, a former Civil War general and Indian fighter who took charge of military security for the devastated city. His contact in the nation's capitol was Secretary of War General W. W. Belknap, whom Sheridan wired to report ordering rations, tents, and two companies of infantry from nearby forts, orders that were seconded by Belknap. Six months later, on October 23, Sheridan wrote to tell the mayor of Chicago—not the secretary of war or the president—that he was disbanding "the volunteer organization of military on duty since the fire." On December 20, he submitted his final report to the secretary of war and responded to criticism of the federal military intervention by stating that "I never for one moment thought of infringing or abrogating any of the civil laws; that my only desire was to aid the civil authorities of this city to carry the heavy burdens which had fallen on them by an unparalleled calamity."[1] We found no record of any public presidential statement about these events.

By contrast, on April 18, 1906, Theodore Roosevelt reacted to word of the San Francisco earthquake with a telegram to California governor George Cooper Pardee, saying, "Hear rumors of great disaster through an earthquake in San Francisco but know nothing of the real facts. Call upon me for any assistance I can render."[2] When information was forthcoming, so, too, was aid.

In this case, the information included strong visuals. "This was the first disaster to be photographed on a large scale, by professionals and amateurs," notes historian John Allen. "There are tens of thousands of photographs."[3] The nature of the technology, however, meant that the photographic record was available only after the event, and that it was experienced as sequential printed images consumed not by an amassed public, but by individual newspaper readers.

Unlike the Chicago Fire, the San Francisco earthquake evoked a response from the president; however, Roosevelt communicated not with the public or the people of California, but with the state governor and the head of the American Red Cross. By contrast, in a manner consistent with the trends increasing the amount of presidential discourse that we noted in chapter 1, when the missions of the space shuttles *Challenger* and *Columbia* ended tragically, when the Murrah Federal Building was blown up in Oklahoma City, and after the tragedies of September 11 and Hurricane Katrina, the president spoke for and to the nation.

We have chosen "national eulogy" as the name for this genre to capture its unique blend of eulogistic content and elements that reconstitute the nation.[4] National eulogies are addresses to the nation about the meaning of events that have shaken the citizenry. Whereas the inaugural reconstitutes the audience as the people, when successful, the national eulogy transforms the wounded polity into a resilient nation.

Like the inaugural, the national eulogy is a type of epideictic discourse in which performance—proper execution—is vital. If this rhetorical act is done well, the president amasses rhetorical capital to create a reservoir of respect and gratitude that can be used to buttress other initiatives—legislative or military initiatives, for example.

In some important ways, the national eulogy performs functions similar to those of the inaugural address of an ascendant vice president; whereas in those inaugurals the president must help the people confront the death of the late president in a way that reassures them that the community and its institutions will survive, here the president must make sense of the deaths and the events that produced them in a way that establishes that the nation and its ideals are strong and secure.

There are elements of national eulogy in the inaugural of Lyndon Johnson that we examined in chapter 3. That speech helped to heal the nation with the successful installation of a new president and the assurance that Johnson would pursue Kennedy's agenda. Johnson's successful investiture confirmed that the institutions of democracy had survived Kennedy's assassination. By contrast, national eulogies heal by combining the act of eulogizing with the act of reclaiming the symbols assaulted by a catastrophic, death-dealing, symbol-challenging event.

Like many other rhetorical genres, the national eulogy is prompted by a perceived need in the community. A traumatic event disrupts national life. In this televisual age, such moments are dramatized by photographs and video footage, often replayed over and over, that heighten the public's sense of catastrophe and insecurity in the face of death-dealing events. Millions of Americans saw the space shuttle *Challenger* explode; most Americans either watched the second plane plow into the World Trade Center or relived it shortly thereafter. Similarly, millions of Americans saw replays of local news footage of the smoldering Murrah Federal Building in Oklahoma City. That coverage showed images of billowing smoke and rubble, medical personnel struggling to treat the injured, and rescue workers attempting to save those buried by the blast, including the iconic photograph of a severely injured child in the arms of a firefighter. Similarly, twenty-four-hour cable coverage combined with ongoing network news coverage to bring the aftermath of Hurricane Katrina in New Orleans into the nation's living rooms. These were large-scale, nationally experienced events resulting in many deaths. Because the demise of the space shuttle *Columbia* occurred outside the camera's eye, the nation's identification with that event was less intense; accordingly, there was less need for an extended presidential rhetorical act.

The moment created by the events we treat in this chapter is a powerful invitation to presidential response because the calamitous deaths threaten our sense of ourselves as a nation, and that threat is heightened because the public experiences it collectively. This collective experience was particularly disruptive in the case of the *Challenger* explosion because elementary school teacher Christa McAuliffe was part of the crew, which meant that elementary school students and others around the nation were encouraged to watch its launch. To the horror of all, they saw the shuttle explode in midair, causing the deaths of those aboard. The explosion called into question the safety of the space shuttle program and the purpose of space exploration, as well as the assumption that the United States had conquered space. U.S. supremacy in space had signaled a victory in the cold war as it boosted national morale. Because the explosion caused the death of a civilian and was viewed by the amassed public, and because the shuttle was a symbol of the U.S. space program and therefore of the nation, the explosion and resulting deaths were unusually disturbing. In order to begin the process of healing in the aftermath of such a shocking and horrifying event, someone must speak for and to the nation. The president is the likely candidate.

In our earlier chapter on inaugural addresses, we argued that those speeches transcend the historical present by reconstituting an existing community, rehearsing the past, affirming traditional values, and articulating timely and timeless principles that will govern the administration of the incoming president. Whereas the inaugural links the past to the future with the forthcoming presidency as the intermediary, the national eulogy links the present to the future with a central line of argument: that those who died exemplify the best of a nation that will survive this moment because its ideals cannot be undermined by events such as those that took their lives. Whereas in the inaugural the president assumes the right to say what the country's history means, in the national eulogy the president assumes the right to define for the country the meaning of the catastrophe and to assuage the associated trauma.

When presidential action has occasioned the deaths of those who serve the country in the military by sending them into a specific conflict, national eulogies have not been delivered in modern times. So, for example, Ronald Reagan did not craft a national eulogy for the marines who died in Lebanon,[5] nor did George H. W. Bush deliver one for those who died in the invasion of Panama. By contrast, the terrorist attack on the U.S.S. *Cole,* which killed four sailors and injured many more, evoked a national eulogy from Bill Clinton, albeit a somewhat attenuated one for which national television time was not sought.

The low profile of Clinton's speech may have been a result of its timing. The attack occurred on October 12, 2000, in the midst of a presidential campaign pitting Clinton's vice president, Al Gore, against Texas governor George W. Bush. A major speech would have derailed Gore's campaign by placing terrorism high on the national agenda, forcing him to give this issue a central role, a move that would have been difficult so late in the campaign. Raising this new issue would have displaced Gore's focus on Social Security, an issue on which he was gaining traction in October and which may have produced his popular vote lead in the final election count.[6] Emphasizing terror would also have raised the question of whether the Clinton-Gore team had responded appropriately to the terrorist attack on the World Trade Center in 1993. At the same time, an address to the nation would have required a level of response to the attack that Clinton was either unwilling or unable to undertake. Because the attack occurred in a distant place (the Yemeni port of Aden) and involved military personnel, not civilians, the absence of a major address was not noteworthy. After September 11, however, some might wonder whether the nation would have been better served had President Clinton called on it to stop and consider the meaning of this terrorist attack, thereby putting the issue into political play.

Determining the possible causes of a catastrophe and forging remedies may take time. For this reason, and because the extent of the rhetoric must in some sense be proportionate to the expanse of the tragedy, the president's rhetorical response is likely to be spread out across a series of messages. So, for example, the president may respond briefly to the initial event, then speak at a memorial prayer service, refer to the event in a Saturday radio address, and discuss it in a press conference or in an interview.

When well executed, the national eulogy performs the powerful function of epideictic discourse by unifying the country around the leadership of the speaker. In other words, the capacity of this genre to build rhetorical capital for a president is great. This process was illustrated in April 1995 when Bill Clinton's responses to the bombing of the Alfred P. Murrah Federal Building in Oklahoma City resurrected his faltering presidency. By early April 1995, the incumbent's presidency was on the ropes. In the fall of 1994, the Democrats had been swept from power in both the House and the Senate. For the first time in forty years, the House was in Republican hands. At a press conference telecast by only one of the major networks the night before the bombing, Clinton's depleted store of political capital was evident in an exchange premised on it:

> Q. President Clinton, Republicans have dominated political debate in this country since they took over Congress in January. And even tonight, two of the major television networks declined to broadcast this event live. Do you worry about making sure that your voice is heard in the coming months?

In response, Clinton defensively asserted his centrality to government and governance, saying, in part, "The Constitution gives me relevance.

The power of our ideas gives me relevance. The record we have built up over the last 2 years and the things we're trying to do to implement it give it relevance. The President is relevant here, especially an activist President."[7]

The immediate effect of Clinton's handling of the bombing was a 5 percentage point jump in the Gallup poll. Indeed, 84 percent of the public approved of Clinton's response to the calamity. Clinton's effective reaction also quieted speculation about his political viability and relevance.

When a national eulogy builds rhetorical capital, the incumbent is likely to draw on it to construct premises for other presidential claims in dissimilar genres. Thus, for example, George W. Bush built much of the rhetoric of his first term, including the campaign rhetoric of his bid for reelection, on his response to September 11. Likewise, Clinton drew evidence from the actions of an individual at the Murrah Federal Building to attack the Republican Congress for what he cast as its ill-treatment of government workers. In his State of the Union address of the following January, he introduced a survivor of the bombing, Richard Dean. Harnessing the power of epideictic discourse to deliberative ends, Clinton deployed the example of this heroic federal worker to create a synecdochic moment to indict the Republicans in Congress. He explained that Richard Dean was "a 49-year-old Vietnam veteran who's worked for the Social Security Administration for 22 years now." When the Murrah Federal Building was bombed, Dean "reentered that building four times. He saved the lives of three women." But, added Clinton, his "story doesn't end there. This last November, he was forced out of his office when the Government shut down. And the second time the Government shut down he continued helping Social Security recipients, but he was working without pay." On behalf of Dean and others like him, Clinton challenged those in the chamber: "Let's never, ever shut the Federal Government down again."[8]

As a genre, the eulogy that citizens and presidents alike deliver to commemorate the dead has elements in common with the national eulogy. In a eulogy, as noted in chapter 3, death must be recognized and acknowledged, which is the beginning of healing. The speech must facilitate the transformation of physical into spiritual being, the process by which body becomes spirit and the enduring meaning of the lives of the deceased can emerge. Spiritually, they die only in the flesh; they live on in memory and in the legacy they leave. Moreover, the community that the act that caused their deaths has temporarily called into question lives on in a commitment to make their accomplishments meaningful, to carry on their mission, and to reaffirm the values represented by their lives.

Four key differences characterize national eulogies and distinguish them from individual eulogies. First, although all eulogies adopt a personal tone, in the national eulogy, the personal has a different dimension because the president assumes a different role, an intercessory role in which, like priest or pastor, the president speaks to us as individuals. In this capacity, the president may explicitly pray in our name, invite us to pray, and speak to the nation about its faith in itself as well as in God. Second, the president makes sense of the event by helping the citizenry to come to terms with calamity, evil, or terrorism and to see these events in a larger, ongoing national perspective, and by addressing such questions as why the tragedy happened and what meaning it has for the nation. Third, a national eulogy argues that those who died symbolize the best of the nation; in this genre, they are surrogates for the rest of us. Their nobility is our nobility. This argument enables the president to transform symbols of destruction into symbols of resurrection and renewal. Finally, except in unusual circumstances, the national eulogy explains how the president and the government will ensure that the tragedy will not be repeated.

EULOGISTIC RHETORIC

The national eulogy is delivered by the president in a role that can best be described as the national priest of our civil religion, who can not only perform the sacred functions vital to repairing the nation, but can also redefine the event and translate it into a reaffirmation of the health and unity of the nation and of the durability of its values. In this televisual age, the national eulogy takes the form of oral discourse predicated on the intimate relationship among the dead, the nation, and the leader who speaks for the nation and who can begin to heal its wounds. If the rhetorical act is to unify and comfort us as well as enhance our appreciation of presidential leadership, the priestly role cannot be tainted by self-interest.

The historical touchstone for the national eulogy is Pericles' funeral oration for the Athenian warrior dead, as recreated by Thucydides, a speech that celebrates their deaths as an affirmation of Athenian values. Its lines of argument and stylistic characteristics recur in Abraham Lincoln's Gettysburg Address.[9] Both addresses illustrate the power of symbols to create a people's political identity, a power that is also evident in national eulogies. In the contemporary cases we treat here, however, the deaths over which we grieve are civilian, not military. That those who died did not, like military personnel, choose to put their lives on the line creates a special need. They are the victims of disaster or of the malevolence of terrorists, and they were supposed to be protected by the nation and its government.

When a death-dealing catastrophe occurs and is experienced almost simultaneously via television by the citizenry, the people turn to the president as the leader able to speak for and to them. Because speeches delivered under these circumstances cannot benefit from the weeks or months of preparation of other major presidential addresses, a president's earliest responses become a test of rhetorical dexterity. In these early moments, success is not assured. In short, what is required is not just speech, but speech of a special kind. Reagan's eloquent tribute to the crew of the space shuttle *Challenger* heightened his standing as president. Bush's initial statements after September 11 started the rhetorical act of response on shaky ground, but he recovered his footing days later with the speech at the National Cathedral.

Confronted with this kind of catastrophe, the president must begin the rhetorical act of national eulogy with elements of a traditional eulogy. By doing so, he sets the stage for deployment of the other arguments central to the genre. The initial speeches delivered by Reagan and George W. Bush on the losses of *Challenger* and *Columbia* include such traditional eulogies.

In his address to the nation on January 28, 1986, Reagan acknowledged the deaths of the seven *Challenger* crew members, personalized the event, and identified it as a moment of national significance: "Today is a day for mourning and remembering. Nancy and I are pained to the core by the tragedy of the shuttle *Challenger*. We know we share this pain with all of the people of our country. This is truly a national loss." By adding the words, "We mourn their loss as a nation together," he completed the constitution of his audience as a national community.[10]

In eulogistic fashion, Reagan named each of the *Challenger* Seven and celebrated their courage, stating that they were "aware of the dangers, but overcame them and did their jobs brilliantly." He then defined their legacy, "that special spirit that says, 'Give me a challenge, and I'll meet it with joy.'... We're still pioneers. They, the members of the *Challenger* crew, were pioneers," linking the crew to the history of the nation.[11]

Reagan addressed the schoolchildren who watched live coverage of the shuttle's launch and saw the fatal explosion. In the process, he redefined the symbolism of the event by calling it "part of the process of exploration and discovery," again linking this event to world and national history. He shifted the time from past to future and asserted the crew's immortality when he added, "The *Challenger* crew was pulling us into the future, and we'll continue to follow them."[12] That the launch and explosion had both been covered by television was reframed as evidence of national values: "We don't hide our space program. We don't keep secrets and cover things up. We do it all up front and in public. That's the way freedom is, and we wouldn't change it for a minute."[13]

Finally, in keeping with the high style expected in epideictic discourse, Reagan delivered a memorable conclusion that transformed physical death into spiritual life: "The crew of the space shuttle *Challenger* honored us by the manner in which they lived their lives. We will never forget them, nor the last time we saw them, this morning, as they prepared for their journey and waved goodbye and 'slipped the surly bonds of earth' to 'touch the face of God.'"[14]

The deaths of the crew on the space shuttle *Columbia* were less vivid to the nation than those on *Challenger* because it disintegrated upon its reentry into the earth's atmosphere, out of the view of cameras. In a context created by the public's memory of the *Challenger* explosion and Reagan's moving response to it, George W. Bush delivered a national eulogy on February 1, 2003. Addressing the nation from the Cabinet Room, Bush told the families of the bereaved, in words that linked their deaths to the nation, "All Americans today are thinking as well of the families of these men and women who have been given this sudden shock and grief. You're not alone. Our entire nation grieves with you." He asserted that the dead would live on both in memory and in the continuing space program: "And those you loved will always have the respect and gratitude of this country. The cause in which they died will continue."[15]

Bush's attempt to symbolically transform the tragedy is less satisfying than Reagan's because it does not make real an alternative symbol for the shattered vessel and lives. It does, however, move the dead from physical to spiritual life:

> In the skies today we saw destruction and tragedy. Yet farther than we can see, there is comfort and hope. In the words of the prophet Isaiah, "Lift your eyes and look to the heavens. Who created all these? He who brings out the starry hosts one by one and calls them by name. Because of His great power and mighty strength, not one of them is missing."

The conclusion personalized this comfort: "The same Creator who names the stars also knows the names of the seven souls we mourn today. The crew of the shuttle *Columbia* did not return safely to Earth. Yet we can pray that all are safely home."[16] Whereas Reagan asserted that the dead had "touched the face of God," Bush's prayer that they are safely home suggests the possibility that they are not.

Like Reagan's speech, Bush's address is brief. It performs the functions that we expect of a eulogy with language that comforts and unifies. It suffers by comparison with Reagan's *Challenger* speech in part because it would be difficult to rise to those heights of eloquence under circumstances that are so similar. This example once again illustrates the ways in which context—in this case, rhetorical context—alters the meaning and interpretation of presidential discourse.

Bill Clinton gave his major speech on the bombing of the Murrah Federal Building at a prayer service held on the state fairgrounds in Oklahoma City. True to eulogistic expectations, he used the metaphor of a tree planted that morning at the White House to affirm that the memory of the dead will live on: "So this morning before we got on the plane to come here, at the White House, we planted a tree in honor of the children in Oklahoma."[17] Just as Reagan turned the *Challenger* deaths into a symbol of a life beyond, Clinton moved from present to future with a symbol of rebirth and remembrance: "It was a dogwood with its wonderful spring flower and its deep, enduring roots. It embodies the lesson of the Psalms that the life of a good person is like a tree whose leaf does not wither." The speech closed with reassurance based in religious belief articulated by the priest of U.S. civil religion: "My fellow Americans, a tree takes a long time to grow, and wounds take a long time to heal. But we must begin. Those who are lost now belong to God. Some day we will be with them. But until that happens, their legacy must be our lives."[18]

In classic epideictic high style, George W. Bush's speech at the National Cathedral on September 14 also asserted that the dead live on, in the retelling of their stories in the speech and in the president's assurance that "[w]e will read all these names. We will linger over them and learn their stories, and many Americans will weep."[19]

IN A PRIESTLY ROLE[20]

When presidents invoke God in the inaugural, it is to suggest that they recognize a higher power and seek to place the nation under its protection. In the national eulogy, the president instead leads a national service for the deceased. Some presidents are more comfortable than others in explicitly incorporating the language of religion and God into the words of comfort required of the priestly role. Some draw God into the eulogy effortlessly; others shy away from such evocation. In Reagan's eulogy for the *Challenger* crew, the only direct reference to God comes at the end, as they are said to have "touched the face of God." Here Reagan is not quoting the Bible, the usual move of Clinton and Bush, but a prayer written by a Canadian pilot. By contrast, as we have just indicated, in his eulogy for the crew of *Columbia*, Bush comfortably uses scripture to reassure his audience. Similarly, Clinton's first public response to word of the bombing in Oklahoma City initiates the rhetorical act of national eulogy by asking Americans to "pray for the people who have lost their lives, to pray for the families and the friends of the dead and the wounded, to pray for the people of Oklahoma City." It closes by asking that "God's grace be with them."[21]

Clinton's speech in Oklahoma City wove the elements of the national eulogy into a message of comfort and reassurance. He spoke for the nation by saying, "I am honored to be here today to represent the American people." In the speech, he represented a unified nation: "Today our nation joins with you in grief. We mourn with you. We share your hope against hope that some may still survive." He acknowledged the deaths by saying, "Our words seem small beside the loss you have endured."[22]

Linkages between justice and God permit presidents to tie their responses to terrorist attacks to the notion that justice will triumph. At the prayer service, Clinton resurrected his presidency with a speech that was explicitly sermonic: "Let us teach our children that the God of comfort is also the God of righteousness." The promise of justice is forecast in biblical language: "Those who trouble their own house will inherit the wind. Justice will prevail. . . . As St. Paul admonished us, let us not be overcome by evil but overcome evil with good."[23]

TRANSFORMING DEATHS INTO SYMBOLS OF
NATIONAL RESILIENCE

As the nation turns to the chief executive for leadership, it asks two questions: what does this catastrophe mean, and how is the country to act in order to ensure that it does not recur? Providing satisfactory answers builds rhetorical capital for the president, as illustrated by Clinton's response to the Oklahoma City bombing and George W. Bush's response in speeches at the National Cathedral and to Congress after the terrorist attacks of September 11. Unsatisfying responses weaken a president, a phenomenon exemplified by the public's response to George W. Bush's faltering reactions to Hurricane Katrina.

In Clinton's case, information about the perpetrator was not yet available, but he asserted that the meaning for the audience was clear: "Let us let our own children know that we will stand against the forces of fear. When there is talk of hatred, let us stand up and talk against it. When there is talk of violence, let us stand up and talk against it. In the face of death, let us honor life. As St. Paul admonished us, Let us 'not be overcome by evil but overcome evil with good.'"[24] Reagan treated the explosion of *Challenger* as an accident, a failure of technology, but transformed the tragedy into a symbol of the openness of a democracy. George W. Bush likewise treated the tragedy of *Columbia* as a failure of technology, but expressed its meaning this way: "Mankind is led into the darkness beyond our world by the inspiration of discovery and the longing to understand."[25] Such explanations are closely related to the transformation of symbols claimed by terrorists into symbols of national courage and resilience.

The need for a national eulogy is heightened when those who died can be seen as symbols for the institutions or ideals that others, especially terrorists, wish to destroy by their acts. This is another reason that a national eulogy ordinarily is not delivered when deaths occur in war or military action. The death of a soldier is in service of the community she or he has chosen to protect. The community is preserved, not sundered, by such deaths. Indeed, some would argue that these sacrifices are an indispensable part of maintaining a state.[26] Although we recognize their sacrifice and mourn their loss, in the United States at least, the deaths of those in the military, however regrettable, do not ordinarily create the need for a rhetoric of explanation, healing, and resolve.

Implicit in many national eulogies is the notion that those who have died were killed because of what they symbolize. In the case of terrorism, the president's task of identifying and transforming the symbolism of their deaths is eased because the terrorists have selected their target precisely because of its power to stand as a symbol of the nation.

Some speeches strongly signal that they are focused on reclaiming an attacked symbol. Speaking before Congress on September 20, 2001, George W. Bush said, "Terrorists attacked a symbol of American prosperity. They did not touch its source. America is successful because of the hard work and creativity and enterprise of our people. These were the true strengths of our economy before September 11th, and they are our strengths today."[27]

In Clinton's speech in Oklahoma City, as in Reagan's eulogy for the crew of *Challenger* and Bush's National Cathedral address, the dead represent the best of us. Clinton, for example, defines the American family as "innocent children, in that building, [there] only because their parents were trying to be good parents as well as good workers; citizens in the building going about their daily business; and many there who served the rest of us."[28]

In the national eulogy's construction of reality, the deaths require transformation because the "terrorists" have made those who died and the places where they died symbols of something larger. During his trial, for example, we learned that Oklahoma City bomber Timothy McVeigh viewed the bombing, in part, as a response to the assault by the Bureau of Alcohol, Tobacco and Firearms on the Waco, Texas, compound of the Branch Davidians in 1993. The date of the bombing was selected by McVeigh because it was the anniversary of the battle of Lexington and Concord. When the person who destroyed a building lives to detail the meaning of the act, he expands our understanding of what he sought to destroy. Similarly, to those who attacked on September 11, the workers in the World Trade Center towers and the Pentagon were symbols of U.S. capitalism and foreign policy.

To recover the dead as representative Americans, symbols of our values, the national eulogy rejects the terrorists' construction of the meaning of the buildings destroyed and the people who died in them. In Oklahoma City, this process of reclamation was aided by the defining image through which the media telegraphed the event: a photograph of a firefighter carrying a dying child from the rubble. The perpetrators are wordlessly indicted by that evocative visual image: they are child killers. The government symbolized by the adult protectively bearing the child is humane.

The terrorist act assumes that each person killed is a symbol of what needs to be destroyed; the president reclaims those symbols, transforming each into a symbol of what needs to be preserved. In the process, those who were killed become metaphors of courage and determination, whose selfless example expresses the best of what it means to be an American. Part of this process of reconstruction occurs long after the initial presidential rhetoric in the form of permanent memorials erected on the site. These, too, are symbols of commemoration, resurrection, and renewal.

Symbols are also reconstructed in Reagan's speech about the *Challenger* disaster. Whereas the visual images of the explosion suggest failed aspirations and the painful deaths of those incarnating the nation and its space program, in Reagan's eulogy, the astronauts have not died. They have instead "'slipped the surly bonds of earth' to 'touch the face of God.'" Indeed, when Reagan's speech was rebroadcast on the evening of the catastrophe, one of the television networks superimposed the image of the astronauts waving goodbye on the end of the speech. In the process, the network, like the speech, displaced the image of the exploding shuttle with an image of hope and heroism.

FORESTALLING A REPETITION OF THE CATASTROPHE

One of the ways in which national eulogies suggest that the system works is by assuring the public that presidential or government action will prevent a recurrence of the catastrophe. This means bringing the perpetrators to justice in the case of terrorist attacks and ensuring that the tragedy is not repeated in the case of the losses of the space shuttles and the deaths in New Orleans after Hurricane Katrina. Were it not for this element, the national eulogy might be heard to say that the nation mourns the deaths and reclaims its symbols, but stands vulnerable to a repetition of the catastrophe.

Determining appropriate action takes time. So, for example, in the early days following September 11, Bush telegraphed resolve without forecasting specific action: "This conflict was begun on the timing and terms of others. It will end in a way and at an hour of our choosing."[29] It took almost a week after the *Challenger* explosion for Reagan to announce that he was setting up a presidential commission to "review the circumstances surrounding the accident, determine the probable cause or causes, and develop recommendations for corrective action." The reason for action is summed up in Reagan's statement that "we must devote our energies to finding out how it happened and how it can be prevented from happening again."[30]

One of the problems George W. Bush confronted in delivering the national eulogy following the second loss of a space shuttle was that this earlier reassurance by Reagan had now been called into question, and with it, Bush's credibility to assert that his actions would prevent a repetition. Unlike Reagan, Bush did not personally forecast the administrative response to the demise of *Columbia*. Instead, the day after its disintegration on reentry, the NASA administrator reported at a press conference that he had informed the president as soon as contact with the shuttle was lost, and that the president had "specifically offered the full and immediate support to determine what the appropriate steps were thereafter to be taken." He told reporters that the president had called the surviving family members "and spoken to them to express our deepest national regrets. We have assured them that we'll begin the process immediately to recover their loved ones and understand the cause of this tragedy."[31] This rhetoric shifted attention and accountability from Bush to NASA, and here the transfer succeeded. There was no public or press outcry blaming Bush or faulting him for the proposed resolution. As we note below, Bush's attempt to shift responsibility to the storm and to state and local governments after the devastation of Hurricane Katrina was less successful.

The responses of Reagan and Bush to the demise of the shuttles suggested that they would place the blame for failure on a system or a piece of the shuttle technology, not on people. A focus on finding individuals at fault would require them to argue that someone had acted intentionally or with culpable incompetence. Since the responsible agency is located within the executive branch, such a move would also call its competence into question.

Whereas in the shuttle speeches the presidents suggested malfunction as a cause and sought administrative remedies in the form of investigations, in cases of terrorism, the presidents focused on bringing perpetrators to justice. Clinton responded to the Oklahoma City bombing with a brief speech that same day that combined the roles of decisive executive, spokesperson for the nation, and national priest. He spoke for the nation in labeling the act as "an attack on innocent children and defenseless citizens," characterizing it as "an act of cowardice" and defining it as "evil." He also asserted, "The United States will not tolerate it. And I will not allow the people of this country to be intimidated by evil cowards." Those responsible would be found and punished. "Let there be no room for doubt: We will find the people who did this," said Clinton. "When we do, justice will be swift, certain, and severe. These people are killers, and they must be treated like killers."[32] Here is the rhetorical structure that George W. Bush would follow after the events of September 11.

Illustrating the characteristics of the national eulogy by selecting statements from speeches obscures the interrelationship of those elements as well as the presence of those elements in various messages. To show how the notion of the rhetorical act makes it possible to see the existence of the four generic elements we have identified as they play out across messages, we now turn to two rhetorical acts by the same president, one, in our judgment, ultimately successful, the other not so. The first is the national eulogy delivered by George W. Bush after September 11; the second is the speech he delivered in Jackson Square in New Orleans in the aftermath of Hurricane Katrina.

BUSH RESPONDS TO SEPTEMBER 11

On September 14, 2001, three days after the terrorist attacks on the World Trade Center towers and the Pentagon, George W. Bush spoke at the National Cathedral in Washington, DC. Bush's earlier decision to declare September 14 a national day of prayer and remembrance was the context that defined the character of the event. In this eloquent national eulogy, the president spoke for the nation: "We are here in the middle hour of our grief," he began. "So many have suffered so great a loss, and today we express our nation's sorrow." "To the children and parents and spouses and families and friends of the lost, we offer the deepest sympathy of the Nation," he intoned later.[33]

Like other national eulogies, this speech confirmed the fact of death and confronted the mortality of the deceased and of the audience. The confrontation ascribed meaning to the lives lost: "They are the names of men and women who began their day at a desk or in an airport, busy with life. They are the names of people who faced death and in their last moments called home to say, 'be brave,' and 'I love you.' They are the names of passengers who defied their murderers and prevented the murder of others on the ground. . . . They are the names of rescuers, the ones whom death found running up the stairs and into the fires to help others."[34]

The priestly role of the president is evident in the National Cathedral setting and in the invocation of "God" through "prayer": "We come before God to pray for the missing and the dead," said Bush, "and for those who love them."[35] In these rhetorical acts, the president assumes the right to speak to God on behalf of the nation. "On this National Day of Prayer and Remembrance, we ask Almighty God to watch over our Nation and grant us patience and resolve in all that is to come." In the process, Bush forecast a future: "We thank Him for each life we now must mourn, and the promise of a life to come." And he placed the nation in God's hands: "May He bless the souls of the departed. May He comfort our own. And may He always guide our country."[36]

The loss of innocent life challenges faith in God. The speech breathes the assumption that God exists and will hear the supplications of a grieving people voiced by their president. When Bush reported that a woman at St. Patrick's Cathedral in New York had told him on the day of the attacks, "I prayed to God to give us a sign that He is still here,"[37] his speech, with its invocations and prayers, as well as the unified nation personified in the faces of those in the audience, constituted a rejoinder to her doubts, a sign that God was there, in the National Cathedral, and there as well with her at St. Patrick's.

The address offered a second answer to the woman's request: "God's signs are not always the ones we look for."[38] The speech did not directly answer the implied question—what are God's signs in this moment? But the structure of the speech implied an answer. September 11 revivified our national character, created national unity, and brought us back to prayerful invocation of God.

George W. Bush's responses to the attacks on the World Trade Center and the Pentagon illustrate the unfolding character of the rhetorical act that culminates in a speech that completes the national eulogy. Bush's first remarks at the Emma Booker Elementary School in Sarasota, Florida, at 9:30 A.M. EDT, opened in a fashion that seemed to suggest a reluctance to return to the nation's capital: "Ladies and gentlemen, this is a difficult moment for America. I, unfortunately, will be going back to Washington after my remarks." In that statement, however, Bush began the process of assigning meaning to the attacks, describing the events of the morning as "a national tragedy. Two airplanes have crashed into the World Trade Center in an apparent terrorist attack on our country." He then reported ordering the full resources of the federal government to help the victims and their families and to hunt down "those folks who committed this act." The president's message failed to inform the public that Bush had activated U.S. defenses to protect the country—a significant lapse, since planes remained unaccounted for. At the same time, describing the perpetrators as "folks" in a speech that had opened by thanking "the folks here at the Booker Elementary School for their hospitality"[39] created an odd linguistic conflation of the assembled teachers and schoolchildren and the attackers.

Instead of suggesting that he was in command, the president's demeanor hinted that, in the words of ABC anchor Peter Jennings, he was "clearly shaken."[40] "He had not looked determined on September 11, or had looked a whole bunch of other things as well," noted *New York Times* reporter Frank Bruni, "tentative, tense, shocked."[41] His pledge of decisive action in response to the attacks somewhat redeemed his statement: "Terrorism against our nation will not stand."[42]

At Barksdale Air Force Base later in the day, the president spoke again. By reassuring the public that all government resources had been mobilized—"We have taken all appropriate security precautions to protect the American people"—his words accomplished what his earlier statement had failed to do. He said that freedom had been attacked and would be defended: "The resolve of our great Nation is being tested. But make no mistake: We will show the world that we will pass this test."[43]

Given the information available to the president at that time, a fully formed national eulogy would not have been appropriate. Precisely what had occurred, how many and who had died, and who was responsible remained unclear. Still later that day, President Bush spoke from the Oval Office. Much of that speech repeated key ideas from his earlier remarks, but the conclusion foreshadowed a fully developed national eulogy. In words that reflect the role of national priest, Bush said,

> Tonight I ask for your prayers for all those who grieve, for the children whose worlds have been shattered, for all whose sense of safety and security has been threatened. And I pray they will be comforted by a power greater than any of us, spoken through the ages in Psalm 23: "Even though I walk through the valley of the shadow of death, I fear no evil, for You are with me."[44]

Then he moved toward the role of commander in chief to forecast that the country would respond to vanquish this enemy:

> This is a day when all Americans from every walk of life unite in our resolve for justice and peace. America has stood down enemies before, and we will do so this time. None of us will ever forget this day. Yet we go forward to defend freedom and all that is good and just in our world.[45]

The speech at the National Cathedral picked up where this earlier speech left off. In the earlier speech, the president acknowledged that the nation had been hurt. In this speech, he said, "On Tuesday our country was attacked with deliberate and massive cruelty." In a televisual age, the president evoked the pictures imprinted in the public memory: "We have seen the images of fire and ashes and bent steel. ... But our responsibility to history is already clear: to answer these attacks and rid the world of evil."[46]

The honored dead and those who struggled to save them became symbols of goodness: "We see our national character in rescuers working past exhaustion, in long lines of blood donors. . . . in eloquent acts of sacrifice." To carry the point home, the abstractions were embodied in exemplars. "Inside the World Trade Center, one man, who could have saved himself, stayed until the end at the side of his quadriplegic friend. A beloved priest died giving the last rites to a firefighter."[47]

The speech assumed that the people were united in mourning the loss and in drawing resolve from this assault on the nation: "Today we feel what Franklin Roosevelt called the warm courage of national unity. . . . Our unity is a kinship of grief and a steadfast resolve to prevail against our enemies." "Our purpose as a nation is firm." American flags "are displayed in pride and wave in defiance."[48]

The events of September 11 are cast as transformative: "This Nation is peaceful, but fierce when stirred to anger. . . . It is said that adversity introduces us to ourselves. This is true of a nation as well." What have we learned about ourselves? "In this trial, we have been reminded, and the world has seen, that our fellow Americans are generous and kind, resourceful and brave. . . . [W]e are freedom's home and defender."[49] The resourceful and brave are juxtaposed against those who attacked with "stealth and deceit." The generous and kind stand in contrast to those who attacked with "deliberate and massive cruelty."[50] By prayerfully invoking God throughout the speech, the president further heightened the contrast between the nation and those who attacked it.

The nation's response will confirm that it controls its own destiny: "This conflict was begun on the timing and terms of others. It will end in a way and at an hour of our choosing."[51] Will we triumph? "Grief and tragedy and hatred are only for a time. Goodness, remembrance, and love have no end."[52] The remembrance promised earlier has now been elevated: it is endless. We, the praying community, united in the voiced convictions of the president, will triumph, because the attackers and what they stand for are evil, and as the speech suggests throughout, we, the people of a believing, mourning nation, are filled with love and are good.

The rhetorical act continued. On the evening of September 14, after delivering the speech in the National Cathedral, the president visited Ground Zero in New York City. "Grabbing a bullhorn, Bush told the chanting, cheering crowd, 'I can hear you. The rest of the world hears you. And the people who knocked down these buildings will hear all of us soon. The nation sends its love and compassion to everybody who's here. Thank you for your hard work. Thank you for making the nation proud, and may God bless America,' Bush added, raising his arm. The workers responded with a resounding, energetic chant of 'USA, USA!'"[53]

Bush's address to the joint session of Congress on September 20, 2001, completes the rhetorical act of national eulogy begun at the National Cathedral by reprising his earlier themes.[54] Indeed, the first two paragraphs of transcribed text could be inserted into the speech at the National Cathedral. In the middle of the last sentence of these opening words, however, Bush shifts to his role as executive, and later in the speech, he assumes the role of commander in chief. He makes the initial transition with words most commonly spoken in the State of the Union address: "My fellow citizens, for the last nine days, the entire world has seen for itself the state of our Union, and it is strong."[55]

In some of these addresses, questions about the meaning of the events are raised explicitly. In his September 20 speech to Congress, Bush said, "Americans have many questions tonight. Americans are asking, who attacked our country? The evidence we have gathered all points to a collection of loosely affiliated terrorist organizations known as al Qaeda." Why was the country attacked? "Americans are asking, why do they hate us?" The speech did not say that they hate our policies; instead,

> They hate our freedoms—our freedom of religion, our freedom of speech, our freedom to vote and assemble and disagree with each other. . . . These terrorists kill not merely to end lives but to disrupt and end a way of life.

How would the president ensure that the country is no longer vulnerable to this threat? "Americans are asking," he acknowledged, "how will we fight and win this war? We will direct every resource at our command—every means of diplomacy, every tool of intelligence, every instrument of law enforcement, every financial influence, and every necessary weapon of war—to the disruption and to the defeat of the global terror network."[56]

In contrast to the speeches on September 11 and the National Cathedral speech, here the president was addressing Congress in his role as the executive and commander in chief. "[Y]ou acted," he told the assembled members, "by delivering $40 billion to rebuild our communities and meet the needs of our military." He spoke of God, but not to God. Instead, he spoke to other nations: "On behalf of the American people, I thank the world for its outpouring of support." He spoke for the American people to offer an answer to their question, "why do they hate us?": "They hate what we see right here in this chamber, a democratically elected government." He spoke as the custodian of a vast bureaucracy: "Today dozens of federal departments and agencies, as well as state and local governments, have responsibilities affecting homeland security. These efforts must be coordinated at the highest level." To accomplish this, he took specific action: "So tonight I announce the creation of a Cabinet-level position reporting directly to me—the Office of Homeland Security."[57]

In his role as priest, the president can declare war on evil; in his role as commander in chief, he can declare war on terror in general and on al Qaeda in particular. The response he offered to ensure that the country would not be attacked again was for all practical purposes a declaration of war: "We will direct every resource at our command . . . to the disruption and to the defeat of the global terror network." "Our war on terror begins with al Qaeda, but it does not end there. It will not end until every terrorist group of global reach has been found, stopped, and defeated."[58]

This speech builds its deliberative premises on a foundation laid with epideictic material, but at its core it is a justification for action, not an invitation to contemplation. Whereas the speech at the National Cathedral heals, this speech marshals the citizenry. By closing out the rhetorical act that is the national eulogy in a speech that summons the nation to war, Bush uses epideictic rhetoric in the service of deliberative rhetoric. What links the two is that the final argument in the National Cathedral speech—we will prevent this from happening again—is the claim on which the call to war is premised. Ultimately, as Bush's enhanced standing in the polls suggested, after a faltering start, this national eulogy succeeded in uniting the nation behind the president as priest and as commander in chief.[59]

BUSH RESPONDS TO HURRICANE KATRINA

In contrast to his national eulogy after September 11, the rhetorical act that George W. Bush constructed in the two and a half weeks after Hurricane Katrina hit New Orleans failed for several reasons.

On August 27, 2005, as Hurricane Katrina approached the Gulf Coast, President Bush declared a national emergency in Louisiana.

On August 28, the National Weather Service in New Orleans warned of "devastating damage" to New Orleans from the storm.[60] On that date, Bush declared a national emergency in Alabama and Mississippi. On August 29, when Katrina made landfall, President Bush was at his home in Crawford, Texas. Federal, state, and local agencies reported levee failures; surges of water pushed by the storm began overwhelming levees and flood walls protecting New Orleans. Nonetheless, early on August 30, President Bush flew to California, attended a V-J Day commemoration ceremony at Coronado, California, then promoted his administration's prescription drug plan for senior citizens and gave a speech to troops at a Navy base where country singer Mark Wills presented him with a guitar.

On August 31, the president addressed the nation from the Rose Garden at the White House. As evidence of what had been done and what was being done to respond to the emergency on the Gulf Coast, the speech enumerated statistical details: "5.4 million Meals Ready to Eat or MREs, 13.4 million liters of water, 10,400 tarps, 3.4 millions pounds of ice, 144 generators, 20 containers of pre-positioned disaster supplies, 135,000 blankets, and 11,000 cots." The message closed with the words, "The country stands with you. We'll do all in our power to help you. May God bless you."[61] Meanwhile, news footage seemed to give the lie to the assertion that help had been delivered. In dramatic coverage, desperate people without food or water pleaded for the promised aid.

Responses to this speech differed markedly from the reaction to Bush's formal post–September 11 addresses. The *New York Times* of September 1, 2005, editorialized that "he gave one of the worst speeches of his life yesterday, especially given the level of national distress and the need for words of consolation and wisdom,"[62] a reaction suggesting a felt need for a different kind of speech. That view was echoed by blogger Laura Rozen on August 31, 2005: "But for crying out loud, can he put off the laundry list of all the things his wonderful bureaucracy has done so far until the end of the speech and begin by addressing the pain we all feel as this tragedy is unfolding in slow-motion on live TV? We're talking death on a massive scale, and within 2 minutes he's thanking Texas for housing refugees. . . . I love President Bush, but that was a pathetic performance."[63]

From the moment presidents take the oath of office to the moment their successors do the same, a president is never not the president. From the moment a catastrophe affecting the nation takes lives in a way that challenges symbols dear to the country, the president must maintain a rhetoric that is both dignified and decisive. By that standard, President Bush's rhetorical response to Katrina failed.

Instead of transforming those affected by Katrina into symbols of national resilience, Bush focused on the prospect that the home of an influential member of the Senate would be reconstructed. This lapse occurred on September 2, when he made a stop at the Mobile Regional Airport in Alabama to be briefed on the response to Hurricane Katrina.

> We've got a lot of rebuilding to do. First, we're going to save lives and stabilize the situation, and then we're going to help these communities rebuild. The good news is—and it's hard for some to see it now—that out of this chaos is going to come a fantastic Gulf Coast, like it was before. Out of the rubbles of Trent Lott's house—he's lost his entire house—there's going to be a fantastic house. And I'm looking forward to sitting on the porch. (Laughter.)[64]

Similarly, the levity in his extemporaneous comments after a flyover of New Orleans on September 2 was out of keeping with the seriousness of the situation.

> Here's what I believe. I believe that the great city of New Orleans will rise again and be a greater city of New Orleans. I believe the town where I used to come from, Houston, Texas, to enjoy myself, occasionally too much—(laughter)— will be that very same town, that it will be a better place to come to. That's what I believe. I believe the great state of Louisiana will get its feet back and become a vital contributor to the country.[65]

A *USA Today*/CNN/Gallup poll taken on September 5 and 6 found that 42 percent of Americans thought Bush had done "a bad or terrible job responding to the hurricane." "'He's starting to create some vision and some hope,' said Christine Riordan, a leadership expert at Texas Christian University's M. J. Neeley School of Business. 'But it's five days too late.'"[66]

On September 8, 2005, the president issued a proclamation declaring September 16 a national day of prayer and remembrance for the victims of Hurricane Katrina.[67] The proclamation constitutes a written version of the national eulogy, but this form limits its ability to perform the functions we have described. It is an example of the right words in the wrong medium, a medium without the capacity to amass or address the citizenry. Given the current technology and the audience expectations created by it, a national eulogy must be delivered orally. Just as a president must take the oath of office orally, the investiture accomplished in the inaugural address requires oral delivery and our ability to witness the process. Similarly, the national eulogy requires immediacy. Empathy and comfort are intensely personal; we need to see the president and hear these words as they are spoken for national healing to begin.

On September 15, speaking from Jackson Square in New Orleans, Bush tried again. Before we explain why we find that discourse wanting, consider why the situation required a national eulogy: over a thousand people had died, a major city had been devastated, desperate people had been shown on national television calling for help. Moreover, the viewing public had every reason to believe that the government should warn them of imminent natural disasters and protect them from their effects.

Had the government done all that the public perceived it could do and done it valiantly, efficiently, and well, President Bush would have had at his disposal the lines of argument needed to deliver a national eulogy. However, because some argued plausibly that the federal government bore some responsibility for the failure of the levees, and because the Federal Emergency Management Agency (FEMA) failed to deliver aid to New Orleans in an efficient, timely fashion in the aftermath of Hurricane Katrina, Bush could not move effectively from the present crisis to the future and had difficulty assuring the public that such a catastrophe would not recur. He tacitly conceded that difficulty in an interview with Diane Sawyer on *Good Morning America* on September 1, saying, "I want people to know there's a lot of help coming." Later, he added, "We've got to get a handle on the human dimension." [68]

Bush's September 15 speech in Jackson Square in New Orleans has many of the characteristics of a national eulogy. At the outset, he identified those affected by the storm as "fellow citizens" and "fellow Americans," adding that we've "witnessed the kind of desperation no citizen of this great and generous Nation should ever have to know." The core of the eulogy was in this paragraph, in which Bush personalized the suffering of victims and the courage of rescuers and asserted presidential leadership to pledge that appropriate steps would be taken to make right what the storm had destroyed:

> Tonight so many victims of the hurricane and the flood are far from home and friends and familiar things. You need to know that our whole Nation cares about you, and in the journey ahead, you're not alone. To all who carry a burden

of loss, I extend the deepest sympathy of our country. To every person who has served and sacrificed in this emergency, I offer the gratitude of our country. And tonight I also offer this pledge of the American people: Throughout the area hit by the hurricane, we will do what it takes, we will stay as long as it takes, to help citizens rebuild their communities and their lives. And all who question the future of the Crescent City need to know there is no way to imagine America without New Orleans, and this great city will rise again.[69]

Because the adequacy and timing of response to the emergency were in question, Bush then laid out a three-part program, including specific proposals that he would make to Congress, to meet the immediate needs of those affected, to help rebuild Gulf Coast communities, and to ensure that what was rebuilt would be better and stronger than it had been before. He linked the disaster and the response to it to the nation's history; then he tried to speak to the people as national priest to remind them that any American's pain is their pain:

In the life of this Nation, we have often been reminded that nature is an awesome force and that all life is fragile. We're the heirs of men and women who lived through those first terrible winters at Jamestown and Plymouth, who rebuilt Chicago after the great fire, and San Francisco after a great earthquake, who reclaimed the prairie from the Dust Bowl of the 1930s. Every time, the people of this land have come back from fire, flood, and storm to build anew and to build better than what we had before. Americans have never left our destiny to the whims of nature, and we will not start now.

These trials have also reminded us that we are often stronger than we know—with the help of grace and one another. They remind us of a hope beyond all pain and death, a God who welcomes the lost to a house not made with hands. And they remind us that we're tied together in this life, in this Nation, and that the despair of any touches us all.[70]

Finally, Bush made the shift from the past to the future in a way distinctly suited to New Orleans:

In this place, there's a custom for the funerals of jazz musicians. The funeral procession parades slowly through the streets, followed by a band playing a mournful dirge as it moves to the cemetery. Once the casket has been laid in place, the band breaks into a joyful "second line," symbolizing the triumph of the spirit over death. Tonight the gulf coast is still coming through the dirge, yet we will live to see the second line.[71]

At the core of Bush's speech was an effort to displace the notion that government should have ensured that the levees held, evacuated the people who instead died, and adequately fed and sheltered those huddled in the Superdome. Although he stated, "When the Federal Government fails to meet its obligation, I, as President, am responsible for the problem and for the solution," that sentence came paragraphs after one that used the passive voice to place the blame on the impersonal "system":

> Many of the men and women of the Coast Guard, the Federal Emergency Management Agency, the United States military, the National Guard, Homeland Security, and State and local governments performed skillfully under the worst conditions. Yet the system, at every level of government, was not well-coordinated and was overwhelmed in the first few days. It is now clear that a challenge on this scale requires greater Federal authority and a broader role for the Armed Forces, the institution of our Government most capable of massive logistical operations on a moment's notice.[72]

Lost in the passive voice is the question of who failed to coordinate that system. If the public interposes a sound bite from Bush's September 2 speech into the text, "Brownie, you're doing a heck of a job,"[73] then the insurmountable problem this well-crafted speech confronts is clear. Michael Brown, the Bush-appointed head of FEMA, had resigned three days before the speech in Jackson Square.

Interlaced throughout the speech is a subtle effort to deflect blame from FEMA, and from Bush, that hints at the self-interest in the message. The implication of the speech is that no amount of federal effort would have been adequate to the situation. The address's first paragraph makes the "cruel and wasteful storm" (not the inadequately engineered levees or the inadequate government response) the agent responsible for the destruction. The meaning of the death and destruction is that Katrina was "not a normal hurricane," and consequently "the normal disaster relief system" was not up to the job. As a result, "the system" was "overwhelmed." Overwhelmed by what? The storm. Accordingly, the meaning of the disaster is ultimately that "nature is an awesome force and that all life is fragile." His competence at issue, in the end President Bush can only promise that in the future we will be better prepared: "We're going to review every action and make necessary changes so that we are better prepared for any challenge of nature or act of evil men that could threaten our people."[74]

The Bush speech in New Orleans is an instance in which words cannot compensate for deeds. Although the address artfully touches all the bases the national eulogy requires, it fails. Bush acknowledges the tragedy: "[W]e have seen fellow citizens left stunned and uprooted, searching for loved ones and grieving for the dead and looking for meaning in a tragedy that seems so blind and random. ... fellow Americans calling out for food and water ... and the bodies of the dead lying uncovered and untended in the street." In the address, the "meaning" for which they are searching remains unexpressed. Bush honors the rescuers and affirms that "this great city will rise again." He says that to avoid a "repeat of what we've seen," "communities" will have to "change zoning laws and building codes."[75] He proposes a series of specific measures to help the flooded areas and their people, including a Gulf Opportunity Zone and Worker Recovery Accounts. What is missing is a convincing explanation of what went wrong and a rhetoric that transforms the symbols of destruction into those of hope.

The question of how a recurrence will be prevented gains currency from the larger context in which it is set. The speech acknowledges it: "Four years after the frightening experience of September the 11th, Americans have every right to expect a more effective response in a time of emergency."[76] Indeed, they had that right before the terrorist attack, but if the government could not protect the citizens of New Orleans, is it better prepared than it was on September 11 to withstand a terrorist attack?

When Bush said, "I, as President, am responsible," he revealed that he was not speaking in the role required by the national eulogy, that of symbol-transforming priest. Believing that the president can deliver on the promise to protect the country from such events in the future requires us to believe that he has the power and the competence to do so, and that had been called into question by the government response to the event and by the president's praise of "Brownie" and his subsequent resignation. A defensive president cannot be vested in the role of priest. Self-interest or a tacit rhetoric of self-defense is incompatible with the larger role required by this moment.

The September 15 speech had all the elements of the national eulogy; nonetheless, criticism of the Bush administration response persisted. After the speech, according to the results of a poll reported on September 18, "Thirty-five percent (35%) of Americans now say that President Bush has done a good or excellent job responding to Hurricane Katrina and its aftermath. That's down from 39% before his speech from New

Orleans."[77] According to the results of a CNN/USA *Today*/Gallup poll released Monday, September 19, "Just 41 percent of the 818 adults polled between Friday and Monday said they approved of Bush's handling of the aftermath of Hurricane Katrina, while 57 percent disapproved."[78]

There are several possible reasons for these reactions. First, Bush implicitly downplayed the seriousness of the situation when he continued his vacation and pursued his speaking schedule even as the hurricane was devastating the Gulf Coast. Bush's initial reference to the destruction of Senator Trent Lott's second home did not seem appropriate; he further trivialized and personalized the disaster in his comments about partying in New Orleans and seemed not to understand the mass suffering. A president cannot assume the priestly role when his competence in dealing with the tragic event is in doubt and when he is delivering a speech that includes elements designed to deflect blame from himself and his administration. Moreover, to be recognized as the national priest, one must feel the people's suffering and find words to express it.

Second, the national eulogy came too late, particularly given news stories that documented the inadequacy of the emergency response on all levels. Bush's speech of August 31 was an effort to recover from evidence of federal delay and incompetence; that effort is also reflected in the recovery program and policy proposals included in the September 15 speech. Despite these efforts to gain control of the situation, the words of the national eulogy fall on deaf ears when prior events contradict its claims of identification with those who suffer and when inaction and inefficiency belie its pledges to act to make right what had been destroyed.

Third, the lines of argument developed earlier in response to the events of September 11 created a context that affected public response to the president's discourse. In the aftermath of those attacks, the people were told that they were being mobilized for a war on terror; accordingly, the Federal Emergency Management Agency had been repositioned under the Department of Homeland Security. Thus, Hurricane Katrina became a test of preparedness and presidential leadership. Both the president's response and that of FEMA indicated that neither was prepared to forestall a catastrophic event or act quickly and effectively should another terrorist attack occur. What had been President Bush's finest hour now became a frame that heightened his limitations and the inadequacy of preparations to respond to threats in the future.

Every rhetorical act takes place in a context that affects its meaning and power. The public must accept the president as national priest, and to do so, it requires consistency of feeling and attitude in all the words spoken. The national eulogy cannot perform its function if words and actions are discrepant—if the words seek to comfort, but the actions seem inept. Timing, too, is important. As other cases illustrate, the entire rhetorical act can be spread over time, but initial reactions must be consistent with its character and function.

Finally, the slow federal, state, and local responses to the devastation of Katrina created a rhetorical problem heightened by Bush's rhetoric in the aftermath of September 11. Hence, in contrast to Clinton's national eulogy for those killed in the bombing in Oklahoma City, which began to resurrect a failing presidency, Bush's words and actions after Hurricane Katrina contributed to the sliding public approval of his administration.[79] Bush's rhetorical problem was exacerbated because criticism of federal incompetence meant that he had to deflect blame from himself in this speech. The person who delivers the national eulogy cannot be implicated in the act that caused the deaths. Bush had appointed Michael D. Brown, the director of FEMA, and had praised him publicly on September 2. The portion of the September 15 speech that assesses blame and tries to deflect responsibility toward the storm and away from FEMA, Brown, and ultimately, Bush himself creates an internal tension that undercuts the ethos required of a priest. A self-defensive priest is no priest at all.

CONCLUSION

Presidents express themselves in a form we call the national eulogy when a traumatic event results in the death of civilians and by so doing calls the nation's institutions or values into question. In this genre, the president eulogizes the dead while assuming the role of priest to heal the nation's wounds and, in the process, reconstitutes the nation by transforming the symbolic meaning of the deaths into one of national resilience. When a terrorist attack has produced the national trauma, he argues that actions he is taking will protect the nation from future assault. If an individual is implicated, he argues that that person will be brought to justice. When he assigns blame to a process, system, or flawed technology, he calls for an investigation to identify and remedy the problem.

The national eulogy is closely related to the inaugural address because of its epideictic character. Like other epideictic rhetoric, it aspires to high style, even eloquence, and it invites the audience to contemplate and consider. Like eulogies for individuals, these speeches often suggest actions to commemorate the dead and to ensure that their legacy lives on in the future. Whereas the inaugural performatively demonstrates that the person who has taken the oath of office can fulfill the presidential role, the national eulogy is a moment in which the president assumes the mantle of national priest or pastor, ministering to wounds to the body politic, comforting the citizenry in the face of catastrophe, and assuring all of us that our national faith remains strong, that the community created in the nation's original covenant has not been broken or breached, and that in his role as chief executive, the president will ensure that the catastrophe will not recur.

As a eulogy, the speech acknowledges death and begins the process by which physical death becomes spiritual continuity. Whereas terrorists have made the dead symbols of what must be destroyed, President Bush, for example, transforms them into symbols of what must be preserved: the fundamental values that the nation represents. Although national eulogies happen at times of crisis, when presidents respond well to catastrophic events, they are admired and cherished. They show their leadership; they speak to our hearts; they heal our pain; they make us believe that, whatever happens, the nation has a secure future. And when they succeed, they create a reservoir of rhetorical capital on which they can call in future rhetorical acts.

FIVE

Pardoning Rhetoric

On August 9, 1974, Gerald Ford, the nation's only unelected president, took office after Richard Nixon resigned to avoid certain impeachment and removal from office. One month later, at 11:05 A . M . ESt on Sunday, September 8, Ford granted "a full, free, and absolute pardon unto Richard Nixon for all offenses against the United States which he, Richard Nixon, has committed or may have committed or taken part in during the period from January 20, 1969 through August 9, 1974."[1] Ford's unprecedented pardon of his disgraced predecessor dramatically illustrates the nature and scope of the presidential pardoning power, while press, public, and congressional reaction to its timing and its justification reflect the perils in its use.[2]

The pardoning power comes from article 2, section 2 of the Constitution, which vests the president with "power to grant Reprieves and Pardons for offenses against the United States, except in Cases of Impeachment." This power was derived directly from British traditions, which have had a determining effect on its interpretation by the courts.[3] The most extensive treatment of the presidential pardoning power appears in Federalist no. 74, in which Alexander Hamilton described its purposes and the rationales behind them.

The pardoning power was intended as a vehicle to temper justice for the public good. As Hamilton wrote, "The criminal code of every country partakes so much of necessary severity, that without an easy access to exceptions in favor of unfortunate guilt, justice would wear a countenance too sanguinary and cruel."[4] The pardoning power of the executive was a means to mitigate the severity of the judicial system through clemency and, in some instances, to rectify its abuses.

Hamilton also envisioned a second purpose, which was related to timing:

> In seasons of insurrection or rebellion, there are often critical moments, when a
> well timed offer of pardon to the insurgents or rebels may restore the tranquility

of the commonwealth; and which, if suffered to pass unimproved, it may never be possible afterwards to recall.[5]

In such circumstances, the executive would require the power to act quickly and unilaterally in order to "insure domestic tranquility" and "promote the general welfare," clauses that, together with the charge to "take care that the laws be faithfully executed," are the constitutional basis for its exercise. The pardon enabled immediate response to exigencies when time was of the essence. As Hamilton said,

> The dilatory process of convening the legislature, or one of its branches, for the purpose of obtaining its sanction to the measure, would frequently be the occasion of letting slip the golden opportunity. The loss of a week, a day, an hour, may sometimes be fatal.[6]

These purposes required that the pardoning power be unlimited and discretionary. As Hamilton argued, "Humanity and good policy conspire to dictate that the benign prerogative of pardoning should be as little as possible fettered or embarrassed."[7] With the exception of cases of impeachment, excluded by the Constitution, the Supreme Court has held, in words that echo those of Hamilton, that this power is "unlimited"; that it extends

> to every offense known to the law, and may be exercised at any time after its commission. . . . The power of the President is not subject to legislative control. Congress can neither limit the effect of his pardon, nor exclude from its exercise any class of offenders. The benign prerogative of mercy reposed in him cannot be fettered by any legislative restrictions.[8]

The presidential pardoning power is limited to leniency;[9] in addition, the president has no jurisdiction over offenses against state laws or over decrees promulgated by courts in cases between individuals.[10]

The scope of the presidential pardoning power was delineated further in a case decided in 1974. On March 4, 1967, Jimmy Hoffa, president of the International Brotherhood of Teamsters since 1958, began serving a combined sentence of thirteen years upon conviction of obstruction of justice, violation of mail and wire fraud statutes, and conspiracy to defraud a union pension fund. On December 23, 1971, Richard Nixon executed a warrant commuting Hoffa's sentence and making him eligible for immediate release. The warrant included the condition

"that the said James R. Hoffa not engage in direct or indirect management of any labor union prior to March 6, 1980."[11] Hoffa brought suit to
challenge the condition, but in *Hoffa v. Saxbe*, the court ruled that setting
this condition was within the president's pardoning power. The court
"found that any condition attached to a pardon must (a) directly relate
to the public interest and (b) not unreasonably infringe on the individual's constitutional freedoms."[12]

Although pardons are granted to individuals or classes of individuals, they are public acts, not private transactions between the president
and recipients. Courts once held that a pardon was not effective unless
accepted by the individual to whom it was granted,[13] but the Supreme
Court later ruled that a president can make a pardon effective without
the consent of the person pardoned. The recipient, reasoned the Court,
"on no sound principle ought to have any voice in what the law should do
for the welfare of the whole." The Court concluded that the executive
who pardons acts as an agent of society; thus, the pardon is "not a private act of grace from an individual happening to possess power."[14]

Although the founders said little about the pardoning power at the
Constitutional Convention, reservations about the extent of this executive power surfaced in debates at state ratification conventions. For
example, at the North Carolina ratification convention, William Lenoir
foresaw the possibilities that haunted congressional investigations of
Ford's pardon of Nixon:

> This power is necessary with proper restrictions. But the President may be at
> the head of a combination against the rights of the people, and may reprieve
> or pardon the whole. It is answered to this that he cannot pardon in cases of
> impeachment. What is the punishment in such cases? Only removal from office
> and future disqualification. It does not touch life or property. He has power to
> do away with punishment in every other case. It is too unlimited, in my opinion.
> It may be exercised to the public good, but may also be perverted to a different
> purpose.[15]

George Mason also expressed reservations in the Virginia debate on
ratification:

> The President of the United States has the unrestrained power of granting par-
> don for treason; which may be sometimes exercised to screen from punishment
> those whom he had secretly instigated to commit the crime, and thereby pre-
> vent a discovery of his own guilt.[16]

KEY ELEMENTS OF PARDONING RHETORIC

The presidential pardoning power is unilateral and discretionary, and is thus the most unfettered of presidential powers. In pardoning, the president, as the symbolic head of state, following a timeworn testamentary formula, acts at an appropriate moment to temper justice, either for the public good or to extend mercy to individuals. The rhetoric of presidential pardoning has three key elements: (1) the president acts in the presidential role as symbolic head of state; (2) the president demonstrates that this is an opportune time for action; and (3) the president justifies the pardon as being for the public good. The remainder of this chapter will consider these three aspects of this rhetorical genre and will close with a study of Ford's pardon of Nixon.

In pardoning, individual presidents are encouraged to act as symbolic heads of state by the time-tested testamentary formula and the conventions that have developed through its use, both of which invite them to follow the rhetorical patterns of their predecessors. Traditionally, the pardon is laid out in the form of a proclamation, with a series of "whereas" clauses indicating the source of the presidential pardoning power and the circumstances that make such action opportune, followed by a "therefore" clause granting the pardon and a testamentary formula in which presidents swear that they occupy the presidency and that they signed the document on a certain date, as witnessed by the secretary of state. The presidential seal is then attached as further evidence of the document's authenticity. This organization implies a propositional structure, although no justification is required.

In *Lapeyre v. the United States*,[17] the Supreme Court ruled that a proclamation written, signed, countersigned, and sealed in the appropriate form by the president takes immediate legal effect. In the case at issue, a proclamation written on June 24, 1865, was not printed in newspapers for three days. The Court concluded that publication was not essential to the act of presidential proclamation. In other words, a proclamation—the usual form in which pardons are issued—takes effect because, when witnessed by a formally designated government agent who can attest to its authenticity, it follows a formula that only the president can use. The document's legitimacy is established by the affixing of the presidential seal.

The traditional language of a proclamation depersonalizes its author and invites the president to follow archaic usages. Here, more than in any other presidential document, presidents speak with the same institutional voice. For example, the penultimate paragraph of a proclamation of pardon traditionally opens with a "therefore" clause, announcing the "granting" of a specific pardon. For instance, in pardoning those involved in the Whiskey Rebellion on July 10, 1795, George Washington proclaimed,

> Therefore, be it known that I, George Washington, President of the United States, have granted, and by these presents, do grant, a full, free, and entire pardon to all persons (excepting as is hereinafter excepted) of all treasons, misprision of treason, and other indictable offenses against the United States...[18]

Similarly, on September 8, 1974, Gerald Ford proclaimed, "Now, therefore, I, Gerald R. Ford, President of the United States, pursuant to the pardon power conferred upon me by Article 2, Section 2, of the Constitution, have granted and by these presents, do grant a full, free, and absolute pardon unto Richard Nixon." The paragraph then specified the period and the acts covered: "for all offenses against the United States which he, Richard Nixon, has committed or may have committed or taken part in during the period from January 20th, 1969, through August 9th, 1974." In keeping with constitutional limitations, George Washington, too, limited his pardon to "offenses against the United States" and specified that the pardon covered those acts "committed within the fourth survey of Pennsylvania between the said 22d day of August last past..."

In the final paragraph of a presidential pardon, presidents bear witness to their performance of the act; for example, in Washington's case, "in testimony" that he had "hereunto set my hand." The date is specified legalistically: on "this 8th day of September in the year of our Lord, nineteen hundred seventy-four," in Ford's case; on "this 10th day of July A.D. 1795," in Washington's case. In both instances, the presidents reminded immediate readers and successive generations of the legitimizing source of their power by ending the pardons with reference to the numbers of years that had passed since the United States declared its independence: Washington's pardon was issued in "the twentieth year of the Independence of the said United States," Ford's in the year "of the independence of the United States of America the one hundred and ninety-ninth."

The impersonal tone, the archaic language, the reliance on legalistic terminology, and the formality of the document overpower individual style and give presidential pardons a quaint sameness. The suppression of individual style that makes these documents almost interchangeable is evidence of a rhetorical form that empowers even weak presidents. That a proclamation of pardon by a revered founder and first president strikingly resembles one by our only unelected president suggests the institutionalized character of this genre. In the pardon, the institution, not the individual incumbent, speaks; as a result, a president who departs from the institutional formula to personalize the document or the remarks accompanying it weakens its rhetorical force.

A pardon is one of the purest and clearest instances of rhetorical action because, like the public impeachment proceedings described in chapter 11, it must court acquiescence from an audience of citizens. As a rhetorical act, it illustrates the Greek concept of *kairos*—seizing an opportune moment to make the fitting gesture.[19] Justification is unnecessary for the act of pardoning to occur, but in most instances, justification designed to induce approval is implied or detailed in the proclamation of pardon or in the remarks that accompany it.

The presidential statement of pardon, pardons. A president need not explain or justify. Like Grant, a president can simply command that

> all soldiers who have deserted their colors, and who shall, on or before the 1st day of January, 1874, surrender themselves at the military station, shall receive a full pardon, only forfeiting the pay and allowances due them at the time of desertion, and shall be restored to duty without trial or punishment on condition that they faithfully serve through the term of their enlistment.[20]

Pardons lacking any explanation or justification appear when such action enjoys wide popular support.

A special message to Congress informs or recommends; by contrast, a proclamation announces. For example, Thanksgiving Day is proclaimed yearly. Pardons are most often issued as proclamations, a form signaling that the act is self-sufficient, entailing no legislative review or authorization, and effective upon statement or at the point at which the conditions specified in the pardon are met. Occasionally a president will detail the immediate effect of the pardon. "All civil officers are hereby required," said Madison, "according to the duties of their respective stations, to carry this proclamation into immediate and faithful execution."[21]

When the executive informs Congress that a pardon has been issued, the action is warranted by the president's discretionary right under the

Constitution to act for the well-being of the nation. For example, in his third annual message, on December 8, 1863, Lincoln said,

> Looking now to the present and future, and with reference to a resumption of the national authority within the States wherein that authority has been suspended, I have thought fit to issue a proclamation, a copy of which is herewith transmitted. On examination of this proclamation it will appear, as is believed, that nothing will be attempted beyond what is amply justified by the Constitution. . . . The Constitution authorizes the Executive to grant or withhold the pardon at his own absolute discretion, and this includes the power to grant on terms, as if fully established by judicial and other authorities.[22]

Part of the justification for such unilateral, discretionary action is its timing. As his message explains, Lincoln had studied the military situation to ensure that an offer of pardon and amnesty would be made

> when it would materially weaken the enemy. . . . Indeed, choosing the time to announce these measures required an even greater evaluation of conditions [than announcing the Emancipation Proclamation], since their efficacy would be determined by the certainty of victory and the final restoration of the Union. . . . The time was now "ripe" for such action.[23]

Just how presidents have preserved the public good through their pardoning power can be illustrated by its exercise. The prospect of a pardon has been used to prevent the enlargement of a rebellious group by inviting it to cease its agitation against the government, as in the case of the pardons offered to those involved in the Whiskey Rebellion; to reward offenders whose later actions have demonstrated their commitment to the nation's interests, as in the case of the pardon of Lafitte's Barrataria pirates after the battle of New Orleans in the war of 1812; and to heal the wounds of the nation after war, as exemplified by pardons granted by Lincoln, Andrew Johnson, Truman, and Ford.

To engage in overt justification might imply that the pardoning power was not absolute, but instead required assent. Thus, as the verbs used in pardoning reveal, the rhetoric of a proclamation of pardon is the rhetoric of assertion and declaration. Lincoln "proclaims," "declares," "makes known," and in commuting sentences, he "directs."[24] Andrew Johnson "proclaims" and "declares."[25] Washington makes it known that he "has granted," as does Adams.[26] Jefferson "proclaims" a full pardon to certain deserters; Madison "grants" and "proclaims."[27]

The simple fact of being the president constitutes the right to pardon; therefore, in pardoning, presidents state that they are acting as president: "I, George Washington, President of the United States, have granted..." The pardon proclamations of Madison and Jefferson state that the pardons are granted "by the President of the United States."[28]

When Andrew Johnson pardoned soldiers who had fought for the Confederacy in the Civil War, he was asked to "transmit to the Senate a copy of any proclamation of amnesty made by him since the last adjournment of Congress, and also communicate to the Senate by what authority of law the same was made." In resisting that request, Lincoln's successor responded,

> The authority of law by which it was made is set forth in the proclamation itself, which expressly affirms that it was issued "by virtue of the power and authority in me vested by the Constitution and in the name of the sovereign people of the United States."[29]

After noting that the Constitution is the supreme law of the land and quoting the pardon and reprieve provision of article 2, section 2, Johnson rooted his action in presidential precedent:

> The proclamation of the 25th ultimo is in strict accordance with the judicial expositions of the authority thus conferred upon the Executive, and, as will be seen by reference to the accompanying papers, is in conformity with the precedent established by Washington in 1795, and followed by President Adams in 1800, Madison in 1815, and Lincoln in 1863, and by the present Executive in 1865, 1867, and 1868.[30]

A simultaneous assertion of constitutional authority and reminder of precedent occurred more recently when, on September 16, 1974, Gerald Ford announced his program "for the return of Vietnam era draft evaders and military deserters." His proclamation stated that "I, Gerald R. Ford, President of the United States, pursuant to my powers under Article 2, sections 1, 2, and 3 of the Constitution, do hereby proclaim a program to commence immediately..."[31] In the remarks introducing the proclamation, Ford noted,

> I promised to throw the weight of my Presidency into the scales of justice on the side of leniency and mercy, but I promised also to work within the existing

system of military and civilian law and the precedents set by my predecessors who faced similar postwar situations, among them Abraham Lincoln and Harry S. Truman.[32]

PRESIDENTIAL PARDONS: CLEMENCY AND LENIENCY

Presidential pardons may be roughly divided into two groups.[33] Most pardons emerge out of a process of petition and review involving appeals by individuals for mercy based on a variety of humane grounds or in order to rectify an injustice.[34] These pardons represent clemency for persons who have been found guilty of a crime and, in most cases, have been punished for it, including commutation of a death sentence, paroling of a prisoner who has served part of a sentence, or an outright pardon that removes a criminal record. The second group is made up of diverse pardons that extend leniency for the public good under a wide variety of circumstances. In this chapter, our major illustrations will be drawn from these diverse pardons, such as that of ex-president Nixon by President Ford, because these special cases display the nature and extent of the presidential pardoning power more clearly.

The use of the presidential pardoning power to extend mercy to individuals was illustrated on November 29, 1974. Upon signing eighteen executive warrants for clemency, President Ford explained that the individuals being pardoned had already been punished for their violations of the law. He then added, "The power of clemency can look to reasons for these actions which the law cannot."[35]

A similar instance of mercy to individuals that took account of motives was Ronald Reagan's April 15, 1981, pardon of W. Mark Felt and Edward S. Miller, ex-FBI agents who committed illegal acts in conjunction with the events of the Watergate scandals. In the statement accompanying the pardon, Reagan noted that Felt and Miller "came forward to acknowledge [their acts] publicly" and that "they acted not with criminal intent, but in the belief that they had grants of authority reaching to the highest levels of Government." He commented, "To punish them further—after three years of criminal prosecution proceedings—would not serve the ends of justice." Reagan also noted that four years earlier, his predecessor, Jimmy Carter, had unconditionally pardoned thousands who had evaded the draft or violated Selective Service laws. He concluded, "We can be no less generous to two men who acted on high principle."[36]

Pardoning as an act of mercy to individuals was also illustrated by Gerald Ford's announcement of presidential clemency for civilians who had evaded the draft. On December 31, 1974, Ford remarked,

> Each of these cases involves an individual—a judgment of his past and a determination of his future. The responsibility in each decision is a grave one. The [Presidential Clemency] Board and I have carefully considered each case on its individual merits. I believe we have acted with both justice and mercy.[37]

In these instances, presidents concluded that justice had been served; as a result, mercy was now appropriate. Their purpose was to make the judicial system more humane, to respond to the special circumstances of those who had already suffered for their crimes. Thus, although pardoning requires no justification, traditions have grown up around the circumstances under which it is fitting to extend mercy.

The second major category of pardons involves leniency extended for the public good. This exercise of presidential pardoning power is illustrated by amnesties, conditional amnesties, pardons, and conditional pardons.[38] In most instances, these pardons have been granted in conjunction with insurrections and war. For instance, the emphasis on justice tempered for the public good was apparent in George Washington's seventh annual message, in which he explained the amnesty extended to those involved in the Whiskey Rebellion:

> For though I shall always think it a sacred duty to exercise with firmness and energy the constitutional powers with which I am vested, yet it appears to me no less consistent with the public good than it is with my personal feelings to mingle in the operation of Government every degree of moderation and tenderness which the national justice, dignity, and safety may permit.[39]

Such amnesties or pardons routinely link justice, the public good, and acknowledgment of wrongdoing. This linkage was evident in John Adams's proclamation granting pardons to Pennsylvanian insurrectionists:

> Whereas the late wicked and treasonable insurrection ... having been speedily suppressed without any of the calamities usually attending rebellion; whereupon ... the ignorant, misguided, and misinformed in the counties have returned to a proper sense of their duty, whereby it is become unnecessary for the public good that any future prosecutions should be commenced or carried on ...[40]

Similarly, in offering full pardons to deserters in 1807, Thomas Jefferson noted that the offenders "have become sensible of their offense and are desirous of returning to their duty." [41] In 1812, James Madison followed this formula in granting full pardons to deserters, whom he also characterized as "hav[ing] become sensible of their offenses and . . . desirous of returning to their duty." [42] In 1815, in granting pardons to the Barrataria pirates for their critical role in the defense of New Orleans, Madison affirmed that these "offenders have manifested a sincere penitence; that they have abandoned the prosecution of the worse cause for the support of the best." He added,

> Offenders who have refused to become the associates of the enemy in war upon the most seducing terms of invitation and who have aided to repel his hostile invasion of the territory of the United States can no longer be considered as objects of punishment, but as objects of a generous forgiveness. [43]

Similarly, in granting amnesties after the Civil War, Andrew Johnson asserted that he acted "that the authority of the Government of the United States may be restored and that peace, order, and freedom may be established." [44] On September 16, 1974, Gerald Ford proclaimed,

> Desertion in time of war is a major, serious offense; failure to respond to the country's call for duty is also a serious offense. Reconciliation among our people does not require that these acts be condoned. Yet reconciliation calls for an act of mercy to bind the Nation's wounds and to heal the scars of divisiveness.

In justifying this grant of conditional clemency, Ford said, "In furtherance of our national commitment to justice and mercy these young Americans should have the chance to contribute a share to the rebuilding of peace among ourselves and with all nations." [45]

As illustrated in this case and in some other instances, mercy to individuals was linked to the public good. That was also the case in Warren G. Harding's commutations of the sentences of political prisoners. In the summer of 1918, Eugene V. Debs, Socialist party leader and perennial presidential candidate, was arrested for seditious antiwar activity. While in prison, Debs received 941,827 votes in the 1920 election, the highest number he had ever received in his five attempts at the presidency. A. Mitchell Palmer, Woodrow Wilson's "red-baiting" attorney general, recommended that Wilson pardon Debs, but his recommendation was rejected. During the 1920 campaign, Harding indicated a willingness to review the cases of political prisoners and, once elected, set pardoning processes in motion. Opposition forced Harding to defer action until the peace treaties officially ending World War I had been signed, but on December 24, 1921, he commuted the sentences of Debs and twenty-three others: "In each instance, his sole criterion was whether the person had committed any criminal or destructive act in connection with his antiwar activities."[46] On that basis, Harding commuted the sentences even of members of the International Workers of the World (Wobblies). In a letter to his friend Malcolm Jennings, Harding explained, "I thought the spirit of clemency was quite in harmony with the things we were trying to do here in Washington."[47]

As these examples of pardoning demonstrate, the pardoning power is one of the most unfettered of presidential powers. The testamentary formula, the purposes, and the character of the presidential pardon are illustrated in its past exercise.

CONTROVERSIAL PARDONS

Presidential pardons often arouse controversy, but recent presidents have issued pardons that, because of their timing and their self-implicating character, have undermined the presidential pardoning power and become part of the reputation and legacy of the president who issued them. Two of these pardons are illustrative.

On December 24, 1992, George H. W. Bush pardoned six persons involved in the Iran-Contra affair, including former secretary of defense Caspar Weinberger. This pardon raised questions because there was evidence that Bush, who had served as Reagan's vice president while the affair was unfolding, had direct personal knowledge of the illegal exchange of arms for hostages. During the Reagan administration, when this illegal exchange came to light, Lawrence E. Walsh was named independent counsel in charge of investigating Iran-Contra. All of those pardoned were part of ongoing prosecutions, and Walsh reacted to the pardons by claiming that "the Iran-Contra cover-up, which has continued for more than six years, has now been completed."[48] It was also reported that Walsh believed that the pardons were designed to prevent Weinberger's trial, scheduled for January 5, 1993—a trial that could have embarrassed the president, a potential witness in the case.

Even in controversial pardons, presidents employ the conventional arguments that pervade the genre we have described. In his proclamation pardoning Weinberger, as well as former national security adviser Robert C. McFarlane, former assistant secretary of state Elliott Abrams, and three former CIA officials, who had all pleaded guilty or been indicted and convicted in connection with the Iran-Contra investigation, Bush used traditional justifications. He described the pardons as part of a "healing tradition," citing such precedents as James Madison's pardon of the Barrataria pirates, Andrew Johnson's pardon of Confederate soldiers, and Jimmy Carter's pardon of Vietnam-era draft dodgers. Bush called Weinberger "a true American patriot" and noted that he and his wife both suffered from debilitating illnesses, suggesting that this was a time for compassionate mercy. Bush also offered other justifications, saying that first, the "common denominator of their motivation—whether their actions were right or wrong—was patriotism. Second, they did not profit or seek to profit from their conduct." He added a more conventional reason: that they had been punished enough; that "all five have already paid a price—in depleted savings, lost careers, anguished families—grossly disproportionate to any misdeeds or errors of judgment they may have committed."[49]

The timing—Christmas Eve—made this a stealth pardon, occurring at a time when the nation's attention was focused on all the events related to the Christmas holiday rather than on the news. Another aspect of the timing—only a few days before a trial that might have tainted the president's reputation—called attention to the pardon's self-implicating dimensions. That it was issued less than a month before Bush was leaving office and after his successor had been elected meant that this pardon would be a key element in his legacy, an act that would become imprinted on the public memory as part of the rhetorical act of farewell.

Pardons from which presidents or their political parties or friends benefit are bound to elicit controversy, in part because they are most often issued in the closing days of a presidency. Bill Clinton issued 456 pardons during his tenure, 176 of them on his last day in office, including one for financier Marc Rich, a fugitive who had been charged with tax evasion, after clemency pleas from Israeli prime minister Ehud Barak, among many other international luminaries. Denise Rich, Marc's former wife, was a close friend of the Clintons and had made substantial donations to Clinton's presidential library and to Hillary Clinton's Senate campaign. E-mails reveal that several months after her last donation, Republican attorney I. Lewis "Scooter" Libby, Jr., asked her to approach Clinton about pardoning Marc Rich. Clinton agreed to a pardon that required Marc Rich to pay a $100,000,000 fine before he could return to the United States. What makes this pardon controversial is the nature of the activity for which Rich was pardoned—tax evasion—as well as his status as an expatriate who fled to avoid prosecution. Fueling the controversy as well was the perception that international leaders were interceding on Rich's behalf, and that his ex-wife, a major donor to the Clintons, also made special pleas. This example combines bad timing with self-implication—that is, there was a self-interested reason for Clinton to pardon a person whose wealth, via his ex-wife, has benefited him and his wife politically. The pardon would have been controversial at any time, but that it occurred as Clinton was leaving the Oval Office made it particularly problematic.

When a pardon elicits national controversy, the risk to the president is that it becomes a part of the rhetorical act known as a farewell. The act of engaging in a suspect pardon reduces the president to a venal partisan, whereas the act of farewell requires instead that he not only transcend the moment, but also do so in a way that makes the country proud of his presidency. If the pardon can be construed as payback or partisan, it drains presidential capital; if, instead, it is perceived as healing, it enhances presidential capital.

Importantly, last-minute pardons elicit discussions in Congress about whether the presidential pardoning power ought to be limited. A notable instance was a proposal not to permit any pardon after October 1 of the year of a presidential election, which would enable the public to hold the president and his party accountable for his pardoning decisions.

That some pardons are controversial may be a sign of healthy interaction between the executive and legislative branches. Daniel T. Kobil, professor of law at Capital University Law School in Columbus, Ohio, testified before the Subcommittee on the Constitution of the House Committee on the Judiciary, convened to examine the presidential pardon power. Kobil emphasized the interactive character of pardons when he stated that

> clemency provides an opportunity for the executive to initiate or participate in a dialogue regarding the wisdom, efficacy, or constitutionality of our laws. . . . President Jefferson did just that when he granted pardons to persons convicted under the constitutionally-suspect Sedition Act. Similarly, many of President Clinton's grants of clemency can be seen as taking aim at what many today, including judges implementing the laws, view as overly-harsh mandatory sentence standards pertaining to the possession or sale of illegal drugs.[50]

In other words, through acts of pardoning and clemency, the president can call attention to areas in which legal penalties are so stringent that they appear disproportionate, or even to laws that may be unconstitutional.

Although the pardoning power is theoretically unfettered, its use is affected by politics, and presidential willingness to exercise it may be affected by the potential for backlash. Kobil noted the "decrease in the use of clemency during the administration of George H. W. Bush," which coincided with an official stance of being "tough on crime," and commented,

> Presidents who follow President Clinton could be unwilling to use the clemency power at all, in view of its obvious political risks. President Ford's pardon of Richard Nixon may have cost him the 1976 election, sparking a precipitous decline in the use of clemency. President Clinton's undisciplined use of clemency may also exact a high cost in terms of his reputation and historic legacy. If the past is prologue, it does not seem far fetched to speculate that such repercussions could threaten, in practical effect, to wipe out use of the clemency power for the foreseeable future.[51]

Margaret Colgate Love, who served as pardon attorney at the Department of Justice for most of the 1990s, underscored these concerns in her prepared statement at the same hearing: "About 20 years ago the Federal pardon power began to be exercised less frequently and less generously. Gestures of mercy were regarded as inconsistent with a tough time [sic] control strategy and politically dangerous"[52] She added,

> I find a lot to be grateful for in the final Clinton pardons. In the first place, two-thirds of them went to ordinary people who had filed applications with the Justice Department and had waited patiently for the relief they sought, some for a number of years. Twenty of his 36 commutations went to low-level nonviolent drug offenders who had already spent between six and 12 years in prison and who will now have a second chance at living a normal, productive life.[53]

She continued, "Recently, ... the pardon program has lost its independence and integrity within the Department of Justice....[and] has gradually come to reflect the unforgiving culture of federal prosecutors."[54]

As these comments suggest, the pardoning power may fall victim to public opinion about crime and punishment and to the threat of serious repercussions of tempering justice with mercy. George W. Bush's use of the pardoning power is one test of this prediction. On December 21, 2006, he

> issued 16 pardons . . . and commuted the sentence of an Iowa man who had been convicted on drug charges. . . . A White House spokesman, Tony Fratto, said Mr. Bush had issued 113 pardons and commuted three sentences in his nearly six years in office. Mr. Bush has issued the fewest pardons of any president since World War II.
>
> President Bill Clinton issued 457 in eight years in office. Mr. Bush's father issued 77 in four years. President Ronald Reagan issued 406 in eight years, and President Jimmy Carter issued 563 in four years.
>
> The most pardons and commutations, 2,031, were issued by President Harry S. Truman, who served 82 days short of eight years.[55]

One commutation by Bush proved particularly controversial, however, because critics viewed it as a means to ensure that its beneficiary would have no incentive to disclose information that might damage the White House. On July 2, 2007, just before the July 4th holiday and without consulting Department of Justice attorneys, George W. Bush commuted the prison sentence of "Scooter" Libby, who had been convicted of committing perjury and obstruction of justice in a CIA leak case while serving as Vice President Dick Cheney's chief of staff. According to the president's statement, this exercise of the pardoning power was occasioned when a panel of judges ruled that Libby could not defer serving his two and a half-year prison sentence while he appealed his conviction. Bush was careful to distinguish this act of clemency from a full pardon, which would have freed Libby from all punishment and expunged his criminal record.

Bush rehearsed the arguments in the debate about this case in the statement accompanying the commutation, saying, "In preparing for the decision I am announcing today, I have carefully weighed these arguments and the circumstances surrounding the case." He added, "I have concluded that the prison sentence given to Libby is excessive," but attempted to mitigate controversy by saying, "My decision to commute his prison sentence leaves in place a harsh punishment for Mr. Libby. The reputation he gained through his years of public service and professional work in the legal community is forever damaged."[56]

The controversial nature of Bush's decision was underscored by the comments of Margaret Colgate Love. With minor exceptions, she said,

"I can't think of a recent commutation that was granted before at least some prison time was served."[57] Moreover, "experts in federal sentencing law said a sentence of 30 months for lying and obstruction was consistent with the tough sentences routinely meted out by the federal system."[58] Her first argument raised the salience of the timing of the commutation, while the second questioned the accuracy of its central rationale.

In sum, pardoning is public, unilateral, and discretionary. It is a uniquely presidential act, justified by its timeliness and by its capacity to serve the public good. Thus, despite their formulaic character, presidential pardons are instances of rhetorical action, and they can be evaluated with criteria drawn from their performative character, their timing, and their skill in demonstrating that the act is in the national interest. The rhetorical perils of the pardon can be illustrated through a close textual analysis of Gerald Ford's proclamation pardoning Richard Nixon on September 8, 1974, and the remarks that accompanied it.[59]

FORD'S PARDON OF NIXON

The difficulties involved in seizing the opportune moment to act in a fitting way affected Gerald Ford's proclamation of pardon of Richard Nixon and the remarks accompanying it on three levels: the hour at which Ford spoke, its timing in his presidency, and its relationship to his pardons of Vietnam-era draft evaders and deserters.

Quite simply, the time at which Ford spoke and issued the proclamation contradicted his avowed intent to candidly explain the motives for the pardon to the public. Reporters are accustomed to White House efforts to control coverage by releasing damaging or controversial material at "slow news times" or times that lessen public exposure. On Sunday morning, the nation's newspapers are scattered across kitchen tables or lie unread on doorsteps. No additional print news coverage will occur until Monday morning. There is no "drive-time" radio on Sunday, and the Sunday morning television audience is one of the smallest of the entire week. As a result, issuing the pardon on a Sunday morning appeared to be secretive, to belie Ford's claim that his remarks were intended to convince his fellow citizens that the pardon was "necessary surgery—essential if we were to heal our wounded nation." Had Ford genuinely intended to persuade the nation, he would have scheduled a speech in prime time on a weeknight and attracted a large audience with advance announcements. The result of this scheduling was recalled by Ford in his autobiography: "The timing of the announcement—11 o'clock on Sunday morning—was touted as 'proof' of the conspiracy."[60]

The granting of the pardon on September 8, 1974, was problematic in a second sense. If Ford was correct when, in his first speech as president, he said that "the long national nightmare is over," then it was contradictory to say now, "My conscience tells me clearly and certainly that I cannot prolong the bad dreams that continue to reopen a chapter that is closed" (103). If a pardon was required to heal the nation, then Ford should have issued it immediately. As a result, Ford had difficulty explaining why he had waited thirty days to issue the pardon or, conversely, why he had not waited longer to issue it. Early in his remarks, he said that it would not be right "to procrastinate, to agonize, and to wait for a more favorable turn of events that may never come or more compelling external pressures that may as well be wrong as right." This comment called attention to the less than favorable conditions and the less than compelling external pressures at the time of the pardon. Later in the speech, he said, "In the end, the courts might well hold that Richard Nixon had been denied due process, and the verdict of history would even more be [sic] inconclusive," thus acknowledging the inconclusive nature of the pardon, despite his earlier assertion that "someone must write the end to" what he called a "tragedy."

That characterization occurred midway through Ford's remarks, when he said of Nixon and his family, "Theirs is an American tragedy in which we have all played a part." Because the part his listeners had played was that of spectators, not actors, it was an odd statement that, as discussed below, raised a question about the part Ford himself had played and, hence, whether Ford had received the presidency as a quid pro quo for the pardon. Here, our concern with this passage is its relation to the next sentence, in which Ford averred that the tragedy "could go on and on and on, or someone must write the end to it." The inclusion of the third "on" suggested an endlessness contradicted by the nature of the judicial process. At some point, Richard Nixon would have been indicted by the courts, tried, found innocent or guilty, and, if guilty, sentenced. Moreover, this allusion to timelessness, juxtaposed with Ford's statement that "I have concluded that only I can do that [write the end to it], and if I can, I must," reminded his listeners that he had not justified the timeliness of acting then rather than on the first day of his presidency or, conversely, a few months later, when Richard Nixon's legal position would have been clarified. In other words, none of Ford's specific references to timing justified the conclusion that this was the opportune moment for action.

One might well ask why Ford did not pardon Nixon immediately. There is a possible answer in the situation in which Ford found himself and in the content of the speech. Had Ford, an unelected president appointed by his predecessor, who was resigning in disgrace, pardoned Nixon immediately, he would have aroused suspicions that he had secured his office illegally, as a quid pro quo. The legitimacy of his ascent to office would have been in question, and Ford himself would have been subject to impeachment. Not until he had functioned in the presidency and performed its rhetorical duties—delivered an inaugural, signed legislation, and been accepted by the press and the public as the president—could Ford pardon his predecessor without creating a presumption that his ascent was tainted.

Why did Ford not wait until the judicial system had clarified Nixon's position? That question is unanswerable, particularly because, in his confirmation hearings for the vice presidency in 1973, Ford had indicated that he would not consider exercising the pardoning power until the judicial process had worked itself out—timing that was tacitly accepted by Congress.[61] As late as August 28, 1974, in a press conference less than two weeks before the proclamation of pardon, he said that the question of a pardon, while open, was premature: "There have been no charges made. There has been no action by the court. There's been no action by any jury, and until any legal process has been undertaken, I think it's unwise and untimely to make any commitment."[62]

The Nixon pardon can also be seen in relation to other events of the Ford presidency. Since the Vietnam War was theoretically over for the United States, presidential treatment of deserters and draft evaders was as inevitable an issue for Ford as it had been for Lincoln, Andrew Johnson, Wilson, and Truman. He had to decide whether to pardon them and, if so, on what terms. He could not pardon Richard Nixon without raising the issue of pardons for these other Americans. On August 19, 1974, in a speech before the Veterans of Foreign Wars, Ford indicated that he would consider granting clemency to or pardoning on a conditional basis those guilty of offenses related to the Vietnam War. On September 16, a little more than a week after Nixon's pardon, he announced the formation of a Presidential Clemency Board to carry out a program of reconciliation for Vietnam-era draft evaders and military deserters. As a result, comparisons were inevitable and charges of inconsistency unavoidable.

The rhetoric in which Ford encased this act of clemency invited the press and public to compare it with the pardon of Richard Nixon. In his remarks of September 16, Ford reminded the public of his promise of August 19 to "throw the weight of my Presidency into the scales of justice on the side of leniency and mercy."[63] The alliance of justice and mercy recurred when Ford announced his clemency decisions on December 31, 1974, saying, "The Board and I have carefully considered each case on its individual merits. I believe we have acted with both justice and mercy."[64] In his proclamation of September 16, Ford said, "My objective of making future penalties fit the seriousness of each individual's offense and of mitigating punishment already meted out in a spirit of equity has proved an immensely hard and very complicated matter";[65] in this case, making the punishment fit the crime remained his objective. As a result, deserters and draft evaders were given options that included various forms of alternative service.

In contrast, Ford concluded "that Richard Nixon and his loved ones have suffered enough." Moreover, Ford claimed that only by pardoning Nixon could he preserve the principle of equal justice under law:

> The facts, as I see them, are that a former President of the United States, instead of enjoying equal treatment with any other citizen accused of violating the law, would be cruelly and excessively penalized either in preserving the presumption of his innocence or in obtaining a speedy determination of his guilt in order to repay a legal debt to society. (102)

The inconsistency between Ford's treatment of Vietnam-era draft evaders and military deserters and of Richard Nixon prompted the resignation of Ford's press secretary, Gerald terHorst, on the day of the Nixon pardon. In his letter of resignation, terHorst wrote, "I do not know how I could credibly defend that action [the pardon of Nixon] in the absence of a like decision to grant absolute pardon to the young men who evaded Vietnam military service as a matter of conscience."[66] The inconsistency was also apparent to the news media. At a press conference on September 16, one reporter asked, "If your intention was to heal the wounds of the Nation, sir, why did you grant only a conditional amnesty to the Vietnam war draft evaders while granting a full pardon to President Nixon?"[67] The difficulties involved in answering that question were suggested in terHorst's letter of resignation: "Try as I can, it is impossible to conclude that the former President is more deserving of mercy than persons of lesser station in life whose offenses have had less effect on our national well-being."[68] Subsequently, Ford would explain in his autobiography that he "thought people would consider his [Nixon's] resignation from the Presidency as sufficient punishment and shame."[69] The timing of its announcement, its timing in his presidency, and its relationship to the clemency extended to Vietnam-era draft evaders all undermined the Nixon pardon as rhetoric.

Pardoning is an act that only the president, as empowered by the Constitution, can perform. Because Ford came to the presidency through appointment by his disgraced predecessor, there were strong reasons for him to delay issuing a pardon at least until the press and the public had accepted him as the president. When Ford decided to pardon Nixon, however, he undercut his authority to pardon in the remarks accompanying the proclamation and by other actions. By delivering remarks that deviated from the formal, impersonal, archaic, legalistic conventions of his predecessors, Ford failed to enact the traditional presidential role that gives the pardon its performative power. Moreover, by warranting the pardon by his conscience and by the laws of God, rather than by the authority granted him by the Constitution, Ford undermined his legitimacy to issue the pardon.

In his remarks, Ford acknowledged the importance of the Constitution: "I have promised to uphold the Constitution, to do what is right as God gives me to see the right, and to do the very best I can for America." However, he then placed his conscience and the laws of God above the Constitution: "The Constitution is the supreme law of our land and it governs our actions as citizens. Only the laws of God, which govern our consciences, are superior to it." Then, in words bordering dangerously on a claim of theocratic prerogatives, Ford noted, "As we are a nation under God, so I am sworn to uphold our laws with the help of God." (The presidential oath specified in the Constitution does not include the phrase "so help me God"; that addition has become a tradition.) Having defined his loyalty to the Constitution and indicated that only the law of God surpasses it, Ford then made a distinction between his role as president and his role as "a man": "As President, my primary concern must always be the greatest good of all the people in the United States whose servant I am. As a man, my first consideration is to be true to my own convictions and my own conscience." Whereas the act of pardoning would dictate that Ford locate his authority in his role as president, as empowered by the Constitution, he instead located his authority in his conscience and in his role as "a humble servant of God." The next six sentences began with one of two phrases, "My conscience tells me," and "I do believe," and were followed by a seventh that began, "I feel." Midway through this litany of soul baring, Ford made his shift in roles explicit: "I do believe, with all my heart and mind and spirit, that I, *not as President* but as a humble servant of God, will receive justice without mercy if I fail to show mercy" [emphasis added]. He also redefined his constitutional obligations as mandated by his conscience: "My conscience tells me it is my duty, not merely to proclaim domestic tranquility but to use every means that I have to insure it." The entire passage, from the delineation of presidential and personal roles, reads as follows:

> As President, my primary concern must always be the greatest good of all the people of the United States whose servant I am. As a man, my first consideration is to be true to my own convictions and my own conscience.
>
> My conscience tells me clearly and certainly that I cannot prolong the bad dreams that continue to reopen a chapter that is closed. My conscience tells me that only I, as President, have the constitutional power to firmly shut and seal this book. My conscience tells me it is my duty, not merely to proclaim domestic tranquility but to use every means that I have to insure it.
>
> I do believe that the buck stops here, that I cannot rely upon public opinion polls to tell me what is right.
>
> I do believe that right makes might and that if I am wrong, ten angels swearing I was right would make no difference.
>
> I do believe, with all my heart and mind and spirit, that I, not as President but as a humble servant of God, will receive justice without mercy if I fail to show mercy.
>
> Finally, I feel that Richard Nixon and his loved ones have suffered enough and will continue to suffer, no matter what I do, no matter what we, as a great and good nation, can do together to make his goal of peace come true. (102–3)

In these remarks, Ford not only violated the role that legitimized the pardon, but also used imagery that was at odds with the purposes he avowed. In the speech he made on assuming the presidency, Ford had assured the citizenry that "the long national nightmare is over." In that same speech, he developed a tragic view of the presidency, as indicated in our analysis in chapter 3, suggesting that failure was likely, if not inherent, in the office—a view that implied that such nightmares might well recur. The same contradictory conception appeared in his remarks upon issuing the pardon. Early in the speech, Ford said of Nixon and his family, "Theirs is an American tragedy in which we have all played a part." Later in the speech, he added, "I cannot prolong the bad dreams that continue to reopen a chapter that is closed."

The words "an American tragedy" invited the audience to see parallels between Nixon and the protagonist of Theodore Dreiser's novel of that title as well as Sophocles' Oedipus in the Greek plays that are the touchstones in terms of which tragedy is defined and understood. Viewed through the perspective of Dreiser's novel, the allusion suggests that poor boys who aspire to realize the American dream are driven to crimes that inevitably transform the dream into a nightmare, a parallel suggesting that the American dream is fatally flawed. If so, then no one could "shut and seal the book" or "write the end to it."

The allusion's implied analogy between Nixon and Oedipus only heightened their differences. Central to the tragedy of Oedipus, and to all tragedy, is *anagnorisis,* or "recognition," a moment of public acknowledgment of wrongdoing, symbolized by Oedipus's acts of self-mutilation. Oedipus can be said to have suffered enough precisely because his self-mutilation symbolizes the perpetual suffering that such guilty knowledge entails. Oedipus can never find peace because his guilt condemns him to wander, suffering, until his death. By contrast, there had been no public acknowledgment by Nixon of his wrongdoing; he had not been indicted, an act that would have required a vote by the full House of Representatives on the articles of impeachment passed by the House Committee on the Judiciary. Neither his resignation speech, discussed in chapter 12 on farewell addresses, nor his statement in response to the pardon acknowledged guilt or expressed contrition for wrongdoing. Thus, in contrast to Oedipus, there was no evidence that Nixon suffered from any guilty self-knowledge, much less that he had suffered enough.

The contrasting positions of Oedipus and Nixon also show why the implied analogy was inappropriate. No one could wish to punish Oedipus further because the punishment he exacted on himself was greater than any other imaginable penalty, and he evokes our pity because he lives his suffering before our eyes, a suffering ordained for him by the fates. As a result, the comparison violates *kairos;* it is not "fitting."

Moreover, in a speech that could ill afford to give the merest hint of duplicity, the language and imagery of Ford's remarks subtly suggested that he might have made a deal to become president. In a speech on April 29, 1974, with his defenses against complicity in Watergate collapsing around him, Richard Nixon used an odd image, drawn from the rhetoric of Abraham Lincoln, to assert that "ten angels swearing I was right would make no difference."[70] In Nixon's speech, the image functioned rhetorically to assert that he was telling the truth in the face of harsh attacks. By the time of Ford's pardon, both Ford and his audience knew that Nixon had lied. By using the same words, Ford subtly allied himself with Nixon and cast doubt on his own veracity. "I do believe," said Ford, "that right makes might and that if I am wrong, ten angels swearing I was right would make no difference."[71]

The second subtle question raised by Ford's language is whether loyalty to Nixon motivated the pardon. Ford emphasized the virtue of loyalty when he said, "And I have sought such guidance and searched my own conscience with special diligence to determine the right thing for me to do with respect to my predecessor in this place, Richard Nixon, and his loyal wife and family." Later in the speech, Ford said, "My concern is the immediate future of this country. In this, I dare not depend upon my personal sympathy as a long-time friend of the former President." As noted, however, Ford then proceeded to ground subsequent lines of argument in his conscience and personal feelings. By speaking in such terms, Ford heightened the possibility that personal sympathy had indeed shaped his decision. This possibility was particularly evident in his revelation, "I do believe, with all my heart and mind and spirit, that I, not as President but as a humble servant of God, will receive justice without mercy if I fail to show mercy." By extolling loyalty as a virtue, and by singling it out as a virtue to praise, Ford hinted that it might have been the motive for his actions.

Nothing in Ford's language or imagery directly suggested a quid pro quo, but both raised questions about the motivation for the pardon. And once those questions have been raised, Ford's statement, "Theirs is an American tragedy in which we all have played a part," can be heard differently. What part did Ford play in Nixon's tragedy? And when, earlier in the speech, Ford said that the difficult decisions facing him no longer looked the same "as the hypothetical questions that I have answered freely," his words suggested the possibility that the answers given in the pardon were less free than those given in the past, particularly at his confirmation hearings. The same whisper can be heard when, instead of saying, "I have concluded," Ford said, "I am compelled to conclude that many months and perhaps more years will have to pass before Richard Nixon could obtain a fair trial by jury."

Finally, in a section of the speech that is rife with mixed metaphors, Ford hinted that he was shutting off access to further information about

Nixon's past wrongdoing or, possibly, his own culpability: "My conscience tells me that only I, as President, have the constitutional power to firmly shut and seal this book." The apparent referent occurred earlier in the speech when Ford said that the Nixon tragedy "could go on and on and on, or someone must write the end to it." The shift in mood from "could" to "must" jolts the listener. With Ford having cast himself as playwright, one might ask, who wrote the opening scenes? Did Ford have a hand in them? Whatever the invited image, by the end of the speech, Ford had put down the playwright's pen to play the role of a reader who would "shut the book." But here, too, he assumed an odd relationship to the plot, because only he had the power to end "the bad dreams that continue to reopen the chapter that is closed." Just how bad dreams reopen a chapter is difficult to imagine. But Ford went on to tell us that only he had the constitutional power to "firmly shut and seal the book." We know what it means to shut a book, to set it aside, but what is it to seal a book? One speaks of sealing court records or of sealing a document as a sign of authenticity. Lurking in the mixed metaphor is an implication that Ford was sealing access to potentially damaging information. That implication was underscored by an agreement giving Richard Nixon control of the documents and tapes of his presidency, which accompanied the pardon—one more instance of unfortunate timing.

At the close of his remarks, Ford reaffirmed his and the nation's joint commitment "to make [Richard Nixon's] goal of peace come true." The alert listener might well have wondered whether Ford saw himself as president in his own right or as an agent of his predecessor. Why, after all, was it *Nixon's* goal of peace that we were to make come true? Is Ford referring to peace in the world, or the personal peace that a pardon will bring to Nixon? This strange locution that identified as uniquely Nixon's a goal shared by all hints at the troubling possibility that the peace of which Ford spoke was, indeed, Nixon's peace of mind.

A similar possibility underlies an earlier statement in the speech:

> To procrastinate, to agonize, and to wait for a more favorable turn of events that may never come or more compelling external pressures that may as well be wrong as right, is itself a decision of sorts and a weak and potentially dangerous course for a president to follow.

Lost in that sentence is the question, for whom would the turn of events be more favorable? For Nixon? And why, when Ford spoke of alternatives that he faced, did he move from the personal pronouns and adjectives that otherwise characterize the address to an abstract discussion of the course "a president" might follow?

One more anomaly in Ford's speech is worthy of remark. Ford said, "After years of bitter controversy and divisive national debate, I have been advised, and I am compelled to conclude that many months and perhaps more years will have to pass before Richard Nixon could obtain a fair trial by jury." Phrased that way, this comment must refer to the processes by which the offenses known as Watergate were brought to judicial and public scrutiny, here characterized negatively as "bitter" and "divisive," not self-corrective. As indicated in chapter 11, the debate of the House Committee on the Judiciary on the articles of impeachment it passed resulted in remarkable unanimity of opinion among both Republicans and Democrats that those articles were fairly drawn and voted on and that Nixon's conviction was likely, if not certain. To describe this process as "bitter" and "divisive" was to see it from Nixon's perspective, not from the point of view of one charged with understanding its effect on the well-being of the body politic.

The alternative readings we have suggested become more plausible when the prose of Ford's speech is contrasted with the prose of the pardoning proclamation, which stated that "inquiry and investigation on the impeachment of the President extend[ed] over eight months," and that "hearings" and "deliberations" "received wide national publicity" and "resulted in votes adverse to Richard Nixon." Nothing therein suggested that this process was bitter or divisive; in fact, in paragraph four, Ford referred to "the tranquility to which this nation has been restored by the events of recent weeks." Here, characterizations of the process by which Nixon's wrongdoing was discovered and assessed were fair and factual, and its result was tranquility; the dangers of division had a different source. It was the prospect of bringing a former president of the United States to trial that threatened to "cause prolonged and divisive debate." The threat lay in the future, when the judicial system might indict Nixon for his crimes and a trial might occur in which he could be found guilty and sentenced to imprisonment—a time when a pardon would be fitting, even acceptable.

To attribute these differences to a speechwriter would be inaccurate. Ford's commitment to the views in his September 8 remarks was clear in his press conference of September 16, when he was asked about his two pardons, and answered,

The only connection between these two cases is the effort that I made in the one to heal the *wounds involving the charges* against Mr. Nixon. . . . In one case, you have a President who was forced to resign *because of circumstances involving his Administration,* and he has been shamed and disgraced by that resignation. [emphasis added][72]

Here, as in Ford's September 8 speech, the wounds come from those who attacked Nixon, not from his offenses. Like Nixon himself in his farewell address, Ford suggested that Nixon resigned because of changed political circumstances, not because there was explicit evidence of the commission of impeachable offenses, and that the shame and disgrace were not a result of Nixon's actions, but of his being forced to resign.

In effect, Ford accepted two key premises underlying Nixon's resignation speech. The first was that forces other than Nixon were responsible for Watergate; the second was that Nixon's resignation was caused not by his own wrongdoing, but by a changed climate of public opinion. Acceptance of these premises placed Ford in the anomalous position of minimizing Nixon's guilt at a time when the citizenry and Congress had accepted it as fact, and of magnifying Nixon's resignation as punishment at a time when the public and Congress wished to see the judicial process take its course. In other words, Ford abandoned the presidential role that legitimizes pardoning, speaking sometimes in personal terms and sometimes as Nixon's partisan defender.

Finally, by dissociating the pardon from justice, Ford sacrificed the basis on which presidents have traditionally justified the act of pardoning when he said, "I do believe . . . that I, not as President, but as a humble servant of God, will receive justice without mercy if I fail to show mercy." As the executive charged by the Constitution to "take care that the laws are faithfully executed," he undermined his authority to pardon by tacitly admitting that in Nixon's case, he was showing mercy; he could not and did not claim that justice had been done.

Ordinarily, regardless of type, pardons involve the tempering of justice. That entails a public acknowledgment that an offense has been committed, ordinarily by the person(s) who are granted the pardon, and public agreement that they have already been punished in some way or, as in the case of the Barrataria pirates, that they have performed acts of expiation. In Nixon's case, there had been no acknowledgment of crime or guilt. At the time of Ford's pardon, the House Committee on the Judiciary had passed three articles of impeachment, which were the equivalent of a grand jury indictment. At this stage, the indicted person is still presumed innocent. Ford himself acknowledged this when he said that Nixon "would be cruelly and excessively penalized either in preserving the presumption of his innocence or in obtaining a speedy determination of his guilt in order to repay a legal debt to society" (102). His words made it clear that Nixon was still presumed innocent, and they minimized what Nixon owed society for his alleged wrongdoing by referring to it as "a *legal* debt" [emphasis added].

In his autobiography, Ford reported that his legal advisers had cited a Supreme Court opinion stating that "the President has power to pardon for a crime of which the individual has not been convicted and which he does not admit." Moreover, the Court had found that "a pardon 'carries an imputation of guilt, acceptance, a confession of it.'" In Ford's view, then, Nixon's acceptance of the pardon was tantamount to an admission of guilt, but that link was not clear to the press or the public. Ford later acknowledged that he should have made the connection explicit, that he should have pointed to "the Supreme Court's ruling that acceptance of a pardon means admission of guilt."[73]

Nixon's public response to the pardon included the crucial words, "In accepting this pardon," but contained no admission of guilt or statement of contrition.[74] Nixon's statement said only that he "was wrong in not acting more decisively and more forthrightly in dealing with Watergate, particularly when it reached the stage of judicial proceedings." He reserved his "regret and pain" for the "anguish my mistakes over Watergate have caused the nation and the presidency." The most problematic sentence in the statement reads, "I now understand how my own mistakes and misjudgments have contributed to that belief [that my motivations and action in the Watergate affair were intentionally self-serving and illegal] and seemed to support it." The words treated the mistakes, whatever they were, as personal, not presidential, as public relations errors, not as violations of the oath of office. However, one is not impeached for mistakes or misjudgments, but for high crimes and misdemeanors. It was not beliefs or appearances (as implied by "seemed") that compelled Nixon to resign, but rather documented breaches of law and violations of the public trust. Moreover, Nixon was not a mere "contributor"; his own actions were vital to the events leading to the articles of impeachment.

Ford attempted to convince the nation that Nixon had already been punished sufficiently, "that Richard Nixon and his loved ones have suffered enough." In the proclamation of pardon, he called attention to Nixon's reelection in 1972 "by the electors of forty-nine of the fifty states," emphasizing the "unprecedented penalty of relinquishing the highest elective office in the United States." In light of that penalty, he questioned "the propriety of exposing [Nixon] to further punishment and degradation" (104). Ford faced a dilemma: on the one hand, he could hardly argue that he was performing an act of mercy when Nixon's resignation had been voluntary, not a punishment imposed by the system. On the other hand, he faced the difficulty of showing how the pardon of someone still presumed innocent could function for the public good when, in his opening speech as president, he had declared "the long national nightmare . . . over" and when there was public consensus that the judicial process should be allowed to proceed unimpeded. In addition, by turning the Nixon tapes and records over to the ex-president in an agreement that accompanied the pardon, Ford himself ensured that the controversy surrounding Nixon would continue whether he was pardoned or not.[75]

Ford's attempts to justify the pardon were complicated by his efforts to claim that he was being merciful as well as acting for the public good. He said that "allegations and accusations hang like a sword over our former President's head, threatening his health," and he also spoke of Nixon's being "cruelly and excessively penalized" and of a need to "show mercy" to a man who has "suffered enough and will continue to suffer" no matter what is done. These justifications were undermined because they presupposed guilt, which had not been admitted or legally established.

The claim of mercy on the grounds of health aroused suspicion. In her testimony at a congressional inquiry into the pardon, Rep. Bella Abzug (D-NY) indicated the grounds for skepticism:

> Most of the facts respecting Nixon's health were released following the pardon. They appeared to be a well-orchestrated after-the-fact attempt to protect the vitality of the pardon by promoting the notion that Nixon was grievously ill. We are all familiar with the alarming statements issued by Dr. Tkach, Mr. Nixon's personal physician. According to Dr. Tkach, the former president was a ravaged man who had lost his will to fight. However, after Dr. Tkach left San Clemente, Communications Director Kenneth Clausen spent three hours with the former President and said he seemed animated and in no visible pain. Did Mr. Nixon's condition suddenly worsen after the pardon? Or did Mr. Ford receive new infor-

mation about Mr. Nixon's health after his first news conference? The American people have a right to know all this. Certainly, their deep sense of compassion and fair play should not be played upon, if the facts do not warrant it.[76]

The problem of using imminent death as grounds for pardoning had been explained by William Howard Taft:

> There has been a custom in the presidential office of pardoning men who are supposed to be near their death to enable them to go home and die with their families. The difficulty in such cases is in being certain that death is near. I had two notable cases in which I was assured by the prison authorities that death was imminent and that if they were to be released at all, to die, they ought to be released at once. I instituted as thorough an investigation as I could, through the Army and Navy surgeons in the employ of the government and reached the conclusion from the evidence submitted that death was certain. I pardoned them both. One man died and kept his contract. The other recovered at once, and seems to be as healthy and active as any one I know.[77]

Moreover, the personal relationship between Nixon and Ford— Nixon's appointment of Ford as vice president and what Ford called "their long friendship"—turned an act of mercy into a cause for suspicion. The warnings of William Lenoir and George Mason in the constitutional ratification debates were echoed here.

Ford also presented the pardon as motivated by concern for the public good. He said he wished "to do the very best for America." He argued that the judicial process would have undesirable effects on the body politic: "ugly passions would again be aroused, and our people would again be polarized in their opinions, and the credibility of our free institutions of government would again be challenged at home and abroad." He claimed that his concern was "the immediate future of the country." The evidence he presented to show potential damage to the polity, however, was dubious and hypothetical; moreover, the proclamation itself contradicted it. As a result, neither of Ford's rationales for the pardon was particularly persuasive.

That the rhetorical act of pardoning hinges on timing and on fulfilling the performative conditions—that is, acting as the president, following a formula, justifying the timing, and so on—is demonstrated by the arguments with which critics in the press and in Congress attacked Ford's pardon of Nixon. At a hearing before the House Subcommittee on Criminal Justice, Representatives Abzug, Gilbert Gude (R-MD),

Steward B. McKinney (R-Ct), and Barbara Jordan (D-TX) all attacked the timing of the pardon. Gude argued that the legal process should be allowed to run its course; McKinney argued that Ford had prematurely closed the book and should have waited until there was a more complete account of the facts. Abzug called the pardon "premature, confusing, unprecedented," and noted the contradictions between the statements Ford had given in his confirmation hearings and those found in his remarks.[78] Members of the Senate also attacked the pardon. John L. McClellan (D-AR) said, "This pardon is premature," and Sam J. Ervin, Jr. (D-NC), chair of the Senate Select Committee on Presidential Campaign Activities, said, "President Ford ought to have allowed the legal processes to take their course, and not issued any pardon to former President Nixon until he had been indicted, tried, and convicted."[79]

Reporters also raised questions on these grounds in press conferences. On September 16, Ford was asked, "Do you find any conflicts of interest in the decision to grant a sweeping pardon to your life-long friend and your financial benefactor with no consultation for advice and judgment for the legal fallout?"[80] a question directed at Ford's problems in acting as the president in this situation. The failure of Ford's pardoning rhetoric was noted on November 14, 1974, when reporters commented that voters in the November 5 midterm elections had indicated their displeasure at the timing of the Nixon pardon by voting Republicans out of office.[81] In his autobiography, Ford himself admitted the failure of his pardoning rhetoric: "instead of healing the wounds, my decision had only rubbed salt in them."[82]

CONCLUSION

Ford's remarks in conjunction with the proclamation pardoning Nixon illustrate the sense in which pardoning is a rhetorical act that is capable of being performed more or less effectively. The ineptitude of Ford's speech and the negative response to it are strong proof that the presidential pardon, while highly discretionary, must follow traditional forms, must be linked to conventional justifications, must be grounded in the constitutional power of the president, and must be performed at an appropriate moment. Moreover, Ford's pardon of Nixon has made use of the pardoning power by subsequent presidents a matter of greater political risk. In this way, Ford's pardoning rhetoric not only affected his own future, contributing to his defeat in 1976, but also diminished the latitude for subsequent exercise of the presidential pardoning power.

An analysis of pardoning rhetoric suggests that no presidential power is wholly unfettered. Even the unilateral and discretionary act of pardoning needs to be performed properly if presidential power is to be maintained. Were any presidential power wholly unfettered, it would be impossible to claim that the rhetoric involved in its exercise was constitutive either of the institution or of a particular presidency. But because power is always limited, the rhetorical exercise thereof is constitutive in that such power will always be exercised wisely or unwisely, with care for or indifference toward the institution, and with concern for or indifference to the future of the presidency and future presidents.

SIX

State of the Union Addresses

The State of the Union address, formerly known as the annual message,[1] takes its name and function from article 2, section 3 of the Constitution, which provides that the president "shall from time to time give to the Congress information on the state of the Union and recommend to their consideration such measures as he shall judge necessary and expedient." In charging presidents with reporting on the state of the Union, the Constitution offers them the role of national historian, giving them the opportunity to reconstruct the past in order to forge the future. By using history skillfully, they can involve Congress and the people in an affirmation that this is not only the way it was, but also the way it will be. The more eloquent presidents have seized the opportunity to reshape reality and to imprint their conception of it on the nation.

The Constitution does not indicate how these messages are to be delivered; the earliest were oral and delivered at midday. Thomas Jefferson, a diffident speaker committed to reducing the pomp and ceremony of the presidency, chose to send written addresses. From that time until Woodrow Wilson reinstated oral delivery, annual messages were written.[2] In modern times, Supreme Court justices, the Joint Chiefs of Staff, members of the cabinet, and members of Congress are all seated before the president. Members of the public witness the speech from the galleries, and a large viewing audience watches it on television during prime time. The setting ritualistically reaffirms the existence of the three branches of government and that each is playing its constitutionally ordained role.

The annual message is a uniquely presidential genre and, as such, helps to maintain the role of the executive. No one else is charged with this specific responsibility or may deliver this address to the assembled Congress. As Charles Beard wrote, "Whatever may be its purport, the message is the one great public document of the United States which is widely read and discussed."[3] Woodrow Wilson saw the annual message as one of the instruments best suited to the exercise of presidential leadership:

> If the President has personal force and cares to exercise it, there is a tremendous difference between his message and the views of any other citizen either outside Congress or in it; the whole country reads or listens to them and feels that the writer speaks with an authority and a responsibility that the people themselves have given him.[4]

By the sheer fact of its delivery, the address reminds the country that presidents have a unique role in our system of government. They are to view questions in the aggregate and as they pertain to the whole—to the Union. They must report to and advise Congress, the diverse representatives of the people of all states and regions, which implies that the presidency gives its occupant a unique, national vantage point.

On its face, the constitutional provision appears to call for messages that identify problems and justify the policies the president deems best suited to their solution. As the Constitution acknowledges, however, policy proposals grow out of the interpretation of information; that is, out of the executive's assessment of the condition of the nation. Proposals are solutions to problems recognized and defined in that assessment. In other words, facts do not speak for themselves; assessments must be grounded in values. Consequently, State of the Union addresses not only assess and recommend, they also articulate the values underlying assessments.

On January 8, 1790, at the first session of Congress, at a ceremony whose pomp and formality were reminiscent of the Speech from the Throne made by British monarchs, George Washington delivered the first annual message. In it, he made no specific policy proposals; he merely enumerated those topics that he believed required congressional attention. Despite this deference to what he took to be congressional prerogatives, Washington's prestige and the nature of the occasion gave great weight even to implied proposals.

The latitude offered by the constitutional provision has affected presidential practice from 1790 to the present and has produced a body of discourse that varies greatly.[5] Some addresses have been lengthy compendia covering dozens of topics; others have sharply defined a limited number of legislative priorities.[6] Some have outlined only general programs, leaving policy details to Congress; others have laid out specific legislative programs.[7] Some have informed without recommending, in some instances merely calling congressional attention to issues of concern, in others simply indicating administrative implementation of congressional enactments.[8] Some have been coherent wholes; others have been catalogues of unrelated concerns or policies.[9] Some have been delivered orally; others have been written. Some have been addressed to Congress; others have been addressed to the public as well in an effort to marshal popular support for presidential initiatives; some have addressed the increasingly important international audience. Some have made carefully reasoned arguments for policies; others have merely listed areas for potential action. Some have been eloquent exhortations; others have been factual and dull. These addresses also vary depending on when they occur in a presidency. Typically, a president's first address forecasts; the last recapitulates; those in between do both. As a result, each president's annual messages trace the evolution of that presidency, as accomplishments and frustrations are reflected in the extent to which the legislative agenda has been enacted, persists, or has been abandoned.

KEY ELEMENTS OF STATE OF THE UNION ADDRESSES

As we have just noted, the variation among State of the Union addresses is great—so great that it may seem presumptuous to approach them as a genre. Here it is imperative to recall what was said in chapter 1 about generic criticism. Genres do not exist in any fixed and final sense; they are only critics' tools, to be judged by the illumination they provide. In the case of State of the Union addresses, while recognizing their variety, we offer an analysis based on a few key similarities that have existed through time and that reveal the functions of this rhetorical act for the presidency.

Viewed generically, the State of the Union address is characterized by three processes: (1) public meditations on values, (2) assessments of information and issues, and (3) policy recommendations. Each address incorporates, to varying degrees, specific characteristics related to each of these processes. In the course of meditating, assessing, and recommending, presidents also create and celebrate a national identity, tie together the past, present, and future, and sustain the presidential role. In the remainder of this chapter, we use the processes of meditation, assessment, and recommendation to organize our analysis, after which we consider the ways in which these addresses work to create and sustain the presidency.

Structurally, the annual message resembles the loosely defined but clearly recognizable form of the essay. Its underlying organization arises out of links between the three processes we have described. Meditations on values lead to assessments, which are frequently assessments of issues that have persisted through time, and those, in turn, lead to recommendations. The specific assessments and recommendations are the ephemera of U.S. history; the values developed in the public meditations are an enduring record of the creation and development of our national identity.[10]

The first key element of State of the Union addresses is meditation on underlying values. Such public meditations exemplify the symbolic processes by which a collectivity of individuals comes to see itself as an entity—a group, a community, a nation—with an identity that unifies its members and distinguishes them as a group. Public meditations include a retelling of the past that emphasizes shared experience in order to create a collective fiction, an ethos or national character.

The nation's history has made repeated efforts to create a national identity necessary. What became the United States began as thirteen distinct colonies with separate governments, separate histories, and a common resistance to federal power. Sectional differences, rising levels of immigration, the displacements of westward migration, urbanization, and industrialization, and the dispersal of the population over large expanses of territory intensified the need for unifying symbolic events. State of the Union addresses are not the only rhetoric, nor even the only presidential rhetoric, in which meditations on the character of the nation appear, but the annual message has been, from the outset, one symbolic moment in which the head of state has woven the cloth of common national history, character, and identity.

Confronted with the problems of inflation, unemployment, war, poverty—problems beyond the ken of any single citizen—the State of the Union address boldly assures the citizenry that, in the future as in the past, Americans will solve their problems. The address reaffirms that the citizenry can and will "establish a more perfect Union," that Horatio Alger lives on in the national spirit, that the Protestant work ethic endures. This powerful reaffirmation appeared even in the annual messages of failing presidents, such as Andrew Johnson; even in times of national uncertainty, such as the Great Depression; even when problems had long proved intractable, such as the inflation of the 1970s; and even in addresses, such as Ford's in 1975, that began by claiming that the state of the Union was not good. No president, no matter how pessimistic or how severe the crisis, has ever reported that the state of the Union was such that its problems could not be surmounted.

In articulating fundamental values, presidents urge the audience to celebrate a certain national ethos. In his first message, for example, Franklin Roosevelt commented, "Disorder is not an American habit. Self-help and self-control are the essence of the American tradition— not of necessity the form of that tradition, but its spirit" (3:2810). In his seventh message, Truman reminded the nation,

> In all we do, we should remember who we are and what we stand for. We are Americans. Our forefathers had far greater obstacles than we have, and much poorer chances of success. They did not lose heart, or turn aside from their goals. In that darkest of all winters in American history, at Valley Forge, George Washington said: "We must not, in so great a contest, expect to meet with nothing but sunshine." With that spirit they won their fight for freedom. We must have that same faith and vision. (3:2993)

State of the Union addresses often include definitions of exemplary attitudes and conduct for the citizenry. In his third annual message, for instance, Jefferson asked citizens to

> adopt individually the views, the interests, and the conduct which their country should pursue, divesting themselves of those passions and partialities which tend to lessen useful friendships and to embarrass and embroil us in the calamitous scenes of Europe. (1:73)

More than a century later, Wilson echoed Jefferson's views:

> There are some men among us, and many resident abroad who, though born and bred in the United States and calling themselves Americans, have so forgotten themselves and their honor as citizens as to put their passionate sympathy with one or the other side in the great European conflict above their regard for the peace and dignity of the United States. (3:2573)

As they meditate on values, annual messages become instructive. Because any government requires some means of support, early Congresses authorized duties on various items, and if Washington's third message is taken at its word, "enlightened and well-disposed citizens" responded well. Nonetheless, there was some dissatisfaction. Given "proper explanations and more just apprehensions of the true nature of the law," Washington was confident that discontent would "in all [citizens] give way to motives which arise out of a just sense of duty and a virtuous regard to the public welfare" (1:9). In effect, the first president was instructing his fellow citizens about how to respond to government initiatives. Because taxation had helped to precipitate revolt against Great Britain, Washington was also careful to instruct Congress on the importance of popular support for government policy:

> If there are any circumstances in the law which consistently with its main design may be so varied as to remove any well intentioned objections that may happen to exist, it will consist with a wise moderation to make the proper variations. It is desirable on all occasions to unite with a steady and firm adherence to constitutional and necessary acts of government the fullest evidence of a disposition as far as may be practicable to consult the wishes of every part of the community and to lay the foundations of the public administration in the affections of the people. (1:9–10)

Similarly, in his second annual message, after setting down the principles that should control the process of governance, Jefferson said, "By continuing to make these the rule of our action we shall endear to our countrymen the true principles of their Constitution and promote a union of sentiment and of action equally auspicious to their happiness and safety" (1:68). In a letter to Washington dated January 4, 1786, Jefferson wrote that it was axiomatic that liberty is safe only in the hands of the people, but added that the people required "a certain degree of instruction. This it is the business of the state to effect on a general plan."[11]

In public meditation, presidents also explore the meaning of our system of government, and here the link between the past and the future is apparent in most of the addresses. Reflection about the past yields reconsideration of the principles that should govern present decision making about the future. Meditation and reconsideration reassure the audience that the president's legislative recommendations are the product of careful consideration, not partisan passion or momentary whim. Franklin Roosevelt's 1944 address provides a particularly artful illustration of this set of moves:

> This Republic had its beginnings, and grew to its present strength, under the protection of certain inalienable political rights—among them the right of

free speech, free press, free worship, trial by jury, freedom from unreasonable searches and seizures. They were our rights to life and liberty.

As our Nation has grown in size and stature, however—as our industrial economy expanded—these political rights proved inadequate to assure us equality in the pursuit of happiness.

We have come to clear realization of the fact that true individual freedom cannot exist without economic security and independence. . . . In our day these economic truths have become accepted as self-evident. We have accepted, so to speak, a second Bill of Rights under which a new basis of security and prosperity can be established for all—regardless of station, race, or creed.

Among these are:

The right to a useful and remunerative job in the industries or shops or farms or mines of the Nation;

The right to earn enough to provide adequate food and clothing and recreation; . . .

I ask the Congress to explore the means for implementing this economic bill of rights. (3:2881)

Another value celebrated in these messages is bipartisanship. In his 1995 State of the Union address, delivered after Republicans gained control of the Senate, Bill Clinton made this plea: "My fellow Americans, without regard to party, let us rise to the occasion. Let us put aside partisanship and pettiness and pride. As we embark on this new course, let us put our country first, remembering that regardless of party label, we are all Americans." [12] Similarly, in 2002, George W. Bush said, "I'm a proud member of my party. Yet as we act to win the war, protect our people, and create jobs in America, we must act, first and foremost, not as Republicans, not as Democrats but as Americans." [13]

In 2003, George W. Bush celebrated basic national values as ensuring success in the "war on terror":

Throughout the 20th century, small groups of men seized control of great nations, built armies and arsenals, and set out to dominate the weak and intimidate the world. In each case, their ambitions of cruelty and murder had no limit. In each case, the ambitions of Hitlerism, militarism, and communism were defeated by the will of free peoples, by the strength of great alliances, and by the might of the United States of America. [14]

Second, meditations in State of the Union addresses lead to assessments. In this transition from one process to the next, presidents take stock of enduring national issues, such as foreign affairs, commerce, civil rights, or immigration, linking current, past, and future addresses and linking the concerns of their presidencies with those of past and future presidents. The sense that presidents are temporary occupants of an ongoing institution is strong. Herbert Hoover expressed it this way in a speech in Detroit on October 22, 1932:

> No man can be President without looking back upon the effort given to the country by the thirty Presidents who in my case have preceded me. No man of imagination can be President without thinking of what shall be the course of his country under the thirty more Presidents who will follow him. He must think of himself as a link in the long chain of his country's destiny, past, and future.[15]

State of the Union addresses thus become vehicles through which presidents address issues that persist through time. This is most apparent in their final State of the Union addresses, many of which have included farewell remarks. Truman, for example, took stock of enduring issues in his last message, which was also his farewell address to Congress:

> Let all of us pause now, think back, consider carefully the meaning of our national experience. ... The Nation's business is never finished. The basic questions we have been dealing with, these eight years, present themselves anew. That is the way of our society. Circumstances change and current questions take on different forms, new complications, year by year. But underneath the great issues remain the same—prosperity, welfare, human rights, effective democracy, and, above all, peace. (3:3010)

This linking of the past and future combines deliberation with Congress over prudent policies in the present with discussion of how current conditions compare with those in the nation's history. In such assessments, presidents discuss the changing functions of the presidency through time, refining the country's central precepts and reforming its goals. In his fourth annual message, for example, Franklin Pierce explained,

> Our forefathers were trained to the wisdom which conceived and the courage which achieved independence by the circumstances which surrounded them, and they were thus made capable of the creation of the Republic. It devolved

on the next generation to consolidate the work of the Revolution, to deliver the country entirely from the influences of conflicting transatlantic partialities or antipathies which attached to our colonial and Revolutionary history, and to organize the practical operation of the constitutional and legal institutions of the Union. To us of this generation remains the not less noble task of maintaining and extending the national power. We have at length reached the stage of our country's career in which the dangers to be encountered and the exertions to be made are the incidents, not of weakness, but of strength. (1:938)

In 2004, George W. Bush linked the war in Iraq to the nation's past:

We have not come all this way—through tragedy, and trial, and war—only to falter and leave our work unfinished. . . . The work of building a new Iraq is hard, and it is right. And America has always been willing to do what it takes for what is right.[16]

These presidential assessments address questions of continuity and change. How much change, they ask, can there, or should there, be in the system? In 1996, Clinton addressed this question when he said,

The era of big Government is over. But we cannot go back to the time when our citizens were left to fend for themselves. Instead, we must go forward as one America, one nation working together to meet the challenges we face together. Self-reliance and teamwork are not opposing virtues; we must have both.[17]

In 1997, he again spoke of the challenges posed by change:

The new promise of the global economy, the information age, unimagined new work, life-enhancing technology, all these are ours to seize. That is our honor and our challenge. We must be shapers of events, not observers. For if we do not act, the moment will pass, and we will lose the best possibilities of our future.[18]

In 2005, George W. Bush made this assessment, which also linked continuity and change:

Social Security was a great moral success of the 20th century, and we must honor its great purposes in a new century. The system, however, on its current path, is headed toward bankruptcy. And so we must join together to strengthen and save Social Security.[19]

Here assessment leads directly to recommendation, as illustrated below.

George W. Bush's January 24, 2007, State of the Union address illustrates the ways in which these addresses, too, can be part of an extended rhetorical act. In this case, the president used his Saturday radio address of January 20 to introduce the health care reform proposal that would be an important part of his domestic proposals in his State of the Union address.[20] In response, Democrats declared that they would not support his proposals to revise the federal tax code to provide incentives for individuals to buy health insurance. Nonetheless, in his Saturday radio address on February 17, Bush again urged Congress to create a tax break to enable people to purchase private health insurance outside the workplace, a policy that he continued to promote while on the road in Tennessee, urging citizens to support his proposal in order to prompt congressional consideration.[21]

With assessments of the need for change, the third element of State of the Union addresses emerges: the recommendation of legislative initiatives and their justification. Bush's 2007 address illustrates this element as well. In assessing the need for change, presidents confront the gap between the promises of the founding documents and the country's performance. The Constitution is an amalgam of concepts that have taken on meaning as they were called into question, defined, and put into practice. In the recommendations found in annual messages, one hears a government in the act of creating itself. That is palpable in the early addresses. "A free people ought not only to be armed, but disciplined," said Washington in his first annual message, "to which end a uniform and well-designed plan is requisite; and their safety and interest require that they should promote such manufactories as tend to render them independent of others for essential, particularly military, supplies," and he added, "Uniformity in the currency, weights, and measures of the United States is an object of great importance, and will, I am persuaded, be duly attended to" (1:2, 3).

Occasionally, presidents frame their recommendations as indictments of the country for failing to live up to its promises to all of its citizens.[22] For example, in an impassioned moment in his first annual message, Benjamin Harrison asked,

> When and under what conditions is the black [sic] man to have a free ballot? When is he in fact to have those full civil rights which have so long been his in law? When is that equality of influence which our form of government was

intended to secure to the electors to be restored? This generation should courageously face these grave questions, and not leave them as a heritage of woe to the next. (2:1651)

The issue of guaranteeing equality of opportunity has also been framed in economic terms. Theodore Roosevelt, for example, considered the unequal distribution of goods in his fifth annual message:

> We can get justice and right dealing only if we put as of paramount importance the principle of treating a man on his worth as a man rather than with reference to his social position, his occupation or the class to which he belongs. There are selfish and brutal men in all ranks of life. If they are capitalists their selfishness and brutality may take the form of hard indifference to suffering, greedy disregard of every moral restraint which interferes with the accumulation of wealth, and the cold-blooded exploitation of the weak; or, if they are laborers, the form of laziness, of sullen envy of the more fortunate, and of willingness to perform deeds of murderous violence. . . . Individual capitalist and individual wage-worker, corporation and union are alike entitled to the protection of the law, and must alike obey the law. Moreover, in addition to mere obedience to the law, each man, if he be really a good citizen, must show broad sympathy for his neighbor and genuine desire to look at any question arising between them from the standpoint of that neighbor no less than from his own. (3:2155)

Similarly, when Roosevelt argued for a progressive inheritance tax in his seventh annual message, he did so in the name of equality. His citation of Lincoln as precedent illustrates the use of past presidential statements as a major source of evidence:

> Our aim is to recognize what Lincoln pointed out: The fact that there are some respects in which men are obviously not equal; but also to insist that there should be an equality of self-respect and of mutual respect, an equality of rights before the law, and at least an approximate equality in the conditions under which each man obtains the chance to show the stuff that is in him when compared to his fellows. (3:2255)

In his 1948 message, Truman also considered the question of equality in civil rights:

> Our first goal is to secure fully the essential human rights of our citizens. The United States has always had a deep concern for human rights. . . . Any denial

of human rights is a denial of the basic beliefs of democracy and of our regard for the worth of each individual. Today, however, some of our citizens are still denied equal opportunity for education, for jobs and economic advancement, and for the expression of their views at the polls. Most serious of all, some are denied equal protection under our laws. Whether discrimination is based on race, or creed, or color, or land of origin, it is utterly contrary to American ideals of democracy. (3:2952)

Lacking support for legislative action, Truman expressed this concern in his Executive Order 9981 of July 26, 1948, establishing the President's Committee on Equality of Treatment and Opportunity in the Armed Forces, which began the process of their desegregation.

John F. Kennedy responded to the civil rights protests in the spring of 1963 with a televised special message on June 11, in which he adopted a role of national priest similar to that assumed in national eulogies in order to argue that the nation confronted a "moral crisis as a country and as a people," a crisis requiring individual as well as legislative action.[23] Capitalizing on Kennedy's assassination to urge passage of the pending civil rights bill, Lyndon Johnson seized a propitious moment in his first annual message:

> Let me make one principle of this administration abundantly clear. All of these increased opportunities—in employment, in education, in housing, and in every field—must be open to Americans of every color. As far as the writ of Federal law will run, we must abolish not some but all racial discrimination. . . . For this is not merely an economic issue—or a social, political, or international issue. It is a moral issue; and it must be met by the passage this session of the bill now pending in the House. (3:3159)

Then, in three sentences, Johnson summarized his views, appropriating memorable phrases from the speeches of presidents Kennedy and Wilson:

> In establishing preferences, a nation that was built by the immigrants of all lands can ask those who now seek admission: "What can you do for our country?" But we should not be asking: "In what country were you born?" For our ultimate goal is a world without war, a world made safe for diversity, in which all men, goods, and ideas can freely move across every border and every boundary. (3:3160)

In 1997, illustrating the ways in which issues recur through time, Clinton also developed this theme, linking it to attitudes toward immigrants:

> My fellow Americans, we must never, ever believe that our diversity is a weakness. It is our greatest strength. Americans speak every language, know every country. People on every continent can look to us and see the reflection of their own great potential, and they always will, as long as we strive to give all of our citizens, whatever their background, an opportunity to achieve their own greatness. We're not there yet. We still see evidence of abiding bigotry and intolerance in ugly words and awful violence, in burned churches and bombed buildings. We must fight against this, in our country and in our hearts.[24]

Generally, as these cases illustrate, the State of the Union address presents proposed legislation as the solution to a persistent problem with national implications. As part of the process of justifying a legislative program, the address becomes the occasion on which presidents adjust members of Congress and the public to new circumstances. "This country can not afford to sit supine on the plea that under our peculiar system of government we are helpless in the presence of new conditions," said Theodore Roosevelt in his second annual message (2:2056). When presidents argue that the system must respond to new conditions, they do so either in the name of compelling facts reflected in a specific instance or in the name of fundamental premises they believe are shared by their audience. For example, Roosevelt continued, "The power of Congress to regulate interstate commerce is an absolute and unqualified grant." Hence, he concluded that "under the power of Congress to regulate commerce among the separate states," Congress can prevent "monopolies, unjust discriminations which prevent or cripple competition, fraudulent over-capitalization, and other evils in trust organizations and practices" (2:2056). Franklin Roosevelt developed a similar line of argument in 1944 when he proclaimed a new economic bill of rights to complement the political Bill of Rights that had shaped the country to that point.

When legislative proposals constitute major innovations, they are justified in the name of evolution. That point is illustrated well by what Theodore Roosevelt said in his third annual message:

> We have cause as a nation to be thankful for the steps that have been so successfully taken to put these principles into effect. The progress has been by

evolution, not by revolution. Nothing radical has been done; the action has been both moderate and resolute. Therefore the work will stand. There shall be no backward step. If in the working of the laws it proves desirable that they shall at any point be expanded or amplified, the amendment can be made as its desirability is shown.[25] (2:2076)

The issues featured in State of the Union addresses over time reflect the development of the country and its institutions. In them we find the patterns isolated by political scientist Theodore Lowi, who observes that certain public policy concerns have been linked to certain historical periods in the United States. The messages of the founders were concerned with constituent (state-building) policies, such as avoiding entangling alliances and encouraging manufacturing. Through most of the nineteenth century, the messages focused on distributive policies; the development of land and of rivers and harbors was among the topics treated. Then, in the late nineteenth century, questions of regulating resources emerged, such as those leading to the founding of the Interstate Commerce Commission in 1887. During the New Deal, the messages had a redistributive cast, and post–New Deal messages have blended the four types.[26]

Regardless of party or period, however, presidents have read the constitutional provision as an opportunity to link their messages to proposed legislation, almost as if they had rewritten the Constitution to read that the president "shall, from time to time, give to the Congress information on the state of the Union to enable the President to recommend for their consideration such measures as are deemed necessary and expedient."

For instance, in 1964, Lyndon Johnson said, "Wages and profits and family income are also at their highest levels in history—but I would remind you that 4 million workers and 13 percent of our industrial capacity are still idle. We need a tax cut now to keep this country moving" (3:3159). This linkage mirrors that made by Washington when he said,

The militia laws have exhibited such striking defects as could not have been supplied but by the zeal of our citizens. Besides the extraordinary expense and waste, which are not the least of the defects, every appeal to those laws is attended with a doubt on its success. The devising and establishing of a well regulated militia would be a genuine source of legislative honor and a perfect title to public gratitude. I therefore entertain a hope that the present session will not pass without carrying to its full energy the power of organizing, arming, and disciplining the militia, and thus providing, in the language of the Constitution, for calling them forth to execute the laws of the Union, suppress insurrections, and repel invasions. (1:25)

In 2002, George W. Bush said, "For the sake of long-term growth and to help Americans plan for the future, let's make these tax cuts permanent."[27] In 2005, he noted,

America's prosperity requires restraining the spending appetite of the federal government. I welcome the bipartisan enthusiasm for spending discipline. So next week I will send you a budget that holds the growth of discretionary spending below inflation, makes tax relief permanent, and stays on track to cut the deficit in half by 2009.[28]

PRESERVING AND STRENGTHENING THE PRESIDENCY

Through public meditation, assessment, and policy recommendations, State of the Union addresses sustain the presidency. Taken together, meditating on values, assessing conditions to define problems, and recommending solutions in the form of policy proposals constitute an opening move in a struggle for political power between the executive and legislative branches of government. Throughout the history of this country, Congresses and presidents have jockeyed for power, and State of the Union addresses have been an important weapon in that struggle. Even in periods when presidential power was at an ebb, the State of the Union address affirmed the executive's role in the legislative process. The message, regardless of its author, is a way of ensuring that, at least once each year, Congress will acknowledge the president's legislative prerogatives. In this sense, the State of the Union address sustains and maintains the presidency. Its delivery also ensures that once each year the head of the government will pause to consider where the nation stands and where it is going. Moreover, as a yearly vehicle, the message invites an assessment of how one year's agenda is related to those of preceding years.

The submission of a legislative program to Congress implies that the president is committed to the use of power through authorized channels—that extraordinary powers will not be arrogated to the executive. The repeated assertion that these legislative initiatives are constitutional reaffirms that the president is keeping the oath of office by proposing legislation and acting from principles that preserve and protect the Constitution.

In State of the Union addresses, one observes presidents justifying their initiatives on the basis of a changing view of what the Constitution permits. A majority of the arguments found in these addresses advocate or justify actions clearly authorized by the Constitution, such as presidential funding requests and policy recommendations. Particularly in the early days of the republic, presidents called for actions not specifically authorized by the Constitution but potentially warranted by it. In some instances, their recommendations overstepped specific constitutional provisions, in which case, while inviting congressional concurrence in their views, presidents argued that the public well-being required action.

In his first annual message in 1797, John Adams remarked that he had considered convening the national legislature somewhere other than Philadelphia "on account of the contagious sickness which afflicted the city." Fortunately, "without hazard to the lives or health of the members," Congress was able to assemble there (1:40). Crises such as this one, unanticipated by the framers, prompted presidents to ask whether and in what ways they or others were empowered to respond. By 1798, Adams had found an answer. He was grateful, he reported, that "the alarming and destructive pestilence with which several of our towns have been visited" had disappeared (1:44). Because the illness had ravaged some seaports and interrupted public and private business, Adams thought it his duty

> to invite the Legislature of the Union to examine the expediency of establishing suitable regulations in aid of the health laws of the respective States; for these being formed on the idea that contagious sickness may be communicated through the channels of commerce, there seems to be a necessity that Congress, who alone can regulate trade, should frame a system which, while it may tend to preserve the general health, may be compatible with the interests of commerce and the safety of the revenue. (1:44)

The argument that circumstances necessitate congressional action is common in State of the Union addresses. "Congress witnessed at their late session the extraordinary agitation produced in the public mind by the suspension of our right of deposit at the port of New Orleans, no assignment of another place having been made according to treaty," noted Jefferson in his third message. Through "friendly and reasonable representations," the "right of deposit was restored." This crisis brought a significant realization, said Jefferson: "We had not been unaware of the danger to which our peace would be perpetually exposed whilst so important a key to commerce of the Western country remained under foreign power" (1:69). This realization was a key rationale for the Louisiana Purchase.[29]

When proposed policies will have significant consequences, presidents reveal those consequences in an attempt to counter potential objections. The Louisiana Purchase, for example, was expected to add $13,000,000 to the public debt. Using arguments familiar to modern readers, Jefferson claimed that this obligation could be met by the "ordinary annual augmentation of impost from increasing population and wealth," by "economies which may still be introduced into our public expenditures," and without "recurring to new taxes" (1:71).

The first invocation of extraconstitutional power occurred under Jefferson, known in his battles with Alexander Hamilton as a "strict constructionist." On June 22, 1807, during a congressional recess, a British ship shot at the U.S.S. *Chesapeake*. Several of the *Chesapeake*'s crew were killed and four were captured, one of whom was executed. Jefferson responded to these events by purchasing military matériel to cope with the emergency. In his annual message, on October 27, Jefferson justified his actions:

> The moment our peace was threatened I deemed it indispensable to secure a greater provision of those articles of military stores with which our magazines were not sufficiently furnished. To have awaited a previous and special sanction by law would have lost occasions which might not be retrieved. I did not hesitate, therefore, to authorize engagements for such supplements to our existing stock as would render it adequate to the emergencies threatening us, and I trust that the Legislature, feeling the same anxiety for the safety of our country, so materially advanced by this precaution, will approve, when done, what they would have seen so important to be done if then assembled. Expenses, also unprovided for, arose out of the necessity of calling all our gunboats into actual service for the defense of our harbors; all of which accounts will be laid before you. (1:92)

Implied in this statement is a claim that Jefferson later made explicit in his writings: that in an emergency, when the safety of the country cannot be secured under the written law, the written law may be set aside temporarily to save the system of government constituted by that written law. "To lose our country by a scrupulous adherence to written law," wrote Jefferson, "would be to lose the law itself, with life, liberty, property, and all those who are enjoying them with us." [30]

These examples illustrate that annual messages are part of the maintenance and evolution of the presidency and of its powers. Because its end is legislative enactment—that is, because power must be shared—the State of the Union address stresses cooperation with Congress and is conciliatory in tone. Because congressional collaboration is essential if recommendation is not to be an empty exercise, the message presupposes, applauds, or pleads for teamwork and often tacitly invites the eavesdropping national audience to make its support for legislation known to the members of Congress.

Jefferson's pledge of cooperation in his first message was subtle and elegant:

> Nothing shall be wanting on my part to inform as far as in my power the legislative judgment, nor to carry that judgment into faithful execution. The prudence and temperance of your discussions will promote within your own walls that conciliation which so much befriends rational conclusion, and by its example will encourage among our constituents that progress of opinion which is tending to unite them in object and in will. (1:63–64)

In his seventh message, Madison said, "In all measures having such objects my faithful cooperation will be afforded" (1:139). Andrew Jackson, whose relations with Congress were often troubled, concluded his fifth annual message by saying,

> Trusting that your deliberation on all topics of general interest to which I have adverted, and such others as your more extensive knowledge of the wants of our beloved country may suggest, may be crowned with success, I tender you in conclusion the cooperation which it may be in my power to afford them. (1:388)

Tensions with Congress were reflected in the tone of his seventh address:

> With these observations on the topics of general interest which are deemed worthy of your consideration, I leave them to your care, trusting that the

legislative measures they call for will be met as the wants and best interests of our beloved country demand. (1:445)

Wilson's break with the tradition of written messages, in place since Jefferson, occurred in part because he believed that oral delivery created a climate conducive to cooperation. On April 8, 1913, he appeared in person to deliver his first major address, a special message on tariff reform, before both houses of Congress. He opened that tradition-breaking address with these words:

I am very glad indeed to have this opportunity to address the two houses directly and to verify for myself the impression that the President of the United States is a person, not a mere department of the government hailing Congress from some isolated island of jealous power, sending messages, not speaking naturally and with his own voice—that he is a human being trying to cooperate with other human beings in a common service.[31]

Although proposals in the State of the Union address presuppose cooperation between the executive and the legislature and a posture of bipartisan leadership, some addresses have not been conciliatory. Truman's 1948 message, for example, was a blueprint for the coming campaign. Truman aide George Elsey had recommended that the address "be controversial as hell, must state the issues of the election, must draw the line sharply between Republicans and Democrats. The Democratic platform will stem from it, and the election will be fought on the issues it presents."[32] The speech was crafted to achieve those ends.

Truman was in conflict with Congress through most of his tenure, and his annual messages reflect that conflict. In his fifth message, for example, he said, "At present, largely because of the ill-considered tax reduction of the Eightieth Congress, the Government is not receiving enough revenue to meet its necessary expenditures" (3:2975). Despite this ongoing tension, there were cooperative and conciliatory remarks in his other addresses. In his fourth, for example, he said that he hoped for the cooperation of farmers, labor, and business and added that every segment of the population had "a right to expect that the Congress and the President will work in the closest cooperation with one objective— the welfare of the people of this Nation as a whole. In the months ahead I know that I shall be able to cooperate with the Congress" (3:2967). Later, his appeals became even more explicit. In his sixth message,

Truman asked "the Congress for unity in these crucial days" in a passage that had overtones of a lecture:

> When I request unity, what I am really asking for is a sense of responsibility on the part of every Member of this Congress. Let us debate the issues, and let every man among us weigh his words and deeds. There is a sharp difference between harmful criticism and constructive criticism. If we are truly responsible as individuals, I am sure that we will be unified as a government. Let us keep our eyes on the issues and work for the things we all believe in. Let each of us put our country ahead of our part, and ahead of our own personal interests. I had the honor to be a Member of the Senate during World War II, and I know from experience that unity of purpose and of effort is possible in the Congress without any lessening of the vitality of the two-party system. Let us all stand together as Americans. (3:2983)

Presidential appeals for cooperation and bipartisanship, as noted above, are surprisingly direct and personal; indeed, these addresses evince the kinds of stylistic markers ordinarily associated with oral delivery, even in speeches written to be read.[33]

If the citizenry can be mobilized behind a proposal, the likelihood of congressional cooperation increases. Conscious of the power of popular support, presidents in the electronic age have attempted to reach both Congress and the people.[34] In 1944, for example, Franklin Roosevelt delivered his annual address to Congress at noon, but repeated the same message over radio in the evening. He introduced the radio address this way:

> Only a few of the newspapers can print this message in full, and I am very anxious that the American people be given the opportunity to hear what I have recommended to Congress for this fateful year in our history—and the reasons for those recommendations. Here is what I said.[35]

He then redelivered the message read earlier to Congress.

Televised addresses have become the norm in the modern presidency, but Eisenhower reported that he had rejected a proposal for his address to be televised in prime time. His concern was the balance of power between the executive and Congress: "On January 7, 1954, I delivered my annual State of the Union message. Three days earlier I disapproved a suggestion that I deliver this message, for the first time in history, at night on television: such an innovation, I felt, would reflect badly on the Congress."[36]

As we have illustrated, State of the Union addresses, which assert presidential legislative leadership while seeking congressional cooperation, also perform symbolic functions for the presidency as an institution. Because they include meditations on the values underlying assessments and recommendations, and because the address is an annual ritual, arbitrarily called into existence by the calendar, annual messages are a complex rhetorical genre, with purposes that are both ceremonial and deliberative. As a result, the State of the Union address presents a problem to critics as well as to presidents, even when approached generically: how to balance its ceremonial and deliberative purposes. Anthony Dolan, Ronald Reagan's chief speechwriter, put it this way: "It's a difficult, difficult speech to do, because you have all the competing claims of the nation's business, and at the same time, the stylistic demands of coherence and grace."[37] Political scientist Jeffrey Tulis notes that "it is difficult in practice for a single speech to be inspirational and highly specific at the same time."[38] Articulating the values from which assessments are made and describing the character of the occasion call forth ceremonial rhetoric. Asserting legislative leadership by setting policy priorities necessitates deliberative rhetoric. The importance of ceremonial elements is indisputable: if the president's meditations fail to rehearse the values that form the criteria on which assessments are made, the policy recommendations have no clear basis. Initiating policies, however, is similarly crucial if the president is to assert legislative leadership, particularly insofar as that leadership involves constituent opinion and the pressure it can exert on members of Congress. If policies are not proposed, the speech comes to resemble the inaugural, and presidential legislative leadership must be asserted by other means, if at all.

We end our analysis of the State of the Union address with a case study that focuses on the annual messages of Ronald Reagan as contrasted with those of Lincoln, Wilson, and Franklin Roosevelt.[39]

REAGAN'S INFLUENCE

Ronald Reagan's seven annual messages illustrate the problem of balancing the concerns we have just outlined.[40] Reagan's speeches were ceremonial successes. Throughout his tenure, he adopted a positive tone, managing present problems by framing them as challenges or by justifying them in terms of cherished values, such as asking Americans to weigh the increasing federal deficit against the values of peace, freedom, and security. He used anecdotes, living persons, and events, such as the deaths of the *Challenger* space shuttle crew, to extol basic values and to redefine the people as heroes, techniques that have been institutionalized by his successors. Reagan retold national history to applaud the country as the "last and greatest bastion of freedom" and reinforced his version of the past with the words of his predecessors, such as Washington, Eisenhower, and Kennedy. In short, his public meditations were exemplary. Consider the conclusion to his 1987 address:

> Our revolution is the first to say the people are the masters and government is their servant. Don't ever forget that. Someday, you could be in this room, but wherever you are, America is depending on you to reach your highest and be your best, because here, in America, we the people are in charge. . . .
>
> We the people. Starting the third century of a dream and standing up to some cynic who's trying to tell us we're not going to get any better.
>
> Are we at the end? Or are we at the beginning? Well, I can't tell it any better than the real thing, a moment recorded by James Madison from the final moments of the Constitutional Convention, September 17, 1787. As the last few members signed the document, Benjamin Franklin—the oldest delegate at 81 years, and in frail health—looked over towards the chair where George Washington daily presided. At the back of the chair was painted the picture of a sun on the horizon. Turning to those sitting next to him, Franklin observed that artists found it difficult in their painting to distinguish between a rising and a setting sun.
>
> I know if we were there, we could see those delegates sitting around Franklin, leaning in to listen more closely to him. Then Dr. Franklin began to share his deepest hopes and fears about the outcome of their efforts, and this is what he said: "I have often . . . looked at that picture behind the President without being able to tell whether it was rising or setting. But now at length I have the happiness to know that it is a rising and not a setting sun."
>
> You can bet it's rising because, my fellow citizens, America isn't finished, her best days have just begun.[41]

This passage is typical of Reagan's State of the Union addresses, but it also captures the essence of the public meditations we have described, meditations that reaffirm and redefine our national identity and values and that instruct the citizenry about the nation's beginnings as a means to confirm its future. It perfectly fulfills ceremonial functions while rehearsing the values underlying the president's assessments.

Reagan's 1987 message, however, like his others, was short on policy proposals, sharply tilting the character of the address toward the ceremonial and away from the deliberative. As a result, Reagan's State of the Union addresses did not enhance his legislative leadership. From his first address in 1982 to his last in 1988, Reagan followed a consistent pattern of setting out positions but avoiding detailed policy proposals,[42] in effect describing the legislative ends of which he approved, but neglecting to specify the means by which they could be achieved.[43] For the most part, he identified only those policies the administration would eschew. Insofar as he attempted to exert legislative leadership, he delivered special messages,[44] prepared separate written documents for delivery to Congress,[45] or delegated policy details to his staff and cabinet.

Reagan's rhetorical choices reflect his presidency. For the most part, he did not emphasize the presidential role of legislative leader, preferring to devote his efforts to raising the morale of the citizenry. As he left office with the highest approval ratings of any president in the preceding forty years, some concluded that he had not risked his personal popularity to achieve legislative ends, preferring to avoid conflict and to heighten a sense of national unity.[46]

Reagan's choices also highlight the problems posed for presidents by this rhetorical genre. The electronic media have shortened the average American's attention span, with the result that orally delivered presidential speeches are expected to fall within the half-hour limit of shorter television programs, a length that makes it extremely difficult to develop and justify major policy proposals.[47] Thus, it may be that Reagan's emphasis on the ceremonial was well adapted to the constraints of the orally delivered State of the Union address broadcast to the national audience by television. His decision to adapt this message to televisual constraints, however, created audience expectations of the president as national cheerleader, with a concomitant loss of tolerance for the president as initiator of a national legislative program, a role that inevitably generates disagreement and usually erodes a president's personal popularity among some segments of the populace.[48] The variation among annual messages, even within the modern presidency, indicates that presidents have wide latitude in balancing these diverse but related functions.[49]

ELOQUENT EXAMPLES

Some presidents have succeeded in combining deliberative and ceremonial functions in State of the Union addresses that are eloquent, artistic wholes. The addresses of Abraham Lincoln, Woodrow Wilson, and Franklin Roosevelt, among others, illustrate how reporting on events can become a vision of the future and how legislative initiatives can become proposals that make the future described possible.

In his first message, Lincoln listed the policy decisions he had made in response to the Civil War, such as continuing to blockade ports held by insurgents. He also specified the principles that guided him. He had taken care that the "insurrection . . . not degenerate into a violent and remorseless revolutionary struggle" (2:1064). Although presented as a report on the progress of the war, the narrative about the war at the close of the speech was an argument for Southern responsibility for the conflict, an argument that right was on the side of the Union, and an affirmation that the Union was prevailing.

The report began by subtly affixing blame: "The last ray of hope for preserving the Union peaceably expired at the assault upon Fort Sumter." But, he continued, "What was painfully uncertain then is much better defined and more distinct now, and the progress of events is plainly in the right direction" (2:1064). As the speech developed, Lincoln described difficulties and causes for discouragement and then, in each instance, asserted that they had been overcome, implying that the frustrations currently felt by Congress and the public would also be resolved. For example, as he reported,

> The insurgents confidently claimed a strong support from north of Mason and Dixon's line, and the friends of the Union were not free from apprehension on the point. This, however, was soon settled definitely, and on the right side. South of the line noble little Delaware led off right from the first. Maryland was made to seem against the Union. Our soldiers were assaulted, bridges were burned, and railroads torn up within her limits, and we were many days at one time without the ability to bring a single regiment over her soil to the capital. Now her bridges and railroads are repaired and open to the government; she already gives seven regiments to the cause of the Union, and none to the enemy; and her people, at a regular election, have sustained the Union by a larger majority and a larger aggregate vote than they ever before gave to any candidate or any question. (2:1064)

Underlying this progression was an argument grounded in repentance and an invitation to his audience to renew their compact with the Union:

> An insurgent force of about 1,500, for months dominating the narrow peninsular region constituting the counties of Accomac and Northampton, and known

as the Eastern Shore of Virginia, together with some contiguous parts of Maryland, have laid down their arms, and the people there have renewed their allegiance to and accepted the protection of the old flag. (2:1064–65)

One commentator has noted the synthesis of values, assessment, and recommendations in Lincoln's speech: "Under Lincoln's pen, the annual message reached one of its highest peaks of prestige and consequence."[50] Woodrow Wilson is similarly praised, on ceremonial grounds, as "able to combine an almost poetic simplicity and soaring eloquence with a moral earnestness that impressed his listeners as well as his readers,"[51] but he was also able to link that eloquence to assessments and recommendations, as illustrated by his summary of the events of World War I in his fifth message in order to prepare Congress and the nation for his views of the peace (3:2580–87).

Franklin Roosevelt was also able to link values, assessments, and recommendations. In his twelfth address, for example, he reviewed U.S. military choices in World War II in order to justify his decisions:

> The tremendous effort of the first years of this war was directed toward the concentration of men and supplies in the various theaters of action at the points where they could hurt our enemies most. . . .
>
> Always—from the very day we were attacked—it was right militarily as well as morally to reject the arguments of those shortsighted people who would have had us throw Britain and Russia to the Nazi wolves and concentrate against the Japanese. Such people urged that we fight a purely defensive war against Japan while allowing the domination of all the rest of the world by Naziism and Fascism. . . . Therefore, our decision was made to concentrate the bulk of our ground and air forces against Germany until her utter defeat. (3:2883–84)

His review was followed by specific recommendations to Congress, along with appeals to the nation:

> The only way to meet these increased needs for new weapons and more of them is for every American engaged in war work to stay on his war job. . . . This is no time to quit or change to less essential jobs.
>
> There is an old and true saying that the Lord hates a quitter. And this Nation must pay for all those who leave their essential jobs. . . . And—again—that payment must be made with the life's blood of our sons. . . .
>
> Last year, after much consideration, I recommended that the Congress adopt a national service act. . . . I now call upon the Congress to enact this measure for

the total mobilization of all our human resources for the prosecution of the war. (3:2889)

Artistically, Roosevelt's annual messages are unified wholes, and in striving for clarity and appeal as he addressed both Congress and the public, he peppered his speeches with vivid metaphors, parallel constructions, and familiar quotations from the Bible.[52]

In the annual messages of these three great presidents, one sees the integration of ceremonial and deliberative functions and the simultaneous assertion of symbolic and legislative leadership.[53]

Clinton's State of the Union addresses offer a contrast. His messages were famous for being laundry lists of specific plans and policies appealing to various constituencies. One critic noted that "the one unchanging element in Clinton's oratory is its mutability—his ability to shift political positions, to change primary colors, and to steal the Republicans' fire even as he gives them a bipartisan Trojan Horse."[54] That effort to appeal to a wide variety of constituencies was echoed in a column by Thomas Friedman, who wrote of the 1999 address that Clinton "left almost no constituency untickled by his 77-minute goody-bag of proposals."[55] Reporter Dan Balz commented, "Saving his presidency has become a regular subtheme of Clinton's State of the Union speeches. That was the case in 1995 after Republicans took control of Congress. It was true again in 1996 when he used the State of the Union address to turn around his political standing and lay the foundation for his reelection campaign."[56]

CONCLUSION

In a general sense, each annual message is rooted in a president's most recent inaugural. The inaugural lays down the principles that will govern a presidency while demonstrating the president's commitment to the country's basic principles. In State of the Union addresses, presidents revive the principles to which they committed their presidencies and show how those principles will be reflected in their legislative programs. Linking of the past and the future, as well as reflection on broad themes, is conducted against the backdrop of those principles.

Given the ritualistic character of the annual message and the need to celebrate the values underlying its assessments and recommendations, ceremonial rhetoric is appropriate, but given the constitutional mandate and a need to establish presidential legislative leadership, deliberative rhetoric is needed to justify policy recommendations and to establish legislative priorities.

When presidents fulfill the ceremonial functions of the State of the Union address, they define and redefine the national ethos and the nation's values, and they instruct the citizenry and Congress in their roles as members of the polity. In so doing, they weave the fabric of a shared national heritage and identity.

When the president makes proposals, the reasons given and the legislative outcomes sought reveal that presidency and our system of government as constructed by that administration. The laying out of a legislative program defines the relationship between the president and Congress in the system of checks and balances and defines the presidency in relation to the Constitution. These messages also describe appropriate responses to presidential initiatives for citizens and members of Congress. In effect, they refine the inaugural's definition of the people to specify how they should behave. In the aggregate, then, these messages are an ongoing cultural dialogue about the nature and purposes of our political system.

The State of the Union address is a rhetorical act maintaining the presidency. By placing the message of the president before Congress and requiring congressional attention, the address sustains the identities of the two branches. At the same time, the message invites a policy dialogue between the branches and encourages a cooperative relationship between them. By referring to the statements of their predecessors in these addresses, presidents imply that the presidency is continuous, rather than an aggregation of discrete individuals. Reliance on the past also reassures the listening citizenry by implying that as the nation weathered problems then, so, too, will it overcome them now.

The president's legislative proposals emerge out of a political philosophy developed in a public meditation on the meaning of our system of government. That meditation links national history to present assessment and future recommendations. Although many State of the Union addresses treat a long list of apparently unrelated topics, the overall structure of these addresses is problem-solution, the hallmark of deliberative, policy-making rhetoric. As such, this rhetorical genre exudes reassurance that the nation's problems can be solved, particularly with this system of government led by this president and supported by the people. Because the solutions require the joint action of Congress, the president's tone is ordinarily conciliatory and compromising, including calls for and offers of cooperation. Cooperatively, the president and Congress begin a process of deliberation about what problems are amenable to legislative treatment and what are the proper functions of government. As these addresses appear, they define the role of the president in legislative enactment and delineate the appropriate grounds for presidential initiatives.

The State of the Union address is central to the maintenance of the presidency in two ways. First, the address is delivered on a formal, ceremonial occasion that recognizes the president as both symbolic and real head of state. That role gives the president great persuasive force, particularly as the occasion also offers the opportunity to act as national historian, keeper of the national identity, and voice of national values. Second, the address marks the occasion on which the president has the greatest opportunity to exercise legislative leadership, linking national history to present assessments and recommendations for future policy. In this address, the president has the opportunity to appeal forcefully for congressional cooperation, to buttress such appeals with pleas for popular support, and to link the legislative agenda to cultural values underlying the system of government.

Presidents' State of the Union addresses are directly related to their inaugural addresses. Thus, those rhetorical genres and the relationships between them constitute one major part, not only of the presidency through time, but of individual presidencies, including their strengths and weaknesses.

SEVEN

Veto Messages

Presidential veto messages are not found in anthologies of public discourse, nor are they candidates for inclusion in volumes of masterpieces of presidential rhetoric. In most instances, veto messages illuminate the character of the presidency as one part of an interactive rhetorical system by illustrating the use of persuasive resources by individual presidents. As part of the system of checks and balances, the veto message is one means by which presidents act to preserve the system of which they are a part and to sustain the legislative agenda developed in their State of the Union addresses. Veto messages typically appear at moments of historical and political import, moments that mark controversial policy making and reflect power struggles between the president and Congress. Because the veto power is part of the legislative power of the presidency, this chapter is a companion to our preceding analysis of State of the Union addresses. Here veto messages are analyzed as a means to understand more fully the president's rhetorical role in the legislative process and the ways in which presidential use of the veto has enlarged the power of the executive branch.[1]

In one important respect, veto messages are unique: they are the single genre of presidential rhetoric whose central characteristics follow directly from constitutional provisions. Like the State of the Union address, the veto message is a product of the Constitution. Article 1, section 7 says that if the president approves a bill, "he shall sign it, but if not he shall return it, with his Objections to that House in which it shall have originated, who shall enter the Objections at large on their journal, and proceed to reconsider it." The constitutional provisions define this form of presidential discourse, determining its purposes, major lines of argument, predominant strategy, and structure as well as the persona and tone usually adopted by the president. The Constitution makes the veto and its accompanying message an integral part of the legislative process, and the function of the veto—to prompt reconsideration—brings the executive and the legislature into potential conflict. The intensely interactive character of the veto creates a moment at which it is possible to assess the relationships between the president, Congress, and the people and to use the exercise of the veto as a measure of presidential activism. Thus, the veto message is a response to a specific piece of legislation, it is framed around presidential objections, and it is designed to provoke congressional reconsideration. These three key elements shape the characteristics of the veto message as a rhetorical act, and we use them as an organizational plan in the analysis that follows. The history of its use, however, is a key part of the story of the making of the imperial presidency.

At the outset, it should be noted that the veto is but one option available to presidents when presented with a piece of legislation passed by both houses of Congress. If, despite earlier reservations, the president supports a measure or wants to be associated with it, it can be signed at a public ceremony in the presence of its authors and key congressional leaders, accompanied by a speech praising Congress and explaining how the bill contributes to the well-being of the nation. Neither the ceremony nor the accompanying rhetoric is required by the Constitution, but such ceremonies are becoming a fixture of the modern presidency because, in a televisual age, they offer dramatic news bites showcasing an activist president surrounded by endorsing representatives from Congress.[2]

Taking credit for popular legislation may on occasion be such an attractive prospect that a president who initially opposed a bill finds it advantageous to identify with it at a signing ceremony. Despite his earlier opposition, for example, Richard Nixon took public credit for passage of the bill enabling eighteen-year-olds to vote. He did not wish to present Congress with a veto that he knew would be overridden, and the political disadvantages of alienating millions of new voters overcame his initial resistance.[3]

A president can also sign a bill without fanfare. This occurs most often when the bill's enactment is politically necessary but distasteful. For example, when presidents sign enabling legislation to raise the national debt ceiling, they are likely to do so unobtrusively or to bury the act in a flurry of ceremonies celebrating the passage of more popular legislation.

A president who disapproves of a piece of legislation but lacks a strong rationale for rejecting it, or considers rejection politically inexpedient, may allow a bill to become law without his signature. Former president William Howard Taft explained that "some Presidents have allowed bills to become law without their signature, with the idea, I presume, that objections to a bill prevented affirmative approval and yet were not of such character as to justify a veto."[4] Thus, although he had denounced the bill in a letter to a member of Congress, Grover Cleveland allowed the Wilson-Gorman tariff to become law.[5] In 1989, George H. W. Bush allowed an act prohibiting flag desecration to become law without his signature, although he opposed the act on the grounds that a constitutional amendment was needed to achieve its ends.

Presidents can also register a formal protest when signing a bill into law or submit a message to Congress narrowing the interpretation of the act; such signing statements are the subject of chapter 8. Andrew Jackson, the first to adopt this tactic, wrote a note above his signature that drew congressional attention to his interpretive message.[6] The president can also take action in the ten-day period after an act is passed to limit the measure's effect. For example, only after establishing much of the national forest system by proclamation did Theodore Roosevelt sign a bill that he otherwise supported but that contained a provision, of which he strongly disapproved, restricting the use of federal lands.[7]

Finally, presidents can veto a bill by "pocketing" it within ten days of congressional adjournment or by returning it unsigned with objections. Either veto may be accompanied by a message, but the Constitution requires only that any bill rejected by a means other than pocketing be returned to Congress with a statement of the reasons for presidential disapproval.[8] Such veto messages are the focus of the remainder of this chapter.[9]

Although it is conventional usage, the label "veto message" is a misnomer. Nowhere does the Constitution use the word "veto," literally meaning "I forbid." Because the framers of the Constitution were familiar with the legal history of the veto and because the term "veto" appeared in both the Randolph proposal (Virginia plan) and the Pinckney plan, which were the bases for the nineteen resolutions reported to the Constitutional Convention on June 13, its omission is noteworthy. The resolutions of the convention, sitting as a committee of the whole, dropped the term, saying instead that "the national executive shall have a right to negative any legislative act, which shall not be afterwards passed unless by 2–3 parts of each branch of the national legislature."[10] Because Congress can reconsider and override a veto, the act, despite its name, cannot forbid; however, the power to veto is a significant barrier to congressional action. During the first fifty years of the republic, not one bill became law over a presidential veto. As of November 1987, as we worked on our earlier study of presidential rhetoric, only 100 presidential vetoes had been overridden, and by the summer of 2005, that number had increased to only 106. During that time there were 1484 regular vetoes and 1066 pocket vetoes, for a total of 2,550.[11] Because the pocket veto takes place after Congress has adjourned, it cannot be overridden.[12]

GROUNDS FOR VETOES

Veto messages are framed around presidential objections, and from the time of George Washington, objections to bills have been made on two major but interrelated grounds: constitutionality and expediency. The first reflects the quasi-judicial character of the veto, the second its legislative function. Washington was reluctant to use the veto power and did so only twice. In his first veto on April 5, 1792, he grounded his objections in the Constitution.[13] His message invited congressional reconsideration, and the revised bill met with his approval. His second veto on February 27, 1797, was based in part on expediency. In that message he described the proposed bill as "inconvenient and injurious to the public" and as not appearing "to comport with the economy." Moreover, he applied his military experience in evaluating the effects of the legislation.[14]

Washington's references to inconvenience and public injury were not the norm in early vetoes. As presidential scholar Andrew Rudalevige notes, in the eight vetoes in the following twenty-eight years, "Presidents rejected only those statutes they deemed unconstitutional, believing that policy differences with Congress were not legitimate cause for the veto pen."[15]

Increased use of the veto coincided with the shift to policy-based vetoes. Andrew Jackson rejected twelve bills, including the rechartering of the Bank of the United States (BUS), in part on policy grounds. The assertion of power in Jackson's aggressive use of the veto, most notably in his bank veto, reshaped the relationship between the legislative and executive branches. "Jackson's 'little bank war' produced several novel constitutional doctrines, most of which we take for granted today," argues political parties and organizations scholar Scott James. These doctrines include the notion that "the presidency is an equal and autonomous branch of government; that only the president speaks with a national voice and, as such, more effectively embodies the popular will in politics; and that the president is the responsible head of the administration (and is therefore justified in ensuring that the executive branch is responsive to presidential direction)." At the same time, "[i]n his veto message, Jackson indicted the BUS as 'inexpedient' and contrary to 'sound policy.' In so doing, the president was directly expressing his personal programmatic judgment."[16]

The presidential veto is, of course, an integral part of the checks and balances built into the federal system. Legislatively, by preventing immediate passage of a bill, it checks congressional action, but because the veto cannot forestall enactment permanently, it is a balancing mechanism that invites additional, calmer, more thoughtful consideration from legislators. In this sense, the veto message is part of a rhetoric designed to preserve the system, casting the president in the role of conservator. That is particularly true when the president's objections are based on constitutional grounds. Generally, this conserving function is reflected in statements expressing fears about deviation from precedents or Supreme Court opinions or about violating the Constitution. In his highly controversial veto message of August 16, 1841, John Tyler defined this conserving function:

> I readily admit that whilst the qualified veto with which the Chief Magistrate is invested should be regarded and was intended by the wise men who made it a part of the Constitution as a great conservative principle of our system, without the exercise of which on important occasions a mere representative majority might urge the Government in its legislation beyond the limits fixed by its framers or might exert its just powers too hastily or oppressively, yet it is a power which ought to be most cautiously exerted, and perhaps never except in a case involving the public interest or one in which the oath of the President, acting under his convictions, both mental and moral, imperiously requires its exercise.[17]

In his last annual message, which was also his farewell address, James Polk addressed himself at length to an analysis of the presidential veto power. In a complex and tightly reasoned argument, Polk laid out the justifications for exercise of the presidential veto and described its vital role in the system:

> It is not alone hasty and inconsiderate legislation that he is required to check; but if at any time Congress shall, after apparently full deliberation, resolve on measures which he deems subversive of the Constitution or of the vital interests of the country, it is his solemn duty to stand in the breach and resist them. . . . Any attempt to coerce the President to yield his sanction to measures which he

can not approve would be a violation of the spirit of the Constitution, palpable and flagrant, and if successful would break down the independence of the executive department and make the President, elected by the people and clothed by the Constitution with power to defend their rights, the mere instrument of a majority of Congress.[18]

In answer to assertions "that there is greater safety in a numerous representative body than in the single Executive, ... and that the Executive veto is a 'one-man power,' despotic in its character,"[19] Polk recalled the systemic limitations on the power of each branch and on the states as sovereign entities. He concluded, "That the majority should govern is a general principle controverted by none, but they must govern according to the Constitution, and not according to an undefined and unrestrained discretion, whereby they may oppress the minority."[20] He argued further, "The people, by the Constitution, have commanded the President, as much as they have commanded the legislative branch of the Government, to execute their will,"[21] and, "If the Presidential veto be objected to upon the ground that it checks and thwarts the popular will, upon the same principle the equality of representatives of the States in the Senate should be stricken out of the Constitution,"[22] as should the power of the vice president to break a tie in the Senate. Moreover, he pointed out that if the principle of majority rule were to be followed absolutely, the whole system would have to be remodeled, so "that no bill shall become a law unless it is voted for by members representing in each House a majority of the whole people of the United States."[23] Thus, Polk's argument grounds the presidential veto in the principles of checks and balances that pervade the Constitution. The recognition of the systemic character of this power was apparent in Tyler's earlier veto message, in which he described the presidential posture this way: "The duty is to guard the fundamental will of the people themselves from (in this case, I admit, unintentional) change or infraction by a majority in Congress."[24]

Presidents have frequently expressed a willingness to use the veto to preserve the system of which they are a part. In some instances, they have acted in extraordinary ways. Franklin Pierce vetoed the Indigent Insane Act on May 3, 1854, despite overwhelming popular support for the legislation. "I have been compelled to resist the deep sympathies of my own heart in favor of the humane purpose sought to be accomplished and to overcome the reluctance with which I dissent from the conclusions of the two Houses of Congress,"[25] he wrote, and attributed his decision to do so to "that earnestness which springs from my deliberate conviction that a strict adherence to the terms and purposes of the federal compact offers the best, if not the only, security for the preservation of our blessed inheritance of representative liberty."[26] Preservation of the system took precedence over personal disposition and popular will.

A modern president, Dwight Eisenhower, acted similarly when he vetoed a bill that he favored in order to protect the political process. Shortly after the passage of the Natural Gas Act, evidence emerged that lobbyists might have corrupted the legislative process. On February 17, 1956, Eisenhower vetoed the bill on the grounds that it should not become law until the circumstances surrounding its passage could be investigated. Because he favored the substance of the bill, Eisenhower asked Congress to pass comparable legislation quickly.

Use of the veto to preserve the system has extended to economic matters. In the aftermath of the Civil War, succeeding Congresses passed numerous bills to recompense Union veterans and their dependents, which produced a special fiduciary threat to the system. These private relief bills, sponsored by members who collaborated in responding to the demands of their individual constituents, inundated post–Civil War presidents. Bills such as these account for the extraordinary numbers of vetoes by Grant, Cleveland, and Benjamin Harrison. In one veto message, Cleveland wrote,

> I am so thoroughly tired of disapproving gifts of public money to individuals who in my view have no right or claim to the same. . . . I have spoken of their "apparent" congressional sanction in recognition of the fact that a large proportion of these bills have never been submitted to a majority of either branch of Congress, but are the result of nominal sessions held for the express purpose of their consideration and attended by a small minority of the members of the respective Houses of the legislative branch of Government.[27]

Facing Congresses that, despite the costs, were unwilling to reject the demands of their constituents on an emotional issue, these presidents were compelled to take unpopular stands.

Members of Congress have acknowledged the system-preserving function of the presidential veto through their own inaction. Early in the nineteenth century, consideration was given to amending the Constitution to permit a simple majority of Congress to override the presidential veto, but sufficient support could not be marshaled.[28]

James Polk believed that presidential reluctance to use the veto power was a greater danger than its exercise:

> No President will ever desire unnecessarily to place his opinion in opposition to that of Congress. He must always exercise the power reluctantly, and only in cases where his convictions make it a matter of stern duty, which he can not escape. Indeed, there is more danger that the President, from the repugnance he must always feel to come in collision with Congress, may fail to exercise it in cases where the preservation of the Constitution from infraction, or the public good, may demand it than that he will ever exercise it unnecessarily or wantonly.[29]

Although he did not live long enough to exercise the veto power, William Henry Harrison, in his inaugural address, offered an extended rationale for using that power in cases in which legislation was in the judgment of the president constitutional but violated the rights of individuals or of sections of the country. Referring to Congress, he argued that

> it was impossible to expect that bodies so constituted should not sometimes be controlled by local interests and sectional feelings. It was proper, therefore, to provide some umpire from whose situation and mode of appointment more independence and freedom from such influences might be expected. Such a one was afforded by the executive department constituted by the Constitution. A person elected to that high office, having his constituents in every section, State, and subdivision of the Union, must consider himself bound by the most solemn sanctions to guard, protect, and defend the rights of all and of every portion, great or small, from the injustice and oppression of the rest. I consider the veto power, therefore, given by the Constitution to the Executive of the United States solely as a conservative power, to be used only first, to protect the Constitution from violation; secondly, the people from the effects of hasty legislation where their will has been probably disregarded or not well understood, and, thirdly, to prevent the effects of combinations violative of the rights of minorities.[30]

James Polk agreed, as he made clear in his inaugural address:

> That the blessings of liberty which our Constitution secures may be enjoyed alike by minorities and majorities, the Executive has been wisely invested with a qualified veto upon the acts of the Legislature. It is a negative power, and is conservative in its character. It arrests for the time hasty, inconsiderate, or unconstitutional legislation, invites reconsideration, and transfers questions at

issue between the legislative and executive departments to the tribunal of the people.[31]

When a veto has been overridden, the president has three rhetorical choices. He can say nothing; he can reiterate his objections; or he can say the obvious—that he intends to carry out the intent of Congress.

POST-VETO DISCOURSE

The use of post-veto rhetorical action to reiterate earlier objections dates at least back to Herbert Hoover, who on May 28, 1930, wrote the Senate saying that he was "returning this bill (S. 476) without approval. The bill establishes a new basis for pension of Spanish War Veterans. I am in favor of proper discharge of the national obligation to men who have served in war who have become disabled and are in need. But certain principles are included in this legislation which I deem are opposed to the interest both of war veterans and of the public."[32] On June 3, 1930, Hoover held a press conference to respond to a congressional vote overriding his veto, at which he defended it by saying,

> I favored a liberalizing of the Spanish War veterans' pensions, because they have not been on a parity with the other services. But even yet I have not changed my opinion that it should have been worked out in a way that rich and well-to-do people with substantial incomes should not draw pensions from this Government. I made no suggestion at any time of a pauper provision against veterans, or anything akin to it.
>
> I do not believe yet that we should alter the principles which have been held for Civil War veterans all of these 70 years, providing for the 90-day requirement of service.[33]

A more recent illustration of this dynamic occurred during the first Truman administration. In the 1946 elections, the Republicans had gained control of both houses of Congress. The following year, they passed the Taft-Hartley Act, which "outlawed union-only workplaces, prohibited certain union activities, forbade unions to contribute to political campaigns, established loyalty oaths for union leaders, and allowed court orders to stop strikes that could affect national health or safety."[34] Truman vetoed it, but Congress overrode his veto.

The advent of radio made it possible for Truman to go to the airwaves after vetoing the bill in order to explain his decision to the public and to enlist public support to dampen congressional enthusiasm for overriding his veto. In a nighttime radio address, he defended his veto of the Taft-Hartley Act by indicting it as

> a bad bill. It is bad for labor, bad for management, and bad for the country. I had hoped that the Congress would send me a labor bill I could sign. I have said before, and I say it now, that we need legislation to correct abuses in the field of labor relations. Last January I made specific recommendations to the Congress as to the kind of labor legislation we should have immediately. I urged that the Congress provide for a commission, to be made up of representatives of the Congress, the public, labor and management, to study the entire field of labor management relations and to suggest what additional laws we should have.
>
> I believe that my proposals were accepted by the great majority of our people as fair and just.
>
> If the Congress had accepted those recommendations, we would have today the basis for improved labor-management relations. I would gladly have signed a labor bill if it had taken us in the right direction of stable, peaceful labor relations—even though it might not have been drawn up exactly as I wished.
>
> I would have signed a bill with some doubtful features if, taken as a whole, it had been a good bill.
>
> But the Taft-Hartley bill is a shocking piece of legislation.
>
> It is unfair to the working people of this country. It clearly abuses the right, which millions of our citizens now enjoy, to join together and bargain with their employers for fair wages and fair working conditions.
>
> Under no circumstances could I have signed this bill. The restrictions that this bill places on our workers go far beyond what our people have been led to believe. This is no innocent bill.[35]

Similarly, when Eisenhower wanted to explain his veto of the Farm Act, he addressed the nation on April 16, 1956, via radio and television simultaneously.

At some moments in the nation's history, presidents think it important to publicly accept an override as a way to exemplify democracy in action. Truman did that when he lost the divisive fight over the passage of the Taft-Hartley Act. At the opening of a press conference on June 26, 1947, Truman read a statement that said, in part,

> The Taft-Hartley labor bill has been passed by the Congress over the President's veto.

I have expressed my objections to this legislation and my concern as to its effects. Nevertheless, it is now the law of the land. It has become law in accordance with the constitutional processes of our Government. We must all respect its provisions.

For my part, I want to make it unmistakably clear that, insofar as it lies within my power as President, I shall see that this law is well and faithfully administered.

I have already received the assurances of the present members of the National Labor Relations Board that they will seek to give the new act the fairest and most efficient administration within their power.[36]

Truman used the Taft-Hartley Act as a campaign issue in 1948, however, choosing to ignore the majority of his party who had voted to override his veto.[37]

The significance of presidential veto power and its interactive character were reflected in a statement by John F. Kennedy in the first Kennedy-Nixon debate in 1960:

We were threatened by a veto if we passed a dollar and a quarter [minimum wage]—it's extremely difficult, with the great power that the president does [sic], to pass any bill when the president is opposed to it. All the president needs to sustain his veto of any bill is one-third plus one in either the House or the Senate.

Richard Nixon responded:

I would say further that to blame the President in his veto power for the inability of the Senator and his colleagues to get action in this special session uh—misses the mark. When the president exercises his veto power, he has to have the people behind him, not just a third of the Congress. Because let's consider it. If the majority of the members of the Congress felt that these particular proposals were good issues—the majority of those who were Democrats—why didn't they pass them and send to the President and get a veto and have an issue? The reason why these particular bills in these various fields that have been mentioned were not passed was not because the President was against them; it was because the people were against them. It was because they were too extreme.[38]

Interaction between the president and Congress often begins with a threat to veto legislation. Clinton's most famous and dramatic threat occurred in a State of the Union address forecasting his health care reform package in January 1994, when he said, as he pulled out a pen, "If you send me legislation that does not guarantee every American private health insurance that can never be taken away, you will force me to take this pen, veto the legislation, and we'll come right back here and start all over again."[39] Seizing on health care reform as an issue and arguing that the Clinton plan would produce rationing and government control of medical decisions, the Republicans forestalled Democratic efforts to pass a bill and created an issue that, in the 1994 elections, helped Newt Gingrich lead the Republicans to control of the House for the first time in 40 years.

Although the executive veto was designed in part to protect the community and the presidency from constitutional abuse by legislative majorities, expediency, rather than constitutionality, has dominated justifications in veto messages throughout our history. The emphasis on expediency is an inevitable by-product of the veto as an exercise of legislative power.

THE PRESIDENT AS LEGISLATOR

Presidential vetoes raise objections to legislation. Consequently, as commentators and analysts have recognized from the beginning, the veto power gives the president a legislative role.[40] In this legislative role, the president engages in a form of deliberative rhetoric, and the crux of deliberative rhetoric is expediency, the key issue in all rhetoric on matters of policy. (Throughout this chapter, "deliberative rhetoric" refers to rhetoric regarding policy, whose characteristics follow from that concern. "Deliberation" can also refer to thoughtful consideration, usually signified by careful, logical argument.) As Aristotle wrote,

> The political orator aims at establishing the expediency or the harmfulness of a proposed course of action; if he urges its acceptance, he does so on the ground that it will do good; if he urges its rejection, he does so on the ground that it will do harm; and all other points, such as whether the proposal is just or unjust, honourable or dishonourable, he brings in as subsidiary and relative to this main consideration.[41]

In other words, because the veto is a legislative power, it was inevitable that presidential objections would tend to focus on whether proposed legislation could achieve the ends for which it was enacted and whether it was timely, prudent, and beneficial to the nation.[42]

Although veto messages are deliberative rhetoric, and although the veto is an integral part of the executive's legislative function, the role of the president in the veto message is both distinctive and complex. It is distinctive because, in addressing issues of expediency, the president legislates, but does so as the representative of the whole people. It is complex because, as discussed below, in weighing legislation enacted after the thoughtful consideration of both houses of Congress and in weighing constitutional issues, the president plays a role with judicial overtones.[43] Finally, exercise of the veto power becomes part of the ongoing struggle for dominance between the executive and legislative branches of government.

The debates on the Constitution suggest that the framers envisioned the veto chiefly as protection against congressional encroachment on executive power. Constitutional scholar Edward Campbell Mason noted that although the veto had been used to protect the powers of the executive, it had more often, and as significantly, been used to prevent Congress from enlarging its powers unconstitutionally. Such an argument for vetoing is signaled, particularly in the period before the Civil War, by reference to the "necessary and proper" clause of article 1, section 8 of the Constitution.[44] This use of constitutionality as grounds for objection links the presidential functions of preserving and legislating.

The enlarged role of the president as legislator, a major development in U.S. history, has expressed itself through assertive use of the veto power and in strongly worded appeals for enactment of presidential proposals in State of the Union addresses. Alexander Hamilton envisioned in the veto power a broadened legislative role for the president, one that he thought would be "a salutary check upon the legislative body, calculated to guard the community against the effects of faction, precipitancy, or of any impulse unfriendly to the public good, which may happen to influence a majority of that body."[45]

As noted, early presidents made only sporadic and limited use of the veto.[46] For Andrew Jackson, however, the veto was a central tool of presidential power. Faced with "mounting enthusiasm for public spending," he asked Secretary of State Martin Van Buren "to watch Congress and bring to the White House the first vulnerable bill to meet his eye." When a bill passed to build a turnpike through "the strongest Jackson district" in Kentucky, Jackson issued a veto that predicated "his case on the welfare of the common man" and on the belief that "an unrestrained improvement policy" would increase taxes.[47] The veto was sustained.

The most famous presidential veto message is Jackson's message of July 10, 1832, objecting to the rechartering of the Bank of the United States.[48] This message is significant for a number of reasons. First, the stance Jackson took was consistent with his assertion that the president is the representative of all the people, in contrast to elected legislators who represent smaller constituencies. Throughout his presidency, Jackson vigorously claimed the rights of the executive in legislating; he powerfully interposed his judgment on matters of public policy.[49] In addition, Jackson claimed some of the judicial power that Jefferson recognized was implicit in the veto. In his bank veto message, Jackson enunciated the view that determining constitutionality was not the exclusive province of the Supreme Court, but belonged equally to members of Congress and the president. His comments reaffirm the important role of rhetorical interaction among the three branches:

> It is as much the duty of the House of Representatives, of the Senate, and of the President to decide upon the constitutionality of any bill or resolution which may be presented to them for passage or approval as it is of the supreme judges when it may be brought before them for judicial decision. The opinion of the judges has no more authority over Congress than the opinion of Congress has over the judges, and on that point the President is independent of both. The authority of the Supreme Court must not, therefore, be permitted to control the Congress or the Executive when acting in their legislative capacities, but to have only such influence as the force of their reasoning may deserve.[50]

Jackson's vigorous assertion of his legislative prerogatives was disturbing to Congress. During the debate of July 11 and 12, 1832, senators criticized Jackson's use of the veto. Henry Clay, for example, said,

> The veto is an extraordinary power, which, though tolerated by the Constitution, was not expected by the convention to be used in ordinary cases. It was designed for instances of precipitate legislation in unguarded moments. . . . We now hear quite frequently, in the progress of measures through Congress, the statement that the President will veto them urged as an objection to their passage. The veto is hardly reconcilable with the genius of representative government. It is totally irreconcilable with it, if it is to be frequently employed, in respect to the expediency of measures, as well as their constitutionality.[51]

Clay's comments document the effect of a threatened veto on the legislative process in Congress and the resentment of members toward what they saw as encroachment on their prerogatives.[52]

Given the precedent set by his predecessors, by 1855, Franklin Pierce was willing to assert that the exercise of the veto power is part of the president's constitutional duty. In a message expressing his objections to a French Spoliation Claims Act, he wrote,

> When, however, he entertains a decisive and fixed conclusion, not merely of the unconstitutionality, but of the impropriety, or injustice in other respects of any measure, if he declares that he approves it, he is false to his oath, and he deliberately disregards his constitutional obligation.[53]

Because the veto message must contain objections, its overarching strategy is refutation, and it is deductively argued and structured. Although philosophical comments sometimes appear, veto messages must address the provisions of a specific bill, a requirement that produces substantive variation in the arguments that appear in them. Like State of the Union addresses, and unlike inaugural and farewell addresses, veto messages speak to particular issues, but all veto messages share key characteristics, which include similar purposes achieved through similar means, as discussed below. Their diversity emerges because the evidence used in these messages ranges as widely as the subjects of legislation, although here, as elsewhere in their discourse, presidents tend to rely heavily on earlier presidential rhetoric, buttressed by appeals to the Constitution and statements of the founders.

In this respect, the veto messages of James Madison are significant because they initiated a pattern that persists into the present. Specifically, the lines of argument found in his vetoes were treated as precedents by his successors. For example, the arguments Madison used to justify his veto of an act establishing a national bank on January 30, 1815, particularly the bank's freedom "from all legal obligation to cooperate with public measures,"[54] reappeared in Andrew Jackson's 1832 veto of a similar act,[55] and the arguments he used in vetoing congressional legislation providing for internal improvements on March 3, 1817,[56] were adopted by a number of his successors.

As part of the legislative process, the veto message is, in some respects, the counterpart of the State of the Union address.[57] Whereas the State of the Union address offers a legislative program, the veto message limits the extent to which Congress can alter the president's agenda. The State of the Union address gives reasons for enacting legislation; veto messages explain why specific measures should not be enacted. By using the veto message to invite legislative reformulation, the president is able to engage Congress in a dialogue about the legislative agendas advanced in State of the Union addresses. To the extent that the president and Congress agree on goals, their dialogue can focus on the best means to achieve those goals.

Because, upon return of a bill, the originating house is asked to reconsider it, and because the president's objections must be entered on its journal, the veto is an invitation for reconsideration based on an analysis of the president's objections. In effect, the Constitution calls for a dialogue between branches, which is noteworthy because this is the only point in the relationship between the president and Congress, other than impeachment, at which such a dialogue is explicitly ordered. Clinton, for example, in his message vetoing a military authorization bill in December 1995, invited reconsideration and a bill he could sign: "I welcome separate action on the pay raise. I want it to be effective January 1, and I will sign it as soon as I get it."

STYLE AND TONE

Consistent with this purpose of inviting reconsideration, the tone and style of the veto message depict the president as a legislator-judge who stands above the fray, free from partisan considerations, executing the obligation to "preserve, protect, and defend the Constitution" and expressing the views of all the people.[58] Hence, although the veto has an important legislative function, the posture adopted by presidents in vetoing is adjudicative—that of a national legislator-judge who has arrived at a conclusion through thoughtful consideration and examination of the facts. In their veto messages, presidents speak as impartial evaluators and appeal to the past—the founders, debates on the Constitution, Supreme Court opinions, the actions of their predecessors—and frequently address posterity and the Court as well as Congress. Consistent with this quasi-judicial posture, and with the presentation of objections, veto messages tend to be carefully reasoned and tightly argued. The implied audience is a reading, not a hearing, one.

The style and tone of veto messages are rhetorical responses to a political problem. The veto is controversial because, on its face, it appears to be a denial of the will of the duly elected representatives of the people and, hence, smacks of executive despotism. Feeling some discomfort in asserting their legislative role, early presidents emphasized the interactive character of these exchanges. For instance, in a veto message of January 30, 1815, James Madison wrote,

> In discharging this painful duty of stating objections to a measure which has undergone the deliberations and received the sanction of the two Houses of the National Legislature I console myself with the reflection that if they have not the weight which I attach to them they can be constitutionally overruled, and with a confidence that in a contrary event the wisdom of Congress will hasten to substitute a more commensurate and certain provision for the public exigencies.[59]

Although they may claim to speak as representatives of the whole people, presidents do not thwart the will of elected representatives casually. The typical veto message expresses reluctance and regret at this action, praises Congress for its efforts, indicates agreement with specific parts of the legislation, or expresses approval of the ends the bill seeks to achieve. Even the most strident, partisan, and polemical veto messages contain assurances that the vetoes are not partisan acts, but decisions made after careful examination, mature consideration, and full deliberation; decisions made studiously, "objectively, free from the emotional strains of the time."[60]

Because these messages are designed to prompt congressional reconsideration, they must speak in a tone consistent with that purpose. Because it would not invite or foresee reconsideration, a fiercely partisan, highly polemical document would, in some sense, violate the intent of the Constitution. With few exceptions, veto messages are deferential and conciliatory.[61] After his party lost control of Congress in the midterm elections of 1994, however, Clinton's veto threats were frequent and expressed in extremely partisan terms. In his weekly radio address, for example, he said, "Anyone on Capitol Hill who wants to play partisan politics with police for Americans should listen carefully. I will veto any effort to repeal or undermine the 100,000-police commitment. Period."[62] Similarly, his veto messages contain partisan language not present in those of earlier presidents:

> Republicans in the Congress have resorted to extraordinary tactics to try to force their extreme budget and priorities into law. In essence, they have said they will not pass legislation to let the Government pay its bills unless I accept their extreme, misguided priorities.[63]

Because the president is assessing legislation already considered by Congress, the language of these messages usually resembles that of an opinion by a third party. Speaking as representatives of the whole people, presidents emphasize the national welfare, the public good, and what is wise, just, and fair for all the citizenry. Their objections tend to be couched in language that asks Congress to transcend sectional and partisan concerns. The executive veto is a check against the enactment of ambiguous and poorly conceived legislation and protection against the tyranny of congressional majorities that, in some instances, reflect regional or partisan dominance.

Because members of Congress must transcend sectional concerns and party allegiances in order to override a presidential veto, the alliances in the House and Senate that reconsider an act are likely to differ from those that initially considered and passed it. In his veto of August 22, 1911, of the Arizona Enabling Act, William Howard Taft recognized

> that the majority of a people, unrestrained by law, when aroused and without the sobering effect of deliberation and discussion, may do injustice to the minority or to the individual when the selfish interest of the majority prompts. Hence arises the necessity for a constitution by which the will of the majority shall be permitted to guide the course of the government only under controlling checks that experience has shown to be necessary to secure for the minority its share of the benefit to the whole people that a popular government is established to bestow.[64]

The requirement of a two-thirds vote to override a presidential veto is a mandate for thoughtful consideration, an invitation to transcend differences for the common good. In that requirement for overriding a veto, as well as for conviction by the Senate on impeachment charges and for treaty ratification, lies the hope that action will be taken only if it transcends sectional or partisan interests to benefit the nation as a whole. The president's nonpartisan stance, carefully reasoned arguments, and dispassionate tone in the veto message invite comparable rhetoric from Congress.

The veto messages of Andrew Johnson are of considerable rhetorical interest in this respect. Johnson, after all, was the president who faced an article of impeachment based on his "harangues" that allegedly "demeaned the dignity of the Congress" (see chapter 11). By contrast to the campaign speeches that formed the basis for that article, his veto messages were cogently argued and elegantly phrased. This contrast calls attention to the various personae created by presidential speechwriters. For example, when Johnson vetoed the Tenure of Office Act in 1867 (the veto that occasioned his impeachment), Rep. James G. Blaine (R-ME) praised his veto message:

> The veto message was a very able document. In all official papers of importance the President appeared at his best, having the inestimable advantage of Mr. Seward's calm temper and of his attractive and forcible statement of the proper argument. Few among the public men in the United States have rivaled Mr. Seward in the dignity, felicity, and vigor which he imparted to an official paper. . . . In the veto message under consideration his hand was evident in every paragraph; and if it had been President Johnson's good fortune to go down to posterity on this single issue with Congress, he might confidently have anticipated the verdict of history in his favor.[65]

The contrast between Johnson's veto messages and his extemporaneous speeches was striking. For example, Johnson's veto of the Freedmen's Bureau Act, on February 19, 1866, was calm and reasoned. It concluded this way:

> I will cheerfully cooperate with Congress in any measure that may be necessary for the protection of the civil rights of the freedmen, as well as those of all other classes of persons throughout the United States, by judicial process, under equal and impartial laws, in conformity with the provisions of the Federal Constitution.[66]

The veto was sustained. In an abusive harangue at a gathering celebrating that event, however, Johnson demonstrated the stark differences between his personal style and sentiments and those expressed in the ghostwritten veto message:

> Does not the murder of Lincoln appease the vengeance and wrath of the opponents of this Government? Are they still unslaked? Do they still want more blood? I am not afraid of the assassin attacking me where a brave and courageous man would attack another. I dread him only when he would go in disguise, his footsteps noiseless. If it is blood they want let them have courage enough to strike like men.[67]

The significance of Johnson's personal style was illustrated in the debate on his veto of the Tenure of Office Act. On January 18, 1867, Senator Charles Sumner (R-MA) said,

> In holding up Andrew Johnson to judgment, I do not dwell on his open exposure of himself in a condition of beastly intoxication while he was taking his oath of office; nor do I dwell on the maudlin speeches by which he has degraded the country as it was never degraded before; nor do I hearken to any reports of pardons sold, or of personal corruption. This is not the case against him, as I deem it my duty to present it in this argument. These things are bad, very bad; but they might not, in the opinion of some Senators, justify us on the present occasion.[68]

The constitutional injunction to provide objections to a bill that would enable its reconsideration created such strong systemic constraints that, with the help of ghostwriters, even a president whose personal style was hyperbolic, emotional, and vituperative produced veto messages reflecting the generic characteristics we describe.

On some occasions, veto messages are addressed both to the present and to posterity, most commonly when an override is expected. Andrew Johnson, for instance, confronted a Congress so hostile to his views on Reconstruction that appeals to its members were likely to be futile. Accordingly, his messages were addressed to posterity in the hope that his constitutional views would one day be vindicated. Similarly, in 1879, Rutherford B. Hayes made a principled argument about substantive riders attached to appropriations bills that enunciated his firm views on constitutionality. That argument was an appeal to Congress, but it was also an appeal to posterity to rectify this flaw in the constitutional relationship of the executive and Congress. Comparable arguments may be found in Truman's September 22, 1950, message on the Internal Security Act and in Nixon's message in support of his veto of the War Powers Resolution of 1973. Carter's comments on the so-called legislative veto are also illustrative.[69]

In the jockeying for power that follows a veto, presidents gain an advantage by presenting their arguments dispassionately, but those in Congress who want to discredit them nevertheless label presidential objections as partisan. This was illustrated in the congressional debates on Jackson's vetoes of the Maysville Road bill and of legislation rechartering the Bank of the United States. Subsequently, it was illustrated in debates over Andrew Johnson's vetoes of Reconstruction acts, Theodore Roosevelt's vetoes of the James and Rainy River Dams,

Franklin Roosevelt's veto on March 27, 1934, of an appropriations bill that included veterans' pensions, and Harry Truman's veto of the Taft-Hartley Act.

As numerous examples illustrate, the veto message is pivotal in power struggles between the executive and Congress because it checks congressional action. When the president and Congress share a legislative goal and a cooperative past, and when presidential objections are based on expediency, the veto message is likely to be part of an ongoing process through which mutually acceptable legislation becomes law. When the grounds are constitutional or ideological, the chances of conflict are greater, as the message is more likely to be a statement of principle, admitting of little or no compromise, addressed to the public and posterity.[70] Such conflicts may also produce lawsuits that draw the Supreme Court into the struggle.

VETOES AS CAMPAIGN RHETORIC

Highly partisan discourse emerges when a president of one party is using the veto as a means of demonstrating the incompetence of the opposition party controlling Congress. For example, the veto messages of Truman, Ford, and Clinton in both presidential and midterm election years previewed lines of argument used in the upcoming campaigns to urge voters to oust the opposition party from Congress and sustain the incumbent party in the White House. Two of Clinton's election-year vetoes are illustrative. In each case, it would be difficult to distinguish much of the veto message from a campaign speech. Here the confrontational tone does not invite reconsideration, but rather mobilization of the like-minded against those who passed the offensive legislation.

> By refusing to permit women, in reliance on their doctors' best medical judgment, to use their [sic] procedure [for late-term abortions] when their lives are threatened or when their health is put in serious jeopardy, the Congress has fashioned a bill that is consistent neither with the Constitution nor with sound public policy.[71]
>
> By sending me this bill, the Congress has instead chosen to weaken public education and shortchange our children. The modifications to the Education IRAs that the bill would authorize are bad education policy and bad tax policy.[72]

Twice Clinton vetoed bills containing the funds to keep the government running in order to make the point that his budgetary priorities differed from those of the Republican Congress. In the second instance, he vetoed a bill containing reductions in the rate of Medicare growth with the same pen Lyndon Johnson had used to sign Medicare into law. These vetoes in 1995 set in place a central argument for Clinton's reelection bid: that the Republicans, led by Robert Dole and Newt Gingrich, had tried to cut Medicare, but Clinton had preserved it.

The most strongly worded veto messages occur when a congressional override is virtually certain. Examples include Andrew Johnson's vetoes of the first two Reconstruction acts; Franklin Roosevelt's 1943 veto of a revenue act, overridden on February 25, 1944; and Truman's 1947 veto of the Taft-Hartley Act. In these instances, the presidents spoke to the American people, recognizing that the only hope of having their vetoes sustained lay in mobilizing public pressure on members of Congress.

The response to a veto can reveal the president's standing with Congress and the public.[73] By overriding Richard Nixon's veto of the War Powers Resolution, Congress not only demonstrated its desire to curtail presidential war powers, but also showed that Nixon's power had been severely weakened by the Watergate scandal. Similarly, when Ronald Reagan vetoed the Highway Act in 1987, the override that followed was taken as a signal that his presidential authority had been lessened by the Iran-Contra scandal.[74]

A president who loses popular support in a midterm election is vulnerable to a Congress willing to pass controversial legislation, confident that it can override a presidential veto without fear of retribution from constituents. For example, Andrew Johnson's power lessened as popular outcry against him increased:

> [Johnson] had been stubborn and bitter. He would yield nothing; vetoed the measures upon which Congress was most steadfastly minded to insist. ... It came to a direct issue, the President against Congress: they went to the country with their quarrel in the congressional elections, which fell opportunely in the autumn of 1866, and the President lost utterly. Until then some had hesitated to override his vetoes, but after that no one hesitated. 1867 saw Congress go triumphantly forward with its policy of reconstruction *ab initio*.[75]

Andrew Jackson's contest with Congress over the Bank of the United States stands in sharp contrast to Johnson's experience. Both Jackson's supporters and opponents distributed copies of his veto message in the election of 1832. His supporters believed that it would attract adherents; his opponents believed that, if publicized, such an egregious usurpation of power would cause his defeat. The election became a referendum on that veto. Jackson interpreted his reelection as evidence that his veto had majority support. In his statement to the cabinet on September 18, 1833, Jackson said, "On that ground the case was argued to the people; and now ... the people have sustained the President, notwithstanding the array of influence and power which was brought to bear."[76]

When the party coveting the White House believes that support for a position can be marshaled in an upcoming election, it may pass legislation with confidence that a veto can be overridden and that the elicited veto will discredit the incumbent president. In March 1934, for example, Congress passed an appropriations bill restoring the pensions of Spanish-American war veterans to the 75 percent level. When Franklin Roosevelt vetoed the act, he handed the Republicans an election issue they relished; for the first time in Roosevelt's presidency, with an eye on the veterans' vote in the upcoming election, Congress overrode a veto. Demonstrating that two can play at this game, Roosevelt engaged in a dramatic test of presidential popularity and suasive power by speaking before a joint session of Congress in an effort to sustain his veto. On May 22, 1935, with the country listening on a national radio hookup, the president forcefully defended his veto. The veto was sustained.[77]

Both Congress and the president have sought to expand their powers in the pas de deux that is the veto process. Presidents have sought additional power through the de facto item veto or signing statement, discussed in chapter 8. In the modern period, Congress attempted to create a veto of its own as a means to circumscribe presidential power. In 1932, Congress gave Herbert Hoover the authority to restructure the government, but added conditions such that Congress retained the right to scuttle his plans if a majority of the legislators disapproved. Known as the legislative veto, this tactic became a prominent weapon in the 1970s as Congress attempted to restrain what it viewed as Nixon's abuses of executive power. The War Powers Resolution, for instance, contained built-in legislative veto provisions, as did a number of other laws governing regulatory agencies, the sales of arms, and the export of U.S. technology and nuclear fuel. In 1983, however, the Supreme Court ruled that such provisions were unconstitutional.[78] More recent informal agreements between Congress and the first Bush administration on provisions for continuing humanitarian aid to the Nicaraguan Contra forces circumvented the Court's ruling.[79]

Presidential efforts to enlarge the veto power and congressional efforts to limit presidential action reflect the integral part the veto plays in the power struggle between the executive and legislative branches, to which the Court is sometimes a party. The number of vetoes and the percentages of them sustained or overridden are measures of conflict between executive and legislature. Andrew Johnson, one of only two presidents to be impeached, used veto after veto to try to thwart congressional plans for Reconstruction. Johnson has the dubious distinction of having the largest absolute number (15 of 29) as well as the largest percentage (over 50) of his vetoes overridden. The extent of that conflict becomes apparent through comparison. Truman, for example, vetoed 250 measures; 12 of his vetoes were overridden. Ford used the veto 66 times; 12 vetoes were overridden.[80]

Another way of looking at the role of veto messages in legislative-executive power struggles is to consider willingness to veto and the justifications used in accompanying veto messages as indicators of a given president's conception of executive power. Presidents have shown varying dispositions for action, including rhetorical action. John Adams, William Howard Taft, and Calvin Coolidge were rhetorically restrained presidents; Andrew Jackson, Theodore Roosevelt, Woodrow Wilson, and Franklin Roosevelt represent the opposite extreme. Presidents' conceptions of the institution they occupy affect their views of the role of presidential rhetoric, including the veto message. Taft, for example, described his conception of the presidency this way:

> The true view of the Executive function is, as I conceive it, that the President can exercise no power which cannot be fairly and reasonably traced to some specific grant of power or justly implied and included within such express grant as proper and necessary to its exercise. . . . There is no undefined residum [sic] of power which he can exercise because it seems to him to be in the public interest.[81]

In his view, however, executive powers could be expanded by specific grants of power by the legislature.

Theodore Roosevelt espoused a quite different view: "I acted for the common well-being of all our people, whenever and in whatever manner was necessary, unless prevented by direct constitutional or legislative prohibition."[82] His philosophy had a rhetorical dimension: in a speech delivered at Osawatomie, Kansas, he said, "Words count for nothing except in so far as they represent acts."[83] Like Roosevelt, Lincoln was a presidential activist, and described his conception of executive power this way: "I felt that measures, otherwise unconstitutional, might become lawful by becoming indispensable to the preservation of the Constitution through the preservation of the nation."[84]

Presidents who are activists are more likely either to call Congress into special session, as did Woodrow Wilson and Franklin Roosevelt did three times each, or to delay calling Congress into session, as did Lincoln. Each such exertion of presidential power encouraged or forestalled rhetoric from the legislative branch. Activist presidents are more likely to seek out occasions to veto as a means of asserting their authority, as illustrated by Andrew Jackson's veto of the Maysville Road bill and Franklin Roosevelt's request to his staff to find something for him to veto.[85]

Andrew Jackson invited passage of the Maysville Road bill in order to veto it. His first annual message stated his determination to retire the annual debt, which would be more difficult if money were appropriated for internal improvements. Fearful that the bill's supporters would alter it if they anticipated a Jackson veto, Secretary of State Martin Van Buren passed the word that the president had not yet made up his mind. When the bill appeared in its anticipated form on May 27, 1830, Jackson vetoed it.[86] That the veto was politically motivated is indicated because several days later, Jackson signed acts appropriating money for surveys for an extension of the Cumberland Road.[87] Jackson's determination to adhere to his legislative agenda was evident in an allusion he made to his first annual message in the veto message: "The act which I am called upon to consider has ... been passed with a knowledge of my views on this question, as these were expressed in the message referred to."[88] Jackson's notes for the Maysville veto message make it clear that he viewed such action as responsive to the public will:

> The voice of the people from Maine to Louisiana during the last canvass [has] ... cried aloud for reform, retrenchment for the public expenditures, and economy in the expenditures of the Government—they expect the public debt to be speedily paid, not increased by appropriations for local not national concerns.[89]

The congressional debate on the Maysville veto divided along sectional and party lines; it did not center on the merits of the bill, but on Jackson's performance as president.

Presidential activists are disposed to use all the tools available to them, including rhetoric. Wilson, for example, delivered his first State of the Union address in person; Franklin Roosevelt flew to the 1932

Democratic convention to deliver his acceptance address and went to Congress in person in 1935 to deliver a veto message. Presidential activists are more likely to submit a comprehensive legislative agenda to Congress in their first annual messages, more likely to remind Congress in subsequent State of the Union addresses that parts of that agenda remain to be enacted, and more likely to veto acts that threaten to alter their agenda. Activists are more comfortable using rhetoric to achieve their ends, which, in turn, disposes them to engage in more ceremonial rhetoric, as illustrated both by Abraham Lincoln's decision to deliver an address at the dedication of the cemetery at Gettysburg and by Ronald Reagan, who sought out televisual occasions to present his patriotic, optimistic messages.

The disposition to be active rhetorically affects veto messages. Those not disposed to use rhetoric as a tool of presidential power are less likely to produce veto messages even when faced with a hostile Congress. They are likely to speak only when they perceive that a compelling ideological or constitutional issue has arisen. This approach was illustrated by Ronald Reagan, who through two terms in office produced relatively few veto messages, despite facing Congresses with a majority of the opposing party in one or both houses.[90]

An analysis of the vetoes of Cleveland and Franklin Roosevelt, the presidents with the highest total number of vetoes, reveals some subtle differences in their conceptions of presidential activism. Whereas Cleveland concentrated on pension, military, and naval relief bills, Franklin Roosevelt's veto messages range across most congressional legislative activity. He vetoed bills concerning religious periodicals, cemetery approaches, homing pigeons, parking meters, and flood control as well as ones treating issues central to most presidencies.

An activist president is also more inclined to break new ground in the use of the veto. Thus, it is not surprising that Jackson's bank veto was precedent setting and precedent shattering, or that it was Franklin Roosevelt who, for the first time, vetoed a revenue act. Similarly, as discussed in chapter 8, Jackson invented a rhetorical way to attenuate an act, and Truman made notable use of that device.

Reflecting their varying dispositions for action, including rhetorical action, presidents' conceptions of the importance of the veto power have differed substantially. For Woodrow Wilson, the veto was a president's most powerful prerogative, and he concluded that the president was not powerful in his function as head of the executive branch, but rather gained his power as a branch of the legislature.[91] By contrast, presidents such as John Adams, Franklin Pierce, James Buchanan, and Chester Arthur treated the veto power as extraordinary.

THE VETO IN STRUGGLES OVER IMMIGRATION

The role of the veto in executive-legislative relations can be illustrated by the history of immigration legislation. Immigration has been a national concern from the earliest days of the nation. In March of 1819, customs collectors were required to report the numbers of immigrants to the Department of the Treasury. In 1882, Congress enacted a law providing for a head tax on those arriving by sea and empowering customs officials to prevent the landing of any "convict, lunatic, idiot, or any person unable to take care of himself or herself without becoming a public charge."[92] Throughout the 1880s and 1890s, the immigration laws were amended to protect U.S. workers from competition from cheap immigrant labor.

The annual messages of nineteenth-century presidents often contained reports, filed originally by the secretary of the treasury, on the number of immigrants. A review of these addresses calls attention to other concerns raised by increasing immigration. On December 4, 1893, Grover Cleveland, for example, noted the success of the Marine Hospital Service in "preventing the entrance and spread of contagious diseases" from foreign ports.[93] In his fourth annual message, on December 3, 1888, Cleveland pointed out the international complications of immigration and recommended reorganization of the immigration process. Specifically, he was concerned that immigrants were "evading the duties of citizenship" while making prompt claims for "national protection" and demanding U.S. "intervention on their behalf."[94] On December 6, 1904, in his annual message, Theodore Roosevelt argued that "we should not admit any man of an unworthy type, any man concerning whom we can say that he will himself be a bad citizen or that his children and grandchildren will detract from instead of add to the sum of the good citizenship of the country."[95] These messages illustrate that the nation was engaged in an ongoing dialogue about the policies that should govern immigration.

Congress repeatedly attempted to define the quality of the individuals who would be admitted to the country by setting up entrance tests. Some were skill-related tests; proposed literacy tests fell into this category. Both Cleveland and Taft vetoed acts that called for literacy tests, and Woodrow Wilson twice vetoed such measures. The first three vetoes were sustained; the fourth, handed down in 1917, was overridden.

Wilson's January 28, 1915, veto message on an act mandating literacy tests for immigrants illustrates the elements of veto messages that we have described and shows a rhetorically skilled president using all the available means of persuasion at his disposal to make his veto effective.[96] That it was sustained, and that a later veto of a similar act was overridden, also illustrates the role that the climate of public opinion plays in a president's success or failure in exerting presidential power through vetoing.

In the first line of his 1915 veto message, Wilson announced his intent: "It is with unaffected regret that I find myself constrained by clear conviction to return this bill without my signature." He then indicated his awareness of his role in preserving the system as well as his respect for Congress as a branch of government:

> I feel it a serious matter to exercise the power of the veto in any case. . . . This particular bill is in so many important respects admirable, well-conceived, and desirable. Its enactment into law would undoubtedly enhance the efficiency and improve the methods of handling the important branch of the public service to which it relates. (2481)

Wilson's invitation to Congress to reconsider coincides with his explanation of the constitutional basis for his veto: "But candor and a sense of duty with regard to the responsibility so clearly imposed upon me by the Constitution in matters of legislation leave me no choice but to dissent" (2481). His tone was neutral, reflective, thoughtful. He explained that his veto was prompted by tradition and the character of the government, elements of the presidential function of preserving the system:

> In two particulars of vital consequence this bill embodies a radical departure from the traditional and long established policy of this country, a policy in which our people have conceived the very character of the government to be expressed, the very mission and spirit of the Nation in respect of its relations to the peoples of the world outside their borders. (2481)

Consistent with the constitutional requirement that the president provide reasons for a veto, Wilson, drawing support from the language of the founding document, claimed that the bill closed the gates to those whose opportunity for constitutional agitation, "for what they conceived to be the natural and inalienable rights of men," existed nowhere else. Without indicating its source, Wilson also marshaled an argument used in Taft's veto of a similar act on February 14, 1913. The act, Wilson argued, "excludes those to whom the opportunities of elementary education have been denied, without regard to their character, their purpose, or their natural capacity" (2481). Here both Wilson and Taft were drawing on what had become stock criteria for evaluating immigrants: their characters, their purposes, and their natural capacities. This was a veto message that could not have been issued in the early 1870s, before these lines of argument had become commonplace assumptions.

Wilson's veto message not only embodied the qualities and arguments we have identified in veto messages throughout U.S. history, but also included a line of argument that was uniquely Wilsonian. He argued that the people had not spoken on this issue, as literacy tests had not been incorporated into the platform of either party. Accordingly, he wanted instructions from those "whose fortunes with ours and all men's are involved" (2482). By contrast, in 1913, Taft did not appeal either to the people or to the Constitution, but to a principle that he believed should be upheld. That principle was stated in a letter Taft appended to his message, written by Charles Nagel, secretary of commerce. Nagel argued that illiteracy was not an inherent characteristic of immigrants; it was, instead, an indication of the disadvantages of their previous lives. Illiterates quickly learned, he noted, once they entered the country and were able to take advantage of educational opportunities.

Wilson's appeals to the parties and to a referendum of the citizenry exhausted arguments against the literacy test. In 1915, Wilson had enough power for his veto to be sustained by Congress. By 1917, when his second veto was overridden, his power had begun to wane. Literacy tests had been approved by both houses of Congress four times—convincing evidence that the will of the people was being expressed in this legislation. In addition, by 1917, the ethnocentrism that tends to accompany war made any legislation inhibiting immigration more palatable. Moreover, the cases for both sides had been developed exhaustively. By 1917, the changed climate of opinion tipped the balance in favor of literacy tests.

The history of Wilson's vetoes of literacy acts illustrates the interaction between the president and Congress, which, in turn, takes place in a changing historical context. Although we have tended to treat veto messages as responses to acts of Congress, we are mindful that this complex of circumstances, as well as the disposition to activism of specific presidents, is at work in these encounters.

CONCLUSION

The veto message, a special kind of deliberative rhetoric, is a creature of the Constitution. Because presidents must return vetoed acts to Congress with their objections, veto messages must be strategically refutative and deductively structured. Because the president is responding to legislation, lines of argument based on expediency predominate. When constitutional issues are the grounds for objection, presidents act as conservators of the system. When issues of expediency predominate, presidents act as legislators, but as representatives of the entire citizenry. Because the purpose of the veto message is to prompt reconsideration, presidents speak as dispassionate legislator-judges and in a tone and a style that tend to be conciliatory. Because a veto interdicts congressional enactment, however, it becomes a pivotal moment in struggles for power between the executive and legislative branches. For this reason, veto messages reveal the comparative powers of the executive and legislative branches at different times, and they are one indicator of presidential conceptions of the institution of the presidency. Similarities among veto messages bespeak the power of the constitutional provisions; their differences reflect the variation in legislative concerns and the rhetorical activism of the incumbent president.

A study of presidential veto messages reveals one means by which presidential powers have grown; in this case, exercise of the veto power has enlarged the executive role in the legislative process. Tracing presidential use of the veto power and examining the messages in which extensions of power have been explained and justified are ways to understand how such change has occurred. One can also study conflicts between the executive and the legislature as manifested in veto messages. A president's willingness to veto and the justifications used for doing so are indicators of presidential activism. Veto messages are to some extent a constitutive element both of the institution of the presidency and of individual presidencies. Even more than inaugurals and State of the Union addresses, however, veto messages constitute an important part of our system of government, including its checks and balances and interbranch struggles for power.

The effort to enlarge presidential power still further has produced a new rhetorical genre, which is the subject of the next chapter.

EIGHT

The Signing Statement as De Facto Item Veto

In the summer of 2006, hearings by the Senate Committee on the Judiciary and a report by the American Bar Association's Task Force on Presidential Signing Statements and the Separation of Powers Doctrine drew public attention to the special form of presidential discourse that we consider in this chapter. A de facto item, or "constitutional," veto occurs when, after signing legislation, a president issues a statement taking exception to one or more of its provisions.[1] Because these documents are issued when or shortly after the president signs a piece of legislation, the press and legal scholars usually call them "signing statements." This label breeds confusion by focusing attention on when they are issued rather than on what they accomplish.

Most signing statements are not de facto item vetoes. Some simply thank or acknowledge those who played an important role in passing the legislation. "I applaud the Congress' swift, unanimous, and bipartisan passage of this bill," noted Bill Clinton in a signing statement on the Church Arson Prevention Act of 1996.[2] Others indicate presidential displeasure without taking exception to the legislation. "I am disappointed that the Congress did not accept the Department of the Interior's recommendation that performance of a formal new area study precede establishment of this Historic Site," noted George H. W. Bush on signing the bill establishing the Ulysses S. Grant National Historic Site in St. Louis.[3] Of the 276 signing statements issued by Ronald Reagan, only 71 include "provisions questioning the constitutionality of one or more of the statutory provisions signed into law." For George H. W. Bush, that number is 146 of 214 signing statements, and for Bill Clinton, 105 of 391 signing statements. By September 20, 2006, when the Congressional Research Service issued the report from which these numbers are drawn, George W. Bush had issued 128 signing statements, "110 of which (86%) contain some type of constitutional challenge or objection."[4]

We focus here on "signing statements" that circumscribe the signed legislation. This genre's salient characteristic was identified as the third of three important functions delineated in a legal memo written by Walter Dellinger, assistant attorney general and head of the Office of Legal Counsel, to Bernard N. Nussbaum, counsel to President Clinton. According to Dellinger, signing statements perform three "useful and legally significant functions":

> (1) explaining to the public, and particularly to constituencies interested in the bill, what the President believes to be the likely effects of its adoption, (2) directing subordinate officers within the Executive Branch how to interpret or administer the enactment, and (3) informing Congress and the public that the Executive believes that a particular provision would be unconstitutional in certain of its applications, or that it is unconstitutional on its face, and that the provision will not be given effect by the Executive Branch to the extent that such enforcement would create an unconstitutional condition.[5]

Once rare, the de facto item veto has become increasingly common in recent times. "Only in the last 50 years have signing statements emerged as a principal means for the White House to assert constitutional objections to acts of Congress," noted legal historian Christopher May in 1994. "Prior to 1945, the number of signing statements that raised constitutional issues was negligible. From 1789 to 1945, only 15 such statements were issued, an average of about one a decade."[6]

The de facto item veto is one area of presidential rhetoric in which words are not necessarily deeds. "Of the 93 statutes whose validity was challenged in presidential signing statements between 1789 and 1981," notes May, "only 12 were disregarded by the President. In the remaining 81 cases, representing 87 percent of the total, the Chief Executive either had no occasion to execute the law or chose to honor the statute despite his constitutional reservations."[7] In other words, presidents who assert that they are not obligated to follow a provision in question may nonetheless do so voluntarily.

In the genre on which we focus in this chapter, the president circumscribes legislation he has recently signed by taking exception to specific provisions on constitutional grounds. In the process, in the name of exercising the president's constitutional obligations, he deploys lines of argument legitimized by past presidents.

What makes the signing statement as de facto item veto distinct is not the lines of argument that it employs. Indeed, it rarely claims any powers not exercised and defended elsewhere in the history of the presidency, often in other, more traditional presidential genres of discourse. These powers include certain privileges, responsibilities, powers, or prerogatives based in the constitutional structure of separation of powers or designation of the president as commander in chief; control of what happens in the executive branch and, as a result, the right to refuse authority granted to the president in legislation or to refuse to comply with provisions that circumscribe the power of the executive; and the right, rooted in the oath of office and the requirement to faithfully execute the laws, to take exception to legislation that is held to violate the Constitution.

LINES OF ARGUMENT DRAWN FROM PAST PRESIDENTIAL RHETORIC

To demonstrate that the de facto item veto is drawing on already claimed presidential prerogatives, we briefly examine past invocations of three arguments found in other genres and commonly reprised in the de facto item veto. We then explore the evolution of this genre. After doing so, we suggest that this rhetorical form is distinct because of when it occurs (after the signing of legislation), what it does not do (veto and return the offending legislation to the originating house of Congress with objections), its audience, and the style that it adopts. Specifically, it is a rhetoric of construal that claims to protect presidential power while instructing the executive branch to follow the president's reading of the legislation and setting down premises to defend the president's action if it is challenged in the courts. Finally, we argue that in the presidency of George W. Bush, the genre has taken a form substantially different from that adopted by his predecessors. We refer to this form as public embrace and private repudiation.

To demonstrate that the lines of argument employed in signing statements are neither novel nor unprecedented, we briefly note early uses of three arguments now commonly found in the de facto item veto: (1) that a president can act on his understanding of what is and is not constitutional; (2) that presidents can refuse to disclose information to Congress; and (3) that in times of war, presidents may assume the power needed to protect the nation.

Throughout the history of the presidency, those holding the office have acted on the assumption that the constitutionally prescribed oath of office gives the president authority to interpret the Constitution in

order to "preserve, protect and defend" it and the constitutional prerogatives of the executive. The premise that the president can and, indeed, in some circumstances, must determine what is and is not constitutional and act accordingly drew support from the debates on ratifying
the Constitution when James Wilson, one of the framers and a future
Supreme Court justice, noted that the president "could shield himself
and refuse to carry into effect an act that violates the Constitution."[8]
Early in the country's history, presidents employed that line of argument when working within two of their most powerful constitutionally
licensed genres, the pardon and the veto.

Because he regarded the Sedition Act as unconstitutional, Thomas
Jefferson pardoned those convicted under it. "But the executive, believing the law to be unconstitutional, were [sic] bound to remit the execution of it; because that power has been confided to them by the Constitution," Jefferson explained in a letter to Abigail Adams.[9]

Similarly, in his most famous veto message, Andrew Jackson offered
a clear defense of the right and obligation of each of the branches to
interpret the Constitution. "It is as much the duty of the House of Representatives, of the Senate, and of the President to decide upon the constitutionality of any bill or resolution which may be presented to them
for passage or approval as it is of the supreme judges when it may be
brought before them for judicial decision," Jackson declared in his veto
of the rechartering of the Bank of the United States.[10] Although the
Supreme Court had earlier held in *McCulloch v. Maryland*[11] that the bank
was constitutional, Jackson's veto was premised on the argument that
it was not.

In both of these cases, the president's right to act on his interpretation of the Constitution was bolstered because the genre in which he
claimed the right was constitutionally sanctioned and exclusively presidential. By giving the president the absolute power to reprieve and pardon, the Constitution accepts the possibility that the pardoning power
may be used on the grounds that the president views the conviction as
unconstitutional. By authorizing a president, who does not approve of a
bill, to "return it, with his Objections," the Constitution opens the way
for the president to offer constitutional objections.

The argument that the president has an executive privilege that
permits him to protect the information found in the executive branch
also has a history that antedates its uses in contemporary signing statements. From the early days of the republic, Congress acknowledged
that there were circumstances under which the president should not

be asked to provide information. When Congress requested information, it did so with the qualification "if not incompatible with the public interest." Over time, as historian Arthur M. Schlesinger, Jr., noted, that concession was transformed by presidents into an assertion of executive right. "[C]ongressional power began to suffer attrition after the Spanish-American War," he observes. "The notion began thereafter to arise that the formula by which Congress was accustomed to request information about foreign affairs . . . was less a matter of congressional courtesy than of executive right."[12]

The presidential conviction that Congress cannot compel the executive to provide information explains why presidents respond to the requirements of the War Powers Resolution of 1973 with letters submitting information "consistent with" rather than "in compliance with" the act. To "comply" would undercut the presidential contention that the act unconstitutionally infringes on the president's power as commander in chief.[13]

The argument that a president has the right to assume extraordinary powers in times of war was advanced most clearly by Abraham Lincoln.[14] Slightly more than a month after being sworn in as president, Lincoln faced insurrection. On April 12, when Fort Sumter was fired on, Congress was not in session. The newly installed president used the power the Constitution gave him to call Congress into session on July 4, 1861—timing rich with symbolism. On April 27, responding to a threat in Maryland, Lincoln authorized General Winfield Scott to suspend the writ of habeas corpus along the military line between Philadelphia and Washington, D.C.

In his July 4 special message, Lincoln argued, in a fashion reminiscent of Jefferson,

> It was decided that we have a case of rebellion, and that the public safety does require the qualified suspension of the privilege of the writ which was authorized to be made. . . . [T]he Constitution itself, is silent as to which, or who, is to exercise the power; and as the provision was plainly made for a dangerous emergency, it cannot be believed the framers of the instrument intended, that in every case, the danger should run its course, until Congress could be called together; the very assembling of which might be prevented, as was intended in this case, by the rebellion.[15]

Lincoln told Congress that he had acted on the assumption that once in session, Congress would ratify his actions: "These measures, whether strictly legal or not, were ventured upon, trusting, then, as now, that Congress would readily ratify them."[16] The sixteenth president also issued the Emancipation Proclamation in the name of "the power in me invested as Commander-in-Chief, of the Army and Navy of the United States in time of actual armed rebellion against authority and government of the United States."[17]

In his first inaugural address, Lincoln had denied that the Supreme Court's powers were dispositive. "[T]he candid citizen," he said, "must confess that if the policy of the government, upon vital questions, affecting the whole people, is to be irrevocably fixed by decisions of the Supreme Court . . . the people will have ceased, to be their own rulers, having, to that extent, practically resigned their government, into the hands of that eminent tribunal."[18]

In sum, when signing statements adopt these three lines of argument, they are adopting claims made in other genres long before the signing statement gained currency as a regularly used presidential rhetorical genre.

EVOLUTION OF THE DE FACTO ITEM VETO

Whereas we found that the genres we treated in other chapters had distinctive rhetorical characteristics from their inception, the process of signing legislation and then registering exception developed over time. On May 30, 1830, for example, Andrew Jackson approved and signed a bill, but in a message to the Senate and House, noted that "the phraseology of the section which appropriates the sum of $8,000 for the road from Detroit to Chicago may be construed to authorize the application of the appropriation for the continuance of the road beyond the limits of the Territory of Michigan." Jackson then added, "I desire to be understood as having approved this bill with the understanding that the road authorized by this section is not to be extended beyond the limits of the said Territory."[19]

Twelve years later, John Tyler advanced this emergent form by signing an apportionment bill and then notifying the House that he had deposited with his secretary of state "an exposition of my reasons for giving it my sanction." Unsurprisingly, the House responded to word of the "exposition" by passing a resolution requiring that it be transmitted to the House. What they found was a document that did not say that Tyler would interpret the legislation in a specific way, which was Jackson's move in 1830, but rather one in which he expressed doubts about the constitutionality of the measure he had just signed. "That Congress it-self has power by law to alter State regulations respecting the manner of holding elections for Representatives is clear, but its power to command the States to make new regulations or alter their existing regulations is the question upon which I have felt deep and strong doubts," wrote the president. Nonetheless, Tyler noted that in signing he was "yielding *my* doubts to the matured opinion of Congress"[20] [emphasis in the origi-nal]. By the turn of the twenty-first century, "yielding" had given way to categorical presidential assertion of the right to interpret legislation and to act on that interpretation.

The House did not respond favorably to Tyler's exposition. "A select committee of the House," notes congressional scholar Louis Fisher,

> issued a spirited protest, claiming that the Constitution gave the President only three options upon receiving a bill: a signature, a veto, or a pocket veto. To sign a bill and add extraneous matter in a separate document could be regarded "in no other light than a defacement of the public records and archives."[21]

Recall that Tyler expressed reservations, but yielded to Congress. His exposition assumed that he would do as the legislation requires. None-theless, in that document, the president had charted new rhetorical ground by signing while asserting constitutional reservations instead of vetoing because of constitutional concerns. Lincoln made a related move when he signed a bill into law while attaching the veto message he would have issued had the legislation not accommodated his objections.[22]

As we note in chapter 9, on war rhetoric, in international affairs, the president has always claimed wide latitude to act without congressional authorization. Unsurprisingly, the strongest claims to executive rights in the de facto item veto are made in matters related to international af-fairs or in times of war. In this regard, both the content and the process of Woodrow Wilson's rejection of a provision of the Jones Merchant Marine Act of June 5, 1920, are noteworthy. To take exception to the section of the Jones Act that instructed him to end certain treaty provi-sions, Wilson sent his secretary of state a letter indicating that he would not comply: "[I]t is clearly not the Constitutional right of Congress to direct the President to do anything whatever, particularly in regard to foreign affairs," Wilson told Secretary of State Bainbridge Colby in that letter.[23]

Three weeks later, Wilson's Department of State issued a state-ment taking exception in a language of barely veiled outrage: "The

Department of State has been informed by the President that he does not deem the direction in section 34 of the *so-called* Merchant Marine Act an exercise of *any* Constitutional power possessed by Congress" [emphasis added].[24] By issuing the document from the Department of State, Wilson established that he had instructed his subordinates to abide by his interpretation and at the same time insulted Congress by refusing to address his objections directly in his own voice. Congress was out of session when the statement was issued. Although he criticized Wilson's stance while campaigning for the presidency that fall, once elected, Warren G. Harding followed suit and refused to do as Congress had instructed.

We can surmise that the public and Congress were Wilson's intended audience, both because the Department of State's document was released to the press and because the statement not only offers arguments, but also couches them in a language of outrage. The treaties "contain no provisions for their termination in the manner contemplated by Congress," argues the statement. Hence, a language of "termination" by Congress is "misleading." Moreover, "[t]he action sought to be imposed upon the Executive would amount *to nothing less than* the breach or violation of said treaties" [emphasis added]. That the action is illegitimate is highlighted by the verb form (i.e., "sought to be imposed" rather than "imposed"). The principles involved in the exception are expressed categorically as well. "Such a course [as that in the legislation] would *be wholly irreconcilable* with the historical respect which the United States has shown for its international engagements and would *falsify every profession* of our belief in the binding force and the reciprocal obligation of treaties in general"[25] [emphasis added].

By the time Wilson's secretary of state issued word of Wilson's exception to the Jones Act, the signing statement as de facto item veto had developed six characteristics that distinguish it from related rhetorical forms: (1) in it, the president signs the legislation before him and then takes exception to part of it, in the process forgoing the option to veto it; (2) it is issued shortly after signing; (3) it stipulates the meaning of the signature attached to the legislation using a rhetoric of construal; (4) in it, the president speaks as the executive branch defending its constitutional prerogatives; (5) the de facto item veto instructs the executive branch to follow the president's construal of the signed legislation; and (6) the justification for the exception can be used if the de facto item veto is challenged in court. Specifically, it is a rhetoric of construal that expands presidential power while addressing the executive branch and the courts. As a rhetoric of construal that argues that it protects legitimate and established presidential powers while instructing the executive branch to follow the president's interpretation of the law and setting down the arguments to be used if the move is challenged in court, the de facto item veto does not envision the public as a potential part of its audience.

Two kinds of construal lie at the core of this rhetoric of exception taking. First, presidents posit an interpretation of the Constitution that requires them to take exception. Second, they construe the legislative provision to which they are taking exception as a constitutional problem that the executive must resolve through this process of exception taking.

One form of the second kind of construal takes place when there is ambiguity in the language of legislation and the president moves into the breach to specify its meaning. George H. W. Bush did this in a signing statement that said, "Article II, section 3, of the Constitution grants the President authority to recommend to the Congress any legislative measures considered 'necessary and expedient.' Accordingly, in keeping with the well-settled obligation to construe ambiguous statutory provisions to avoid constitutional questions, I will interpret section 506 so as not to infringe on the Executive's authority to conduct studies that might assist in the evaluation and preparation of such measures."[26]

In other cases in which the meaning of the legislation is plain and places a requirement on the president, the signing statement simply reinterprets congressional intent. One way to interpret a requirement that the president considers unconstitutional is to construe the mandate as a request or recommendation, not as a mandate or requirement. Harry Truman, for example, said in his signing statement on the General Appropriation Act of 1951, "I do not regard this provision as a directive, which would be unconstitutional, but instead as an authorization, in addition to the authority already in existence under which loans to Spain may be made."[27]

Similarly, Jimmy Carter said, "I believe that Congress cannot mandate the establishment of consular relations at a time and place unacceptable to the President. In order to protect this constitutional prerogative of the President, I will therefore regard section 108 as a recommendation and not a requirement."[28] In asserting the same prerogative, Ronald Reagan used words identical to those of Carter.[29]

In his signing statement on the Ethics Reform Act of 1989, George H. W. Bush said, "To avoid Constitutional concerns, I will view as advisory the section calling for the President to recommend to the Congress equal rates of pay for different positions. I will similarly construe as advisory the provisions allowing officials lacking executive powers to issue interpretive opinions purporting to insulate Federal employees from the consequences of potentially violative acts."[30]

Thus, in de facto item vetoes, presidents argue that they are protecting existing presidential powers that Congress has no right to circumscribe. The rhetoric is declarative. There is no invitation to Congress to reconsider.

In their signing statements, presidents also telegraph their conviction that the right they are invoking is based in ample precedent. In the process, they assert their right to interpret by interpreting. The rhetoric is performative. So, for example, Eisenhower noted in a statement on July 24, 1959, that he had signed a bill amending the Mutual Security Act of 1954

> on the express premise that the three amendments relating to disclosure are not intended to alter and cannot alter the recognized Constitutional duty and power of the Executive with respect to the disclosure of information, documents, and other materials. Indeed, any other construction of these amendments would raise grave Constitutional questions under the *historic* Separation of Powers Doctrine. [emphasis added][31]

In matters of national security, presidents bolster their assertion of the right to withhold information by citing Supreme Court precedent. "The Supreme Court of the United States has stated that the President's authority to classify and control access to information bearing on the national security flows from the Constitution and does not depend upon a legislative grant of authority," states George W. Bush in a signing statement, while arguing that "situations may arise, especially in wartime, in which the President must act promptly under his constitutional grants of executive power and authority as Commander in Chief of the Armed Forces while protecting certain extraordinarily sensitive national security information."[32] Everyone who recalls Lincoln's actions in the Civil War can then read that context back into the assertion that wartime creates special demands and with them confers special powers on the president.[33]

By indicating what the president takes the legislation to mean, in effect, the signing statement instructs the executive branch to adopt that meaning and to act in accordance with the president's interpretation.

In some cases, the instructions are explicit. George H. W. Bush, for instance, signed the Departments of Commerce, Justice, and State, the Judiciary, and Related Agencies Appropriations Act, 1992, while "directing the Secretary of State to ensure that this provision does not interfere with my constitutional prerogatives and responsibilities."[34] After signing the Cuban Liberty and Democratic Solidarity Act of 1996, Clinton directed "the Secretary of State and Attorney General to ensure that this provision is implemented in a way that does not interfere with my constitutional prerogatives and responsibilities."[35] Still, as we noted earlier, until the mid-twentieth century, the de facto item veto was deployed infrequently.

Were the public their intended audience, these statements would be delivered orally, not in writing, and would forsake technical, even arcane, language unfamiliar to the general public. "I will construe such requirements to be precatory rather than mandatory," George H. W. Bush wrote of provisions in the National Defense Authorization Act of 1991, which he said "derogate from the President's authority under the Constitution to conduct United States foreign policy, including negotiations with other countries."[36] "While I support the underlying intent of these sections," wrote Bill Clinton, "the President's constitutional authority over foreign policy necessarily entails discretion over these matters. Accordingly, I will construe these provisions to be [sic] precatory."[37] The use of terms such as "precatory" suggests that a reviewing Court may be the ultimate audience for these statements.[38]

GEORGE W. BUSH'S DE FACTO ITEM VETOES

Until the administration of George W. Bush, the de facto item veto did not displace the veto in the president's list of preferred options. In the first term of the forty-third president, however, the veto disappeared altogether, to be replaced by routine use of the de facto item veto. As of May 2006, in the sixth year of his presidency, Bush had not issued a single veto message, but instead had taken exception to legislation that he signed in over 750 signing statements. The first veto message of the Bush presidency, defending his circumscription of federally funded stem cell research, was not issued until the summer of 2006.

We see a central set of differences between the signing statements of George W. Bush, which simply assert presidential authority, and those of his predecessors, which make an argument for the assumed authority. To illustrate, we compare two de facto item vetoes, one by Ronald

Reagan and one by George W. Bush. There are dramatic differences in the language of these two signing statements on appropriations acts, the first Reagan's Statement on Signing a Bill Authorizing Fiscal Years 1982 and 1983 Appropriations for Certain Federal Agencies,[39] the second Bush's Statement on Signing the Science, State, Justice, Commerce, and Related Agencies Appropriations Act, 2006.[40] Both authorize the funding of the Department of State and several independent agencies. Both reinterpret a congressional requirement as a request. But there the similarities end.

The first difference between the two is the level of descriptive detail about the provision to which the president is taking exception. Reagan explains that he is addressing "those provisions of S. 1193 concerning the opening and reopening of United States consulates abroad." Specifically, he observes that after "lengthy review, the Department of State closed the seven consulates in question because the services they provided were disproportionately small in relation to the costs of maintaining them."[41]

Bush simply notes, "The executive branch shall construe as advisory the provisions of the act that purport to direct or burden the Executive's conduct of foreign relations, including the authority to recognize foreign states and negotiate international agreements on behalf of the United States, or limit the President's authority as Commander in Chief."[42] Bush then lists the provisions by number and heading, but does not describe the specific content to which he objects.

Not detailing the nature of the questioned provisions suggests that Bush is writing for an audience that can fill in those blanks. This is insider rhetoric. By contrast, Reagan is raising the level of information that his audience has and supplying context. He is engaging in traditional persuasion, not simple assertion of authority.

Reagan's is a rhetoric that not only describes the offending legislative provision, but also explains why adopting it is a bad idea. This second distinction is critical. Reagan is engaged in reason giving, not assertion: "The enrolled bill ... would require the State Department to operate and maintain these consulates and preclude the opening of any new U.S. consulates until the seven are reopened." The invited inference is that Congress is being unreasonable.[43]

Unlike Bush, Reagan offers an extended explanation to justify his conclusion that he will regard the challenged provision "as a recommendation and not a requirement." This line of rhetorical demarcation is drawn when Reagan explains why he believes he has the authority, in effect, to disregard this part of the bill. "Under the Constitution," he notes, "the President has the power to appoint consuls as well as ambassadors and other public ministers." But he is not making the claim that this right is explicit in the Constitution. "Accordingly," he adds, "I believe that Congress cannot mandate the establishment of consular relations at a time and place unacceptable to the President." From this explanation, he draws the concluding statement of the message: "In recognition of this constitutional prerogative of the President, I shall therefore regard section 103 as a recommendation and not a requirement."[44]

Finally, the voice in which the president speaks differs between the two documents. Reagan tells his audience what he believes ("I believe that Congress cannot mandate . . . I shall therefore regard . . ."[45]); Bush speaks as the executive branch ("The executive branch shall construe . . ."[46]). Reagan seems to make a claim for his tenure in office, Bush for the remaining history of the presidency.

George W. Bush's first veto of July 19, 2006, dramatically illustrates the difference between the reservations expressed in the signing statements we have cited and those in a traditional veto. His veto of HR 810, the Stem Cell Research Enhancement Act of 2005, uses plain, accessible English to argue that the legislation upends the "balance between the needs of science and the demands of conscience" that Bush says he established in his 2001 policy on stem cell research. The audience implied by the veto is the public, particularly those who share Bush's belief that the bill passed by the House and Senate is unethical. "If this bill were to become law," writes Bush, "American taxpayers for the first time in our history would be compelled to fund the deliberate destruction of human embryos. Crossing this line would be a grave mistake and would needlessly encourage a conflict between science and ethics that can only do damage to both and harm our Nation as a whole."[47]

These distinctions suggest that, unlike Bush, Reagan was making an argument to a future court that might turn to his statement as part of the legislative history of the signed act. The utility of this strategy was confirmed when, in *Bowsher v. Synar*, the Supreme Court struck down part of the Gramm-Rudman Deficit Reduction Act for giving Congress authority properly held by the executive. In the process, the Court noted that "[i]n his signing statement, the President expressed his view that the Act was constitutionally defective because of the Comptroller General's ability to exercise supervisory authority over the President."[48] After citing this example, however, the Congressional Research Service goes on to note that "[w]hile these citations by the Court lend credence

to [the] validity of signing statements as constitutional presidential instruments, it does not appear that the statements were in fact relied
upon in any determinative degree by the Court." [49]

To facilitate Court use of them, Reagan's attorney general Edwin
Meese III published Reagan's signing statements in the U.S. *Code Congressional and Administrative News* so that "the presidential statement on
the signing of a bill will accompany the legislative history from Congress so that all can be available to the court for future construction of
what that statute really means." [50] In this regard, Reagan's approach is
akin to Lincoln's. By contrast, Bush is simply asserting a prerogative in
a code to be read by the executive branch and to be decoded if there is a
court challenge of his exception taking in this instance.

There are other noteworthy differences between some of George W.
Bush's de facto item vetoes and those of his predecessors. In the term
of the forty-third president, a new kind of de facto item veto emerged,
practiced when the item being objected to had been unsuccessfully
fought by the administration during the legislative process and was
now part of a bill presented for the president's signature. We call this
Bush strategy "public embrace and private repudiation." With this
move, Bush gained through assertion of executive power what he had
failed to secure through suasion in the legislative arena or the court of
public opinion. On the three occasions that we explore in the remainder
of this chapter, Bush objected to a provision of a bill while the bill was
being considered, embraced the legislation publicly upon its passage,
and then quietly took exception to the provision in a signing statement.

The rhetorical act of interest begins either with efforts to secure
the concession during the legislative process or with a public signing
ceremony or media event after the bill's passage. We begin here with
the public embrace. At the media event, the president poses with the
sponsors of the legislation, and there does not appear to be a flicker of
light between them. The signing statement, however, is a private repudiation, taking categorical exception to something in the legislation the
president seemingly embraced in public. In the cases we note here, the
contested provision is favorably viewed by Congress and the public.
And, importantly, by the time the press has spotted the exception in the
signing statement, the president has been given credit for his embrace
of the legislation, and the news agenda has moved on.

Bush is not the first president to take exception to a provision he had
opposed during the legislative process. Reagan, for example, did just

that when the Immigration Reform and Control Act of 1986 reached his desk with antidiscrimination language that the administration had opposed. The disjunction between the public rhetoric of the photo opportunity and the signing statement is present in this instance, as it is in the Bush examples.[51] However, when Robert Pear of the *New York Times* reported on the ceremony at which Reagan signed the legislation, he also reported on the exceptions contained in the signing statement and the objections to those exceptions voiced by the sponsor of the problematic provision, Rep. Barney Frank (D-MA).[52] He was able to do so because the signing statement was issued on the day of the public event celebrating the bill. We call the Reagan strategy public embrace and quasi-public repudiation. By contrast, Bush has engaged in a strategy of public embrace and private repudiation.

Additionally, whereas the Reagan White House drew attention to that signing statement, the Bush administration did not do so when it took exception to the torture provisions in the McCain amendment to the Department of Defense appropriations bill in 2005. Passed by the Senate 90–9 and the House 308–122, the legislation, banning "cruel, inhuman, or degrading" treatment of any detainee held by the United States anywhere, was veto-proof. At a White House media event on December 15, the leading proponent of the bill, Senator John McCain (R-AZ), declared victory. "We've sent a message to the world that the United States is not like the terrorists," he said. Smiling and seated side by side, the president and the senator seemed to be on the same page at the event. "We've been happy to work with him to achieve a common objective, and that is to make it clear to the world that this government does not torture and that we adhere to the international convention [related to] torture, whether it be here at home or abroad," noted Bush.[53]

Behind the comity of the occasion was a stark political fact: McCain had gotten what he wanted in the legislation; Bush had not. "The announcement of a deal at the White House yesterday was a setback for the administration," noted an article in the *Washington Post*, "which had pressed the senator either to drop the measure or modify it so that interrogators, especially with the CIA, would have the flexibility to use a range of extreme tactics on terrorism suspects. In the end, McCain, bolstered by strong support in both houses of Congress, was willing to add only two paragraphs that would give civilian interrogators legal protections that are already afforded to military interrogators."[54]

There were no reporters present two weeks later, on December 30, when Bush quietly signed the legislation. His aides then posted a signing statement on the White House Web site and officially filed it in the *Federal Register*. Its eighth paragraph asserted the right to nullify the provision over which he and McCain had fought and in defense of which McCain had secured a veto-proof majority in both the House and the Senate. As Deb Riechmann, a White House reporter for the Associated Press, notes, the timing of the release made it difficult for the press to cover the statement in depth.

> The White House issued the signing statement, addressing torture, after 8 P.M. Friday, Dec. 30th, while the president and his entourage were in Crawford, Texas. It was between Christmas and New Year's Eve—a time when people tend to be preoccupied with the holidays. It hit my Blackberry at 8:18 P.M., after I'd left the Crawford filing center, prompting me to pull into a gas station to fire up my laptop and take a look.
>
> It was difficult to reach anyone back in Washington on that day, and at that late hour. Still, worried that something could be buried in the statement, I reached out to one of our congressional reporters who had covered the issue on Capitol Hill. Although on a ski trip, the congressional reporter forwarded the statement to Hill staffers who had been working on the issue. We wanted them to take a quick look to see if anything looked amiss, but nobody got back to us because they were on vacation. I ended up using a quote from the signing statement in a very straightforward story that made no reference to the controversy over his signing statements.[55]

Whereas the language of the public McCain-Bush event was accessible and plain, the language of the signing statement was technical and obscure. Whereas the president's statement while on camera with McCain personalized his relationship to the bill ("*this* Government [emphasis added]"[56]), the signing statement depersonalized it ("*The* executive branch shall construe [emphasis added]"[57]). Whereas the statement at the White House spoke in straightforward subject-verb-object fashion ("we adhere to the international convention"[58]), the signing statement was full of syntactic underbrush. Compare Bush's public statement that "the Government does not torture"[59] with the paragraph from the signing statement quoted below, in which, without mentioning torture, he reserved the government's right to use it to protect the "American people from further terrorist attacks."[60] Indeed, without going back to read the legislation, the reader would be unlikely to know the content of

"Title X in Division A of the Act" at all. The relevant section of the signing statement read as follows:

> The executive branch shall construe Title X in Division A of the Act, relating to
> detainees, in a manner consistent with the constitutional authority of the Presi-
> dent to supervise the unitary executive branch[61] and as Commander in Chief
> and consistent with the constitutional limitations on the judicial power, which
> will assist in achieving the shared objective of the Congress and the President,
> evidenced in Title X, of protecting the American people from further terrorist
> attacks.[62]

In a manner that increases the likelihood that the exemption will not
be noticed, the paragraph then includes a rash of additional technical
material:

> Further, in light of the principles enunciated by the Supreme Court of the
> United States in 2001 in *Alexander v. Sandoval,* and noting that the text and
> structure of Title X do not create a private right of action to enforce Title X, the
> executive branch shall construe Title X not to create a private right of action.
> Finally, given the decision of the Congress reflected in subsections 1005(e) and
> 1005(h) that the amendments made to section 2241 of title 28, United States
> Code, shall apply to past, present, and future actions, including applications for
> writs of habeas corpus, described in that section, and noting that section 1005
> does not confer any constitutional right upon an alien detained abroad as an en-
> emy combatant, the executive branch shall construe section 1005 to preclude
> the Federal courts from exercising subject matter jurisdiction over any existing
> or future action, including applications for writs of habeas corpus, described in
> section 1005.[63]

Not until midway through the next week did the press—in this case,
Charlie Savage of the *Boston Globe*—report the views of opponents on
the effects and implications of the signing statement:

> Legal academics and human rights organizations said Bush's signing statement
> and his stance on the wiretapping law are part of a larger agenda that claims
> exclusive control of war-related matters for the executive branch and holds
> that any involvement by Congress or the courts should be minimal.[64]

Public embrace and private repudiation also characterized Bush's response to another controversial piece of legislation: the reauthorization

of the USA PATRIOT Act. In a public signing ceremony on March 9, 2006, he offered detailed and extended praise for the PATRIOT Act. Nowhere in his remarks did he express a hint of reservation about the legislation. Indeed, at the end of his remarks, he stated, "it's my honor to sign the USA PATRIOT Improvement and Reauthorization Act of 2005."[65] "But after the reporters and guests had left," notes Charlie Savage in an article published in the *Boston Globe* two weeks later, "the White House quietly issued a 'signing statement,' an official document in which a president lays out his interpretation of a new law." Savage noted that the reauthorization of the PATRIOT Act had "contained several oversight provisions intended to make sure the FBI did not abuse the special terrorism-related powers to search homes and secretly seize papers. The provisions require Justice Department officials to keep closer track of how often the FBI uses the new powers and in what type of situations. Under the law, the administration would have to provide the information to Congress by certain dates."[66]

In that signing statement, Bush, in effect, nullified the act's requirement that his administration report to Congress on the information gathering it conducted by asserting the president's right to deny Congress information. Specifically, the statement declared,

> The executive branch shall construe the provisions of H.R. 3199 that call for furnishing information to entities outside the executive branch, such as sections 106A and 119, in a manner consistent with the President's constitutional authority to supervise the unitary executive branch and to withhold information the disclosure of which could impair foreign relations, national security, the deliberative processes of the Executive, or the performance of the Executive's constitutional duties.[67]

Although the form of the de facto item veto does not provide a ready avenue for congressional response, those responsible for the legislation in question or those in the committees responsible for congressional oversight do sometimes take note of the exception-taking process. Senators McCain and John Warner (R-VA), for example, responded to Bush's signing statement that reserved the right to take exception to the McCain amendment on torture by issuing a joint statement saying, "We believe the President understands Congress's intent in passing by very large majorities legislation governing the treatment of detainees included in the 2006 Department of Defense Appropriations and Authorization bills. The Congress declined when asked by administration officials to include a presidential waiver of the restrictions included in our legislation. Our Committee [Armed Services] intends through strict oversight to monitor the Administration's implementation of the new law."[68] Senator Arlen Specter (R-PA), chair of the Senate Committee on the Judiciary, reacted to Bush's use of such signing statements by holding a hearing on them in June 2006 and by proposing legislation the following month to give Congress standing to sue if a signing statement indicated that the president did not intend to enforce the signed legislation.

Specter's proposal generated controversy. Speaking on National Public Radio's *Justice Talking*, Harvard law professor Lawrence Tribe commented,

> Well, it's not Congress' business, really, to challenge it. Congress may feel insulted, but when Congress passes a law, for example, to protect detainees from being abused in certain ways, being subjected to water-boarding or some other technique, and if the president disregards that or says I interpret it to mean something other than what it really means, and proceeds to do the things to detainees that Congress has said he must not do, it will be the detainees or those who represent their interests who go to court and challenge the president. The only role that Congress has in overseeing presidential power is to conduct hearings, use the subpoena power, find out what the president is doing, use the power of the purse, and in sufficiently extreme cases, use the power to impeach and remove from office.[69]

CONCLUSION: POTENTIAL FUTURE DEVELOPMENTS

The de facto item veto is a form of rhetoric that asserts a wider presidential share of interbranch powers in the name of protecting existing presidential powers. Whereas the veto is subject to override, there is no ready constitutional mechanism, other than impeachment or refusing funding, that the legislature can draw on to curb this form of presidential assertion of authority. As we will note in a moment, no one ordinarily has the standing to sue the president over the exception taken.

Still, in one notable case during the Bush administration, those who authored the legislation in question aggressively pushed back and, as a result, secured an administration commitment to enforce the legislation as drafted. Passed by Congress in 2002, the Sarbanes-Oxley Act included strong whistle-blower provisions that protected those who reported corporate malfeasance from retaliation. Writing in the

Washington Post, Kathleen Day recounts, "As Bush signed the legislation, he praised it for providing needed investor protections. More quietly, he issued a 'signing statement' saying that he interpreted the whistle-blower sections as extending protections only to employees who gave information to members of Congress engaged in an ongoing investiga-tion. A few weeks later, the Labor Department filed a brief asserting the same interpretation."

The authors of the provisions, senators Charles Grassley (R-IA) and Patrick Leahy (D-VT), protested both to the White House and to the Labor Department, which is charged with enforcing the act. In the process, they made it "clear that Congress intended a much broader interpretation." Grassley argued that the position taken in the signing statement meant, in effect, that protection was available only to those "who are lucky enough to find the one member of Congress out of 535 who happens to be chairman of the appropriate committee who also just happens to already be conducting an investigation, even though the problem identified may not have come to light yet." Grassley char-acterized that reading as "nonsense." Under pressure from the authors, the White House Counsel (not the president) wrote a letter conceding the point.[70]

Rarely has a person or organization had the standing necessary to challenge a de facto item veto in court. When Reagan's exception to the 1984 Competition in Contracting Act was challenged, however, the federal courts rejected the Reagan administration's argument that the law was unconstitutional.[71]

One of the reasons that we see this genre as a special exertion of presidential power through rhetoric is that its exception taking is not subject to a ready response from either of the other two branches of government. Signing statements of this sort ordinarily do not, in the language of legal scholars, "present a justiciable controversy." Law pro-fessor Douglas Kmiec, who helped direct the Office of Legal Counsel in the Reagan administration, explains that the circumstances under which a person could have the standing to move against a provision in a signing statement in court are specific. "[S]igning statements interpret statutes, and statutes confer rights and define liabilities. It is conceiv-able that someone could claim a statutory injury from being denied a benefit under law by virtue of a presidential signing statement which, say, more restrictively interpreted the class of statutory beneficiaries than Congress intended. [T]he excluded beneficiary would have an 'in-jury' caused by the restrictive interpretation which would be redressible

by the Court—injury, causation and redressibility being the main elements of standing."[72]

The American Bar Association's Task Force on Presidential Signing
Statements made a similar point when it noted, "At present, the standing element of the 'case or controversy' requirement of Article III of the
Constitution frequently frustrates any attempt to obtain judicial review
of such presidential claims of line-item veto authority that trespass
on the lawmaking powers of Congress." Accordingly, the task force
recommended that Congress "enact legislation that would enable the
President, Congress, or other entities to seek judicial review.... [S]uch
legislation would confer on Congress as an institution or its agents ...
standing in any instance in which the President uses a signing statement
to claim the authority, or state the intention, to disregard or decline to
enforce all or part of a law, or interpret such a law in a manner inconsistent with the clear intent of Congress."[73] This is the remedy supported
by the chair of the Senate Committee on the Judiciary, Arlen Specter
(R-PA), who noted that Congress could pass legislation giving Congress
the standing to sue over exceptions in signing statements. "If Congress
had the power to sue, ... the Supreme Court could determine whether
the president's objections are valid under the Constitution."[74]

Congress has other recourses as well. It can respond to presidential exception taking by exercising the power of the purse. This, notes
Kmiec, is what the chair of the House Committee on the Judiciary, Peter Rodino (D-NJ), did during the Reagan years when he "threatened
to deny funding for the entire Department [of the Attorney General]
unless Meese would implement the disputed provision." "The Attorney
General," he writes, "relented even though the ... issue remains judi-
cially disputed and not finally resolved by the Court."[75]

Ultimately, Bruce Fein, partner of Fein and Fein, argued before the
Senate Committee on the Judiciary on June 27, 2006, that "[i]f all other
avenues have proved unavailing, Congress should contemplate impeachment for signing statements that systematically flout the separation of powers and legislative prerogatives."[76] This response is unlikely,
of course, when the House and Senate are controlled by the president's
party.

In the contest of the branches over their shared powers, the de facto
item veto is a presidential trump card the president plays to circumscribe recently signed legislation by taking exception to specific provisions on constitutional grounds. What is distinctive about the genre
is not the lines of argument it employs. There are ample precedents for

them. Indeed, this rhetorical form rarely claims any powers not exercised and defended elsewhere in the history of the presidency. Instead, this genre is distinct because of when it occurs (after the signing of legislation), what it does not do (veto and return the offending legislation to the originating house of Congress with objections), its audience, and the style that it adopts. In the presidency of George W. Bush, however, the genre has been adapted to a strategy of public embrace and private repudiation that marks his de facto item vetoes as different from those of the past. At the same time, by all but forgoing the veto for this alternative, the Bush administration has elicited calls for a legislative and judicial check on this rhetorically created exercise of power.

NINE

Presidential War Rhetoric

Executive war powers have been broadened over time by their exercise, by congressional complicity, and by Supreme Court sanction. Many scholars have traced and interpreted the events that have led to this broadening, with differing results,[1] but one lesson recurs throughout the history of the presidency. Political scientist Edward Keynes phrases it this way:

> Future presidents should recall one of the Vietnam War's most important lessons—the nation should not wage a long, protracted, undeclared war without fundamental prior agreement between Congress and the president and broad, sustained public support for the government's decision to send the nation's sons and daughters off to war.[2]

In Keynes's warning, one hears what is central to war rhetoric: the need for the public and Congress to legitimize presidential use of war powers for an end that has been justified. Each message seeking congressional support for initiating military action thus has the authorization of the president's assumption of the role of commander in chief as its central persuasive purpose. If that authorization occurs, Congress formally vests the president with the broad powers of the commander in chief.

Particularly when wars go badly, as in Vietnam and Iraq, rhetorical efforts to sustain support for the war and for the presidential role as commander in chief illustrate the ways in which genres are constituted in rhetorical acts.[3] So, for example, in the face of mounting concerns about the war in Iraq, in November and December of 2005, George W. Bush made four speeches linking the war on terror to the conflict in Iraq, a linkage disputed by many Democrats and increasingly called into question by the public.[4] Again in September 2006, in the week before the fifth anniversary of the September 11 attacks, Bush made a set of speeches linking the war on terror to the conflict in Iraq.[5]

This chapter examines the rhetoric by which presidents seek to justify to Congress and to the citizenry their exercise of war powers.

Presidential war rhetoric is intimately related to the ongoing struggle between the president and Congress, refereed by the courts, over what the Constitution permits the president to do.

In identifying those messages that constitute presidential war rhetoric, we follow the language of the War Powers Resolution of 1973, defining this genre pragmatically as discourse justifying "the introduction of United States Armed Forces into hostilities, or into situations where imminent involvement in hostilities is clearly indicated by circumstances, and ... the continued use of such force in hostilities or in such situations."[6] In this chapter, we examine the historical background to consider how earlier war rhetoric has influenced later discourse, describe five recurring elements defining this genre, and present a case study to illustrate that these elements persist because the functions such rhetoric performs have not changed.

Historically, disputes over presidential prerogatives have occurred because article 1 of the Constitution reserves to Congress the power to "declare War, ... to raise and support Armies, ... provide and maintain a Navy, ... [and] make Rules for the Government and Regulation of the land and naval forces," whereas article 2 designates the president as "Commander in Chief of the Army and Navy of the United States, and of the militia of the several states, when called into the actual service of the United States."

That presidents have a significant advantage in exercising military power independent of the legislature can be demonstrated statistically. In the course of U.S. history, war has been declared only five times, in 1812, 1846, 1898, 1917, and 1941. Major military actions in Korea, Vietnam, Kuwait, and Iraq have been carried out without declarations of war, and more than one hundred military ventures involving combat troops have been conducted without any form of congressional authorization.[7] Since the turn of the twentieth century, presidents have introduced troops into Korea, Vietnam, Mexico, Russia, Lebanon, the Dominican Republic, Grenada, and Panama, among other places, without statutory authorization, a resolution of support, or a declaration of war.

Although just what war powers inhere in the executive has been a matter of contention, the president's favorable position in relation to Congress arises in part from the powers implicit in executive functions.[8] All agree that the president is responsible for the defense of the nation, although just what actions that responsibility permits is sometimes in dispute. Most founders shared the views expressed in Federalist no. 23, in which Alexander Hamilton wrote that "there can be no limitation of that authority which is to provide for the defense and protection of the community ... in any matter essential to the formation, direction, or support of the national forces."[9] The Supreme Court supported this view when ruling on the actions Lincoln took independent of Congress. The Court held that "if a war be made by invasion of a foreign nation, the President is not only authorized but bound to resist force by force. He does not initiate the war, but is bound to accept the challenge without waiting for any special legislative authority."[10]

Divisions of opinion arise over the line to be drawn between appropriate actions in defense of the nation and offensive use of the nation's military capabilities. The constitutional provision giving Congress the power to declare war implies a process through which that body authorizes the president to assume the office of commander in chief. The result has been a rhetorical genre justifying military action and calling for congressional authorization of military action by the executive. Such authorization can take the form of a resolution, a statute, or a declaration of war. Although presidential rhetoric has always sought to justify military action and to evoke congressional and public approval, such justification now appears less frequently in speeches seeking congressional authorization for future actions and more frequently in speeches seeking congressional ratification of actions already undertaken.

The founders hoped that the rhetorical process implied by the Constitution would ensure that a decision to wage war would be arrived at thoughtfully, not rashly or emotionally. As James Wilson said in the Philadelphia ratification debates,

> This system will not hurry us into war; it is calculated to guard against it. It will not be in the power of a single man, or a single body of men, to involve us in such distress; for the important power of declaring war is vested in the legislature at large.... [F]rom this circumstance we may draw a certain conclusion that nothing but our national interest can draw us into war.[11]

Thomas Jefferson expressed similar views in a letter to James Madison in 1789: "We have already given in example one effectual check to the Dog of War by transferring the power of letting him loose from the Executive to the Legislative body, from those who are to spend to those who pay."[12] As envisioned by the founders, decisions about waging war were to be made through a cooperative process manifested in reciprocal acts. The first, implicit in the separation of powers in the Constitution, was a request or recommendation to declare war or authorize military action by the president; the second was a congressional resolution, statute, or declaration of war.

The cooperative process involved in the decision to wage war illustrates the separation of powers characteristic of our system. Constitutionally, Congress has the right to declare war unilaterally, even to pass a declaration of war over a presidential veto. The president, however, controls diplomatic exchanges as well as the sources of official information regarding foreign relations; furthermore, as commander in chief, the president would have to prosecute any war that Congress declared.[13] On the other hand, a president can, through the exercise of diplomatic and executive powers, precipitate a situation in which Congress, even against its wishes, is practically compelled to support presidential war policy.

One dramatic incident illustrates the restraint inherent in this relationship:

> An associate of President Cleveland was once present when a delegation from Congress arrived at the White House with this announcement: "We have about decided to declare war against Spain over the Cuban question. Conditions are intolerable." Cleveland responded in blunt terms: "There will be no war with Spain over Cuba while I am President." A member of Congress protested that the Constitution gave Congress the right to declare war, but Cleveland countered that the Constitution also made him commander in chief. "I will not mobilize the army," he told the legislators. "I happen to know that we can buy the Island of Cuba from Spain for $100,000,000, and a war will cost vastly more than that and will entail another long list of pensioners. It would be an outrage to declare war."[14]

War with Spain over Cuba would be deferred until William McKinley became president.

The constitutional provisions mandating joint consideration are thwarted when presidents act without congressional authorization. Congress may ratify such executive initiatives through resolutions of support; at a minimum, Congress must decide whether to support a presidential initiative by funding its continuation. Ratification in some cases may appear to be a formality, as illustrated by congressional approval of Lincoln's actions at the outset of the Civil War, but even that delegation of congressional power proved controversial. In 1863, when the ex post facto ratification of Lincoln's actions was challenged, the Supreme Court not only upheld the executive's power to act, but also concluded that Congress had the power to acquiesce in such a delegation of power and had acted *"ex major cautela,"* that is, deliberately and cautiously, in passing an act "approving, legalizing, and making valid all the acts, proclamations and orders of the President ... as if they had been issued and done under the previous express authority and direction of the Congress of the United States."[15] This decision is a key example of Supreme Court approval of congressional acquiescence to a presidential initiative taken without consultation with Congress; in effect, the Court sanctioned a delegation of legislative power to the executive.

The history of presidential war rhetoric illustrates processes at work in all forms of rhetorical action. Rhetorical genres are linked to purposes; that is, they arise to perform certain functions, to accomplish certain ends in certain kinds of situations. A given genre persists only so long as it remains a functional response to exigencies. In effect, any rhetorical genre is constantly under pressure, and as conditions or purposes change, and as rhetorical action establishes new precedents, advocates alter and expand existing genres or develop substitute forms better suited to achieve their ends.

Presidential war rhetoric illustrates both rhetorical continuity and adaptation to altered circumstances. Despite the shift from prior to subsequent justification of military action, and despite broadened justifications based on precedent, presidential war rhetoric throughout U.S. history manifests five pivotal characteristics: (1) every element in it proclaims that the momentous decision to resort to force is deliberate, the product of thoughtful consideration; (2) forceful intervention is justified through a chronicle or narrative from which argumentative claims are drawn; (3) the audience is exhorted to unanimity of purpose and total commitment; (4) the rhetoric not only justifies the use of force, but also seeks to legitimize presidential assumption of the extraordinary powers of the commander in chief; and, as a function of these other characteristics, (5) strategic misrepresentations play an unusually significant role in its appeals. Each of these characteristics helps presidents recast situations of conflict in terms that legitimize their initiatives, usually as entailed in the executive's constitutional right to defend the nation. In the following pages, we consider each of these five characteristics.

A PRODUCT OF THOUGHTFUL DELIBERATION

Military intervention is a life-and-death matter. Accordingly, it is crucial that this decision be presented as the outcome of thoughtful consideration, not of anger or impetuosity. The constitutional mandate for rational deliberation, implied in the separation of powers, is reflected in the language of presidential speeches requesting Congress to declare war or to authorize the introduction of armed forces. In such speeches, presidents emphasize the seriousness of their responsibility in making such a recommendation. In Madison's war message of June 1, 1812, for example, the decision whether to go to war against Great Britain was characterized as "a solemn question which the Constitution wisely confides to the Legislative Department of the Government."[16] In like manner, in 1917, in his speech requesting a declaration of war against Germany, Wilson said,

> It is a distressing and oppressive duty, Gentlemen of the Congress, which I have performed in thus addressing you.... It is a fearful thing to lead this great peaceful people into war, into the most terrible and disastrous of all wars, civilization itself seeming to be in the balance.[17]

Like other presidents, Wilson also stressed that a decision to declare war must be made on rational, not emotional, grounds:

> The choice we make for ourselves must be made with a moderation of council and a temperateness of judgment befitting our character and our motives as a nation. We must put excited feelings away. Our motive will not be revenge or the victorious assertion of the physical might of the nation, but only the vindication of right, of human right, of which we are only a single champion.

On March 28, 1898, McKinley commented on the sinking of the U.S.S. *Maine* in Havana Harbor:

> The appalling calamity fell upon the people of our country with crushing force, and for a brief time an intense excitement prevailed, which in a community less just and self-controlled than ours might have led to hasty acts of blind resentment. This spirit, however, soon gave way to the calmer processes of reason and to the resolve to investigate the facts and await material proof before forming a judgment as to the cause, the responsibility, and, if the facts warranted, the remedy due. This course necessarily recommended itself from the

outset to the Executive, for only in the light of a dispassionately ascertained certainty could it determine the nature and measure of its full duty in the matter.[18]

Appended to the message was the finding of the court of inquiry: "That no evidence has been obtainable fixing the responsibility for the destruction of the *Maine* upon any person or persons."[19] On April 11, however, McKinley asked Congress for a declaration of war.

This sober language of thoughtful consideration is reflected in congressional replies. Declarations of war are expressed in formal, legalistic prose that directs the president to assume the nation's military leadership. The December 6, 1898, declaration of war against Spain, for example, stated:

> Be it enacted by the Senate and House of Representatives ... First, That war be, and the same is, hereby, declared to exist ... Second, That the President of the United States be, and hereby is, directed and empowered to use the entire land and naval forces of the United States, to such extent as may be necessary to carry this Act into effect.[20]

The 1917 declaration expanded the executive's extraordinary military powers to economic matters when it stated that to "bring the conflict to a successful termination, all of the resources of the country are hereby pledged by the Congress of the United States."[21] Congressional actions during World War II gave Franklin Roosevelt virtual control of the entire economy as well as of the conduct of the war.

Congressional resolutions authorizing presidential actions are similarly formal and, ordinarily, equally broad in scope. The 1955 Formosa Resolution empowered the president "to employ the Armed Forces of the United States as *he deems necessary* for the specific purpose of securing and protecting Formosa and the Pescadores against armed attack" [emphasis added]; the 1957 Middle East Resolution declared, "To this end [to preserve the independence and integrity of Middle Eastern states], *if the President determines the necessity thereof*, the United States is prepared to use armed forces to assist any nation or group of nations requesting assistance against armed aggression from any country controlled by international communism" [emphasis added]; and the Gulf of Tonkin Resolution stated, "The United States is ... prepared *as the President determines* to take all necessary steps, including the use of force to assist any member or protocol state of the Southeast Asia Collective

Defense Treaty requesting assistance in defense of its freedom" [emphasis added].[22]

In a speech to the nation announcing allied military action in the Persian Gulf on January 16, 1991, George H. W. Bush said, "This military action, taken in accord with United Nations resolutions and with the consent of the United States Congress, follows months of constant and virtually endless diplomatic activity on the part of the United Nations, the United States, and many, many other countries." Subsequently, he added, "The United States, together with the United Nations, exhausted every means at our disposal to bring this crisis to a peaceful end."[23]

USE OF NARRATIVE

The second element of presidential war rhetoric, the use of narrative, may appear odd, because rational decision making implies carefully developed arguments and evidence. Yet in presidential war rhetoric, rather than being laid out explicitly and deductively, justification for military intervention ordinarily emerges in a two-step process that, as illustrated below, links argumentation to exhortation, the third element in war rhetoric. The justification is embodied in a dramatic narrative from which, in turn, an argument is extracted. That argument claims that a threat imperils the nation, and indeed, civilization itself; that the threat emanates from the acts of an identifiable enemy; and that, despite a patient search for alternatives, the threat necessitates a forceful, immediate response. Central to this justificatory rhetoric is the president's power to characterize the circumstances impelling action. The resulting narrative tends to recast the conflict as aggression by the enemy, which legitimizes presidential initiatives as actions to defend the nation while exhorting the audience to action by simplifying and dramatizing the events leading to the decision to wage war.

In what is usually an extended narrative, sometimes interspersed with argumentative claims, presidents describe a threat that imperils the kinds of cherished national values rehearsed and reinvigorated in presidential inaugural addresses. Moreover, the threat they describe imperils the continued existence of the nation and, as noted, civilization itself. In 1812, Madison represented Great Britain's actions as "hostile to the United States as an independent and neutral nation."[24] In 1846, James Polk called on Congress "by every consideration of duty and patriotism to vindicate with decision the honor, the rights, and the interests of our country" by declaring war on Mexico.[25] In his message to a special session of Congress on July 4, 1861, Lincoln said,

> And this issue embraces more than the fate of these United States. It presents to the whole family of man the question whether a constitutional republic, or democracy—a government of the people by the same people—can or can not maintain its territorial integrity against its own domestic foes.[26]

The threat is frequently amplified in order to rebuff implications of self-interest, as illustrated by McKinley's address to Congress on April 11, 1898. After an extended narrative,[27] McKinley drew the following conclusions:

> The forcible intervention of the United States as a neutral to stop the war, according to the large dictates of humanity and following many historical precedents where neighboring states have interfered to check the hopeless sacrifices of life by internecine conflicts beyond their borders, is justifiable on rational grounds. ... in the cause of humanity and to put an end to the barbarities, bloodshed, starvation, and horrible miseries now existing there, and which the parties to the conflict are either unable or unwilling to stop or mitigate.... we owe it to our citizens in Cuba to afford them that protection and indemnity for life and property which no government there can or will afford.... The present condition of affairs in Cuba is a constant menace to our peace.... the lives and liberty of our citizens are in constant danger.... In any event, the destruction of the Maine, by whatever exterior cause, is a patent and impressive proof of a state of things in Cuba that is intolerable.... The issue is now with the Congress. It is a solemn responsibility. I have exhausted every effort to relieve the intolerable condition of affairs which is at our doors. Prepared to execute every obligation imposed upon me by the Constitution and the law, I await your action.[28]

Similarly, Theodore Roosevelt's 1904 justification of military intervention in the Caribbean in his corollary to the Monroe Doctrine illustrates the way presidents define the threat to which they are responding:

> Chronic wrongdoing, or an impotence which results in a general loosening of the ties of civilized society, may in America, as elsewhere, ultimately require intervention by some civilized nation, and in the Western Hemisphere the adherence of the United States to the Monroe Doctrine may force the United States,

however reluctantly, in flagrant cases of such wrongdoing or impotence, to the exercise of an international police power.[29]

In 1917, Wilson claimed that the Imperial German government had "put aside all restraints of law or of humanity" and argued that its "submarine warfare against commerce is a warfare against mankind."[30] Subsequently, Eisenhower explained his 1958 intervention in Lebanon by saying "that the action taken was essential to the welfare of the United States. It was required to support the principles of justice and international law upon which peace and a stable international order depend."[31] On May 2, 1965, in an address justifying U.S. intervention in the Dominican Republic, Lyndon Johnson said, "There are times in the affairs of nations when great principles are tested in an ordeal of conflict and danger.... At stake are the lives of thousands, the liberty of a nation, and the principles and values of all the American Republics."[32]

In chronicling the events leading to a decision to go to war, presidents identify a specific adversary whose aims must be thwarted at all costs. Madison described the British as having "wantonly spilt American blood within the sanctuary of our territorial jurisdiction," called attention to British "intrigues having for their object a subversion of our Government and a dismemberment of our happy union," and, after a narrative detailing specific injuries, concluded, "We behold, in fine, on the side of Great Britain a state of war against the United States, and on the side of the United States a state of peace toward Great Britain."[33] Polk vilified the Mexican government, which, he said, had "violated their plighted faith and refused the offer of a peaceful adjustment of our difficulties," and ended his narrative by branding Mexico as an aggressor: "The grievous wrongs perpetrated by Mexico upon our citizens throughout a long period of years remain unredressed, and solemn treaties pledging her public faith for this redress have been disregarded." As a result, he said,

> War actually existing and our territory having been invaded, ... [i]n further vindication of our rights and defense of our territory, I invoke the prompt action of Congress to recognize the existence of war, and to place at the disposition of the Executive the means of prosecuting the war with vigor, and thus hastening the restoration of peace.[34]

In like manner, in a press conference on June 28, 1950, Secretary of State Dean Acheson defended Truman's decision to send troops to Korea by describing the invasion from the North as "the most cynical, brutal, naked attack by armed forces upon an undefended country that could occur." [35]

On occasion, as illustrated in Wilson's 1917 speech, a distinction is made between the adversary nation's government, identified as the enemy, and its people, who remain our friends.

On January 16, 1991, announcing the start of the Gulf War, George H. W. Bush said, "This conflict started August 2d when the dictator of Iraq invaded a small and helpless neighbor. Kuwait—a member of the Arab League and a member of the United Nations—was crushed; its people, brutalized. Five months ago [President of Iraq] Saddam Hussein started this cruel war against Kuwait. Tonight the battle has been joined." [36]

On November 27, 1995, Bill Clinton addressed the nation to announce military action in Bosnia:

> When I took office, some were urging immediate intervention in the conflict. I decided that American ground troops should not fight a war in Bosnia because the United States could not force peace on Bosnia's warring ethic groups, the Serbs, Croats, and Muslims. Instead, America has worked with our European allies in searching for peace, stopping the war from spreading, and easing the suffering of the Bosnian people. We imposed tough economic sanctions on Serbia. We used our air power to conduct the longest humanitarian airlift in history and to enforce a no-fly zone that took the war out of the skies. We helped to make peace between two of the three warring parties—the Muslims and the Croats. But as the months of war turned into years, it became clear that Europe alone could not end the conflict. This summer, Bosnian Serb shelling once again turned Bosnia's playgrounds and marketplaces into killing fields. [37]

On March 17, 2003, George W. Bush addressed the nation, stating that Saddam Hussein must leave Iraq within 48 hours:

> For more than a decade, the United States and other nations have pursued patient and honorable efforts to disarm the Iraqi regime without war. The regime pledged to reveal and destroy all its weapons of mass destruction as a condition for ending the Persian Gulf war in 1991. Since then, the world has engaged in 12 years of diplomacy. We have passed more than a dozen resolutions in the United Nations Security Council. We have sent hundreds of weapons inspectors to oversee the disarmament of Iraq. Our good faith has not been returned. [38]

The chronicle of events in the narrative demonstrates that the existing threat has resulted from causes for which the United States bears no responsibility. Despite exhaustive efforts to find other means to resolve conflict, the threat persists; thus, military intervention is unavoidable. In this rhetoric, aggressors have choices, but the United States acts out of necessity. Infusing these claims is the posture of "forbearance," which supports the claim that the decision was arrived at thoughtfully and allows presidents to contend that every other possibility was attempted before they reluctantly opted for the use of force. In 1812, Madison spoke of his efforts "to make every experiment short of the last resort of injured nations" and concluded that these efforts had only encouraged the British enemy: "Our moderation and conciliation have had no other effect than to encourage perseverance and to enlarge pretensions." He even linked U.S. patience to an exhortation:

> Whether the United States shall continue passive under these progressive usurpations and these accumulating wrongs, or opposing force to force in defense of their national rights, shall commit a just cause into the hands of the Almighty Disposer of Events . . . is a solemn question. . . . I am happy in the assurance that the decision will be worthy the enlightened and patriotic councils of a virtuous, a free, and a powerful nation.[39]

Past forbearance becomes the basis for powerful emotional appeals. In 1846, in a speech noteworthy for its duplicity, Polk described himself as "determined to leave no effort untried to effect an amicable adjustment with Mexico." He even argued that the patient search for an alternative had exacerbated the threat:

> Our forbearance has gone to such an extreme as to be mistaken in its character. Had we acted with vigor in repelling the insults and redressing the injuries inflicted by Mexico at the commencement, we should doubtless have escaped all the difficulties in which we are now involved.[40]

Similarly, after describing attempts to avoid war, Wilson said,

> There is one choice we cannot make, we are incapable of making; we will not choose the path of submission and suffer the most sacred rights of our nation and our people to be ignored or violated. The wrongs against which we

now array ourselves are not common wrongs; they cut to the very roots of human life.[41]

In announcing that U.S. troops would go to Korea, Truman said, "The attack upon Korea makes it plain beyond all doubt that Communism has passed beyond the use of subversion to conquer independent nations and will now use armed invasion and war."[42] On April 28, 1965, announcing that he was sending U.S. troops into the Dominican Republic, Lyndon Johnson noted,

> We have appealed repeatedly in recent days for a cease-fire between the contending forces of the Dominican Republic in the interests of all Dominicans and foreigners alike. I repeat this urgent appeal tonight.[43]

On April 30, he reported,

> We took this step when and only when we were officially notified by police and military officials of the Dominican Republic that they were no longer in a position to guarantee the safety of American and foreign nationals and to preserve law and order.[44]

On March 19, 2003, George W. Bush announced the beginning of military action against Iraq:

> The people of the United States and our friends and allies will not live at the mercy of an outlaw regime that threatens the peace with weapons of mass murder. We will meet that threat now, with our Army, Air Force, Navy, Coast Guard, and Marines, so that we do not have to meet it later with armies of firefighters and police and doctors on the streets of our cities.[45]

These narratives and the arguments that can be drawn from them are powerful elements in presidential war rhetoric because they dramatize and simplify the causes of war while providing the evidence and arguments warranting the use of force.

On only one occasion has war resulted from an invasion of U.S. territory: Japan's attack on ships and planes at Pearl Harbor on Oahu, Hawaii, on December 7, 1941. In response, Franklin Roosevelt delivered a memorable and eloquent speech on December 8 seeking a congressional declaration that war already existed between the United States and

Japan. Despite the attack, the speech includes a characteristic narrative of efforts to avoid war:

> The United States was at peace with that Nation and, at the solicitation of Japan, was still in conversation with its Government and its Emperor looking toward the maintenance of peace in the Pacific. Indeed, one hour after Japanese air squadrons had commenced bombing in the American Island of Oahu, the Japanese Ambassador to the United States and his colleague delivered to our Secretary of State a formal reply to a recent American message. And while this reply stated that it seemed useless to continue the existing diplomatic negotiations, it contained no threat or hint of war or of armed attack.

A somewhat different narrative heightens the danger as the president describes a foe that is moving steadily across the Pacific ever closer to U.S. shores:

> Yesterday the Japanese Government also launched an attack against Malaya.
> Last night Japanese forces attacked Hong Kong.
> Last night Japanese forces attacked Guam.
> Last night Japanese forces attacked the Philippine Islands.
> Last night the Japanese attacked Wake Island. And this morning the Japanese attacked Midway Island.

At the same time, Roosevelt needed to rouse an ill-prepared nation's fighting spirit and to dispel any feelings that the United States would not be able to prevail in this struggle. He indicated that he had already acted; he also pledged ultimate success:

> As Commander in Chief of the Army and Navy I have directed that all measures be taken for our defense.... No matter how long it may take us to overcome this premeditated invasion, the American people in their righteous might will win through to absolute victory.

He was blunt in describing the threat: "Hostilities exist. There is no blinking at the fact that our people, our territory, and our interests are in grave danger." He was equally direct in asserting ultimate triumph: "With confidence in our armed forces—with the unbounding determination of our people—we will gain the inevitable triumph—so help us God."[46] Both a clear sense of the threat and confidence in the future are essential to arousing the nation's fighting spirit.

In this case, the passage of the declaration of war was a foregone conclusion. Investiture as commander in chief had already occurred, as authorized by the Constitution. The more important function of this speech was characterizing the threat clearly while mobilizing the nation to action to resist. These variations resulted from the unique circumstances that the president faced.

As rhetorical critic Hermann G. Stelzner has demonstrated, this was a carefully crafted speech whose every word was chosen for its effect. In addition, Stelzner points to the language Roosevelt used to characterize the Japanese and its implications: the attack marks "a date which will live in infamy"; "the Japanese Government has deliberately sought to deceive the United States by false statements"; their actions are a "form of treachery"; and this was an "unprovoked and dastardly attack."[47] These are not just fighting words; they are characterizations of the Japanese people as willing to commit acts worthy of infamy, as engaging in deliberate deception and lies, as treacherous, and as capable of unprovoked and dastardly deeds. If the character of the Japanese was as described, how could Americans trust the Japanese, whether immigrants [Issei], Japanese-Americans [Nisei], or second-generation citizens [Sensei] living in the United States? What Stelzner notes is that the characterizations in this speech made it easier for the president and the nation subsequently to approve placing all Japanese on U.S. soil, whether citizens or not, in so-called relocation camps.[48] This analysis calls attention to the ways in which war rhetoric mobilizes the public and demonizes the enemy. Such rhetoric has domestic implications, such as the creation of hostile attitudes toward U.S. Muslims since the beginning of the war with Iraq in 2003.

EXHORTATION TO UNIFIED ACTION

The third characteristic of presidential war rhetoric is an exhortation to intense commitment, because thoughtful consideration must lead not only to a rational decision, but also to unified action. Once the dramatic narrative, filled with emotionally charged language, has set the stage for this process, rhetoric justifying military intervention exhorts, attempting to spur the audience to respond with unanimity, to join a just cause in defense of humanity and civilization. Thus, presidential war rhetoric constitutes the audience as a united community of patriots that is urged to repulse the existing threat with all available resources, assured that, with the help of Providence, right will prevail.[49]

In his first annual message to Congress in 1845, for example, Polk quoted Andrew Jackson's address of February 6, 1837, in order to arouse intense public reaction and to lay the groundwork for the forbearance argument he would develop in his 1846 appeal to Congress for a declaration of war against Mexico:

> The length of time since some of the injuries have been committed, the repeated and unavailing applications for redress, the wanton character of some of the outrages upon the property and persons of our citizens, upon the officers and flag of the United States, independent of recent insults to this Government and people by the late extraordinary Mexican minister, would justify in the eyes of all nations immediate war.[50]

Exhortation is most evident in presidential proclamations issued following congressional declarations of war. In 1812, Madison proclaimed,

> I do specially enjoin on all persons holding offices, civil or military, under the authority of the United States that they be vigilant and zealous in discharging the duties respectively incident thereto; and I do moreover exhort all the good people of the United States, as they love their country, as they value the precious heritage derived from the virtue and valor of their fathers, as they feel the wrongs which have forced on them the last resort of injured nations, and as they consult the best means under the blessing of Divine Providence of abridging its calamities, that they exert themselves. . . .[51]

Polk used identical language in his proclamation of May 13, 1846.[52]

Facing divided public opinion on the Vietnam War, Lyndon Johnson and Richard Nixon made such exhortation painfully explicit. On May 17, 1966, Johnson appealed to Democrats within and outside Congress:

> Put away all the childish divisive things, if you want the maturity and the unity that is the mortar of a nation's greatness. . . . As Commander in Chief, I am neither Democrat nor Republican. The men fighting in Vietnam are simply Americans. Our policy in Vietnam is a national policy.[53]

On November 3, 1969, Nixon said, "Let us be united for peace. Let us also be united against defeat. Because let us understand: North Vietnam cannot defeat or humiliate the United States. Only Americans can do that."[54] On April 30, 1970, Nixon's announcement of the Cambodian "incursion" concluded,

> I ask for your support for our brave men fighting tonight halfway around the world—not for territory—not for glory—but so that their younger brothers and their sons and your sons can have a chance to grow up in a world of peace and freedom and justice.[55]

On November 27, 1995, in announcing military action in Bosnia, Clinton said,

> And so I ask all Americans and I ask every member of Congress, Democrat and Republican, to make the choice for peace. In the choice between peace and war, America must choose peace. ... Because previous generations of Americans stood up for freedom and because we continue to do so, the American people are more secure and more prosperous. And all around the world, more people than ever before live in freedom. More people than ever before are treated with dignity. More people than ever before can hope to build a better life. That is what America's leadership is all about.[56]

The particulars of the narrative and the argument it embodies are intimately related to the fourth element in war rhetoric, approval of presidential assumption of the office of commander in chief. In order to gain such approval, presidents must present detailed information to establish that they have carefully gathered the requisite information and thoughtfully deliberated about whether the existing conditions require war. As Franklin Roosevelt's so-called Quarantine speech, delivered in Chicago on October 5, 1937, illustrates, when evidence of such informed deliberation on the part of the president is not apparent, presidential appeals are subject to rebuff. Substituting broad assertions for a detailed narrative of the progress of the Spanish Civil War, of the significance of the rejection by Germany of the war reparations section of the Treaty of Versailles, and of the invasion of China by Japan, among other threatening world events, Roosevelt said,

> Without a declaration of war and without warning or justification of any kind, civilians, including women and children, are being ruthlessly murdered with bombs from the air. ... Innocent peoples and nations are being cruelly sacrificed to a greed for power and supremacy which is devoid of all sense of justice and humane consideration.[57]

Opponents quickly responded; some condemned the speech as "war-mongering and saber-rattling." Isolationist members of Congress threatened impeachment; the American Federation of Labor passed a resolution against involvement in foreign wars.[58] The president quickly retreated. Speechwriter Sam Rosenman concluded that Roosevelt's mistake lay in "trying to lead the people . . . too quickly, and before they had been adequately informed of the facts or spiritually prepared for the event."[59] Between the time of the Quarantine speech and Japan's attack on Pearl Harbor, Roosevelt's speeches moved more systematically to make a detailed case for the threat these foreign wars posed for the nation.[60]

INVESTITURE AS COMMANDER IN CHIEF

It is noteworthy that, like the inaugural address, war rhetoric is a rhetoric of investiture. In identifying a threat to the community and to its fundamental values, presidents implicitly argue that now is the appropriate time for them to assume the office of commander in chief. Presidential war rhetoric legitimizes that role in the face of the identified threat and seeks support for its assumption from Congress and the public.

In 1898, for example, McKinley asked Congress

to authorize and empower the President to take measures to secure a full and final termination of hostilities between the Government of Spain and the people of Cuba . . . and to use the military and naval forces of the United States as may be necessary for these purposes.[61]

Such requests initiate the cooperative process that the framers thought would necessarily occur when the Constitution separated the power to declare war from the power to make war. They believed that they were providing presidents with the power to repel attack without giving them the power to initiate warfare independently. Presidential innovations, however, especially as ratified by Congress and sanctioned by the Supreme Court, have created precedents that presidents have used to claim expanded executive war powers.

The expansion of war powers began with George Washington's pioneering use of a proclamation. A 1778 treaty with France had committed the United States to guaranteeing French possessions in the Americas. When Britain engaged France in war, France expected the United States to come to its defense. Although the citizenry was intensely anti-British, Washington was determined to keep the nation out of conflicts between the great powers of Europe. Accordingly, he issued a proclamation of neutrality. That proclamation touched off a sharp debate on constitutional issues. Did the president have the authority to issue a proclamation of neutrality? Hamilton, under the pen name Pacificus, argued that diplomacy was inherently an executive function. Madison, under the pen name Helvidius, countered that the Constitution had not given the president the power to declare neutrality. As the power to declare war resided with Congress, it was for that body to decide whether the country would remain neutral and at peace. Madison could not muster the votes to challenge the administration, and the proclamation was enforced. In 1794, Washington obtained congressional ratification of his action through the passage of neutrality legislation, thereby setting a pattern that other presidents would follow.[62]

The pattern is this: A president develops and implements an alternative to the constitutional formula of inviting congressional authorization for future military action and is able to withstand opposition to that exercise of presidential power. Subsequently, Congress approves the presidential action and, implicitly, the right of a future president to exercise the powers of the commander in chief through this alternative mode. In many instances, the courts have ratified such presidential actions. Constitutional scholar Edward Keynes contends that "[b]y amalgamating the constitutionally distinct congressional war powers with the presidential office of commander in chief, the courts have acted as a midwife to the birth of constitutional dictatorship in the United States."[63]

Jefferson's response to the British attack on the U.S.S. *Chesapeake* without calling Congress into session, described in chapter 6, represents another step in the expansion of presidential war powers. By contrast, that expansion was eased by the negative example of James Madison in the War of 1812. Historian Abbot Smith comments,

> No one, so far as I know, has ever given Madison credit for an attempt to conduct policy strictly according to the letter and spirit of the Constitution, yet this is really what he tried to do. ... The failure of this wholly constitutional, republican, and pacific method of handling foreign policy is evident. It diminished the prestige of the United States, because for years the country permitted itself, upon its own showing, to be pushed around by England and France. ... Such conduct diminished the reputation of Madison personally and of the

presidency as an office, for despite all the tenets of pristine republicanism the country wanted then, and has always wanted since, to follow a strong leader in times of crisis.[64]

As noted below, that war was very unpopular, among the most unpopular in our history.

Polk's actions gained congressional and popular support for an activist conception of the role of commander in chief because the Mexican War resulted in the acquisition of large amounts of territory, territory whose acquisition most Americans viewed as the nation's "manifest destiny." Polk's successful prosecution of the war legitimized his activist view of executive war powers. He expanded those powers by using his defensive prerogatives to provoke an attack in order to claim that a state of war already existed. In his request to Congress for a declaration of war on May 11, 1846, Polk admitted that he "had ordered an efficient military force to take a position 'between the Nueces and the Del Norte,'" in territory that, he neglected to mention, was claimed by Mexico.[65] This move, he explained, "had become necessary to meet a threatened invasion of Texas by the Mexican forces, for which extensive military preparations had been made." On the basis of the resulting skirmish, which his own actions had incited, Polk asked Congress to declare that war already existed:

> A party of dragoons of 63 men and officers were on the same day dispatched from the American camp up the Rio del Norte, on its left bank, to ascertain whether the Mexican troops had crossed or were preparing to cross the river, "became engaged with a large body of these troops, and after a short affair, in which some 16 were killed and wounded, appear to have been surrounded and compelled to surrender."

Accordingly, said Polk, "war exists, ... exists by the act of Mexico herself," and he asked Congress "to recognize the existence of the war."[66]

Similarly, Lincoln responded to Confederate military actions and used that response to establish a state of war.[67] In his message to Congress of July 4, 1861, Lincoln stated that he had had "no choice ... but to call out the war power of the Government and so to resist force employed for its destruction."[68] Moreover, although nothing in the Constitution authorized him to do so, Lincoln assumed the right as president to act militarily when Congress was not in session. Because he believed that the Union remained unbroken, he saw the Confederate actions as "a domestic insurrection." Accordingly, a declaration of war would have been improper because it would have recognized the independence and sovereignty of the Confederacy. His July 4 speech was a request to Congress to ratify the actions he had already taken.

The expanded war powers exercised by earlier presidents are transformed by their successors into precedents. The right of a president to use force abroad to protect U.S. lives and property is an example. The U.S. Court of Appeals entered the disputes over presidential war powers in 1860. In *Durand v. Hollins*, it sanctioned the extension of the presidential right to defend the nation, finding that

> as it respects the interposition of the Executive abroad, for the protection of the lives or property of the citizen, the duty must, of necessity, rest in the discretion of the president. Acts of lawless violence, or of threatened violence to the citizen or his property, cannot be anticipated and provided for; and the protection, to be effectual or of any avail, may, not infrequently, require the most prompt and decided action.[69]

Somewhat later, at the turn of the twentieth century, McKinley helped to suppress the Boxer Rebellion when he sent U.S. troops to China. In that case, under the guise of protecting U.S. lives and property, the president intervened in the internal affairs of another sovereign nation. Invoking this precedent, Theodore Roosevelt sent U.S. forces into several Caribbean countries and installed provisional governments without prior congressional sanction. Although protection of U.S. citizens and property remained the pretext, the result in the Roosevelt and Taft administrations was a series of challenges to sovereign states.[70]

This line of argument resurfaced in 1958 when Eisenhower justified sending troops into Lebanon "to protect American lives and by their presence there to encourage the Lebanese government in defense of Lebanese sovereignty and integrity."[71] It recurred in 1965, when Lyndon Johnson justified sending marines into the Dominican Republic to prevent what he described to Congress and the public as a threatened Communist takeover, and in 1970, when Nixon justified the invasion of Cambodia as an effort to destroy what he called North Vietnamese "sanctuaries" that he argued "clearly endanger the lives of Americans who are in Vietnam now."[72] It was used by Ford in 1975 to send troops to rescue the *Mayaguez* from the Khmer Rouge and by Reagan in 1983 to invade Grenada.

In some instances, presidents have warranted their initiatives in congressional actions, particularly Senate ratification of treaties. Truman, for example, treated ratification of the United Nations Charter as implicit endorsement of his right to send troops to Korea. In his announcement of that decision on June 27, 1950, he said,

> The Security Council called upon all members of the United Nations to render every assistance to the United Nations in the execution of this resolution. In these circumstances I have ordered United States air and sea forces to give the Korean Government troops cover and support.[73]

Similarly, in a 1966 memorandum, Leonard C. Meeker, legal adviser to the Department of State, contended that Lyndon Johnson had a right to intervene in Vietnam under the 1954 South East Asia Treaty Organization (SEATO) treaty.[74]

Presidents have also contended that the speed of communications and, hence, of warfare requires swift, unilateral executive responses to situations of conflict. The declaration of war that Madison requested on June 1, 1812, was not forthcoming until June 18; McKinley called for a declaration of war on April 11, 1898, and Congress acted on April 25. By contrast, the requests by Polk and Wilson were met immediately, as was that of Franklin Roosevelt following the bombing of Pearl Harbor. Modern presidents have invoked the rapidity with which aggression occurs to explain why they did not seek prior congressional authorization for military action. Truman's decision to send troops to Korea and his failure to seek a congressional resolution of support, for example, were defended on the grounds that if he had waited for congressional approval, countries vital to U.S. security would have been overrun by the time action could have been taken.[75] Gerald Ford argued that when "a crisis breaks, it is impossible to draw Congress into the decision-making process in an effective way." During the Da Nang evacuation, which occurred during the Easter recess in 1975, "not one of the key bipartisan leaders of the Congress was in Washington. . . . [T]wo were in Mexico, three were in Greece, one was in the Middle East, one was in Europe, and two were in the People's Republic of China."[76] Moreover, Ford contended, Congress is beset by distractions, requires a long time to reach consensus, and may leak sensitive information.

Presidents have also found ways to circumvent congressional control of military appropriations. When Theodore Roosevelt wanted to send the fleet around the world in 1907, for instance, an influential senator declared that Congress would not appropriate the money. The president replied that he had the funds to send the fleet to the Pacific, and if Congress so chose, it could leave it there.[77] More often, members of Congress have been confronted with unacceptable alternatives: either to withdraw financial support and court public retaliation for imperiling U.S. troops or to appropriate funds in support of continued military action.[78] On May 4, 1965, in asking Congress for an additional $700 million for military operations in Vietnam, Lyndon Johnson made a vote for this appropriation an explicit authorization of his decision to send large numbers of troops there. He also linked a vote in favor of the bill to support for troops already in the field:

> This is not a routine appropriation. For each member of Congress who supports this request is also voting to persist in our effort to halt Communist aggression in South Vietnam. Each is saying that the Congress and the President stand united before the world in joint determination that the independence of South Vietnam shall be preserved and the Communist attack will not succeed.... Nothing will do more to strengthen your country in the world than the proof of national unity which an overwhelming vote for this appropriation will clearly show. To deny and delay this means to deny and to delay the fullest support of the American people and the American Congress to those brave men who are risking their lives for freedom in Vietnam.[79]

In such circumstances, members of Congress find themselves in a dilemma. The political costs of denying support to troops in the field are high; at the same time, the passage of appropriations bills can be construed as congressional endorsement of the president's military initiatives.[80] In these cases, presidents act independently, then effectively coerce Congress into accepting their actions, a reversal of the constitutional allocation of war powers.

The rhetorical model in the Constitution is that of a president going to Congress to request authorization to act as commander in chief; the model that has developed over time, however, is that of a president assuming that role and then asking for congressional ratification. As a result, what began as a genre based on reciprocity and cooperation has become a genre crafted to compel congressional approval as well as public support of unilateral executive action. The history of the War Powers Resolution, passed in 1973 over the veto of Richard Nixon, demonstrates that a cooperative genre has been superseded by a justificatory genre designed to compel legislative ratification. The efficacy of that resolution in limiting presidential war powers remains in doubt, however; its constitutionality has not been tested, although court action in 1983 rendered unconstitutional those provisions interpreted as constituting a legislative veto of executive action. Since its passage, it has never been invoked successfully.

The War Powers Resolution requires three different forms of presidential rhetoric. The first, consultation before military intervention, carries an escape clause: the president is to consult Congress "in every possible instance."[81] Presidents quickly surmised that it was not "possible" to consult Congress beforehand. There are other loopholes in this requirement as well: the resolution does not specify who in Congress is to be consulted or how the consultation should take place.

Second, the resolution states that after authorizing deployment of armed forces "into hostilities or into situations where imminent involvement in hostilities is clearly indicated,"[82] the president must report to Congress. How and when such reports must be made, and what information they have to include, is not specified.

Finally, the resolution sets a limit on how long troops can be deployed without authorization from Congress. Unless congressional approval is obtained, the troops must be withdrawn within sixty days, a number that becomes ninety if the president believes that the additional time is required to safely remove the troops. The sixty-to-ninety-day provision becomes active on the day of the report to Congress.[83]

On May 12, 1975, Gerald Ford learned that the S.S. *Mayaguez* had been seized off the coast of Cambodia and was being towed to the Cambodian port of Kompong Som. At the time of its seizure, the ship was in international waters.[84] Ford honored the consultation provision of the War Powers Resolution by having his aides inform twenty-one congressional leaders of his plans "to prevent the ship and her crew from being transferred to the mainland."[85] After issuing the order "to launch four air strikes against military installations near Kompong Som,"[86] Ford also met with the bipartisan congressional leadership. At that meeting, Ford recounted, "West Virginia Senator Robert Byrd wanted an assurance from me that I would comply with the War Powers Act and give Congress a full written report on every aspect of the incident. I told him I would carry out the provisions of the act *even though I seriously questioned its applicability*" [emphasis added].[87] In the rescue mission, forty-one U.S. military personnel died and fifty were wounded. In his report to Congress, Ford indicated that he had acted under "the President's Constitutional Executive power and his authority as

Commander-in-Chief of the United States Armed Forces"[88] His explanation took the form of identical letters to the Speaker of the House and the president pro tem of the Senate.

Before launching the mission on April 25, 1980, to try to free the hostages being held at the U.S. Embassy in Iran since November 1979, Jimmy Carter engaged in minimal consultation with a single member of Congress, Senate majority leader Robert Byrd (D-WV). Like Ford, Carter submitted an after-the-fact report to Congress that invoked his authority as commander in chief.

In identical letters addressed to the Speaker of the House and president pro tem of the Senate, Ronald Reagan reported on September 29, 1982, that he had dispatched marines to Lebanon to participate in the multinational force requested by the government of Lebanon to restore "Lebanese sovereignty and authority, and thereby further the efforts of the Government of Lebanon to assure the safety of persons in the area and bring to an end the violence which has tragically occurred." He explained that the report was the by-product of his "desire that the Congress be fully informed on this matter" and noted that the report was "consistent with the War Powers Resolution." Consistent with the rationale offered by Ford and Carter before him, he asserted that "[t]his deployment of the United States Armed Forces is being undertaken pursuant to the President's constitutional authority with respect to the conduct of foreign relations and as Commander-in-Chief of the United States Armed Forces."[89]

Reagan used the same justification in his report to Congress on the U.S. deployment of troops to Grenada in 1983. This report offered the first example of the rhetorical use of export of terror as a justification for military action. Grenada was, said Reagan, "a Soviet-Cuban colony, being readied as a major military bastion to export terror and undermine democracy."[90]

The first invocation of "imminent danger" as a justification for military intervention occurred in 1989, when George H. W. Bush used it as one of three arguments for the use of 24,000 U.S. troops to remove General Manuel Noriega from power in Panama. The other justifications were restoring the legitimately elected government of Panama and bringing Noriega to justice after his indictment by a Florida grand jury for drug distribution.[91]

Although he said that he did not need it, George H. W. Bush sought and received congressional authorization to launch the Gulf War. As he signed the congressional resolution, however, he made a signing statement (see chapter 8 on the de facto item veto) that redefined its import: "As I made clear to congressional leaders at the outset, my request for congressional support did not, and my signing this resolution does not, constitute any change in the long-standing positions of the executive branch on either the President's constitutional authority to use the Armed Forces to defend vital U.S. interests or the constitutionality of the War Powers Resolution."[92] George W. Bush used nearly identical language on signing into law a congressional resolution authorizing the use of U.S. armed forces against Iraq on October 16, 2002.[93]

Bill Clinton, like many of his predecessors, did not secure congressional consent before bombing Baghdad in 1993 in retaliation after learning of a plan to assassinate former president George H. W. Bush, or for his use of force in Somalia, Haiti, or Bosnia.

Once invested as commander in chief, the president cannot abandon that role casually. In a joint press conference on May 26, 2006, with Prime Minister Tony Blair of Great Britain, George W. Bush said that "he regretted some personal mistakes, like declaring 'bring 'em on.'" He also mentioned his declaration that he wanted Osama bin Laden "dead or alive." "Bush termed his words 'kind of tough talk, you know, that sent the wrong signal to people.' He added that 'I learned some lessons about expressing myself maybe in a little more sophisticated manner' and that 'in certain parts of the world it was misinterpreted.'"[94] The problems Bush identified were moments in which he stepped out of the role of commander in chief and assumed the role of a Texas sheriff.

STRATEGIC MISREPRESENTATION

The final characteristic of war rhetoric is strategic misrepresentation, which plays an unusually significant role in this genre.[95] To put that claim in perspective, we readily acknowledge that no rhetorical act can reveal the whole truth; even highly informative discourse addressed to experts can reflect the "reality" it seeks to encompass only selectively, obscuring, at least through emphasis, some elements of whatever is being discussed.[96] Presidential war rhetoric, however, evinces an unusual tendency to misrepresent the events described therein in ways strategically related to the president's desire to stifle dissent and unify the nation for immediate and sustained action. That tendency, we believe, has little to do with presidential character, but rather reflects the unusual rhetorical situation in which presidents find themselves in this discourse.

Because the president assumes extraordinary, even near-dictatorial, powers in assuming the office of commander in chief, and because war rhetoric seeks unanimity of conviction and action, the temptation to misrepresent events is heightened. In effect, presidents seek a degree of support that, except as a response to invasion, is virtually impossible in a democracy, but one that is vital to legitimizing their extraordinary powers as commander in chief. Any form of protest calls into question these unusual presidential prerogatives. Accordingly, presidents are inclined to preempt dissent through misrepresentation—for example, by transforming the dramatic narrative justifying the use of force into melodrama. The thoughtful consideration on which war rhetoric is based entails the careful weighing of evidence and the examination of competing claims and alternatives, a process that is unlikely to generate the unanimity of response that presidents desire. Thus, war rhetoric joins the claim that such deliberation has occurred and is occurring with misrepresentation that, in effect, undercuts fully reasoned deliberations. Presidents' unique access to data from diplomatic sources and intelligence services allows them to misrepresent events in ways that will facilitate a unified response.

The potential for misrepresentation has its origins in the president's power to determine when defensive action is required. In 1827, the Supreme Court interpreted the president's constitutional powers to mean that the authority to decide whether defensive military action is required

> belongs exclusively to the President, and that his decision is conclusive upon all other persons. We think that this construction necessarily results from the nature of the power itself. . . . The power itself is to be exercised upon sudden emergencies, upon great occasions of state, and under circumstances which may be vital to the existence of the Union.[97]

Of more importance, only the president has access to the information that makes it possible to determine whether circumstances warrant the use of armed forces, and only the president can speak authoritatively with a single voice to characterize those circumstances as a threat to basic national and human values. By selecting the information they will make available to Congress, presidents exercise a powerful rhetorical function. In his 1921 study of executive war powers, Clarence Berndahl concluded that a president may withhold certain information, the disclosure of which would vitally affect the action of Congress. He may, if he is desirous of war, reveal only such information as will tend to inflame congressional opinion, or he may select a moment for his disclosures and recommendations when opinion is excited and ready to hear the worst.[98]

The potential for rhetorical and factual abuse in this discourse was appreciated early on. James Madison was aware of the extraordinary executive control of information and the intense emotional reaction to situations of conflict:

> The management of foreign relations appears to be the most susceptible of abuse of all the trusts committed to a Government, because they can be concealed or disclosed, or disclosed in such parts and at such times as will best suit particular views; and because the body of the people are less capable of judging, and are more under the influence of prejudices, on that branch of their affairs, than of any other.[99]

Indeed, early in the nation's history, Jefferson and Madison charged that in order to arouse the war temper of Congress and of the country, John Adams had selectively disclosed facts in his speech of May 16, 1797, to suggest that France was the republic's only enemy of significance.[100]

Similar charges have been made throughout the nation's history. Samuel Eliot Morison, for example, claims that "the most unpopular war that this country has ever waged, not even excepting the Vietnam conflict, was our second war with Great Britain. The declaration on June 18, 1812, passed by only 79 to 49 in the House, and 19 to 13 in the Senate." Indeed, Madison's defense of the war on the basis of "'Free Trade and Sailors' Rights' seemed mere hokum to Federalists and to the ship-owning community generally; they were making big money in neutral trade, and the number of impressments of native-born American seamen was small."[101] Federalist dissent was intense and unremitting, and was finally quelled only by Andrew Jackson's fortunate victory in 1815 at New Orleans.

Despite strong support for action to fulfill the United States' "manifest destiny," Polk felt compelled to create an incident that would justify war with Mexico in order to acquire the land he desired. In the rhetoric leading to the war, he deliberately misrepresented events so as to paint the Mexicans as the aggressors. Further attempts to prevent dissent are illustrated by the maneuvers of Polk's supporters to railroad passage of a declaration of war against Mexico through Congress. Their methods, as well as the conditions that prevented dissenters from being more effective, are described by historian Frederick Merk.[102] Noting the ways in which manipulation of facts suppressed dissent, he cites a statement by John C. Calhoun to the effect that "not 10 percent of Congress would have voted the war bill if time had been given to examine the documents [accompanying Polk's message]."[103] Later, when all the facts became known, the House of Representatives, including Abraham Lincoln, voted to censure Polk in a statement that called the war "unnecessary and unconstitutionally begun by the President of the United States."[104]

Although an official investigation could not determine who had been responsible for the sinking of the U.S.S. *Maine*, William McKinley obtained a declaration of war by fanning popular resentment against Spain. Historian Frank Freidel describes the failure of dissenters to prevent or end U.S. military action against Filipinos fighting for independence following the Spanish-American War, but also notes their accomplishments, in large part a result of their dissemination of information about the horrors committed by U.S. troops while suppressing the Philippine Insurrection: "In the end they brought about a considerable degree of national revulsion, and in consequence an end to this sort of imperialist venture."[105]

In addition to recounting attacks on U.S. shipping by U-boats, Woodrow Wilson in 1917 used the fabricated Zimmerman letter to imply a German threat to U.S. sovereignty. In his speech requesting a congressional declaration of war, he said, "That it [the German government] means to stir up enemies against us at our very doors the intercepted note to the German Minister at Mexico City is eloquent evidence."[106] Before that speech, Wilson had used Germany's policy of unrestricted submarine warfare to invoke a statute, which he claimed legitimized armed neutrality, to arm and authorize American merchantmen to fire on sight.[107] Congressional authorization was not requested.

Before the U.S. entry into World War II, Franklin Roosevelt acted to circumvent congressional actions limiting his military powers. When the isolationist Congress resisted the president's initiatives, Roosevelt's efforts to aid Great Britain took the form of executive actions that thwarted the expressed intent of the 1940 Neutrality Act. Opposing Roosevelt's efforts to embargo arms to the aggressor nations while providing them to their victims, Congress embargoed arms to all belligerents. The Lend-Lease program came into being through an executive agreement under which the United States transferred fifty old but recently refitted destroyers to Britain in exchange for bases in the Atlantic and Caribbean.

A specific case from this period illustrates the kinds of misrepresentations that are typical of presidential war rhetoric. On September 11, 1941, in a radio speech to the nation, Roosevelt described an incident in which a German U-boat had fired torpedoes at the destroyer U.S.S. *Greer.* Claiming that the Germans had committed an act of piracy, Roosevelt linked his response to Jefferson's actions against the Barbary pirates 150 years earlier. In his narrative, Roosevelt failed to point out that for more than three hours the *Greer* had been broadcasting the U-boat's position to an attacking British plane. The British plane dropped depth charges; the submarine fired two torpedoes; the destroyer dodged, returning fire.[108] Historian Merlo Pusey comments that "the story of the *Greer* was the closest [Roosevelt] could come to a blood-stirring atrocity, and he made the most of it, distorting the facts so as to lend justification to what he was doing."[109]

With U.S. troops massing in the Persian Gulf in the fall of 1990, the nation was on the brink of an undeclared war with Iraq over its invasion of Kuwait. George H. W. Bush's administration not only needed to provide a principled justification for action, but also to demonize Saddam Hussein and the Iraqi military. To that end, Bush focused public attention on a compelling narrative, although it was a story based on fabrications.

On October 10, 1990, a fifteen-year-old using the assumed name "Nayirah" appeared before the Congressional Human Rights Caucus. "I just came out of Kuwait," she said.

> "While I was there, I saw the Iraqi soldiers come into the hospital with guns. They took the babies out of the incubators, took the incubators, and left the children to die on the cold floor." After her testimony, Representative John Porter [R-IL] said, "We've had scores of hearings about human rights abuses throughout the world ... we have never heard in all this time, in all circumstances, a record of inhumanity and brutality and sadism as the ones that the witnesses have given us today.... [A]ll countries of the world ... must join together and take whatever action may be necessary to free the people of Kuwait."[110]

Although Bush initially indicated some doubt about the accuracy of this story, commenting that it had not been authenticated, on October 28, while rallying troops en route to Iraq, he said that twenty-two babies had died and that "the hospital employees were shot and the plundered machines were shipped off to Baghdad."[111] The story became a staple of the drive to mobilize public support for the impending war. In a speech at Mashpee, Massachusetts, on November 1, for example, Bush said of Saddam Hussein and his troops,

> They've tried to silence Kuwaiti dissent and courage with firing squads, much as Hitler did when he invaded Poland. They have committed outrageous acts of barbarism. In one hospital, they pulled twenty-two premature babies from their incubators, sent the machines to Baghdad, and all those little ones died.[112]

The story, which Bush repeated in subsequent speeches and interviews, legitimized the comparison of Saddam Hussein and Hitler and refuted charges that the conflict was actually about U.S. dependence on Middle Eastern oil. What went unnoticed was a fact uncovered by *Harper's* publisher John R. MacArthur long after the war was over: that "Nayirah" was the Kuwaiti ambassador's daughter and a member of the royal family of Kuwait.[113] Subsequently, Amnesty International concluded that no babies had been removed from incubators. The president's assertion, "This aggression is not going to stand," was built in part on a deception about babies and incubators. Bush used the heartrending story to reframe the conflict as a moral one in which no compromise was possible, in which the U.S. military action was a battle against evil.[114] In addition to reframing the conflict, the story became a powerful engine to mobilize public support for the war.

A cover story in *Time* on July 21, 2003, explored the process by which a similar line of argument became part of George W. Bush's State of the Union address of January 28, 2003. In that address, Bush stated, "The British government has learned that Saddam Hussein recently sought significant quantities of uranium in Africa." That claim was part of the justification for military action based on Iraq's possession of weapons of mass destruction. According to the article, "Last week the White House finally admitted that Bush should have jettisoned the claim." The authors added, however, that "the controversy over those 16 words would not have erupted with such force were they not emblematic of larger concerns about Bush's reasoning for going to war in the first place."[115] A related sidebar looked like this:

WHAT ELSE MAY HAVE BEEN WRONG?
The White House has admitted the Niger allegation should never have made it into the State of the Union, but other key charges from Bush's address remain unproved.

WHAT HE SAID

"We know that Iraq in the late 1990s had several mobile biological weapons labs. These are designed to produce germ warfare agents."

WHAT WE NOW KNOW

U.S. forces found two trailers that could be bioweapons labs but no trace of pathogens. The CIA claims they're labs, but some State Department intelligence analysts disagree.

WHAT HE SAID

"Our intelligence sources tell us that he has attempted to purchase high-strength aluminum tubes suitable for nuclear weapons production."

WHAT WE NOW KNOW

In May an Iraqi scientist led U.S. troops to centrifuge blueprints that he buried in his rose garden in 1991. But no evidence of a recent nuclear program has been found.

WHAT HE SAID

"Evidence from intelligence sources, secret communications and statements by people now in custody reveal that Saddam Hussein aids and protects terrorists, including members of al Qaeda."

WHAT WE NOW KNOW

U.S. and Kurdish forces in northern Iraq destroyed camps belonging to Ansar al-Islam, linked to al-Qaeda, but found no proof of the ties to Saddam that Bush alleged. Al-Qaeda deputy Abu Musab Zarqawi, who sought medical attention in Baghdad, is still at large.

Once again, the need to mobilize the nation and to gain broad public support for military action produced strategic deceptions.

Because presidents are ultimately in charge of the intelligence-gathering capacity of the federal government, and because as commander in chief, the president leads the generals who run the war, the president ordinarily has access to information that is not readily available to those who would challenge his claims about what is happening in the war zone. When members of Congress gain information directly from the military in the field, they increase their standing to challenge the president because they are now doing so with what is ordinarily a privileged source of information. So, for example, when Rep. John Murtha (D-PA), the senior Democrat on the House Defense Appropriations Subcommittee and chair of the committee when the Democrats controlled Congress, gave a floor speech on the war in Iraq on November 17, 2005, the speech exploded into the national media, in part because this hawkish former marine, known as a champion of the military, was calling for withdrawal from Iraq within six months. Of special note was the kind of insider, on-the-ground information in the speech. "The speech was filled with devastating information," wrote investigative journalist Seymour Hersh. "For example, Murtha reported that the number of attacks in Iraq has increased from a hundred and fifty a week to more than seven hundred a week in the past year. He said that an estimated fifty thousand American soldiers will suffer 'from what I call battle fatigue' in the war, and he said that the Americans were seen as 'the common enemy' in Iraq."[116]

As these examples illustrate, because they claim extraordinary powers as commanders in chief, presidents seek an extraordinary mandate. In the absence of invasion, they are strongly tempted to circumvent congressional interference and to silence or preempt dissent by misrepresenting the situation on the basis of information to which only they are privy, so that it appears that an attack, or its equivalent, has occurred. Such a characterization not only stifles dissent, but also warrants immediate and unilateral action by the president.

Thus, in presidential war rhetoric, presidents attempt to prove that military action is or was the only appropriate response to a clear, unavoidable, and fundamental threat. Although the events that precipitate intervention are concrete and time-bound, the values being defended are timeless and enduring. Its tone is exhortative, calling on Congress and the citizenry to put aside dissent and unite in committing themselves to protect these fundamental values. It is a rhetoric of immediacy, calling for action now. At its center is a narrative detailing the events that constitute the threat and showing that military intervention has become a last resort. In such rhetoric, presidents ask the audience—Congress and the public—to empower them to act as commander in chief, leading a battle to preserve the nation and civilization itself. Because they seek a unanimity of commitment and action that is unlikely short of an invasion, and because they seek approval for the assumption of powers so great that they conflict with the principles of democratic government, presidents frequently succumb to the temptation to misrepresent events in ways that will stifle dissent and arouse the "war temper" of Congress and the public.

As we have shown, the characteristics of war rhetoric that we have described can be found in presidential discourse justifying military intervention throughout U.S. history. In concluding this argument, we analyze an example of modern presidential war rhetoric in order to demonstrate how the characteristics apparent from the beginning have persisted into the present.

The commitments that eventuated in U.S. military intervention in Vietnam began under Harry Truman and continued under Dwight Eisenhower. John F. Kennedy introduced the first U.S. military personnel, but substantial, direct military involvement began under Lyndon Johnson. In a speech to the American people on radio and television on August 4, 1964, Johnson described two attacks on the U.S.S. *Maddox* in the Gulf of Tonkin, justified the retaliatory air strikes he had ordered against North Vietnam, and requested a congressional resolution empowering him to deploy further U.S. military might in Southeast Asia. This speech illustrates clearly that, despite a shift in its timing and an increase in the grounds available to justify independent military initiatives by the executive, presidential war rhetoric remains fundamentally unchanged.[117]

At the outset of the speech, Johnson grounded his right to order military action in the executive powers implicit in national sovereignty. He acted and spoke as "President and Commander in Chief," fulfilling his "duty to the American people" to "report ... renewed hostile actions against the United States" that "required" him "to order the military forces of the United States to take action in reply." He said that he had acted in self-defense when "*renewed* hostile actions" [emphasis added] left him no choice but to respond with force. A narrative followed. Johnson related the story of an August 2 attack on the *Maddox*, "the initial act of aggression," followed by another attack two days later. The retaliation he had ordered had resulted in the sinking of two of the attacking boats, with no loss of U.S. lives.[118] He framed these incidents as the culmination of a series of hostile actions, described as "repeated acts of violence against the Armed Forces of the United States," which, in turn, he placed in a larger context: "Aggression by terror against the peaceful villagers of South Viet Nam has now been joined by open aggression on the high seas against the United States of America" (927). He linked the conflict to larger values, "the struggle for peace and security in southeast Asia" and "support of freedom" (927).

Johnson's speech is a paradigmatic example of rhetoric establishing legitimacy for the assumption of extraordinary military powers. Johnson spoke as president and commander in chief, claiming from the outset the executive powers that some court opinions argue are implicit in national sovereignty.[119] As he developed the narrative, he claimed to have done what was "required" by his constitutional duty to defend the nation. All of his actions were in self-defense, taken in response to aggression. Moreover, that aggression was a threat not just to the nation, but also to fundamental values of freedom and peace.

Following the narrative that established the need for forceful response to a threat, Johnson shifted his justification for action from the inherent powers of the executive to democratic and constitutional grounds by claiming bipartisan support. Johnson related that he had "today met with the leaders of both parties in the Congress of the United States and . . . I shall immediately request Congress to pass a resolution making it clear that our government is united in its determination." (927). He strengthened that argument by noting that Senator Barry Goldwater (R-AZ), the Republican presidential nominee, who would be his opponent in the fall election, had "expressed his support" (928). Finally, Johnson reaffirmed that his decision was the result of thoughtful consideration. He reassured his audience by indicating that it was "a solemn responsibility to have to order even limited military action" (928).

Johnson's speech rehearsed the constitutional formula, based on inherent executive powers and on a narrative establishing that a malign enemy has attacked, threatening basic values and compelling the president to assume the role of commander in chief and respond with force. Assumption of such extraordinary, near-dictatorial powers compelled the president to defer to democratic bases for legitimacy, in the form of bipartisan congressional support. In addition, because the support needed to justify these extraordinary powers would have been difficult to obtain were all the facts known, Johnson strategically misrepresented what had occurred in the Gulf of Tonkin, so a complex international incident, involving repeated provocations of the North Vietnamese by the United States, became a simple case of repeated aggression against the United States,[120] a characterization whose accuracy was apparently validated by bipartisan support. Writing many years after the event, Senator Thomas Eagleton took note of what he called "speculation that the attacks were not accurately reported by the administration," but commented, "In August 1964, Congress had no alternative but to believe the truth of the administration's report of Tonkin Gulf hostilities and to base its action on that report."[121]

As this example illustrates, modern presidents continue to observe the constitutional forms legitimating presidential assumption of the extraordinary powers of the commander in chief, but those forms are used to justify prior, unilateral presidential action through a narrative based on sources of information to which only the president is privy.

CONCLUSION

The constitutional provisions separating the war powers imply a co-operative rhetorical process in which presidents request and recommend and Congress authorizes. The process itself implies a rhetoric of thoughtful consideration, demonstrating that the decision to use force is a last resort, compelled by the seriousness of the threat posed by the acts of a malign adversary. When the original formula is followed, presidents ordinarily set forth the evidence and arguments for that conclusion in a detailed narrative, requesting congressional action empowering them to wage war and exhorting the nation to mobilize. In a formal and solemn document authorizing military action, Congress empowers the president to act as commander in chief.

Despite major advances in death-dealing weaponry and in the speed of communications, the essential elements of presidential war rhetoric persist because its functions—demonstrating that military decisions have been made rationally and seeking approval of the assumption of the office of commander in chief—have not changed. The basic form of presidential war rhetoric has remained relatively unchanged precisely because, as we have shown, it is easily adapted to the needs of modern presidents. The original formula is well suited to recasting of the events leading to military intervention as aggressive acts by an implacable enemy such that presidential initiatives appear to be an exercise of the constitutional obligation to defend the nation. The narratives characteristic of earlier rhetorical efforts are also easily adapted to simplify and dramatize events in ways that capitalize on the executive's privileged access to information while stifling dissent and enlisting the strongest possible support. Strategic misrepresentations permeate past and present presidential war rhetoric precisely because, apart from the unanimity created by an invasion, no set of circumstances can ensure congressional and public assent to sending men and women to their deaths or to the assumption of near-dictatorial powers by the president in a democracy.

As noted, two shifts in presidential war rhetoric have occurred through time. Previous exercise of presidential war powers, followed by congressional acquiescence and judicial ratification, has enlarged the warrants available to justify unilateral executive initiatives. These precedents have also altered the timing of presidential war rhetoric; this discourse increasingly seeks after-the-fact ratification for military actions already undertaken rather than authorization for future intervention. As our analysis shows, however, changes in the warrants available and in the timing of presidential war rhetoric have not exceeded the capacity of this genre to justify the executive use of force and to empower the president to assume the office of commander in chief.

Like inaugurals, State of the Union addresses, and veto messages, war rhetoric is constitutive both of the institution of the presidency and of individual presidencies; like veto messages, it is constitutive of our system of government; and more than any other rhetorical genre, this form displays the power struggles inherent in a system of checks and balances. War rhetoric also illustrates the evolving powers of the presidency and demonstrates that such evolution frequently occurs with the cooperation of the other branches of government—in this instance, through Congress's delegation of its war powers and Supreme Court sanction of such delegation. Presidential war rhetoric also reveals that the role of commander in chief, given its extraordinary powers and the need they engender for unanimity, are a continuing threat to the nation's democratic principles.

TEN

Presidential Rhetoric of Self-Defense

In this chapter and the next, we discuss the rhetoric of presidential self-defense and impeachment. Other chapters in this book treat State of the Union addresses and veto messages, genres that highlight rhetorical relationships among the branches of government. Interbranch relationships are pivotal to understanding the symbolic functions those genres perform, the lines of argument selected, and the success or failure of these rhetorical efforts. In the case of impeachment rhetoric and rhetoric intended to forestall impeachment, these relationships are even more important.

The rhetoric of State of the Union addresses and veto messages differs significantly from the rhetoric of inaugural addresses, national eulogies, and farewell addresses. Inaugurals and farewells are like monologues in the sense that no specific action is asked of the audience; instead, these addresses evoke contemplation. Those addressed are the people, a group so massive and diverse that unified action in any ordinary sense is impossible. Moreover, inaugurals, national eulogies, and farewells constitute the audience as the people, and the unity of consciousness and the sense of national identity created are among their primary functions.

Conversely, State of the Union addresses and veto messages are part of a dialogue or debate between the executive and legislative branches. In most instances, such discourse is a response to prior rhetoric and demands a specific rejoinder. Members of Congress are expected to introduce the legislation called for in a president's first annual message; subsequent annual messages are part of a dialogue to determine an appropriate legislative program for the times and circumstances. A presidential veto message is a response to the enactment of legislation by Congress and fulfills the constitutional requirement that the president's objections be made explicit. Congress must respond by overriding the veto, or the legislation dies.

In the State of the Union address, the president addresses Congress as a constitutional equal. The members of Congress, like the president, are elected representatives who have taken an oath of office, and they are empowered to act on the president's proposed legislative program. Through time, the legislative initiative has come to devolve primarily on the president, who has the advantage of being able to speak as an individual, whereas Congress, lacking party discipline, finds it difficult to unite sufficiently to initiate policy. In veto messages, the president responds to a majority vote of Congress. If Congress is to win the debate that has been joined, it must reach a new level of agreement; regional, ideological, even party differences must be transcended if the two houses are to override the veto.

In this and the following chapter, we discuss the rhetorical advantage that presidents have in interbranch and public discourse, an issue we believe to be essential if one is to understand the rhetorical and, hence, the political power presidents wield. Whatever their constitutional status, the three branches of government are not equal rhetorically. Once invested in office, presidents ordinarily are at a significant rhetorical advantage because they speak with a single voice, whereas Congress and the Supreme Court rarely do. Dissenting opinions are a routine part of most Supreme Court decisions. Congressional action follows debate that includes conflicting views of legislative intent, and, as a practical matter, legislation must speak for itself to the courts and to those who must implement its provisions.[1] Presidents can speak whenever, wherever, and on whatever topic they choose, whereas Congress and the Court cannot speak without following established procedures and securing a majority vote of their members. For these reasons, among others, the constitutionally coequal branches of government are not rhetorical peers.

The significance of this rhetorical inequality is most sharply illustrated in presidential rhetoric responding to charges of misconduct. There is an enormous difference between the rhetorical status of presidents so charged, but not yet formally accused, and that of presidents against whom formal charges have been brought in impeachment proceedings. Further, two strikingly different defenses, one personal, the other presidential, are available to a president depending on the nature of the accusations made. Until Congress is able to formulate accusations of potentially impeachable offenses or to initiate formal impeachment proceedings, presidents are usually in a rhetorically superior position from which they can act to forestall the emergence of a formal congressional action moving toward impeachment.

Once formal impeachment proceedings have begun, however, that relationship shifts dramatically. The president then confronts as accuser a constitutionally designated coequal branch of government. The president no longer controls the terms of the debate, but must respond to specific charges. Moreover, because of the nature of the charges, one important option, the personal apologia described below, ordinarily is foreclosed, thus diminishing the persuasive powers of the president. Once impeachment proceedings begin, there is an immediate jury—a House committee, the House as a whole, or the Senate—that judges the charges and reaches a verdict, while the citizenry watches and judges the proceedings.[2] Finally, the president's usual absence from these rhetorical settings reduces the opportunity to use the symbolic power of the presidency in self-defense. The presidential rhetoric of self-defense prior to impeachment is the subject of this chapter; the rhetoric of presidents so charged, that of the next.[3]

Although few presidents have escaped charges of misconduct or corruption,[4] there have been seven instances in which some sort of formal charge of violating the oath of office has elicited a rhetorical response. Presidents Andrew Jackson, John Tyler, and James Buchanan responded to formal actions by Congress, such as a committee report or a censure resolution; presidents Andrew Johnson, Richard Nixon, and Bill Clinton responded to formal impeachment proceedings. Abraham Lincoln's statement of self-defense, by contrast, was made in response to resolutions passed by a convention of New York Democrats who condemned him for suspending habeas corpus and for placing the antiwar agitator Clement L. Vallandigham under military arrest.[5] In this chapter, we examine those presidential responses in some detail and contrast them with another instance of presidential self-defense, Ronald Reagan's speech of March 4, 1987. Although no formal charges had been leveled against Reagan, we have included an analysis of his speech here because it illustrates a particular strategy, the personal apologia, that is available as a form of presidential self-defense under only some circumstances.[6] By its very existence, Reagan's speech responding to the conclusions of the Tower Commission, a group appointed by Reagan himself to investigate the Iran-Contra affair, indicates the importance of the commission's report. In this chapter, then, we look at the responses presidents have made to formal charges of violating the oath of office, short of impeachment, whether by Congress or a citizens' group; a speech by Reagan that clearly illustrates the personal apologia as a strategy of presidential self-defense; and two brief statements by Clinton prior to formal impeachment proceedings against him.

THE PERSONAL APOLOGIA

There are two kinds of defenses a president can offer to charges of misconduct: a forensic response or a personal apologia. The personal apologia is a strategic response to an accusation. An effective apologia is a single, unified response to a series of charges that shifts the focus from the accuser(s) to the defender and presents the character of the accused in ways that are appealing to the audience. When this type of address is delivered by a president, it suggests that the charges, if proved, would not constitute impeachable offenses and that they do not call executive leadership into question.

The substance of some apologias is autobiographical material that makes the original charges appear implausible or irrelevant.[7] Famous examples of this strategy include Cardinal Newman's Apologia pro Vita Sua,[8] Socrates' responses to Miletus in Plato's "Apology," and Richard Nixon's response to charges of a secret campaign fund in the so-called Checkers speech in 1952, the most famous and successful personal apologia in U.S. political history.

When evidence for the argument it contains is drawn from the intimate details of the rhetor's life, the apologia is a peculiarly personal rhetorical document. This particular form of self-defense both opens rhetorical possibilities and imposes limitations on a president who chooses to exercise it. The audience, as citizens, knows that the president is a fallible human being. Consequently, personal peccadilloes as such are not treated as impeachable offenses, although they may create a climate more conducive to impeachment, as occurred in the case of Andrew Johnson. Lies about personal improprieties, however, may lay the foundation for impeachment proceedings, as occurred in Clinton's case. On the other hand, instances of presidential misconduct—that is, violations of the oath of office—are not likely to be transcended by the kind of defense that is the core of the personal apologia. As Lincoln argued in the case analyzed below, the attack of the New York Democrats was not on him as a person, but on actions he had taken in his role as president. A personal attack might have been ignored; an attack on the presidency had to be defended on constitutional grounds.

A similar distinction was made by Truman in his reply to a congressional subpoena issued on November 13, 1953, after he had left office. In refusing to honor the subpoena, Truman quoted constitutional authorities and his predecessors to assert executive privilege and concluded,

> It must be obvious to you that if the doctrine of separation of powers and the independence of the Presidency is to have any validity at all, it must be equally applicable to a President after his term of office has expired when he is sought to be examined with respect to any acts occurring while he is President.[9]

He continued to draw a sharp distinction between his presidential and his personal roles: "If your intention, however, is to inquire into any acts as a private individual either before or after my Presidency and unrelated to any acts as President, I shall be happy to appear."[10]

Ronald Reagan's speech of March 4, 1987, responding to the Tower Commission report on the Iran-Contra affair, is an instance of a successful personal apologia by a president. The Tower Commission report contained a series of accusations against the president, suggesting mismanagement of his subordinates such that foreign policy initiatives were carried out in undesirable, potentially illegal ways, contrary to laws and policies enacted by Congress. Whether the charges made in the report might become the bases for articles of impeachment lay in the future, at issue in the Iran-Contra hearings being held by a joint congressional committee during the summer of 1987. As a result, in March 1987, Reagan was responding to charges of mismanagement, but he was not yet in a situation that threatened him with removal; consequently, the personal apologia was an option available to him.

A personal apologia admits that the charges made warrant a response. In some instances, there is an admission of error—for example, there was an appearance of evil, mistakes were made, subordinates acted improperly—but the errors are blamed on qualities of character that are presented as admirable. Reagan's speech followed this pattern. He admitted that errors had occurred: "I've studied the board's report. Its findings are honest, convincing, and highly critical, and I accept them."[11] Speaking of the policy of trading arms to Iran for hostages in Lebanon, he said, "It was a mistake" (220). However, Reagan never suggested that he, as the president, had committed errors, and he remained in his presidential role only to a limited extent, saying, "I take full responsibility for my own actions and for those of my administration.... It happened on my watch" (220). Later, he added, "I didn't know about any diversion of funds to the contras. But as President, I cannot escape responsibility" (221).

The crux of Reagan's response was a presentation of his own character. He defended his delay in speaking to the U.S. public by saying that he was waiting for the complete story, a defense that suggested that he was ignorant of what had been going on, a recurring theme in the speech. That defense was supported by an appeal to his character: "I'm often accused of being an optimist, and it's true I had to hunt pretty hard to find good news in the board's report, . . . but I was very relieved to read this sentence, '. . . the board is convinced that the president does indeed want the full story to be told'" (220). Listeners were told about the president's feelings: "As angry as I may be about activities undertaken without my knowledge. . . . And as personally distasteful as I find secret bank accounts. . . . My heart and my best intentions still tell me . . . ," and, of most importance, "I let my personal concern for the hostages spill over into the geopolitical strategy of reaching out to Iran" (220).

Finally, at the end of the speech, listeners were offered a moral lesson, directly related to Reagan's character:

> Now what should happen when you make a mistake is this: You take your knocks, you learn your lessons, and then you move on. That's the healthiest way to deal with a problem. . . . You know, by the time you reach my age, you've made plenty of mistakes if you've lived your life properly. So you learn. You put things in perspective. You pull your energies together. You change. You go forward. (222)

These last statements were canny choices in a personal apologia, simultaneously revealing Reagan's character and rehearsing for the audience the way it should respond to the speech. These comments may not be eloquent pleas, they may not ring through the ages as rhetorical master touches, but, coupled with Reagan's personal popularity, they were persuasive. They presented Reagan as a man who acted and, hence, erred; as a man who learned from his errors; as a man who was mentally healthy; and as a man who was not destroyed by facing evidence of his own fallibility. Listeners also discovered, or rediscovered, what would be appropriate behavior on their part: to learn the lesson and move on, to put the president's mistakes in perspective (and proceed with the business of the country, not congressional investigations), to change, and to move forward. These comments also framed the audience's interpretation of what Reagan did in the speech, suggesting that he had admitted mistakes (he had not), learned from them, and was acting decisively to change the situation, in ways detailed in the second half of the speech.

Reagan's speech did not respond to charges that might have led to impeachment. He skirted such issues by saying of the transfer of funds to the Nicaraguan Contras, "The Tower board was not able to find out what happened to this money, so the facts here will be left to the continuing investigations of the court-appointed independent counsel and the two congressional investigating committees.... As I told the Tower board, I didn't know about any diversion of funds to the contras" (221).[12] Because his legal situation was ambiguous, and because many details of the affair were not known, Reagan had the rhetorical option of the personal apologia available to him. That option is not ordinarily available to presidents charged with violations of their oath of office. As Reagan framed the issue, he had been charged with poor foreign policy and a poor management style. These he explained in terms of admirable qualities of character that were fully intelligible to listeners. But anger, distaste, disappointment, "heart," and personal concern for individuals are not adequate responses to charges that the president has failed "to preserve, protect, and defend the Constitution" or "to see that the laws are faithfully executed."[13] That is why Richard Nixon could successfully employ the personal apologia as a vice presidential candidate in 1952, but could not use it when charged with impeachable offenses related to the Watergate scandal.

FORENSIC RESPONSES

In contrast to Reagan, Richard Nixon attempted to forestall impeachment in 1973 and 1974 by denying that any misconduct had occurred and, as evidence of misconduct emerged, by ascribing it to others. Whereas Reagan cast himself as a spectator waiting for the results of the Tower Commission report and the congressional investigations, Nixon cast himself as an investigator who first delegated to White House Counsel John Dean the task of finding out what had actually occurred and who then disclosed those findings in all appropriate ways.[14] Throughout this process, however, Nixon was mindful, he said, of protecting the prerogatives of the presidency. Protecting the presidency, he argued, required that he not disclose certain information that others considered germane to their investigations. His posture of proclaimed innocence and his repeated attempts to suggest his willingness to get to the bottom of the issue are evidence that the strategy Nixon adopted for himself was not the personal apologia, but rather the standard forensic defenses we have come to recognize because of our exposure to them in courts of law.

When a president has been formally charged with misconduct, the rhetorical picture changes. When the charges are ill-founded and largely political, as they were in the case of Andrew Johnson, a personal apologia may still be possible as part of an overall defense, but in the face of such serious charges, a forensic defense is also required. As noted in the next chapter, a kind of personal apologia is included in Dale Bumpers's defense of Bill Clinton, an option made possible by the personal character of the charges and the partisanship revealed in the process of voting on articles of impeachment.

Instances of presidential self-defense before formal impeachment proceedings reveal the arguments typically developed in such rhetoric. Such arguments are found in the case of Abraham Lincoln, who defended actions he had taken in wartime in response to accusations originating outside Congress, as well as in the responses of Jackson, Tyler, and Buchanan to charges brought by members of Congress.

Lincoln's statement of self-defense is significant not only because it was a response to the accusations of ordinary citizens, albeit gathered at a state Democratic convention—Lincoln used the resolutions passed at the convention as the occasion to respond to the general case against him—but also because it was a defense of extraordinary actions taken in wartime. Because of the special circumstances surrounding it, Lincoln's response is a test case for disclosing typical lines of argument that presidents use in defending themselves against charges of misconduct. In addition, this special case illustrates the importance of public opinion in the presidential rhetoric of self-defense.

Ordinarily, formal objections to the behavior of a president originate in Congress, but in this instance, charges of misconduct were brought in the form of resolutions passed by a convention of Democrats meeting in Albany, New York. The resolutions were sent to Lincoln in May of 1863; he responded to them in a letter dated almost a month later.[15] The charges involved the imprisonment of Clement L. Vallandigham of Ohio, who had lost his congressional seat in the 1862 elections and whose crime was making speeches exhorting soldiers to desert and urging others not to support the Union's military efforts. Lincoln had suspended the right to a writ of habeas corpus throughout the Union on September 24, 1862, an act that left Vallandigham without legal recourse when he was placed under military arrest.

The resolutions to which Lincoln responded included "a declaration of censure upon the administration for supposed unconstitutional action, such as making military arrests" (311). Like the congressional accusations to which other presidents responded, the declaration of censure challenged his conduct of the presidency. Lincoln explained that he would not have responded to the charges "if there were no apprehension that more injurious consequences than any merely personal to myself might follow" (312). In other words, he was responding in his role as president and in defense of his behavior in that role.

Lincoln's letter was a closely argued brief that addressed each of the charges made in the resolutions. In refutation of those charges, Lincoln argued that (1) his actions in suspending habeas corpus were constitutional; (2) his duties as commander in chief required that in Vallandigham's case, he act in a manner consistent with the actions he took toward deserters; and (3) his actions resembled those of Andrew Jackson after the battle of New Orleans. In addition, Lincoln reaffirmed his role as president of all the people by arguing that there was no partisanship involved in the arrest of the Democratic politician from Ohio, that he had been slow—some might argue too slow—to take such measures, and that the arrest, however justified it may have been, was painful to him.

Lincoln responded with great care to the charge that his actions were unconstitutional. The resolutions showed particular concern for constitutional protections for the citizen on trial for treason and argued, as Lincoln quoted, "'that these safeguards of the rights of the citizen against the pretensions of arbitrary power were intended more especially for his protection in times of civil commotion'" (312). In response, Lincoln argued,

> Ours is a case of rebellion—so called by the resolutions before me—in fact, a clear, flagrant, and gigantic case of rebellion and the provision of the Constitution that "the privilege of the writ of habeas corpus shall not be suspended unless when, in cases of rebellion or invasion, the public safety may require it," is the provision which specially applies to our present case. This provision plainly attests the understanding of those who made the Constitution that ordinary courts of justice are inadequate to "cases of rebellion"—attests their purpose that, in such cases, men may be held in custody whom the courts, acting on ordinary rules, would discharge. . . . its suspension is allowed by the Constitution on purpose that men may be arrested and held who cannot be proved to be guilty of a defined crime, "when in cases of rebellion or invasion, the public safety may require it." (316)

Similarly, he rejected the claim "that military arrests may be constitutional in localities where rebellion actually exists, but that such arrests are unconstitutional in localities where rebellion or insurrection does not actually exist." He responded, "Inasmuch, however, as the Constitution itself makes no such distinction, I am unable to believe that there is any such constitutional distinction" (318). He strengthened the claim of constitutionality through a pair of analogies:

> I can no more be persuaded that the government can constitutionally take no strong measures in time of rebellion, because it can be shown that the same could not be lawfully taken in time of peace, than I can be persuaded that a particular drug is not good medicine for a sick man because it can be shown to not be good for a well one. Nor am I able to appreciate the danger apprehended by the meeting, that the American people will by means of military arrests during the rebellion lose the right of public discussion, the liberty of speech and the press, the law of evidence, trial by jury, and habeas corpus throughout the indefinite peaceful future which I trust lies before them, any more than I am able to believe that a man could contract so strong an appetite for emetics during temporary illness as to persist in feeding upon them during the remainder of his healthful life. (320–21)

Lincoln's claim of constitutionality was also grounded in his view of his duty as commander in chief. He described the events that led to his action this way:

> Mr. Vallandigham avows his hostility to the war on the part of the Union; and his arrest was made because he was laboring, with some effect, to prevent the raising of troops, to encourage desertions from the army, and to leave the rebellion without an adequate military force to suppress it. . . . He was warring upon the military, and this gave the military constitutional jurisdiction to lay hands upon him. (319)

Because the resolutions claimed to "support the administration in every constitutional and lawful measure to suppress the rebellion" (311), Lincoln was able to use his accusers' agreement that the rebellion must be suppressed by military force as the basis for an impassioned comparison justifying his action in this case:

> Long experience has shown that armies cannot be maintained unless desertion shall be punished by the severe penalty of death. The case requires, and the law and the Constitution sanction, this punishment. Must I shoot a simpleminded

soldier boy who deserts, while I must not touch a hair of a wily agitator who induces him to desert? (319–20)

Another justification was drawn from the actions of Andrew Jackson after the battle of New Orleans—an intriguing comparison, given that Jackson became president only after the events described. As Lincoln told the story, after the peace treaty had been concluded following the battle, but before it was announced officially, a man published a newspaper article denouncing the martial law then in effect. Jackson arrested him. When a lawyer procured a writ of habeas corpus from a federal judge, Jackson arrested the lawyer and the judge. After the treaty was announced, the judge called General Jackson into court and fined him $1,000 for having arrested him and the others. Jackson paid the fine, but thirty years afterward, Congress refunded it, principal and interest. Lincoln commented,

It may be remarked—first, that we had the same Constitution then as now; secondly, that we then had a case of invasion, and now we have a case of rebellion; and, thirdly, that the permanent right of the people to public discussion, the liberty of speech and of the press, the trial by jury, the law of evidence, and the habeas corpus, suffered no detriment whatever by that conduct of General Jackson, or its subsequent approval by the American Congress. (323)

Lincoln used Jackson's actions and congressional approval as precedents justifying his own action. These arguments directly refuted the charges made in the resolutions, and they illustrate typical ways of defending the constitutionality of presidential actions.

Moreover, like other presidents charged with misconduct, Lincoln asserted that the actions of his accusers undermined the Constitution and threatened its survival. To do so, Lincoln recalled the conditions that existed when he became president:

The insurgents had been preparing for [rebellion] for more than thirty years, while the government had taken no steps to resist them.... [U]nder cover of "liberty of speech," "liberty of the press," and "habeas corpus," they hoped to keep on foot amongst us a most efficient corps of spies, informers, suppliers, and aiders and abettors of their cause in a thousand ways.... Or if, as has happened, the Executive should suspend the writ without ruinous waste of time, instances of arresting innocent persons might occur, as are always likely to occur in such cases; and then a clamor could be raised in regard to this, which might be at least of some service to the insurgent cause. It needed no very keen perception to discover this part of the enemy's programme, so soon as by open hostilities their machinery was fairly put in motion. (314–15)

The implication was clear: those who condemned the president for acting to save the Union in this emergency were aiding the cause of the Confederacy.

Although he made explicit efforts to praise the New York Democrats as patriots and to acknowledge the beliefs that he and they shared, Lincoln not only implied that his accusers were aiding the rebels, but also condemned their partisanship. Those who had passed the resolutions identified themselves as Democrats. Lincoln responded,

> He on whose discretionary judgment Mr. Vallandigham was arrested and tried is a Democrat, having no old party affinity with me, and the judge who rejected the constitutional view expressed in these resolutions, by refusing to discharge Mr. Vallandigham on habeas corpus is a Democrat of better days than these, having received his judicial mantle at the hands of President Jackson. And still more: of all those Democrats who are nobly exposing their lives and shedding their blood on the battle-field, I have learned that many approve the course taken with Mr. Vallandigham, while I have not heard of a single one condemning it. (321–22)

In other words, Democrats who were true patriots supported the president's actions and recognized them as part of his effort to preserve the Union.

Lincoln also demonstrated that he had been sensitive to the constitutional questions raised by his actions, saying, "I was slow to adopt the strong measures which by degrees I have been forced to regard as being within the exceptions of the Constitution, and as indispensable to the public safety" (315). His statement suggests an executive loath to use the extraordinary powers available to him in emergencies and concerned about the constitutional implications of his actions. Later in the letter, he pointed to a long list of men, including General John C. Breckinridge and General Robert E. Lee,

> now occupying the very highest places in the rebel war service, [who] were all within the power of the government since the rebellion began and were nearly as well known to be traitors then as now. Unquestionably if we had seized and held them, the insurgent cause would be much weaker. But no one of them had

then committed any crime defined in law. Every one of them, if arrested, would have been discharged on habeas corpus were the writ allowed to operate. In view of these and similar cases, I think the time not unlikely to come when I shall be blamed for having made too few arrests rather than too many. (317–18)

Lincoln had been slow to take the actions for which he was censured, so slow that his delay might be viewed as dereliction of duty. A fortiori, he would have been derelict had he not acted in the case of Vallandigham. Lincoln presented himself as a president who took no pleasure in testing the limits of executive power. From such an executive, the citizenry in a democracy had little to fear.[16]

Although it was generated under unusual circumstances, Lincoln's letter made the same basic arguments found in other presidential statements of self-defense. Whether questioned by a group of citizens, as Lincoln was, or formally upbraided or censured by Congress, presidents have responded with three basic lines of argument: (1) they have kept their oath of office to preserve, protect, and defend the Constitution; (2) the actions of their accusers undermine the Constitution; and (3) the president is responsible ultimately to the people and to the Constitution, not to the accusers.

This focus on the presidential oath, on the Constitution, and on the people is a direct by-product of the compact ratified at the inauguration. On that occasion, except under the most unusual circumstances, the country, Congress, and the Supreme Court witness presidents swearing to preserve, protect, and defend the Constitution. If they fail to do so, they have not only violated that oath of office, but have also broken the compact made with the people and with history. A central argument of the inaugural address is that just as presidents inherit the Constitution intact from those who preceded them, they will transmit it intact to those who succeed them.

The single action that the citizenry takes together as a nation is that of electing the president. Members of Congress are elected by sections of the country, not by the country as a whole. Any group that attempts to undo that one collective, national act ultimately assumes the burden of constituting itself as representative of all the people. When the House passes an article of impeachment, it assumes that role. In Federalist no. 65, Alexander Hamilton defined the impeachment trial in the Senate as a confrontation between "an individual accused, and the representatives of the people, his accusers."[17] What the rhetoric of the inaugural accomplished when it enabled popular investiture of the president can be undone only by resignation, by death, by completion of the allotted term of office, or through divestiture by the people's representatives: impeachment by the House and conviction by the Senate. Any accusation that an individual president has acted unconstitutionally has as its logical conclusion a move to impeach and convict.

Article 7, section 2 of the Constitution specifies that conviction divests the convicted individual of the office of the presidency and disqualifies that person from holding or enjoying "any Office of Honor, Trust, or Profit under the United States." In a sense, then, the rhetoric by which a president's accusers engage in the process of securing impeachment in the House and seeking conviction in the Senate is the mirror image of the rhetoric of the inaugural address. Whereas the inaugural invests, the rhetoric of impeachment divests. Jackson, Tyler, and Buchanan successfully parried the rhetoric of divestiture, whereas Andrew Johnson, Nixon, and Clinton tried and failed.

Jackson, Tyler, and Buchanan each faced congressional action. In Jackson's case, the issue involved the Bank of the United States and the extent of executive power. Jackson's secretary of the treasury moved deposits from the Bank of the United States to state banks, and when Jackson let it be known that he had presented a statement to his cabinet defending such a move, the Senate demanded that it be revealed to them. When Jackson refused, they passed a censure resolution. Jackson responded vigorously; the Senate refused to receive or publish his message. Ultimately, a later Congress expunged the censure resolution from the Senate record.

Tyler's conflict with Congress was focused on his economic actions and was occasioned by his vetoes. He faced an accusatory committee report, to which he responded. Buchanan angered Congress by attempting to reform the appointment procedure and, in so doing, removing some of the patronage power dear to its members.

Examples of accused presidents arguing that they have kept their oath of office abound. "I am determined to uphold the Constitution in this as in other respects to the utmost of my ability and in defiance of all personal consequences," declared Tyler.[18] After repeating his oath of office, Jackson contended that he was defending the Constitution.[19]

On April 15, 1834, Jackson referred to the president as the physician of the Constitution, who would try to heal the wounds his accusers had inflicted: "The ambition which leads me on is an anxious desire and a fixed determination to return to the people unimpaired the sacred trust they have confided to my charge; to heal the wounds of the

Constitution and preserve it from further violation."[20] Tyler said that he was called upon to "resist the encroachments of unconstitutional power."[21] Buchanan labeled the proceedings of the House a "violation of the rights of the coordinate executive branch of the Government and subversive of its constitutional independence,"[22] and Jackson termed the censure resolution passed by the Senate "wholly unauthorized by the Constitution."[23]

Instances of presidents arguing that their accusers are undermining the Constitution are also numerous. Buchanan charged the select committee chaired by John Covode (R-PA) with "spreading a drag net without the shadow of authority from the House, over the whole Union, to catch any disappointed man willing to malign my character,"[24] and he argued that the charges against him tended "to degrade the Presidential office itself to such a degree as to render it unworthy of the acceptance of any man of honor or principle."[25] Buchanan also contended that if his accusers accomplished their objectives, the worst fears of the framers of the Constitution about usurpation by the legislative branch would be realized.[26] Similarly, Tyler protested his accusers' effort to break down the constitutional power of the "executive authority of the people of the United States"[27] and claimed that, if unthwarted, their actions would signal an accumulation in "the hands of the House of Representatives or a bare majority of Congress for the time being, [of] an uncontrolled and despotic power."[28] Jackson argued that the Senate was exercising power "in no part . . . conferred on either branch of the Legislature."[29] He continued,

> If by a mere denunciation like this resolution the president should ever be induced to act in a matter of official duty contrary to the honest convictions of his own mind in compliance with the wishes of the Senate, the Constitutional independence of the executive department would be effectively destroyed and its power as effectually transferred to the Senate as if that end had been accomplished by an amendment of the Constitution.[30]

Jackson predicted that if the resolution were allowed to stand, the states would

> fall to mutual crimination and recrimination and give the people confusion and anarchy instead of law and order, until at length some form of aristocratic power would be established on the ruin of the Constitution or the States be broken into separate communities.[31]

Buchanan also forecast dire consequences if the efforts of his opponents were unchecked. In his first protest, he argued that

> they are calculated to foster a band of parasites and informers, ever ready, for their own advantage, to swear before ex parte committees to pretended private conversations between the President and themselves, incapable from their nature of being disproved, thus furnishing material for harassing him, degrading him in the eyes of the country, and eventually, should he be a weak or timid man, rendering him subservient to improper influences.

In a second protest, he said, "If unresisted, they would establish a precedent dangerous and embarrassing to all my successors, to whatever political party they might be attached." [32]

Presidents also protest that the congressional accusations against them are procedural violations of their civil rights. "To make the accuser the judge is a violation of the principles of universal justice, and is condemned by the practice of all civilized nations," said Buchanan. [33] Similarly, Jackson attacked the legitimacy of the Senate's censure resolution: "There is no more settled axiom in that Government whence we derived the model of this part of our Constitution than that 'the lords can not impeach any to themselves nor join in the accusation, because they are judges.'" [34] Tyler treated the attacks on him "as a violation in my person of rights secured to every citizen by the laws and the Constitution." [35] "In the institution of a prosecution for any offense against the most humble citizen," said Buchanan,

> and I claim for myself no greater rights than he enjoys—the constitutions of the United States and of the several States require that he shall be informed in the very beginning of the nature and cause of the accusation against him, in order to enable him to prepare for his defense. There are other principles which I might enumerate, not less sacred, presenting an impenetrable shield to protect every citizen falsely charged with a criminal offense. These have been violated in the prosecution instituted by the House of Representatives against the executive branch of government. Shall the President alone be deprived of the protection of these great principles which prevail in every land where a ray of liberty penetrates the gloom of despotism? [36]

Finally, presidents argue that their responsibility is to the people and to the Constitution, not to their congressional accusers. Buchanan argued, for example, that the president "is the only direct representative on earth of the people of all and each of the sovereign States. To them, and to them alone, is he responsible whilst acting within the sphere of his constitutional duty, and not in any manner to the House of Representatives."[37] Tyler affirmed that it was to the people, Providence, and the law of the land "that I hold myself answerable as a moral agent for a free and conscientious discharge of the duties which they have imposed upon me." He protested against House actions

> in the name of the people, by whose will I stand where I do, by whose authority I exercised the power which I am charged with having usurped, and to whom I am responsible for a fair and faithful discharge according to my own convictions of duty of the high stewardship confided to me by them.[38]

Jackson argued that all branches of government are "servants of the American people, without power or right to control or censure each other in the service of their common superior, save only in the manner and to the degree which that superior has prescribed," adding that the president is accountable "at the bar of public opinion for every act of his Administration."[39]

Although Nixon failed to forestall the impeachment process, he, too, made the arguments described in this chapter. For example, Nixon labeled the charges "wild accusations," "rumor, gossip, innuendo," and "third-hand hearsay charges."[40] Nixon's brief to the Supreme Court invoked the threat of judicial encroachment on the executive by arguing that the very principle of separation of powers meant that the lower court that had ruled against him lacked the power it had claimed.[41] It further predicted that should the arguments of the special prosecutor prevail, "that decision will alter the nature of the American Presidency profoundly and irreparably. If sustained, it will alter, equally irreparably, the delicate balance that has existed between three heretofore separate and coequal branches of government" (403). The brief also argued that his actions were consistent with those of seventeen past presidents, from 1796 to the present (354–55), and charged that "[t]he characterization of the President of the United States as an unindicted co-conspirator, is nothing less than an attempt to nullify the presumption of innocence by a secret, non-adversary proceeding. The presumption of innocence is a fundamental of American justice; the grand jury's procedure is an implication of guilt which corrupts the idea" (390).

Similarly, in producing some of the White House tapes, Nixon said, "In giving you these records—blemishes and all—I am placing my trust in the basic fairness of the American people." [42]

Making the people the ultimate jury is a reminder that the president has been invested with the office by the people: they have witnessed the oath of office, they were constituted as the audience at the inaugural, and they remain the audience as the president's performance in office is attacked. The view embodied in the president's message is that what the people give, only the people can take away. If Congress is to remove the president from office, the people must acquiesce. This is a rhetorical, not a constitutional, requirement, but it looms large in impeachment debates. [43]

These lines of argument typify presidential defenses against charges of misconduct. Each is grounded in the special role of the president in our system of government and in the president's unique relationship to the citizenry. In most cases, as we have demonstrated, these lines of argument are successful in forestalling the process of impeachment. We close this chapter with a look at one such effort that did not succeed.

CLINTON'S FAILED SELF-DEFENSE

The speeches made by Bill Clinton as damaging evidence of his inappropriate behavior emerged exemplify unsuccessful efforts to use personal apologia and forensic responses to forestall impeachment. After testifying before a grand jury convened by Independent Counsel Kenneth Starr as a result of his investigations, Clinton spoke to the nation on August 17, 1998. Seven months earlier, during a press conference, he had wagged his finger and declared to the nation that he did not have "sexual relations" with "that woman," a denial that had been supported by his wife, the White House staff, and other friends and advocates. Now he would admit publicly that his denial was a lie.

The speech began by acknowledging his testimony, but it framed the questions posed by the independent counsel and the grand jury as addressing intimate details of his "private life, questions no American citizen would ever want to answer." Ostensibly, the speech was a moment when, like Reagan, he would "take complete responsibility for all my actions, both public and private." [44] Presumably, because these issues dealt with his private life, taking personal responsibility for them would be all that was required.

Clinton denied that he had lied in the deposition in the Jones case, saying that his answers "were legally accurate," but he now admitted, "I did have a relationship with Ms. Lewinsky that was not appropriate. In fact, it was wrong. It constituted a critical lapse in judgment and a personal failure on my part for which I am solely and completely responsible." He added, "I know that my public comments and my silence about this matter gave a false impression. I misled people, including even my wife. I deeply regret that."[45]

Clinton also denied any obstruction of justice: "But I told the grand jury today, and I say to you now, that at no time did I ask anyone to lie, to hide or destroy evidence, or take any other unlawful action."[46] Whether that was true would be an important issue in his impeachment and trial.

The qualities of personal apologia are most evident in his comments about the reasons for his deceptions. He said that he was motivated "by a desire to protect myself from the embarrassment of my own conduct" and "very concerned about protecting my family." These personal reasons were linked to and buttressed by political reasons: first, that "these questions were being asked in a politically inspired lawsuit, which has since been dismissed"; second, distrust of the "independent counsel investigation that began with private business dealings 20 years ago, . . . about which an independent federal agency found no evidence of any wrongdoing by me or my wife over two years ago."[47] The political dimensions suggested that using his personal life as the basis for impeachment was part of a partisan effort to remove him, partisan because he already had been cleared of these charges by the courts and independent agencies.

There was a brief pragmatic argument: "This has gone on too long, cost too much, and hurt too many innocent people."[48] In other words, it would be best for all if this process came to an end. That argument was linked to his efforts to frame his errors as private and personal.

Clinton stated that this matter was between him and his family and God: "it is private. And I intend to reclaim my family life for my family. It's nobody's business but ours. Even Presidents have private lives." Then, like Reagan, Clinton began to instruct the audience about how to respond:

> It is time to stop the pursuit of personal destruction and the prying into private lives and get on with our national life. Our country has been distracted by this matter for too long. . . . It is time . . . to move on. . . . And so, tonight I ask you to

turn away from the spectacle of the past seven months, to repair the fabric of our national discourse, and to return our attention to all the challenges and all the promise of the next American century.[49]

Clinton's public statement called his character into question. He had lied, and now admitted it; moreover, he had lied to those nearest and dearest to him; a fortiori, to whom would he not lie? Its timing also created doubt; being called to answer questions by a grand jury now compelled him to admit his misleading statements and deceptions. His listeners would doubt that his motives were pure—he was admitting lies because he had no alternative. It would have been very convenient to get off so cheaply—just admit lies, take responsibility for them and one's actions, and forget all about the matter. His appeal to focus on the nation's business seemed highly self-interested in this context.

Less than a month later, on September 11, 1998, Clinton spoke at the annual White House prayer breakfast. He style, tone, and attitude were dramatically different. The speech was far more contrite; the admission that he has done wrong was explicit: "I have sinned." He asked to be forgiven, but acknowledged that sorrow at what he had done was not enough. He said that what was required was "genuine repentance, a determination to change and to repair breaches of my own making—I have repented." That claim might not have been accepted except for what follows: the second requirement was "what my bible calls a 'broken spirit,' an understanding that I must have God's help to be the person that I want to be, a willingness to give the very forgiveness I seek, a renunciation of the pride and the anger which cloud judgment, lead people to excuse and compare and to blame and complain." What this meant, he explained, was a combination of a vigorous legal defense, continuing on the path of repentance, and intensifying his efforts to lead our country "in the hope that with a broken spirit and a still strong heart I can be used for greater good. . . . In this I ask for your prayers and your help in healing our Nation."[50]

The occasion and Clinton's religious background strengthened this message, but once again, its timing was a problem. On the same day, the Starr report, a 453-page summary of the evidence from the independent counsel's investigation, was released over the Internet. The report outlined the case for eleven charges against the president, including perjury, obstruction of justice, and abuse of office. It included many salacious details that distracted from and interfered with public acceptance of Clinton's repentance and made forgiveness difficult. On the other hand, these details, unnecessary to the case for impeachment, were seen by some commentators as a spiteful effort to embarrass and weaken the Clinton presidency. Still others saw them as evidence of the partisanship of the report.

Clinton's efforts to forestall impeachment call attention to the importance of timing and context. Lincoln's self-defense was more effective because of the wartime situation. Reagan's self-defense was more plausible because no efforts had yet begun to move toward impeachment. Clinton's speeches were too little, too late.

CONCLUSION

When faced with accusations short of formal charges of impeachment, presidents remain in a powerful persuasive position relative to their accusers. They are able to respond to the accusations forensically or through a personal apologia, and they have the freedom to define the grounds for debate, to attack their accusers as threatening the system of government itself, and to appeal for final vindication to the people. In most cases, these efforts have been successful. Once formal articles of impeachment are drawn up, however, presidents lose many of these rhetorical advantages, as we shall demonstrate in the next chapter.

ELEVEN

The Rhetoric of Impeachment

Throughout this book, although our analysis has focused on presidential discourse, we have stressed the interdependence of the rhetoric of the three branches of government. In this chapter, in which we discuss the rhetoric of impeachment, the relationship between presidential and congressional rhetoric is so pivotal that our analysis would be incomplete if we did not discuss the rhetoric of Congress, which plays a crucial role in the impeachment process. The reciprocal relationship between the two branches in this instance results from the constitutional provisions that make the houses of Congress the venue for impeachment and conviction. Consequently, this chapter analyzes congressional impeachment rhetoric as well as presidential responses to congressional charges.

In only three instances have formal articles of impeachment been passed by the full House of Representatives or by its Committee on the Judiciary. These three cases differed significantly. In the cases of Andrew Johnson and Bill Clinton, the central facts were not in dispute; in Richard Nixon's, they were. Johnson conceded in his written response to the articles of impeachment that he had addressed a letter to Edwin Stanton saying, "Public considerations of a high character constrain me to say that your resignation as Secretary of War will be accepted."[1] He also admitted that he "did issue and deliver to said Lorenzo Thomas the said writing set forth in the said second article."[2] In response to the eleventh article, he denied that he had said in a speech in August of 1866 that the thirty-ninth Congress was not "a Congress of the United States authorized by the Constitution to exercise legislative power,"[3] but that was a minor point. Similarly, Clinton eventually admitted that he had lied about what he had done and misled those who were investigating him. By contrast, Nixon disavowed the central claim of the first article. He did not, he averred, use "the powers of his high office ... in a course of conduct or plan designed to delay, impede, and obstruct the investigation of" the unlawful entry into the Democratic National Committee's headquarters at the Watergate complex. Nor, he said, did he "cover-up, conceal, and protect those responsible . . . or conceal the existence and scope of other unlawful covert activities."[4]

In the cases of Johnson and Clinton, their trials in the Senate pivoted on whether the actions they had taken were impeachable offenses. In Nixon's case, there was consensus that if he had engaged in the activities alleged in the first three articles, then he should be impeached. So clear was that agreement that ten Republican members of the House Committee on the Judiciary who had voted against the three articles adopted by the committee indicated after the release of transcripts of taped conversations on June 23, 1972, that they had changed their minds on article 1.[5] The transcripts revealed that six days after the Watergate break-in, Nixon had learned of his reelection committee's involvement. The transcripts also revealed that Nixon had instructed his chief of staff, Robert Haldeman, to tell the CIA to thwart the FBI's investigation of this crime.[6] These transcripts were released on August 5, 1974, six days after the committee had concluded its deliberations.[7]

The Nixon impeachment differed procedurally from those of Johnson and Clinton. In Johnson's case, the House began by voting to impeach and then drew up articles of impeachment. In Nixon's case, the House Committee on the Judiciary began by drawing up proposed articles of impeachment. The former procedure sought evidence to support an agreed-upon conclusion; the latter sought evidence to determine what conclusions were warranted. In Clinton's case, the articles of impeachment emerged out of a five-year investigation by Independent Counsel Kenneth Starr, initially charged with investigating allegations about improprieties in the Clintons' Whitewater land deal. That investigation was pursued until Clinton's sexual behavior with Monica Lewinsky came to light. Clinton's deceptions about that relationship ultimately led the House Committee on the Judiciary to consider and vote on articles of impeachment. That process was significantly different from the processes that led to the impeachment of Johnson and to the vote on articles of impeachment against Nixon.

The course followed in the Nixon case was predicated on the need to build consensus, and from its inception the process was designed to ensure public support for its outcome. The ideal toward which Congress aspired was expressed by Peter Rodino (D-NJ), chair of the House Committee on the Judiciary, on February 6, 1974: "Whatever the result, whatever we learn or conclude, let us now proceed, with such care and decency and thoroughness and honor that the vast majority of the American people, and their children after them, will say: That was the right course. There was no other way."[8] By contrast, the Clinton impeachment debates in the House were characterized by intense partisan conflict and harsh attacks. Senate majority leader Trent Lott (R-MS) and minority leader Tom Daschle (D-SD) worked together to stage a speedy and dignified trial that would not become an embarrassing national spectacle. Both understood that the prospect of at least a dozen Democratic senators voting to convict—the minimum necessary for the required two-thirds vote—was exceedingly slim, barring some shocking new revelation about the president's conduct.

This chapter contrasts the rhetoric of unity, fair play, and decorum that characterized the case made by those members of Congress arguing for Nixon's impeachment with the perfervid partisanship and divisive rhetoric of those urging the conviction of Andrew Johnson. Johnson's defenders, and most of Nixon's accusers and defenders, shared a commitment to high standards of rational decision making. By persuading undecided senators to embrace that commitment, Johnson's defenders won his acquittal. By enacting that commitment, the House Committee on the Judiciary created a climate that enabled conservative Democrats and moderate Republicans to join liberal Democrats in voting for three articles of impeachment against Nixon. As a result, in both cases, the outcome muted the fear that Alexander Hamilton expressed in Federalist no. 65, that an impeachment decision would "be regulated more by the comparative strength of parties, than by the real demonstration of innocence or guilt."[9]

In Clinton's case, despite the heated and partisan debates in the House on the articles of impeachment, the trial in the Senate was well argued, and the case made by the thirteen House managers and by Clinton's defenders avoided harsh attacks and partisan appeals. Nonetheless, the votes that followed were surprisingly partisan. Clearly, senators' political commitments strongly influenced how they viewed the evidence for impeachment.[10]

The three impeachments also differ in the use of the personal apologia described in the preceding chapter. In Johnson's case, his counsel were able to present a personal apologia as part of their defense, describing in detail the qualities of Johnson's character that all deplored, but denying that these flaws were grounds for impeachment. That option was available to them because constitutional grounds for impeachment did not exist; the charges were partisan and lacked legal foundation.[11] The final defense of Clinton by former Senator Dale Bumpers followed a similar pattern, admitting personal misbehavior and defects of character, but denying that the president had committed an impeachable offense. In Nixon's case, however, given the nature of the charges and the evidence supporting them, a personal apologia was precluded. In fact, the House Committee on the Judiciary voted down an article based on Nixon's personal conduct and indicted him solely on charges that addressed his conduct as president.

THE IMPEACHMENT TRIAL OF ANDREW JOHNSON

The impeachment trial of Andrew Johnson took place against the backdrop of the Civil War. Johnson had been a Democratic senator from Tennessee and was the only Southern senator to oppose secession from the Union. After Fort Sumter was fired on, a resolution sponsored by Johnson, saying that the North intended only to preserve the Union, not to interfere with slavery where it already existed, was adopted by the Senate. When Union forces reclaimed Tennessee, Lincoln appointed Johnson its military governor, and in 1864, the Republican convention, without guidance from Lincoln, chose him as a compromise vice president in preference to ardent abolitionist Hannibal Hamlin of Maine, who had served during Lincoln's first term. Upon Lincoln's assassination, Johnson became president, and it fell to him to set up interim governments in the reclaimed Confederate states and to supervise the South's reentry into the Union.

After denying representation to eleven of the rebellious states, Congress passed a series of bills to protect freed slaves, sponsored by moderate Republicans. By vetoing these bills, Johnson drove these potential allies into the radical camp. The result was costly. In his impeachment trial, Senator John Sherman (R-OH) argued that Johnson had "abandoned the party which trust [sic] him with power."[12] From that point onward, Congress and the president opposed each other over Johnson's Reconstruction policies, his vetoes, and his pardons.

In 1867, Congress passed the Tenure of Office Act, which took from the president the power to remove a member of the cabinet. The act specified that such presidential action would constitute a "high misdemeanor" and would thus be grounds for impeachment. Secretary of War Edwin Stanton, a carryover from Lincoln's cabinet, opposed Johnson's Reconstruction policies. Believing the Tenure of Office Act to be unconstitutional, and at odds with Stanton, Johnson removed Stanton from office. On February 24, 1868, by a vote of 128–47, the House voted to impeach Johnson, after an attempt to pass articles of impeachment three months earlier had failed.

The effort to impeach Andrew Johnson began in December 1866. In January 1867, a resolution was passed authorizing the House Committee on the Judiciary to "inquire into Johnson's official conduct and determine whether he had done anything impeachable."[13] Despite a wide-ranging inquiry, including investigations of rumors that Johnson had conspired with John Wilkes Booth to assassinate Lincoln, the committee voted in June against recommending impeachment, concluding that no evidence of high crimes and misdemeanors had been uncovered.[14] Because of congressional frustration over Johnson's recalcitrance in vetoing Reconstruction legislation, however, the committee renewed its work in July. Reversing its earlier 4–5 vote, it recommended impeachment on the grounds of general usurpation of power; however, the full House rejected its recommendation.[15]

When the House finally passed articles of impeachment, all charges against Johnson other than those surrounding the removal of Stanton had been dismissed previously by two different House committees and by the full body.[16] Ultimately, eleven articles of impeachment were passed. The first eight dealt with the president's removal of Stanton; the ninth alleged a violation of a rider to the Army Appropriations Act; the tenth, based on a number of speeches Johnson gave on his "swing around the circle" before the 1866 election, charged the president with the intent "to set aside rightful authority and power of Congress" by bringing into "disgrace, ridicule, hatred, contempt, and reproach the Congress of the United States."[17] The eleventh was an omnibus article charging the president with denying the legitimacy of legislation passed by Congress.

When the House passed these articles of impeachment, it created an unprecedented situation, which was admitted by both sides in the Senate trial (9, 327). Never before had the constitutional right of the House to impeach been used successfully against a president. Given the unprecedented character of the proceedings, complicated by the problems of defining what is an impeachable offense, those defending the president as well as those supporting his removal were forced into a contest over the nature of the process in which they were engaged. As a result, definitions were a major preoccupation of the debate. The seven "managers," who represented the House, and the defenders, Johnson's counsel, struggled to determine whether they were engaged in a trial, an inquest, a judicial proceeding, or something else altogether. Seeking to increase the evidentiary burden of the managers, Johnson's defenders claimed that the process was a judicial proceeding, a court (287–91). Seeking to minimize their evidentiary burden, the managers argued that, in this case, the Senate was a law unto itself, bound only by natural principles of equity and justice (30). The defenders attempted to magnify the seriousness of what might constitute an impeachable offense; the managers sought to minimize it. Because the managers had a weak case in legal terms, this struggle over definitions was particularly important.[18] Argument from definitions was inevitable given the ambiguity of the constitutional grounds for impeachment; in this case, it was also a means to encourage those Republicans who had indicated that they might be persuaded to acknowledge procedural defects, which the president's counsel could not criticize directly because such criticism would have been an implicit attack on the constitutionally designated judges of the case, the assembled senators.[19]

Fearful that the justices of the Supreme Court would feel beholden to a president who might have appointed some of them, and recognizing that an inconclusive election might have been decided in the House of Representatives, the founders vested the Senate with special roles. The president can appoint ambassadors, "other public ministers and consuls, judges of the Supreme Court, and all other officers of the United States" only with the advice and consent of the Senate. The Senate is also given responsibility for ratifying treaties and for acting as the jury before whom an impeached president is tried.

The House and Senate perform different rhetorical functions in the impeachment process. To the House is given "the right of accusing," to the Senate "the right of judging," a division that protects the executive "from the prevalency of a factious spirit in either of those branches."[20] The requirement that two-thirds of the Senate must vote to convict provides another systemic protection, one that Hamilton described as "the security to innocence."[21]

The founders considered the Senate more deliberate in action than the House, less subject to the partisan passions that influence those subject to reelection every two years. The Senate's staggered six-year terms give that body a stability lacking in the House, whose composition can be significantly altered by a single election. Such insulation from popular pressure would be particularly important in the case of impeachment, as Hamilton argued. "What other body," he asked, "would be likely to feel confidence enough in its own situation to preserve, unawed and uninfluenced, the necessary impartiality between the individual accused and the representatives of the people, his accusers?"[22]

The popular influence so feared by the founders played an important role in Johnson's case. Senator Richard Yates (R-IL) concluded, "We are not alone in trying this cause. ... [A] deep murmur is heard from thousands of patriot voices; it swells over the western plains. ... [and] it thunders upon us a mighty nation's verdict, guilty" (488). Similarly, the highly partisan climate following the midterm elections of 1994 and resentment over Clinton's reelection in 1996 contributed significantly to his impeachment.

The requirement that two-thirds of the senators concur in convicting the president, coupled with the comparative insulation of senators from immediate public retribution, provided some systemic protection for Andrew Johnson, even in an environment in which partisan passions ran high. By contrast, Clinton's approval ratings remained high during the impeachment process, and public opinion polls suggested that a majority of the public did not wish him removed from office.

Two things made senators more amenable to appeals to act reasonably in Johnson's case. First, the Constitution specifically mandates that "when the President of the United States is tried, the Chief Justice shall preside," a requirement that underscores the seriousness of the occasion and the transformation of the Senate from a legislative into a judicial body. Second, the Constitution stipulates that when trying an impeachment, the senators shall be "on Oath or Affirmation." The oath that senators swore on March 5, 1868, aided Johnson's defenders. Each senator declared, "I do solemnly swear that in all things appertaining to the trial of the impeachment of Andrew Johnson, President of the United States, I will do impartial justice, according to the Constitution and laws. So help me God."[23] What the oath established was that each senator was answerable for his vote, not to his constituents or his party, but to the law, the Constitution, and to God. The "impartial justice" to which each senator was pledged was the justice the president's defenders were calling for. Similarly, in the Clinton impeachment trial, each senator was asked, "Do you solemnly swear that in all things appertaining to the trial of the impeachment of William Jefferson Clinton, President of the United States, now pending, you will do impartial justice according to the Constitution and laws: So help you God?"[24]

Before Johnson's trial, the Senate was deeply implicated in the impeachment process. It attempted to add pro-conviction votes by hurrying through bills admitting Nebraska and Colorado to the Union. When

Johnson vetoed these measures, Congress overrode his veto to admit Nebraska. Moreover, many senators aggressively attacked Johnson in the 1866 campaign and supported efforts in the House to secure his impeachment.[25] Majority leader Charles Sumner (R-MA), for example, labeled Johnson "the successor of Jefferson Davis."[26] The anti-Johnson sentiment in the Senate was obvious before either side's opening statement when the president asked for and was denied forty, then thirty, days to prepare his defense (he was allowed ten). Consequently, had Johnson's defenders pointed to the lack of fairness or equity in the impeachment process to date, they would implicitly have attacked those who would decide the case.

There were other hazards involved in such an attack. If the process itself were discredited, would the public accept a vote to acquit? Would such an attack provide additional ammunition for the claim of the House that the president sought to diminish the legitimate authority of Congress? One article charged Johnson with incendiary rhetoric against Congress, and a direct attack might legitimize that charge. Finally, because the Constitution does not specifically prohibit any of the questionable activities the Senate had engaged in, the defenders lacked constitutional grounds for attacking them.

Nevertheless, there were ample grounds for concluding that Congress had treated Johnson unfairly. The House passed an impeachment resolution before articles of impeachment had been drawn up or debated. The House impeached with an unbecoming haste, just three days after Johnson's attempt to remove Stanton as secretary of war. Members of the Senate who opposed impeachment were urged to resign their places to those who favored it. Although the Constitution prohibits the vice president from voting in an impeachment trial because of the potential for conflict of interest, Benjamin Wade (R-OH), president pro tem of the Senate, who was next in line for the presidency if Johnson was removed, was sworn in and permitted to vote. Finally, that the impeachment vote in the House had followed party lines revealed its partisan nature and political intent. In other words, Johnson's counsel had to operate within a tainted procedure that they could not afford to attack directly.

The arguments of the defenders could succeed only if framed in language and uttered in tones consistent with definitions of the impeachment process calling for the impartiality of the courtroom. If the issues were cast in partisan terms, Johnson would lose, because more than two-thirds of the senators were Republicans. If the defenders responded in kind to the vitriolic attacks of the managers, they would invite reprisal, rather than a judicious verdict, from the senators.

Johnson's defenders were well suited to their task. Benjamin Curtis of Massachusetts had written one of the two dissents from the Dred Scott decision, and he had resigned from the Supreme Court to act as Johnson's counsel. Henry Stanbery of Kentucky had resigned as attorney general in order to defend the president. When Jeremiah Black withdrew as Johnson's counsel because he feared public disgrace, Thomas Nelson of Tennessee and William Groesbeck, a member of the House of Representatives from Ohio from 1857 to 1859, entered the case. William Evarts of New York would later serve as attorney general and as secretary of state.[27]

The temptations offered to the defenders were great. Johnson's character was impugned when manager George S. Boutwell (R-MA) called him "the elect of an assassin" (40), and, in the words of Johnson's counsel Nelson,

> stigmatized [him] as a "usurper," ... as "encouraging murders, assassinations, and robberies all over the southern States"; and finally, by way of proving that there is one step between the sublime and the ridiculous, he has been charged with being "a common scold" and a "ribald, scurrilous blasphemer, bandying epithets and taunts with a jeering mob."[28] (286)

Hostile words were also directed at Johnson's counsel, yet they refused to respond in kind. Nelson parried a personal attack this way:

> I treated the gentleman on the other side with courtesy and kindness. He has rewarded me with insult and with outrage in the presence of the American Senate. It will be for you, Senators, to judge whose demeanor is most proper for you, that of the honorable gentleman who foully and falsely charges me with insinuating calumny, or my course in vindicating the President of the United States in the discharge of my professional duty here. So far as any question that the gentleman desires to make of a personal character with me is concerned this is not the place to make it. Let him make it elsewhere if he desires to do it.[29] (337)

Nor did the defenders respond indignantly to article 10, in which the House charged that "on divers other days and times as well before as afterward," Andrew Johnson did make and deliver, with a loud voice, certain intemperate, inflammatory, and scandalous harangues, and did therein utter loud threats and bitter menaces, as well against Congress as the laws of the United States duly enacted thereby.... [w]hich said utterances, declarations, threats, and harangues, highly censurable in any, are peculiarly indecent and unbecoming in the Chief Magistrate of the United States.

Instead, Groesbeck stepped back to place the charge in a comic frame by suggesting that the article be enacted into law. To the laughter of the Senate and the galleries filled with members of the House and visitors, he made the following proposal:

Be it enacted, That, if the President . . . shall say anything displeasing to Congress . . . or if he shall misquote or carelessly quote the sacred Scriptures, or . . . use bad grammar, then, and in either of such cases, he shall be guilty of a high misdemeanor, and upon trial and conviction thereof shall be fined in any sum not exceeding $10,000, or imprisonment not exceeding ten years. (319)

The genius of this reductio ad absurdum, and of the defenders' consistent reliance on temperate rhetoric, was that they encouraged otherwise partisan individuals to treat the issues dispassionately while inviting their identification with judicial tests of evidence and procedure. In appealing to human fallibility, this particular example was a kind of personal apologia as well.

At the same time, the defenders permitted sympathetic, open-minded Republicans to vent their hostility toward Johnson by agreeing that he was not an ideal president. In effect, they followed the strategy of the personal apologia by separating defects of character from grounds for impeachment. Nelson, who was from Johnson's home state of Tennessee, rehearsed all of Johnson's less attractive qualities while suggesting that what were now viewed as defects were once admired. After characterizing the attacks on Johnson as the product of "all the powers of invective which the able and ingenious Managers can command . . . to fire your hearts and to prejudice your minds against him," Nelson told of Johnson's poverty-stricken youth in Greeneville, and then asked,

Who is Andrew Johnson? Are there not Senators here who are well acquainted with him? Are there not men whose minds go back to the stirring times of 1860 and 1861, when treason was rife in this Capitol . . . ? Where was Andrew Johnson then? . . . Yes, he stood "solitary and alone," the only member from the South who was disposed to battle against treason then; and he now is called a traitor himself!... Then it was that his voice was heard, and again the plaudits of hundreds and thousands shook the very walls of this Capitol in his favor, as they had done on former occasions when he stood here and vindicated the American Constitution and proclaimed the determination of the Government to uphold and to maintain it.... I only ask you here today, if it be possible for you to do so, to place yourselves in Andrew Johnson's position, and to look from his standpoint, and judge in the manner in which he is judged.... I am not addressing mere politicians. I feel that I am addressing judges—the most eminent judges known to the laws and the Constitution of our country—judges sitting upon the greatest trial known to the Constitution. (287)

Nelson recalled Johnson's steadfast behavior during the Civil War to suggest that he was being condemned for the very qualities deemed praiseworthy then. Such an apologetic tactic was apt precisely because the charges damned Johnson on personal grounds and because the case against him was weak or nonexistent on constitutional grounds. In addition, Nelson asked the senators to adopt the role of judge rather than that of politician, and in that role, to see the paradoxical situation in which Johnson found himself.

The laughter evoked by the defenders was a subtle attack on the character of the managers and the fanaticism that seemed to animate them. Johnson's chief counsel, Evarts, was particularly skilled in its use. When Boutwell attacked the president's defenders by characterizing law as a profession which "sharpens and does not enlarge the mind" and described Johnson's offense as so heinous that he ought to be consigned to outer darkness. Evarts responded,

I may as conveniently at this point of the argument as at any other pay some attention to the astronomical punishment which the learned and honorable Manager (Mr. BOUTWELL) thinks should be applied to this novel case of impeachment of the President.... Painfully sensible of my ignorance, being devoted to a profession which "sharpens and does not enlarge the mind" [laughter], I yet can admire without envy the superior knowledge evinced by the honorable Manager. Indeed, upon my soul, I believe he is aware of an astronomical fact which many professors of that science are wholly ignorant of. But nevertheless, while some of his honorable colleagues were paying attention to an unoccupied and unappropriated island on the surface of the seas, Mr. Manager BOUTWELL, more ambitious, had discovered an untenanted and unappropriated region in the skies, reserved, he would have us think, in the final councils of the Almighty, as the place of punishment for convicted and deposed American Presidents [laughter]. . . .

Let it then be provided that in case of your sentence of deposition and removal from office the honorable and astronomical Manager shall take into his own hands the execution of the sentence. With the President made fast to his broad and strong shoulders, and, having already essayed the flight by imagination, better prepared than anybody else to execute it in form, taking the advantage of ladders as far as ladders will go to the top of this great Capitol, and spurning then with his foot the crest of Liberty, let him set out upon his flight [laughter], while the two Houses of Congress and all the people of the United States shall shout "*Sic itur ad astra* [thus journey to the stars]" [laughter]. (347)

The rhetoric of Johnson's defenders pointed out the hyperbole and partisanship of his attackers, that they were not advancing the case for impeachment, and that the motives for the charges were personal. Johnson's accusers made the mistake of using a rhetorical mode that was capable only of reinforcing the committed, but not of persuading the uncertain. Their strategic choices demonstrated either their rhetorical ineptitude or the presumption that the trial was a simple formality leading inevitably to conviction.

The statements of the seven Republican senators who defied party pressure to vote to acquit reflected the success of the defenders' strategy. These key senators accepted the defenders' definitions and adopted their temperate language. Lyman Trumbull of Illinois, for example, wrote that he had made his decision "without giving the least heed to the clamor of intemperate zealots who demand the conviction of Andrew Johnson as a test of party faith" and "governed by what my reason and judgment tell me is the truth, and the justice of the law of this case" (420). James Wilson Grimes of Iowa said, "Nor can I suffer my judgment of the law governing this case to be influenced by political considerations. I cannot agree to destroy the harmonious working of the Constitution for the sake of getting rid of an unacceptable President" (424). Peter Godwin Van Winkle of West Virginia cited legal grounds for his decision (431–33), and John B. Henderson of Missouri said, "We sit in the capacity of a court and also a jury. As a court we must hear all evidence; as a jury we must consider that only which is competent and relevant" (518). Later, he added,

If this were a vote whether Johnson should be elected President, or whether, being in, he is a fit person for the exalted office, our position might be relieved of much embarrassment. The question is simply one of guilt under the charges as presented by the House, and I cannot, in justice to the laws of the land . . . render any other response to the several articles than a verdict of "not guilty." (520)

Edmund Ross of Kansas wrote a book justifying his negative vote.[30] Ultimately, some who voted for impeachment came to agree with the dissenters. James G. Blaine (R-ME), for example, later wrote words that would be cited in Dale Bumpers's defense of Clinton:

> The sober reflection of after years has persuaded many who favored Impeachment that it was not justifiable on the charges made, and that its success would have resulted in greater injury to free institutions than Andrew Johnson in his utmost endeavors was able to inflict.[31]

Speaking during Johnson's trial, William Pitt Fessenden of Maine laid down the criteria for a successful impeachment effort, criteria that explain why Johnson's accusers failed and why the strategies of his defenders were so effective:

> The offense for which a Chief Magistrate is removed from office, and the power intrusted to him by the people transferred to other hands . . . should be of such a character as to commend itself at once to the minds of all right thinking men as, beyond all question, an adequate cause. It should be free from the taint of party; leave no reasonable ground of suspicion upon the motives of those who inflict the penalty, and address itself to the country and the civilized world as a measure justly called for by the gravity of the crime and the necessity of punishment. (452)[32]

What Fessenden described are the dual requirements that characterize any public proceeding: to arrive at a decision and to legitimize the process by which the decision is reached.

The rhetoric surrounding Andrew Johnson's impeachment illustrates the diminished persuasive resources of a president who is absent from the debate, who is under indictment, and who is compelled to respond to specific accusations. Capitalizing on the constitutional requirements for an impeachment trial, including a special senatorial oath, Johnson's defenders framed the event as a trial, not a partisan vote on policy. They never attempted to deny that there were flaws in Johnson's character, although an apologia, recalling his principled actions during the Civil War, pointed out the double standard being applied to his current behavior. They used humor to suggest the hyperbole of the managers' arguments and to call attention to the intensely partisan motivations that energized them. The senators who voted against impeachment responded to these appeals by defining an impeachable offense as a violation of the presidential oath of office and by rejecting partisan disagreement and character flaws as grounds for removal from office.

ARTICLES OF IMPEACHMENT AGAINST RICHARD NIXON

Compared with Andrew Johnson's impeachment, the process that led to the passage of three articles of impeachment against Richard Nixon in 1974 presents a sharply contrasting picture. Nixon's attempts at self-defense in the spring and summer of 1973 have been analyzed by a number of critics.[33] Although they describe the causes of his failure differently, all agree that Nixon chose to defend himself in terms of his office and not as an individual human being or in terms of his own personality. Although there were reasons peculiar to this case that might explain Nixon's choices, the strategies of numerous presidents who preceded him suggest that the personal apologia is not a rhetorical option for presidents faced with well-grounded charges of violating the oath of office. Furthermore, because that option is closed, sources of appeal to the president's character, most particularly grounds for identification, and bases for justifying behavior are also limited. As illustrated by Johnson's case, however, imprudent actions by members of Congress can reopen such possibilities, and as illustrated by Clinton's case, imprudent actions by a special prosecutor or independent counsel can create them.

As they debated the articles of impeachment, members of the House Committee on the Judiciary were acutely aware that their every action would be scrutinized by the public and by Nixon's defenders for signs of partisanship. That both houses of Congress were controlled by Democrats magnified the need not only for fairness, but also for the appearance of fairness. For a Democratically controlled Congress even to contemplate the removal of a Republican president reelected in a landslide was very serious. Accordingly, the committee gave the president's defenders every reasonable opportunity to make their case. The investigative staff was bipartisan. James St. Clair, Nixon's chief counsel, was permitted to propose and question witnesses. At the end of the inquiry, he was invited to sum up Nixon's case. The appearance of fairness was supported by the committee's rejection of two of five proposed articles of impeachment.

Three factors illuminate the dynamics of the debate on articles of impeachment in Nixon's case: the roles assumed by those who accused the president, the nature of the issues, and the rhetorical-political setting of a congressional committee debating on national television, which defined the audience and influenced the character of the debate.

Fundamentally, of course, the accusers and defenders were members of the House, elected representatives and politicians. Although legislator politicians are not always highly regarded, they are uniquely suited to perform certain functions:

> At voicing opinions held by significant numbers of voters back in the constituencies, the United States Congress is extraordinarily effective.... The diversity of the constituencies makes it likely that any given sentiment will find an official voice somewhere.[34]

If the impeachment inquiry was to be seen by the public as something other than a kangaroo court, a charge made by Nixon's press secretary, Ronald Ziegler, it had to produce a decision reflecting diverse constituencies and attitudes. Only such a decision could ensure the assent of the U.S. public. The membership of the House Committee on the Judiciary in the summer of 1974 contributed to that result. Its members were old and young, male and female, African American and white, southern and northern, conservative and liberal, from large and small states, and from rural and urban constituencies.

All of the committee members were lawyers, which added to their credibility on legal matters. As politicians, they might lack credibility, and they were vulnerable to charges of partisanship. Members transformed such potential disabilities into advantages by arguing that Nixon was a politician who should be judged by other politicians, who understand the pressures of campaigns and public life. In other words, they constituted themselves as a jury of his peers. They discussed the problem of partisanship openly and asked whether or not a Democrat could judge a Republican president fairly. Jack Brooks (D-TX) argued that impeachment would bring no political gain to Democrats. If Nixon were removed, he would be replaced by another Republican who might garner stronger support.[35] Similarly, they pondered whether Republicans could condemn their party leader and stain the reputation of their party. M. Caldwell Butler (R-VA) contended that Republicans had always campaigned against corruption; if "the house has to be cleaned," it was they who should do it (69).

The process by which the committee members defined the roles they would assume in reaching a decision was difficult. Article 1 alleged a criminal offense, obstruction of justice, and debate on this article involved a process of discovering just what it meant to "judge" this case. The president's defenders attacked the article for its lack of "specificity." In response, Jerome Waldie (D-CA) began a witty, engaging narrative of the chronology of Watergate (188–89). Initially, other members yielded time so he could continue his "scenario," but gradually, as the debate continued, his narrative style was attacked by both sides;[36] Charles Wiggins (R-CA) referred to it as "Waldie's fable" (222), a characterization supported by Lawrence Hogan (R-MD) (229) and Joseph Maraziti (R-NJ) (242). As the debate developed, the committee came to a tacit agreement that what was required was a serious, factual presentation of relevant evidence in the style of a legal brief. In effect, the committee defined its role legalistically in relation to charges, evidence, and standards of proof.

The committee members also defined themselves as ordinary citizens applying common sense to the issues. This move was most apparent in the debate on article 2, which charged abuse of presidential power. The special character of this charge was expressed by George Danielson (D-CA): "You or I, the most lowly citizen, can obstruct justice. You or I, the most lowly citizen, can violate the statutes of the criminal code. But only the President can violate the oath of office of the President" (337). The strongest argument for this charge was that the pattern of misconduct by the president and his aides demonstrated that the president had failed to "take care that the laws are faithfully executed," an argument made cogently by Robert McClory (R-IL) (341–42, 349, 439). His argument refuted the strictly legalistic view taken by the president's defenders.

The decision to speak in the voice of ordinary citizens produced some of the most eloquent moments in the debate, what Northrop Frye has called "high style in ordinary language."[37] Just before the vote on article 1, Walter Flowers (D-AL) agonized aloud over his decision to vote in its favor. His justification rested almost wholly on his role as an ordinary citizen using common sense:

In approaching this grave matter I said I would be guided by the facts, the Constitution, and my own conscience. I honestly believe I have been faithful to that commitment. I know for certain that I have nothing to gain politically or otherwise from what I must do here. But after weeks of searching through the facts and agonizing over the constitutional requirements, it's clear to me what I must do. . . . I have close personal friends who strongly support President Nixon. To several of these close friends who somehow I hope will see and hear these proceedings, I say that the only way I could vote for impeachment would be on the realization, to me anyway, that they my friends would do the same thing if they were in my place on this unhappy day and confronted with all the same facts that I have. (326)

The most abrasive defender of the president, Charles Sandman (R-NJ), made the relationship between the legal role and the role of citizen explicit while urging the committee not to vote for the articles:

I like to believe that every man that has ever been President of the United States had to be a good man and he had to be a great man or this great country would have never voted for him to be the leader of this country. . . . Now, anybody who feels this way, and I kind of think the country feels this way, they would like to believe their President is a pretty good man, and to do otherwise or to prove to them otherwise, it would take a tremendous amount of proof to do that, and it should, tremendous. (423–24)

The debate involved definitions, particularly what constituted an impeachable offense, but of more importance, it focused on how the committee members could establish themselves as credible judges. As noted, they did so by acknowledging themselves as politicians and party members, but defining themselves as jurors who combined legal expertise with the common sense of the ordinary citizen.

Five articles of impeachment were proposed; three were passed, two rejected. Article 2, charging that the president had violated his oath of office, received the strongest support, with a vote of 28–10; article 1, charging obstruction of justice, also passed, 27–11. Article 3, charging that the president had impeded the constitutionally authorized investigation of the committee by willfully disobeying its subpoena, barely passed by a vote of 21–17. Article 3 threatened what members called the "fragile bipartisan coalition" on the committee, and only two Republicans supported it, while two southern Democrats who had supported articles 1 and 2 voted against it. The committee was least comfortable in asserting the rights of Congress over the president and seemed to recognize that it was least credible in this posture. Article 4, alleging abuse of executive war powers in the secret bombing of Cambodia, also asserted congressional power, but it was defeated by a vote of 12–26, based on arguments that Congress was equally culpable in this abuse and that other presidents had been equally guilty of such abuses, an acknowledgment of the role of precedents in impeachment charges.

Article 5 charged Nixon with tax fraud and with violating the emoluments clause of the Constitution. Although it, too, was defeated resoundingly, the debate was long, and its content echoed the Johnson trial. In this instance, the members threshed out what was for them the distinction between personal misconduct and an impeachable offense. Delbert Latta (R-OH), who was placed on the committee for the period of the inquiry to add pro-Nixon balance and voted against all five articles, said that he found the president "guilty . . . of bad judgment and gross negligence" (554–55). In relation to this charge, the roles the committee members had chosen as legalists and as ordinary citizens were in conflict. For example, in addressing whether or not Nixon committed willful fraud, George Danielson (D-CA) said, "We use good judgment and common sense and we bear in mind at all times that people probably intend to do what they do in the serious matters in this life" (529). As a result, although the members decided, on legal grounds, that the evidence was not conclusive and that the offenses were not impeachable ones, the debate expressed the ordinary citizen's frustration and anger at Nixon-the-person for using fraudulent tactics to avoid payment of taxes.

The rhetorical setting was a debate among the members of a congressional committee broadcast live over national television.[38] Like all congressional committees, the House Committee on the Judiciary functioned under rules of seniority, parliamentary procedure, and special rules adopted by the committee. These rules make congressional debate rather formal and decorous. Because congressional debate had not been easily accessible to the public through the mass media before that time, these procedural rules had unusual effects. In calm times, congressional courtesy may be considered frivolous, but in a situation of constitutional crisis, such civility becomes the vital matter of decorum, essential when a president is being charged with highly indecorous behavior.

Congressional committee structure lends itself to cooperation. Majority and minority members can function together effectively only if conflicting views can be resolved through coalition and compromise, a process facilitated by an atmosphere of mutual respect. The norm of comity—never attacking another member, not even across party lines—contributes to such an atmosphere. Committee structure and habit make it more likely that a vote for impeachment will be bipartisan and that members will cooperate in establishing their credibility as individuals and as a committee. During the debate, the members frequently complimented one another and declared their friendship for those in the opposition. For example, James Mann (D-SC) and Walter Flowers (D-AL) declared their friendship for Charles Sandman (R-NJ), an adamant defender of the president who sarcastically attacked the Democratic majority on several occasions. As a result, the language and tone of the debate were in sharp contrast to the rhetoric of the managers in Johnson's trial. Only one really pointed exchange occurred. When the frustration of the president's defenders erupted, it was in an attack by Delbert Latta (R-OH) on the character of Albert Jenner, the minority counsel, and Latta was sharply rebuked for his behavior by another member of the Ohio delegation, Democrat John Seiberling. This violation of decorum was excised from the written record (199–200).

The broadcasting of the debate on national television opened the impeachment proceedings to the public. In his opening speech, Edward Hutchinson (R-MI), the ranking Republican, said, "Judges and juries deliberate behind closed doors. By the committee's action in opening these discussions it has, in effect, determined that our function is more political than judicial" (4). The decision by the House to allow the debate to be televised was strong evidence that the intended audience included the general public, the constituents in committee members' districts, and other members of Congress. Charles Sandman was correct when he said that an impeachment vote on at least one article was a foregone conclusion (17, 252); as a result, the committee members were rarely the primary audience.

As revealed in the debate on article 2, the committee was unable to develop any new evidence; the thirty-eight volumes of evidence discussed in the debate came from the Watergate special prosecutor, the Senate Select ("Ervin") Committee on Presidential Campaign Activities, and nine witnesses who had testified previously before other tribunals. Consequently, the function of the debate was to educate the public about the evidence and the issues, to test the strengths and weaknesses of the arguments and evidence, to express all possible attitudes and feelings about impeaching the president, and to initiate a process that would end national division. Despite protests from the administration about what it perceived as unfair media coverage, the public was not well informed about the issues related to impeachment.[39] The number of the events involved, the complexity of the issues, and the extended period of time over which the Watergate scandal unfolded made adequate coverage in newspapers or broadcast media impossible. The transcripts of the White House tapes were informative but difficult to read. The Ervin committee hearings televised during the summer of 1973 were fascinating human drama, but as they occurred early in the Watergate investigations, they could not provide a synthesized, coherent picture of what had happened. By contrast, the debate on the articles of impeachment organized the evidence, tested the charges, and rehearsed the available arguments for and against impeachment.

In terms of the norms for public rhetoric, however, there were few signs of adaptation to a mass audience. The evidence was presented at such a rate, and in such detail, that it was difficult to absorb, and a listener had to participate actively and to have considerable background from other sources to follow much of the argument. There was little use of metaphor, analogy, example, or humor, and a minimum of purple prose. What functioned as audience adaptation was more subtle. Because of the diversity of the committee members, each listener could find his or her voice among them, and for this reason, their diversity of regional dialect, attitude, and perspective was significant.

The unifying effect of the debate was partly a result of the cathartic expression of differences and partly a result of the process of inquiry and discussion. The committee's exploration of the available arguments and evidence revealed that there were strong grounds for impeaching the president. But rationality alone will not explain the widespread public approval of the committee's actions that crossed party boundaries. What Americans heard was "the voice of the genuine individual reminding us of our genuine selves, and of our role as members of a society in contrast to a mob."[40] By speaking as jurors, synthesizing their legalistic and civil concerns, the members avoided partisanship, hyperbole, personal attack, and vitriol. They spoke as the people's representatives, not as individuals; they attacked Richard Nixon only in his role as president; and they scrupulously avoided the appearance of congressional usurpation.

The committee was assisted by other factors, not the least of which was Nixon's unfortunate behavior, including his firing of special prosecutor Archibald Cox, which compelled the resignations of Elliot Richardson as attorney general and William Ruckelshaus as deputy attorney general when each, in turn, refused to carry out that order. Such behavior has been described as colliding "with deep-seated American norms about the rule of law, thus creating special pressures on the courts to reassert the primacy of this value in the use of presidential authority."[41] The 8–0 Supreme Court decision in *United States v. Nixon,* announced on July 24, which forced the White House to release key tapes, made a vote for impeachment more acceptable to members of the committee; however, the incriminating tapes became available only on August 5, after the debate was over. They included three conversations held on June 23, 1972, which provided "the smoking gun" demanded by Nixon's defenders: indisputable evidence that the president had known of the Watergate burglary and had participated actively in obstructing justice. Once this evidence became public, Nixon's removal was inevitable. He resigned on August 8, 1974.

THE IMPEACHMENT OF BILL CLINTON

Character flaws were central to the issues in Clinton's impeachment and trial.[42] The proceedings emerged out of the filing of a lawsuit on May 6, 1994, by Paula Corbin Jones in the United States District Court for the Eastern District of Arkansas. Jones alleged sexual harassment and violations of her federal civil rights in 1991 by Clinton when he was governor of Arkansas and she was a state employee.

After the lawsuit was filed, the president's attorneys moved to delay the proceedings, contending that the Constitution required that any legal action be deferred until his term ended, an issue ultimately decided against the president by the Supreme Court in *Clinton v. Jones.*[43] Following the Supreme Court decision, pretrial discovery commenced, in which potential witnesses were subpoenaed for information related to the Jones incident and, over the objections of the president's attorneys, Clinton's alleged sexual approaches to other women. On April 1, 1998, Judge Susan Webber Wright granted summary judgment in favor of Clinton, dismissing the Jones suit in its entirety, finding that Ms. Jones had not offered any evidence to support a viable claim of sexual harassment or intentional infliction of emotional distress. Ms. Jones appealed Judge Wright's decision to the Eighth Circuit Court of Appeals, but before a decision on the appeal was rendered, Ms. Jones and the president settled the case on November 13, 1998.

The name of Monica Lewinsky, who had worked in the White House as an intern in 1995, was included on a list of potential witnesses prepared by the attorneys for Ms. Jones that was submitted to the president's legal team.

On January 15, 1998, Independent Counsel Kenneth Starr, who had been appointed to investigate the Clintons' involvement in the Whitewater land deals, obtained approval from Attorney General Janet Reno to expand the scope of his investigations to include the new allegations, including those related to Lewinsky.

On January 17, Clinton was deposed in the Jones lawsuit. He denied having "sexual relations" with Lewinsky under a definition provided to him in writing by Jones's lawyers, and also said that he could not recall whether he ever was alone with her. On January 21, the *Washington Post*, the *Los Angeles Times*, and ABC News reported that Starr had expanded his investigation of the president to include allegations related to Lewinsky. After repeated media inquiries, on January 26, Clinton asserted in an appearance before the White House press corps, "I did not have sexual relations with that woman, Miss Lewinsky," and denied urging her to lie about an affair.[44]

The president's attorneys failed in their efforts to block Starr's expansion of his investigation, which also included whether the president had lied under oath in his deposition in the Paula Jones litigation. In July 1998, after being granted sweeping immunity from prosecution by Starr, Ms. Lewinsky admitted that she had had a sexual relationship with the president that did not include intercourse, but denied that she had ever been asked to lie about the relationship by the president or by those close to him.

On August 17, the president testified for over four hours before Starr's grand jury on closed-circuit television from the White House. In his testimony, which was later broadcast on television after its release by the House of Representatives, Clinton admitted the Lewinsky relationship, but denied that he had perjured himself in the Paula Jones deposition because he did not interpret his conduct with Lewinsky as constituting sexual relations. On the same evening, he appeared on national television and admitted that he had had an "inappropriate relationship" with Lewinsky and had misled the American people about it.[45]

On September 9, Independent Counsel Starr submitted a detailed report to Congress in which he contended that there was "substantial and credible information that President William Jefferson Clinton committed acts that may constitute grounds for an impeachment" by lying under oath in the Jones deposition and obstructing justice by urging Ms. Lewinsky "to file an affidavit that the President knew would be false."[46] On September 11, the House of Representatives authorized the Committee on the Judiciary to determine whether sufficient grounds existed to recommend to the House that an impeachment inquiry be commenced, and also approved the public release of the Starr report.

On September 21, the Committee on the Judiciary released nearly 3,200 pages of material from the grand jury proceedings and the Starr investigation, including transcripts of the testimony of President Clinton and Ms. Lewinsky. In the days following Clinton's grand jury testimony, calls for impeachment had mounted.

After listening to a panel of experts on impeachment and lawyers for the president, the Committee on the Judiciary voted on December 11 and 12, 1998, to approve four articles of impeachment. The full House approved two of them, rejecting an article based on perjury in the Jones deposition and one containing general charges relating to his unresponsive answers to the committee's questions and abuse of his office. Once again, the House resisted making struggles between the two branches of government the basis for impeachment. The next day, Henry Hyde (R-IL), chair of the Committee on the Judiciary, joined Tom De Lay (R-TX) and majority leader Richard Armey (R-TX) in calling for the president to resign.

Clinton's impeachment trial in the Senate commenced on January 7, 1999. The president's case was outlined in a White House trial memorandum submitted on January 13, which was countered by a House rebuttal. Subsequently, the Senate passed a series of motions to limit evidence primarily to previously videotaped depositions, affidavits, and other documents previously introduced and to close its final deliberations to the public. Each side would have twenty-four hours to present its case without witnesses. The senators would then have two days for a question-and-answer session, after which they would vote on motions to dismiss or requests for witnesses.

Over the first three days in February, House managers deposed Lewinsky, Vernon Jordan, and Sidney Blumenthal. Lewinsky's deposition took place in a hotel suite before a throng of over forty attorneys and congressional aides. Under questioning by Edward Bryant (R-TN), she proved to be an unhelpful witness. She described her present feelings toward the president as "mixed" and claimed that she filed her false affidavit in the Jones case in her own interests, not Clinton's. Most observers left believing that Lewinsky was no victim; accordingly, after her deposition, there was little support for using live witnesses. The Senate voted 70 to 30 against issuing Lewinsky a subpoena to testify. Instead, on a 62 to 38 vote, the Senate authorized each side to show video excerpts of deposition testimony by each of the three witnesses. On

February 6, the managers projected video images of Lewinsky, Jordan, and Blumenthal on four flat screens at the front of the chamber. Clinton's lawyers did the same, offering an uninterrupted twenty-minute clip of Lewinsky that showed her intelligence and near total control of her questioner.

Ultimately, both articles of impeachment were rejected, failing to receive the required votes of two-thirds of the senators.

We shall not analyze the speeches by the thirteen House managers presenting the case for impeachment or the speeches by Clinton's defense counsel Charles Ruff and Greg Craig in the Senate impeachment trial. Both sets of speeches vividly demonstrate that the issue was not the facts, but one's interpretation of them; in particular, whether lying under oath about sexual matters by a president constitutes an impeachable offense. No one committed the errors made by Andrew Johnson's accusers, but neither did those favoring impeachment take steps to ensure fairness and to diminish partisanship, moves that resulted in wide acceptance of congressional decisions in the Nixon impeachment effort.

SENATOR DALE BUMPERS'S DEFENSE OF CLINTON

In order to focus on what we believe are the key rhetorical strategies of defenders and accusers, we turn to the final speech made in Clinton's defense at his trial in the Senate. It was delivered by Dale Bumpers, a fellow Arkansas Democrat, who had served in the Senate for twenty-four years ending in January 1999. The speech illustrates the advantages afforded the president by having someone speak for him, particularly someone with a long career as a lawyer and politician who can address the senators who will decide his case as a peer with a long shared history. It is an example of exceptional rhetorical artistry as well as a powerful argument against a vote for impeachment. In addition, there are many parallels between the strategies of Andrew Johnson's defenders and the choices that Bumpers made in defending Bill Clinton.

As we have seen, two articles of impeachment had been passed by the full House, one alleging that Clinton had provided "perjurious, false, and misleading testimony" before independent counsel Kenneth Starr's grand jury, the other alleging that he had obstructed justice to "delay, impede, cover up, and conceal the existence of evidence" related to the Paula Jones case. Both articles alleged that Clinton had lied.[47]

Consistent with a legal defense, Bumpers stipulated what was known and admitted: that Clinton had engaged in inappropriate sexual behavior with Monica Lewinsky. He conceded that "the President suffered a terrible moral lapse of marital infidelity, . . . a breach of his marriage vows. It was a breach of his family trust. It is a sex scandal. . . . You pick your own adjective to describe the President's conduct. Here are some that I would use: indefensible, outrageous, unforgivable, shameless." Moreover, he noted, "The President has said for all to hear that he misled, he deceived, he did not want to be helpful to the prosecution."[48] Given those admissions, the issue was whether Clinton's lies constituted perjury and whether what he did was an impeachable offense.

Bumpers made three arguments. The first was legal, an effort to address directly the charge of perjury. He divided the issue to argue that there are different kinds of perjury: lies about sex and other criminal lies. After noting the many divorce cases he handled as an Arkansas attorney and guessing that in 80 percent of those that were contested, people lied, he commented, "But there is a very big difference in perjury about marital infidelity in a divorce case and perjury about whether I bought the murder weapon or whether I concealed the murder weapon or not. And to charge somebody with the first and punish them as though it were the second, stands justice—our sense of justice—on its head." He also cited the five prosecutors who testified before the House Committee on the Judiciary "that, under identical circumstances, the identical circumstances of this case, we would never charge anybody because we'd know we couldn't get a conviction." The difference between what Clinton had admitted and what had been alleged under the rubrics of Whitewater, Travelgate, and Filegate culminated in his statement that, after "a five-year, relentless, unending investigation of the President" by the independent counsel, "The President was found guilty of nothing, official or personal."[49]

The legal argument took a political turn when Bumpers introduced a long example from Monica Lewinsky's testimony before the grand jury, followed by the report of the House Committee on the Judiciary, to show how her words had been reinterpreted to suggest perjury, a move that, as a former prosecutor, he described as "wanting to win too badly." That motive implied a partisan effort to construe the evidence in ways that would lead to impeachment. That implication ran through the entire speech, although Bumpers used the term "partisanship" only once, in the conclusion. Instead, he made that argument indirectly, saying that impeachment was designed "to protect the public, not to punish the President," that Madison had feared that a decision on impeachment "would be based on the comparative strength of the parties rather than the innocence or guilt of the President," and that there "is a total lack of proportionality, a total lack of balance in this thing." Bumpers advised the senators, "If you have difficulty because of an intense dislike of the President, and that is understandable, rise above it. He is not the issue. He will be gone. You won't. So don't leave a precedent from which we may never recover and almost surely will regret." Finally, he told them that the people "are calling on you to rise above politics, rise above partisanship. They're calling on you to do your solemn duty. And I pray you will."[50] His implication was that Clinton's lies could be construed as perjury and as an impeachable offense only in a highly partisan climate.

This argument was consistent with Bumpers's second, constitutional argument, that Clinton's actions did not constitute an impeachable offense. Bumpers traced the process by which the impeachment provision of the Constitution was drafted, noting the drafters' efforts to avoid vague terms, such as "maladministration" and "corruption." He showed that they had made a concerted effort to narrow the grounds for impeachment. Finally, to the agreed-upon grounds of "treason and bribery," George Mason had added, "or other high crimes and misdemeanors against the United States," which was approved. The whole was then sent to the Committee on Style and Arrangement for editing, he reported, which deleted the final phrase as redundant. In order to demonstrate that the phrase "high crimes and misdemeanors" referred only to crimes against the state, he traced the history of the phrase back to English law "under a category which said 'distinctly political' offenses against the state." He concluded, "Nobody has suggested that Bill Clinton committed a political crime against the state." Given that history, he argued to the Senate, "if you honor the Constitution, you must look at the history of the Constitution and how we got to the impeachment clause. And if you do that, . . . you cannot convict him."[51]

Bumpers's third argument was practical or expedient: acquittal is the best choice for the country. "If you vote to acquit," he said, "you go immediately to the people's agenda. But if you vote to convict, you can't be sure what is going to happen." Here he paraphrased Senator James G. Blaine, who voted for the impeachment of Andrew Johnson, but who, as we noted, recanted 20 years later: "As I reflect back on it, all I can think about is, having convicted Andrew Johnson would have caused much more chaos and confusion in this country than Andrew Johnson could ever conceivably have created." This argument was buttressed by references to national elections as part of the rule of law, to polls suggesting that the public wanted an end to this process, and an allusion to Gerald Ford's first speech after Nixon's resignation as president: "They [the people] are asking for an end to this nightmare."[52]

Bumpers's speech resonated with the strategies used by William Evarts in defending Andrew Johnson before the Senate. In contrast to the intensity and solemnity of the managers who presented the House case to the Senate, Bumpers began with self-deprecation and humor, and he used jokes to defuse hostility toward the president. He never attacked his opponents; in fact, he described their presentations as eloquent. The carefully developed constitutional argument, the crux of the case, was buttressed by the legal argument, which raised doubts about the appropriateness of interpreting Clinton's lies and evasions as perjury. A careful distinction was made between personal misbehavior and a crime against the state, buttressed by an appeal for compassion based on the seemingly endless investigation of Clinton's actions by the independent counsel, the high legal fees that had bankrupted innocent people, and the punishment visited on Clinton by the shame and humiliation he experienced before his family as a result of his misbehavior and the public revelation of his lies. Finally, Bumpers pleaded that the public wanted this long process to end and, according to polls, without the removal of the president.

Like Evarts, Bumpers did not defend what the president had done; instead, he castigated it with powerful adjectives. Like Evarts's defense, his defense was based on an understanding of impeachable offenses as crimes against the state, not just bad behavior. Like Evarts's, Bumpers's tone was significantly different from that of the managers, who were solemn, intense, and impassioned in their assertions of the seriousness of Clinton's lies and deceptions. Bumpers never disputed those claims, but invited the listening senators to consider them differently, to admit that no one is perfect and that there is a strong motive to lie about sexual improprieties. He was able to evoke laughter at several points in his speech, something that appears not to have occurred in response to the managers' speeches. His tone and style promoted cooler, less impassioned deliberation and a kinder, less punishing view of human imperfections.

All three impeachment cases, then, emphasize the importance of style, tone, and attitude. The removal of a president is the most extreme action that can be taken by Congress. Whatever can be construed as too impassioned, partisan, harsh, or intemperate damages those who seek impeachment and facilitates defense of the president. Insofar as the defenders of the president appear calm, temperate, and nonpartisan and devoted to the good of the nation, their defenses prevail. Those seeking to impeach a president can prevail only when they take every precaution and make every effort to dispel implications of unfairness and partisanship. That, we think, is as it should be.

CONCLUSION

The rhetorical choices made by Nixon's supporters and opponents were in sharp contrast to those made by Johnson's accusers. It is these kinds of choices, as well as the rhetorical relationship between Congress and the president that they reflect, that are the key to understanding why Johnson's impeachment produced an acquittal, which failed to resolve the conflict between branches, while Nixon's precipitated a resignation and began a process of healing, and Clinton's produced an acquittal that failed to resolve or reduce the partisan climate in Congress.

As the impeachment proceedings against Nixon, Johnson, and Clinton illustrate, the ordinary rhetorical conditions of presidential discourse are altered in four significant ways under such circumstances: (1) the president is physically absent from the scene of debate; (2) the president is compelled to respond to specific charges at a particular time and place; (3) in responding to charges that the oath of office has been violated, the president's use of the personal apologia is severely limited; and (4) there is an immediate audience that must reach a formal verdict expressed in a vote.

No president has chosen to be physically present at formal impeachment proceedings, although in theory each might have chosen to appear before the House Committee on the Judiciary or to speak in his own defense in the Senate. Executive privilege has a long history, and presidents historically have refused to answer summonses to appear before Congress or its committees. Even in the case of Andrew Johnson, who was summoned to appear, the Senate accepted that he was symbolically represented before them by counsel.

Absence disadvantages the president rhetorically because the power of the president's presence as a symbol of the nation, a power illustrated in the special rituals through which a president comes before Congress to deliver the State of the Union address, is lost. Some rhetorical advantages accrue to presidents from their absence from the chambers in which the debate occurs, however. Presidents stand in relation to their defenders as a defendant to counsel, and like other defendants, are entitled to have disinterested legal experts assess the situation and develop and execute sophisticated strategies of response. In a Senate trial, the president's counselors are the counterparts of the managers whom the House deputizes to speak for it. It is to the president's advantage to be represented by a group able to present an exhaustive range of arguments without incurring charges of inconsistency. In addition, counsel are able to advance arguments that presidents could not make in their own behalf. In Johnson's case, for instance, one of his defenders admitted that Johnson was unlettered and intemperate, but denied that he was guilty of an impeachable offense. The advantage of being defended by others was magnified in the case of this president, whose rhetorical biography suggests that he would not have spoken effectively in the Senate in his own defense. If he had made inappropriate and indecorous arguments, as seems likely, such arguments would have redounded against him directly and increased the likelihood that he would have been found guilty.[53]

Presidents are further disadvantaged because they no longer control the terms of the debate. Once formal proceedings begin, and in particular, once articles are being debated in committee or in the House or Senate, the president becomes just one actor in an adversarial proceeding, compelled to respond, to justify specific actions named in the articles. In other words, unlike most presidential discourse, defense against impeachment does not occasion a single speech by the president; rather, it is an interchange between accusers and defenders in which responses are compelled and refutation must be anticipated. Moreover, once a president is charged with violating the oath of office, justifications based on personality and character alone will no longer suffice.

Finally, impeachment is a public proceeding, "an official business session of a representative body, including debate and decision on specific issues, conducted before an audience made up of members of the body's constituency."[54] The public proceeding has two interrelated purposes: (1) to make a decision on the matter at hand, in this case, to vote on impeachment; and (2) to gain assent for that decision from the citizenry. In other words, "the body conducting the proceeding must legitimate itself."[55] In this sense, the ultimate arbiter of presidential performance is the people. Just as they must witness and ratify the rhetoric of investiture in the inaugural address, they must witness and ratify the rhetoric of divestiture in impeachment debates and trials. When partisanship is perceived as playing a key role, the process will not garner public approval and acceptance, nor will it heal underlying divisions.

Institutionally, the rhetoric of impeachment is the mirror image of the rhetoric of inauguration. Inaugural rhetoric invests; impeachment rhetoric divests. Despite this close relationship, the two differ significantly in that the latter is the work of two branches of government. Impeachment rhetoric is still more closely related to war rhetoric and is an even clearer instance of the struggle for power between Congress and the president. It follows, then, that impeachment rhetoric is the single rhetorical genre that is partially constitutive of the character and the behavior of both Congress and the president. And, of course, it is the only genre in which a president's right to continue in office can be decided by Congress.

The president's rhetorical standing changes during the impeachment process. While under investigation, the president is under suspicion; while articles are being debated, the president's actions are being scrutinized; once articles have been voted, the president is under indictment, and presidential credibility diminishes. Analysis of presidential rhetoric in this situation underscores the advantage presidents have over the other branches of government under most other circumstances. Unlike the legislature or the judiciary, presidents are able to speak whenever, wherever, and on whatever issue they choose until impeachment compels them to respond to specific charges at a specific time before a specific audience.

TWELVE

Farewell Addresses

The presidential farewell address is produced in response to an institutional need for a ritual of departure. It occurs during a period in which presidents have greater than usual power to redefine the people and the presidency and by so doing to bequeath a legacy to the country. If presidents exploit that privileged time rhetorically, their legacies link the criteria by which they hope their presidencies will be judged to a unifying vision of the country's future—a future shaped by the lessons drawn from the experiences of their administration. The role assumed by outgoing presidents at this moment is profoundly rhetorical. Their practical power virtually spent, in this address more than in any other, presidents must rely on moral suasion.

In this chapter, we examine the institutional needs that prompt the farewell address, the legacy it attempts to bequeath, the moment that facilitates bequeathal, and the role presidents must play and the strategies they must use in order to communicate their visions and make their legacies enduring. Specifically, at the end of the chapter, we attempt to explain why the farewell addresses of Washington, Jackson, Truman, and Eisenhower eloquently concluded their presidencies and why those of Nixon and Carter invited doubts about their administrations and the circumstances under which each was leaving office.

Farewell addresses have an important institutional function. The presidency must be more than a succession of discrete individuals. Presidents symbolically create a sense of continuity not only by claiming in their inaugurals that they understand the lessons of the past, but also by formulating the lessons of their presidencies for later generations in their farewells. As they testify to what they have learned and how it applies to the future, they create a sense that the presidency is being perfected and that the relationships among the branches of government are evolving. In addition, departing presidents reaffirm the meaning of the people and enrich that conception in light of what can be learned from their tenure in office.

That legacy and that new conception of the presidency and of the interrelationships among the elements of our system of government, if articulated clearly and well, become part of the government's ongoing existence, ensuring its continuity. Moreover, in the farewell address, a president projects a conception of the nation and the presidency into the future in an effort to influence the actions of succeeding presidents. Washington's farewell, for example, so clearly enunciates the dangers of foreign alliances that his legacy guided his successors well into the twentieth century.[1]

A farewell signifies both continuity and change. The farewell address suggests that as the nation combines the lessons of the outgoing administration with its founding principles, its system of government not only will survive, but also prosper. Change is sanctioned as a by-product of understanding the past, particularly the meaning of the events of a presidency. Continuity is the outgrowth of reaffirmed principles and of a renewed covenant.

Saying farewell implies a relationship. The relationship between the president and the citizenry is defined by law and custom. Their formal relationship begins with the swearing in of a new president and ends with the swearing in of a successor. The presidential farewell is not a form of permanent leave-taking, but rather a rite of passage, because the outgoing president returns to the role of citizen. Presidents say farewell to the presidency, taking leave of a relationship that has bound them to the people in a special way. "In the years ahead, I will never hold a position higher or a covenant more sacred than that of President of the United States. But there is no title I will wear more proudly than that of citizen," said Bill Clinton.[2]

A farewell address is an anticipatory ritual; the address is delivered days, sometimes weeks, before an outgoing president "lays down" the office, an event that does not occur until a successor is sworn in. As Harry Truman said, "The Presidency of the United States continues to function without a moment's break."[3] The farewell itself is not the act of putting aside the power of the presidency; it signifies transition. Between the delivery of the farewell and the inauguration of the new president, the country has time to ponder the legacy of its outgoing leader before it contemplates the ideas presented in the incoming president's inaugural.

The farewell address meets a symbolic need for a ceremony of transition. In folk wisdom, beginnings require endings. Thus, an inaugural requires a farewell. The rhetorical impulse for delivery of a farewell arises because the U.S. government, unlike some other institutions, has not formalized the ceremonial rhetoric of initiation and departure. For example, a Christian is welcomed into the faith in baptismal rituals and is ushered into the next life with funereal rhetoric. Similarly, the French Academy juxtaposes a eulogy for an academician who has died with a speech welcoming the replacement.[4] By contrast, George Washington's sense that a separate farewell message addressed to the citizenry was needed and appropriate began what has become a tradition in the modern presidency.

The farewell address is a symbolic response to the perceived need for a ritual of leave-taking from an office publicly assumed in the inaugural address and publicly sustained in State of the Union addresses and other presidential rhetoric. Without a farewell address, the transition becomes abrupt; no symbolic process readjusts citizens to the new status of their former leader. The need for closure at the end of a president's tenure in office—the need to complete a term symbolically—means that a presidential farewell usually echoes the rhetoric of the inaugural(s) and invariably reflects the style and lines of argument that have characterized the discourse of a presidency.

Because farewells are not mandated by the Constitution, as are veto messages, or as fixed by custom as are inaugurals, many choices are open. An outgoing president may choose not to make a separate, formal farewell address; however, in virtually every instance, some farewell remarks are made. If one or more formal farewells are to be made, the president can select or create the occasion(s) and the audience(s) to be addressed. The president can issue a farewell to the American people, including Congress and the citizenry, as did Eisenhower, Nixon, and Reagan. The president can deliver a farewell to Congress, which the citizenry overhears, as did Ford[5] and Lyndon Johnson,[6] or deliver a separate farewell to each, as did Harry Truman.[7] Other occasions can also call forth farewell rhetoric. Lyndon Johnson, for example, ended his last press conference with a farewell to the country as well as to the press.[8] A farewell may be delivered orally, or it may be written, as were those of Washington and Jackson as well as Truman's farewell to Congress.

Presidents who included leave-taking rhetoric in their last State of the Union addresses include Grant,[9] Truman, Lyndon Johnson, and Ford. Seven other presidents made more than passing references to their forthcoming departures in their final annual messages: Jefferson,[10] Madison,[11] Monroe,[12] Tyler,[13] Polk,[14] Fillmore,[15] and Arthur.[16] Separate farewells addressed to the citizenry were made by Washington, Jackson, Andrew Johnson,[17] Truman, Eisenhower, Carter, Reagan, and Clinton. Richard Nixon delivered a resignation speech that was, simultaneously, his farewell. In 1981, the release on inauguration day of the U.S. hostages held in Iran prompted a separate farewell statement by Jimmy Carter after he had left office.[18] Similarly, rhetoric that would ordinarily have been private—Nixon's farewell to his staff—became part of the public process of leave-taking because the threat to the system posed by Nixon's near-impeachment made all facets of his departure worthy of press coverage.[19]

Generically, farewells have certain distinctive characteristics: (1) they occur when the president can assume a persona combining the roles of leader and visionary; (2) if the legacy is to be successfully bequeathed, it must be consistent with the character of the president and with the events and rhetoric of the administration; (3) consistent with the character of the farewell as epideictic rhetoric, the legacy must be offered for contemplation rather than action, but may contain warnings; and (4) enduring legacies are encapsulated in a memorable phrase or sentence that reminds the citizenry of an enduring truth about our system of government.

The timing of the farewell is crucial. A farewell is delivered between the election and the inauguration of a successor; that is, when the president is making the transition from president to citizen. In this interval, the president retains the authority of the institution and can consequently, in Truman's words, speak "from the desk" in "the office." The farewell occurs when partisan motivations are at an ebb; as Reagan put it, "Tonight isn't for arguments, and I'm going to hold my tongue."[20] Standing apart from party battles, no longer tainted by self-interest, the president can now speak, in the words of George Washington, as "a disinterested friend," offering what Jackson called "parting counsels." Because a successor has already been elected, the message cannot be read as intervention on behalf of a party, its candidate, or its platform. This privileged moment is one in which a president can offer what Jackson termed "the counsels of age and experience," hoping that they will be received with "indulgent kindness" and "an earnest desire" on the part of the people "to perpetuate in this favored land the blessings of liberty and equal law."[21]

The twilight of incumbency enables the president to assume a special persona. During this period, the president, speaking as the president, can assume a persona crucial to the function of this rhetorical act. This role has its roots in Deuteronomy, a book written as if it were Moses's farewell address to the people of Israel.[22] Moses, alone among the prophets, combined visionary and political or leadership roles.[23] Analogously, at the end of the term of office, the president can integrate a visionary, prophetic function with the role of chief executive. Thus, like the biblical farewells that were ritualistic renewals of the covenant between Israel and Yahweh, the presidential farewell attempts to renew the original covenant between the citizenry and its leaders.

Seizing the opportunity offered by this moment to assume this special persona does not guarantee that bequeathal will occur. Presidents must be able to articulate their visions or legacies in ways consistent with their personal histories and with the achievements and the rhetoric of their administrations. To ensure that the legacy endures, farewells usually include statements of gratitude for support and cooperation, statements implying that the legacy is not just the president's, but has been jointly created by the people, the president, and Congress, intimating that all have a vested interest in perpetuating it. If this is done, the president can draw lessons, usually in the form of warnings, from the collective past. Implicit in these lessons are criteria by which all presidents, including this one, ought to be judged. Hence, the accomplishments of an administration, the criteria by which it should be judged, and the lessons it offers for the future are interwoven to create the legacy.

Thus, for example, Washington argued that during his tenure dangerous alliances had been avoided and a divisive party spirit diminished, and his legacy included warnings against the spirit of faction and against permanent alliances with major European powers. Jackson argued that he had restored constitutional boundaries and warned against violating such limits in the future. Truman claimed that he had responded decisively to the challenges he had faced and warned that similar decisive action would be required in the future to contain the "communist menace." Eisenhower argued that the peace had been kept, but warned that the power concentrated in the military-industrial complex threatened the balance of government power and imperiled that task in the future.

The criteria selected and the warnings developed in farewell addresses are revealing because the failures and successes of each presidency are mirrored in what is excluded from and included in them. Accordingly, Lyndon Johnson's last State of the Union address was an argument that his presidency should be judged by the accomplishments of the Great

Society: Medicare, voting rights, federal assistance to schools, Head Start, job training, and the like. Of these accomplishments he said, "We have finished a major part of the old agenda." By implication, he should be judged not by progress in Vietnam, but by these domestic programs:

> Now, it is time to leave. I hope it may be said, a hundred years from now, that by working together we helped to make our country more just, more just for all of its people, as well as to insure and guarantee the blessing of liberty for all our posterity.[24]

In other words, history should ask not what was accomplished for Southeast Asians, whose "hearts and minds" he had failed to win, but what was achieved for the people of the United States.

In a similar move, Nixon argued that he should be judged by his achievements in foreign affairs and claimed that keeping the peace was the overarching concern of the present and future. In this process, he attempted to redirect public attention from the crises caused by Watergate.

Ford, whose record of accomplishments was mixed, asked the nation to judge him by whether or not he had transmitted the institution of the presidency intact:

> Now, after 30 months as your President, I can say that while we still have a way to go, I am proud of the long way we have come together. I am proud of the part I have had in rebuilding confidence in the Presidency, confidence in our free system, and confidence in our future. Once again, Americans believe in themselves, in their leaders, and in the promise that tomorrow holds for their children.[25]

By this criterion, Ford's presidency had succeeded.

Ordinarily, the criteria established by a president entail warnings. Because he claimed the achievement, noteworthy in his case, of having transmitted the presidency intact to his successor, Ford could warn against limiting presidential power, a natural response to Watergate:

> Because we may have been too careless of these powers in the past does not justify congressional intrusion into, or obstruction of, the proper exercise of Presidential responsibilities now or in the future. There can be only one Commander in Chief. In these times crises cannot be managed and wars cannot be

waged by committee, nor can peace be pursued solely by parliamentary debate. To the ears of the world, the President speaks for the Nation.[26]

Presidents who cannot or do not detail the accomplishments of their terms in office, thereby establishing criteria for judging their presidencies, cannot deliver an aesthetically satisfying, memorable address, as illustrated by Jimmy Carter's farewell, discussed below.

George H. W. Bush made no formal farewell to the nation; however, he delivered farewell discourse in a series of speeches that cohered into a rhetorical act of farewell. This discourse emerged in a radio message on the results of the election on November 7, 1992, and in speeches to small, sympathetic audiences at Texas A&M University on December 15, 1992, and at the United States Military Academy at West Point, New York, on January 5, 1993. In the radio address to the nation, he began to create his legacy: "I hope history will record the Bush administration has served America well. I am proud of my Cabinet and my staff. America has led the world through an age of global transition. We have made the world safer for our kids. And I believe the real fruits of our global victory are yet to be tasted."[27]

Bush's speech at Texas A&M University was more like a traditional farewell. Acknowledging his transition from president to citizen, Bush said,

> In 36 days, I'll hand over the stewardship of this great Nation, capping a career in public service that began 50 years ago in wartime skies over the Pacific. And our country won that great contest but entered an uneasy peace. You see, the fires of World War II cooled into a longer cold war, one that froze the world into two opposing camps. . . . Today, by the grit of our people and the grace of God, the cold war is over. Freedom has carried the day. And I leave the White House grateful for what we have achieved together and also exhilarated by the promise of what can come to pass.[28]

He laid out the meaning of this history: "Here then is the remarkable fact that history will record, a fact that will be studied for years in the [Bush] library right here at Texas A&M University: The end of a titanic clash of political systems, the collapse of the most heavily armed empire in history, took place without a shot being fired. That should be a source of pride for every American." He asserted that "a new and better world is, indeed, a realistic possibility."[29] In order to counter the pessimists, he listed the accomplishments of his administration:

I ask them to consider the last four years when a dozen dreams were made real: The Berlin Wall demolished and Germany united; the captive nations set free; Russia democratic; whole classes of nuclear weapons eliminated, the rest vastly reduced; many nations united in our historic U.N. coalition to turn back a tyrant in the Persian Gulf; Israel and its Arab neighbors for the first time talking peace, face to face, in a region that has known so much war. Each of these once seemed a dream. Today they're concrete realities, brought about by a common cause: the patient and judicious application of American leadership, American power, and perhaps most of all, American moral force.[30]

Bush also offered warnings:

Destiny, it has been said, is not a matter of chance; it's a matter of choice. . . . Our choice as a people is simple: We can either shape our times, or we can let the times shape us. And shape us they will, at a price frightening to contemplate, morally, economically, and strategically. . . . The new world could, in time, be as menacing as the old. And let me be blunt: A retreat from American leadership, from American involvement, would be a mistake for which future generations, indeed our own children, would pay dearly.[31]

At the end, Bush exhorted us to follow in his footsteps: "History is summoning us once again to lead. Proud of its past, America must once again look forward. And we must live up to the greatness of our forefathers' ideals and in doing so secure our grandchildren's futures. And that is the cause that much of my public life has been dedicated to serving."[32]

These views were echoed at West Point. There Bush contrasted the past and the present: "Two hundred years ago, another departing President warned of the dangers of what he described as 'entangling alliances.' His was the right course for a new nation at that point in history. But what was 'entangling' in Washington's day is now essential." Referring to his speech in Texas, he added, "We must engage ourselves if a new world order, one more compatible with our values and congenial to our interest, is to emerge. But even more, we must lead." He also echoed his earlier warnings: "But in the wake of the cold war, in a world where we are the only remaining superpower, it is the role of the United States to marshal its moral and material resources to promote a democratic peace. It is our responsibility, it is our opportunity to lead. There is no one else."[33]

The elements that form Bush's rhetorical act of farewell reflect the motives and purposes of this kind of discourse: the intense need for a ritual of leave-taking, a desire to craft a legacy that will inform future public policy, and a wish to offer warnings based on the president's experience.

Clinton ended his presidency with a farewell tour with stops in New Hampshire, Michigan, Massachusetts, and elsewhere, ending in his home state of Arkansas. He delivered a farewell address to the nation from the Oval Office on January 18, 2001. Finally, he delivered a radio address, which was followed by another farewell address at Andrews Air Force Base, on January 20, 2001, following George W. Bush's inauguration. His Oval Office address is noteworthy for the specificity of his claims of accomplishment:

> Working together, America has done well. Our economy is breaking records with more than 22 million new jobs, the lowest unemployment in 30 years, the highest homeownership ever, the longest expansion in history. Our families and communities are stronger. Thirty-five million Americans have used the family leave law; 8 million have moved off welfare. Crime is at a 25-year low. Over 10 million Americans receive more college aid, and more people than ever are going to college. Our schools are better. Higher standards, greater accountability, and larger investments have brought higher test scores and higher graduation rates. More than 3 million children have health insurance now, and more than 7 million Americans have been lifted out of poverty. Incomes are rising across the board. Our air and water are cleaner. Our food and drinking water are safer. And more of our precious land has been preserved in the continental United States than at any time in 100 years.[34]

Consistent with this focus on domestic and economic accomplishments, he warned, "America must maintain our record of fiscal responsibility."[35]

> Through our last four budgets we've turned record deficits to record surpluses, and we've been able to pay down $600 billion of our national debt—on track to be debt-free by the end of the decade for the first time since 1835. Staying on that course will bring lower interest rates, greater prosperity, and the opportunity to meet our big challenges. If we choose wisely, we can pay down the debt, deal with the retirement of the baby boomers, invest more in our future, and provide tax relief.[36]

The problem with Clinton's speech is that it too closely mimics the campaign speech of a candidate seeking reelection. Alternatively, the speech can be seen as a tacit warning to the country that by rejecting his heir apparent, Vice President Al Gore, for Republican George W. Bush, it has made a serious mistake. Instead of a message for the ages, this speech seems to be a defense of the immediate past and a warning to the incoming president.

The third of Clinton's thoughts about the future comes closer to hitting the mark in both its level of generality and its nonpartisan tone:

Third, we must remember that America cannot lead in the world unless here at home we weave the threads of our coat of many colors into the fabric of one America. As we become ever more diverse, we must work harder to unite around our common values and our common humanity. We must work harder to overcome our differences, in our hearts and in our laws. We must treat all our people with fairness and dignity, regardless of their race, religion, gender, or sexual orientation, and regardless of when they arrived in our country—always moving toward the more perfect Union of our Founders' dreams.[37]

What saves Clinton's speech from the charge that it is self-aggrandizing is his move to credit the citizenry with the accomplishments he claims:

This has been a time of dramatic transformation, and you have risen to every new challenge. You have made our social fabric stronger, our families healthier and safer, our people more prosperous. You, the American people, have made our passage into the global information age an era of great American renewal.[38]

The farewell address is epideictic; it must transcend legislative particulars to articulate the meaning of the events of a presidency.[39] Ideally, the president reformulates the nation's conception of the presidency or of our system of government. Such a reformulation unifies the audience by creating a compelling perspective on the future that rehearses traditional values and renews the covenant underlying our system of government. Although the farewell occurs only at the end of a presidency, this address, in an important sense, is atemporal because its intended audience includes citizens as yet unborn. The farewell speaks to history. Admittedly, presidents issue many messages that they know will be scrutinized by subsequent generations. An occasional veto message or speech of self-defense appeals to history for vindication denied in the present. Such rhetoric, however, also seeks action in the present—personal exoneration on the one hand, a vote to sustain the veto on the other. By contrast, the aim of the farewell, like that of the inaugural, is contemplation. In their farewells, presidents tell us that they are speaking to the future, and they invite history's judgment of their tenure in office.[40] In so doing, they draw on their presidential experience to chart a course for their successors and for the people. They delineate the hazards the country may confront and the benefits it may gain by following that course. As Ronald Reagan commented in 1989, "There is a great tradition of warnings in presidential farewells, and I've got one that's been on my mind for some time."[41]

The epideictic character of farewell addresses is reflected in the priestly function the president performs in them, similar to the role assumed by the president in national eulogies. Until invested with the office, presidents cannot entrust the nation to God or intercede for the nation before God. At the privileged moment of departure, they are able to perform a last priestly function: to ask God to watch over the nation's future. Because God presumably heard their inaugural prayers and guided their administrations, this final supplication is a natural extension of a critical element in the inaugural address. Gerald Ford expressed this idea with great clarity:

> My fellow Americans, I once asked you for your prayers, and now I give you mine: May God guide this wonderful country, its people, and those they have chosen to lead them. May our third century be illuminated by liberty and blessed with brotherhood, so that we and all who come after us may be the humble servants of Thy peace. Amen.[42]

In their inaugurals, presidents acknowledge their dependence on God and entrust the nation to God's care. Correspondingly, in their farewells, they ask God to protect the future of the country for all time. Jackson asked that God "make you worthy . . . to guard and defend to the end of time the great charge He has committed to your keeping."[43] George Washington "fervently beseech[ed] the Almighty to avert or mitigate the evils to which they [his "many errors"] may tend," hoping his country would "never cease to view them with indulgence."[44] Richard Nixon prayed that "God's grace be with you in all the days ahead."[45] Dwight Eisenhower used terms with messianic and millenarian connotations when he prayed that "in the goodness of time, all peoples will come to live together in a peace guaranteed by the binding force of mutual respect and love."[46]

This invocation of God formally renews the covenant in the civil religion that now includes the legacy of a presidency. The future of the nation cannot be assured merely by its learning the lessons of history in a pragmatic sense; the people must also affirm their special relationship to God. With God's grace and God's guidance, the polity can divine the meaning of events and find the way to act rightly. The act of entrusting the country to God signals the end of the privileged moment. It is now the people, their newly elected leader, and their God who must safeguard the covenant.

Each presidential farewell attempts to bequeath a legacy that will be enduring. Leave-takings become eloquent when they are artistic wholes whose content is linked directly not only to the events of a presidency, but also to the style and history of the president. Sometimes the legacy is embodied in a memorable phrase. Washington's farewell, for example, is recalled by his warnings against extremes of partisanship and permanent foreign alliances; Jackson's message is summed up in the statement that "eternal vigilance by the people is the price of liberty." Andrew Johnson ended his address with the words, "The Constitution and the Union, one and inseparable," echoing the theme of his well-known Senate speeches delivered between 1860 and 1862.[47] Eisenhower's farewell spoke of the dangers posed by "the military-industrial complex"; Truman's farewell to the people reflected the phrase with which his presidency was associated: "The buck stops here." Ronald Reagan linked his farewell to "the shining 'city upon a hill,'" noting that he had "spoken of the shining city all my political life."[48] Even Richard Nixon uttered a phrase in his resignation/farewell that ironically recalled the phrase he had made famous in his so-called Checkers speech: "I am not a quitter." A memorable phrase, however, is only the beginning of crafting a farewell address that will make a legacy enduring. As the farewells of Truman, Jackson, Washington, and Eisenhower illustrate, eloquent farewells also merge character, style, and achievements.

ELOQUENT FAREWELLS

Harry Truman's farewell was an artistic masterpiece, a beautifully crafted whole unified by the symbol of the president's desk. Initially, "the desk" identified the place from which he spoke to the radio audience, but it quickly became a symbol for what presidents do and for the continuity of the presidency as an institution:

> I am speaking to you from the room where I have worked since April 12, 1945. This is the President's office in the West Wing of the White House. This is the desk where I have signed most of the papers that embodied the decisions I have made as President. It has been the desk of many Presidents, and will be the desk of many more.[49]

He listed the places to which he had traveled and counted the miles; then he added, "But the mail always followed me, and wherever I happened to be, that's where the office of the President was."[50]

What followed characterized the presidency as a decision-making institution and linked the symbol of the desk to the phrase "the buck stops here":

> The greatest part of the President's job is to make decisions—big ones and small ones, dozens of them almost every day. The papers may circulate around the Government for a while but they finally reach this desk. And then, there's no place else for them to go. The President—whoever he is—has to decide. He can't pass the buck to anybody. No one else can do the deciding for him. That's his job.[51]

Truman reinforced his claim by juxtaposing the problems he had confronted with the solutions he had offered. His broadcast farewell recounted instance after instance in which he had responded decisively. After being told that Roosevelt had died, he said,

> I offered to do anything I could for Mrs. Roosevelt, and then I asked the Secretary of State to call the Cabinet together. At 7:09 P.M. I was sworn in as President. ... The San Francisco conference to organize the United Nations had been called for April 25th. I was asked if that meeting would go forward. I announced that it would. That was my first decision. After attending President Roosevelt's funeral, I went to the Hall of the House of Representatives and told a joint session of the Congress that I would carry on President Roosevelt's policies. ... The war against Japan was still going on. I made the decision that the atomic bomb had to be used to end it. I made that decision in the conviction it would save hundreds of thousands of lives—Japanese as well as American.[52]

In defining the nature of the president's job, Truman stressed its power, responsibility, and difficulty: "There is no job like it on the face of the earth in the power that is concentrated here at this desk, and in the responsibility and difficulty of the decisions."[53] To lessen the possibility that this claim would seem self-aggrandizing, Truman noted that he was informing the citizens of this difficulty so they would better understand the task of his successor: "I want all of you to realize how big a job, how hard a job, it is—not for my sake, because I am stepping out of it—but for the sake of my successor."[54]

Near the end of the speech, the desk reappeared: "So, as I empty the drawers of this desk, and as Mrs. Truman and I leave the White House, we have no regret."[55] He referred to the inadequacy he felt in taking over the presidency from Roosevelt, but added, "Through all of it, through all the years I have worked here in this room, I have been well aware I did not really work alone—that you were working with me. . . . Those are the things we have done together."[56]

Truman was asking that a presidency be judged by whether or not it confronted historic events decisively. Accordingly, he said, "When history says that my term of office saw the beginning of a cold war, it will also say that in those eight years we have set the course that can win it."[57] Of his action in Korea, he said, "So a decision was reached—the decision I believe was the most important in my time as President of the United States. In the days that followed, the most heartening fact was that the American people clearly agreed with the decision."[58] Truman presented the president as one who leads, not follows, public sentiment. Throughout the speech, Truman argued that, unlike some past leaders and administrations, when his administration was faced with a test, it responded decisively: "Where fine men had failed the test before, this time we met the test."[59]

Truman's broadcast farewell was a civics lesson in which, through the homely but original symbol of the desk, he explained the nature of the presidency to the American people. The device is an instance of metonymy, the figure of speech by which the diffuse, ineffable, or spiritual is made concrete, specific, and material. In this form, the nature of the presidency can be understood by the lowliest citizen. Good presidents act. They are able to act because their acts reflect the will of the people; thus, they act with the support of the people. Truman was asking the audience to approve his record—to understand the difficult job he had had and to ratify his actions as instances of presidential decisiveness, a quality the citizenry should applaud in all presidents.

Truman's speech was a satisfying farewell. It left its hearers with a clearly articulated legacy drawn from the events of his tenure as president. It gave them insight into the nature of the presidency as an institution. The legacy was tied to the specific decisions made in his administration and to the qualities of the president who bequeathed it—couched in his colloquial style, associated with his most characteristic phrase, and embodied in a concrete, homely symbol.

Andrew Jackson's farewell also illustrates this synthesis. Like that of Truman, his address was an artistic whole unified around a principle he stated explicitly: "There is but one safe rule, and that is to confine the General Government rigidly within the sphere of its appropriate duties."[60] This principle was reflected in the language Jackson used to describe the functions of government and the role of the people. Jackson's language was admonitory. He asked, "Has the warning voice of Washington been forgotten, or have designs already been formed to sever the Union?"[61] Later, he said, "I have devoted the last hours of my public life to warn you of the dangers."[62]

The central principle of Jackson's speech was mirrored in references to the government's "own sphere of action" and "legitimate authority" and to "the boundaries prescribed by the Constitution." He contrasted these concepts with "assuming a power not given," going "beyond the limits" or "beyond the boundaries of discretion," "usurping the power," "indiscreet extensions," "a wild spirit of speculation," "monopoly and exclusive privileges," an "inordinate thirst for power," the "desire to engross all power," "unlimited dominion," "despotic sway," and exercising "more than its just proportion of influence." Those who behave rightly preserve, perpetuate, secure, watch over, protect, maintain, and regulate. They are, in Jackson's words, "guardians of freedom" whose watchword is this famous principle: "Eternal vigilance by the people is the price of liberty."[63]

Jackson's language implied the sin of trespass, the sin of Lucifer who violated his natural limits by seeking to be God, the sin of Odysseus in sailing through the straits of Gibraltar and, hence, of crossing the boundaries circumscribing human action.[64] In the universe of Jackson's farewell, all will go well as long as the nation recognizes the proper sphere or limits of action—by government, by factions, by individuals. The threat is from immoderation and excess, which generate discord, conflict, dissension, even war—the evil consequences he pointed to again and again.

Like Jackson's, Washington's farewell was concerned with limits. It was also artistically unified; in this instance, by a vision of the United

States that reflected the phrases for which the address is remembered—
"no permanent alliances" and "no foreign alliances."[65] These phrases
summed up the central principle that Washington clearly enunciated
twice during the address. Early on, after detailing the benefits of the
federal Union for all sections of the country, Washington wrote that

> they must derive from union an exemption from those broils and wars between
> themselves which so frequently afflict neighboring countries not tied together
> by the same government, which their own rivalships alone would be sufficient
> to produce, but which opposite foreign alliances, attachments, and intrigues
> would stimulate and imbitter.[66]

Later, after detailing the dangers of involvements in the disputes of
other nations and the advantages of the geographical situation of the
United States, Washington said,

> Why forego the advantages of so peculiar a situation? Why quit our own to
> stand upon foreign ground? Why by interweaving our destiny with that of any
> part of Europe, entangle our peace and prosperity in the toils of European am-
> bition, rivalship, interest, humor or caprice? It is our true policy to steer clear of
> permanent alliances with any portion of the foreign world, so far, I mean, as we
> are now at liberty to do it; for let me not be understood as capable of patroniz-
> ing infidelity to existing engagements.... [L]et those engagements be observed
> in their genuine sense. But in my opinion it is unnecessary and would be unwise
> to extend them.[67]

Two metaphorical patterns support this vision of the Union. On
the one hand, it is an organism. Washington spoke of "this Government, the offspring of our choice," whose public administration must
be "the organ of consistent and wholesome plans, digested by common counsels."[68] "Cultivate peace and harmony with all," Washington urged, and "the fruits of such a plan [of avoiding entanglements]"
would grow.[69] Finally, he said, "With me a predominant motive has been
to endeavor to gain time to our country to settle and mature its yet
recent institutions."[70] The Union was a living thing that required
nurturing.

A second set of metaphors described the conditions needed for such
growth. For Washington, the newly created government was a "political fortress." Washington's warnings against the "baneful effects of

the spirit of party generally" and against permanent alliances spoke to what he perceived as the most serious threats to it: "The point in your political fortress against which the batteries of internal and external enemies will be most consistently and actively ... directed" was the unity of the government.[71] He spoke of the government as a "prop," of unity as "a main pillar in the edifice of your real independence, the support of your tranquility at home, your peace abroad."[72] He asked those addressed to think of their national union as "the palladium of your political safety and prosperity"[73] against which the spirit of faction and party could become "potent engines ... [which] will be enabled to subvert the power of the people."[74] He identified a "method of assault" against liberty. Government, he said, should be liberty's "surest guardian." Similarly, he spoke of "the spirit of encroachments" and of "invasion" of the public weal as "the customary weapon by which free governments are destroyed."[75] He asked, "Who that is a sincere friend can look with indifference upon attempts to shake the foundation of the fabric?" and called on Americans to preserve unity by repelling these dangers.[76]

These metaphors reflect Washington's background. In his view, the nation was an organism; the government an edifice, the nation's political fortress and guardian. The spirit of party or faction was an internal enemy; becoming embroiled in the conflicts of other nations was an external threat—these were the invaders to be repelled. The fortress was a structure within which needed growth could take place; it was also a perimeter within which internal tensions could be contained and controlled. When speaking of the internal threat posed by a spirit of partisanship, he said,

> From their natural tendency it is certain there will always be enough of that spirit for every salutary purpose; and there being constant danger of excess, the effort ought to be by force of public opinion to mitigate and assuage it. A fire not to be quenched, it demands a uniform vigilance to prevent its bursting into a flame, lest, instead of warming, it should consume.[77]

Washington's metaphors comported with his view of human nature. From his perspective, the problems he identified and warned against were nature run wild. For instance, he commented, "This spirit [of party], unfortunately, is inseparable from our nature, having its root in the strongest passions of the human mind."[78] His conditions for the nation's growth also reflected Washington's beliefs about human nature. He said, for example,

> In all the changes to which you may be invited, remember that time and habit are at least as necessary to fix the true character of governments as of other human institutions; that experience is the surest standard by which to test the real tendency of the existing constitution of the country; that facility in changes, upon the credit of mere hypothesis and opinion, exposes to perpetual change, from the endless variety of hypothesis and opinion; and remember especially that for the efficient management of your common interests in a country so extensive as ours, a government of as much vigor as is consistent with the perfect security of liberty is indispensable.[79]

Washington's language reinforced his warnings because it reflected his experience as well as generally shared conceptions of human nature and of how human institutions develop, and because it spoke to the imaginative and sensory capacities of the audience.

So strong is the "great tradition of warnings in Presidential farewells" that Reagan acknowledged it in those words, and he called on parents to teach what is important in U.S. history: "Why the pilgrims came here, who Jimmy Doolittle was, and what those 30 seconds over Tokyo meant." To U.S. children he said, "if your parents haven't been teaching you what it means to be an American, let 'em know and nail 'em on it."[80]

Dwight Eisenhower's farewell added a phrase, "the military-industrial complex," to the U.S. lexicon. His warning against that threat became as memorable as Washington's warnings against permanent foreign alliances because his central idea was summed up in a phrase, and because his vision emerged out of his personal history as well as the events of his presidency and the criterion he developed for judging all presidencies. The notion that the president is a moderator who balances competing forces appears in other farewells. In Eisenhower's, it took this form: "It is the task of statesmanship to mold, to balance, and to integrate these and other forces, new and old, within the principles of our democratic system—ever aiming toward the supreme goals of our free society."[81] It was the president who was in a position to see the larger picture; accordingly, Eisenhower said that

> each proposal must be weighed in the light of a broader consideration: the need to maintain balance in and among national programs.... Good judgment seeks balance and progress; lack of it eventually finds imbalance and frustration.[82]

The military-industrial complex threatened that balance:

> In the counsels of Government, we must guard against the acquisition of un-
> warranted influence, whether sought or unsought, by the military-industrial
> complex. The potential for the disastrous rise of misplaced power exists and
> will persist. We must never let the weight of this combination endanger our lib-
> erties or democratic processes. We should take nothing for granted.[83]

The warning was heightened because it was unexpected, given Eisenhower's past, and because the military language and evidence drawn
from his military experience reinforced his controversial claim. He recalled that a "member of the Senate appointed me to West Point," noted
his war and immediate postwar experience, and discussed the nation's
preeminence, its military strength, and its desire to keep the peace before warning of the dangers of the military-industrial complex.

Eisenhower's warning, however, arose out of actions he had taken
during his second administration. In his 1958 State of the Union address, Eisenhower had called for reorganization of the Department of
Defense, a call made more specific in a special message to Congress on
April 3.[84] Both speeches assigned a high priority to the initiative. In an
era that began with the launching of Sputnik I by the Soviet Union,
Eisenhower saw a need for greater civilian control of the military and
greater military responsiveness to national needs. His proposal became
the Defense Department Reorganization Act of 1958, the most sweeping reform of civilian-defense relationships since the 1947 National Security Act.[85] That act gave the civilian secretary of defense control of
the assignment of weapons to the various military services. It also gave
the secretary the authority to delegate powers to lower-level civilians.
During times of war, the president was given authority to coordinate
all facets of military liaison. The proposal met resistance in Congress
from defenders of the various branches of the military, but Eisenhower
mounted an effective lobbying effort to overcome this resistance. The
warning about the dangers of the military-industrial complex in his
farewell address should be heard against the backdrop of this legislative assertion of greater civilian power.

In the closing section of the speech, he reminded the audience again
of the personal warrant for his claims:

> As one who has witnessed the horror and the lingering sadness of war, as one
> who knows that another war could utterly destroy this civilization which has

been so slowly and painfully built over thousands of years, I wish I could say tonight that a lasting peace is in sight. . . . So much remains to be done.[86]

Finally, he thanked the public for the "many opportunities you have given me for public service in war and in peace."[87]

Style and substance fused to reinforce a warning Eisenhower was uniquely suited to give. The warning was a direct extension of the policies he had pursued while in office, it was grounded in his personal past, and it was couched in language that made it particularly salient.

The farewell does not necessarily end with the close of the formal speech. So, for example, whereas Washington's farewell was indeed his last statement as president, the day after delivering his famous farewell, Eisenhower noted in an extemporaneous moment, "There is becoming a great influence, almost an insidious penetration of our own minds that the only thing this country is engaged in is weaponry and missiles. And, I'll tell you we just can't afford to do that."[88]

In political and legal terms, former presidents become citizens, nothing more. Yet former presidents, particularly beloved former presidents, retain some of their presidential authority. In his Thanksgiving message to the nation as he made the transition to the presidency, Lyndon Johnson said that "the first two citizens to call upon me and to offer their whole support were Dwight D. Eisenhower and Harry S. Truman," indirectly calling on their authority as he took up the reins of government under difficult conditions.[89] Former president Reagan was beloved by many, and he used the remnants of his former authority to issue a special farewell long after he had left the presidency. On November 5, 1994, Reagan released a letter addressed, as presidential speeches often are, to "My Fellow Americans," in which he announced that he had been diagnosed with Alzheimer's disease. Just as Nancy Reagan had used a diagnosis of breast cancer to alert women to its dangers and to methods of detection, Reagan used this letter to create public awareness of this disease. The letter took on characteristics of a presidential farewell as it ended:

In closing let me thank you, the American people for giving me the great honor of allowing me to serve as your president. When the Lord calls me home, whenever that may be, I will leave with the greatest love for this country of ours and eternal optimism for its future. I now begin the journey that will lead me into the sunset of my life. I know that for America there will always be a bright dawn ahead. Thank you, my friends. May God always bless you.[90]

FAILED FAREWELLS

The farewell addresses of Jimmy Carter and Richard Nixon illuminate ways in which the rhetoric of this genre can go wrong and, by so doing, fail to bequeath a legacy.[91] Carter's formal farewell address was unsatisfying for several reasons. His farewell could not perform its symbolic function because, almost from the outset, Carter stepped out of his role as president and, with that move, relinquished the persona that gives the farewell its power. In addition, he failed to link criteria, accomplishments, and warnings, and his warnings about special interest groups were couched in terms that made them seem self-serving.

Carter's most fundamental error was setting aside the role that invests this speech with its special power. By prematurely embracing the role of citizen, he denied his speech the capacity to be a rite of passage. He did this when he said, "For a few minutes now, I want to lay aside my role as leader of one nation, and speak to you as a fellow citizen of the world about three issues."[92]

Within the speech, there was tension surrounding accomplishments Carter would have liked to claim but could not; in particular, his failure to effect the release of the Americans held hostage in Iran. In the address, he said that he would continue "to work hard and to pray for the lives and the well-being of the hostages held in Iran."[93] This piece of unfinished business precipitated a second farewell message, delivered in Plains, Georgia, on January 22, 1981, after the release of the hostages during Ronald Reagan's inauguration. Carter opened that speech by acknowledging that he had no right to speak as president: "Nobody gave me permission to speak, but I'm going to do it this time."[94] He justified the speech by noting, "I have not had a chance yet to make a statement about them [the hostages] and I thought because of the intense interest in these 52 people around the world, that I would say a few words to you about them."[95] What followed was a clear statement of accomplishment, the sort of statement Carter could not make in his formal farewell:

> We've achieved, at the end of this crisis, the two objectives that I set for this nation, and for myself, when they were first seized: to secure their safety and their ultimate release, and to do so on terms that would always preserve the honor and the dignity and the best interests of our nation.[96]

In his formal farewell, Carter spoke as a victim of circumstances, a perspective reflected in his hedged claims about his accomplishments. No longer president, in this later speech he spoke in the authoritative voice characteristic of farewell addresses.

If there was a criterion for judging his presidency implicit in Carter's formal farewell, it was whether or not he had brought us new understanding of the institution of the presidency. The conception of the presidency that he offered was one that viewed this "most powerful office in the world" as the "most severely constrained by law and custom." He defined the president as one who "is given a broad responsibility to lead but cannot do so without the support and consent of the people, expressed formally through the Congress and informally in many ways through a whole range of public and private institutions," and he described the nation as one whose "people have become ever more doubtful of the ability of the government to deal with our problems."[97] Here Carter was redefining the president's ability to meet our expectations. By asking us to lower our expectations of the president, he was asking us to lower the standards by which we judged his presidency. That was a problematic posture because, on its face, it appeared to be a somewhat self-serving excuse for a failed presidency.

What the speech implied, but did not claim explicitly, was that special interest groups had sabotaged his intended legacy, the promises made in his inaugural. In the formal farewell, Carter discussed three issues: the threat of nuclear war, conserving the planet's resources, and human rights. By implication, the nation was asked to judge his presidency by its achievements in these areas, but Carter could only hint at progress on these issues. Speaking in the passive voice, Carter suggested that he deserved credit for decreasing the chance of nuclear war: "The risk of a nuclear conflagration has been lessened."[98] His claim about human rights was similarly oblique, as well as ungrammatical: "One of those constructive forces is the enhancement of human freedoms throughout the strengthening of democracy and the fight against deprivation, torture, terrorism, and the persecution throughout the world."[99] Carter claimed that he had come to comprehend the nature of the presidency, not that he had achieved his goals:

> I understand after four years in this office, as few others can, how formidable is the task the new President-elect is about to undertake.... I know from experience that Presidents have to face major issues that are controversial, broad in scope, and which do not arouse the natural support of a political majority.[100]

Because his speech did not exploit the persona available to presidents at the end of their terms in office, because he did not link the achievements of his administration to the vision he presented, and because the warnings he issued appeared to be an apology for his performance in office, Carter's farewell was unable to bequeath an enduring legacy or to renew the national covenant. Subsequently, in interviews, Carter cited accomplishments that might have been included in his farewell address, such as the Panama Canal treaty, the signing of the 1978 Camp David accords between Anwar Sadat of Egypt and Menachem Begin of Israel, for which both won the Nobel Peace Prize, his human rights stand regarding South Africa, and the SALT treaty negotiations, in addition to environmental and deregulation decisions with significant economic consequences.[101]

Richard Nixon's speech of August 8, 1974, is a special case because, although it was an announcement of his resignation and is usually labeled as such, it also bade the nation farewell. The speech was unprecedented because in Nixon's case, in contrast to other presidents who delivered farewells, his right to hold the office had been publicly repudiated. The House Committee on the Judiciary had demonstrated to its satisfaction, and to the satisfaction of a majority of the country, that Nixon had violated the public trust, that he had arrogated to himself powers not specified by the Constitution, and that he had lied about what he had done. As a result, Nixon approached his farewell as a branded liar who, in his inaugural addresses, had invited the public to ratify a covenant he would not keep. Whereas even such mediocre presidents as Grant could argue that they had preserved, protected, and defended the Constitution and our system of laws, Nixon could not. He had squandered his right to moral leadership. In religious terms, Nixon was a defrocked priest or a false prophet. As a result, he could not assume the role that lends the farewell its special force.

By choosing to deliver a farewell rather than let his one-sentence letter of resignation stand, Nixon grasped at the last opportunity available to him as president to influence history's judgment of him and his administration. The speech he delivered demonstrated the powerful constraints at work in any presidential farewell address. Nixon felt obliged to affirm the Constitution, the continuity of the presidency, and the unity of the president and the people, even as his actions called each into question.

Nixon implied, for example, that his reluctance to resign and his refusal to release requested tapes and transcripts until required to do so by the courts safeguarded rather than subverted the constitutional process. His resignation, he implied, had the same purpose. As long as he had a "political base in Congress," he

> felt strongly that it was necessary to see the constitutional process through to its conclusion; to do otherwise would be unfaithful to the spirit of that deliberately difficult process, and a dangerously destabilizing precedent for the future.[102]

This concern with the future reflected the demand that departing presidents transmit the presidency intact to their successors. Now that his political base had disappeared, he contended "that the constitutional purpose has been served and there is no longer a need for the process to be prolonged."[103]

The irony of Nixon's situation was enhanced because he was the president who had pledged to "bring us together," thus incurring a special obligation to transcend partisan differences and unify the polity. Although Nixon obliquely acknowledged that his actions had caused bitterness and division, he also affirmed the national goal of unity:

> As we look to the future, the first essential is to begin healing the wounds of this nation; to put the bitterness and divisions of the recent past behind us and to rediscover the shared ideals that lie at the heart of our strength and unity as a great and as a free people.[104]

Straining to make the argument characteristic of presidential farewells, Nixon suggested that by resigning, he contributed to the process of unification: "By taking this action, I hope that I will have hastened the start of that process of healing which is so desperately needed in America."[105] Nixon could make no other argument. His illegal actions deprived him of the authority to rehearse the shared values of the country or to offer a unifying vision of the future.

Throughout the speech, Nixon indicated that he understood what must be done to bequeath a legacy. Like other farewells, Nixon's final speech as president proposed criteria by which he hoped history would judge him and, in the process, argued that by those criteria, his presidency had succeeded. His claim, however, was deeply flawed by the hyperbole with which he stated his accomplishments and by the self-contradictory concept of the presidency that he implied. In making such sweeping claims, Nixon might have been attempting to counterbalance the injury he had inflicted on our system of government with a compensating claim of achievement. As a result of his efforts, he was confident "that the world is a safer place today, not only for the people of America, but for the people of all nations and that all of our children have a better chance than before of living in peace rather than dying in war."[106] Whereas other presidents have accompanied statements of accomplishment with statements of appreciation for the support of Congress, the people, and occasionally, their predecessors, Nixon implied that he alone deserved the credit for making the world a safer place. Nixon's preoccupation with foreign affairs—the opening of China, the new relationship with the Soviet Union, ending the Vietnam War—also suggested a desire to distract the nation from the domestic problems engendered by his complicity in Watergate.

Throughout the years since he entered Congress, Nixon said, he had dedicated his career to "the cause of peace not just for America but among all nations," thus responding to the need to claim that he had kept his oath of office. He substituted one oath for another, however. He implied that even if we believed that he had violated his oath of office, he had kept one sacred pledge he made when he became president:

> When I first took the oath of office as President 5 1/2 years ago, I made this sacred commitment: "to consecrate my office, my energies, and all the wisdom I can summon to the cause of peace among nations." I have done my very best in all the days since to be true to that pledge. As a result of these efforts, I am confident that the world is a safer place today.... [These actions] will be my legacy to you, to our country, as I leave the presidency.[107]

This claim was supported by an account of the Nixon administration's accomplishments in China, the Middle East, the Soviet Union, Asia, Africa, and Latin America.

With a single notable exception, active verbs and first-person statements characterized Nixon's speech. In the opening section of the speech, he used the words, "I have done," "I have made," "I have always tried," "I have felt," "I no longer have," "I felt strongly," "I now believe," "I would have preferred," "I have never been a quitter," "I must put the interests of America first," culminating in "I shall resign the presidency effective at noon tomorrow." The verbs of the latter half of the speech were also active and assertive: "We have ended America's longest war," "We have unlocked the doors between the U.S. and the People's Republic of China," "We have opened a new relationship with the Soviet Union."

Nixon broke from this pattern when, in the middle of the speech, he spoke of Watergate. He downplayed his responsibility for damaging the country by framing his statements in the passive voice and by using the objective third person: "I regret deeply any injuries that may have been done in the course of the events that led to this decision [to resign]. I would say only that if some of my judgments were wrong, and some were wrong, they were made in what I believed at the time to be the best interests of the nation."[108] Not "injuries I inflicted" but injuries that "may have been done"; not "I was wrong," but "some of my judgments were wrong"; not "judgments I made" but judgments "were made."

Nixon's language reveals a profound contradiction in the conception of the presidency that permeates his farewell. Nixon expected exclusive personal credit for opening China, improving relations with the Soviet Union, and ending the war in Vietnam; at the same time, he denied personal responsibility for Watergate and the cover-up. Nixon could not simultaneously define the president as personally responsible and accountable and, in the next breath, as neither responsible nor accountable. His concept of the presidency was falsified by its self-contradictory nature. Nixon could either take the blame for Watergate and the cover-up and the credit for his foreign policy, or he could cast himself as the victim of Watergate and the undeserving beneficiary of developments in foreign policy. He could not have it both ways. The insinuations that he unified the country and safeguarded the Constitution by resigning became ironic embellishments on his internally inconsistent view of the presidency.

The material Nixon cited from Theodore Roosevelt was another oblique and ineffective attempt to exonerate himself:

> Sometimes I have succeeded and sometimes I have failed, but always I have taken to heart what Theodore Roosevelt once said about the man in the arena, "whose face is marred by dust and sweat and blood, who strives valiantly, who errs and comes short again and again because there is no effort without error and shortcoming, but who does actually strive to do the deeds, who knows the great enthusiasms, the great devotions, who spends himself in a worthy cause, who at the best knows in the end the triumph of high achievements and who at the worst, if he fails, at least fails while daring greatly."[109]

The use of Roosevelt's statement implied that Nixon should not be judged for his failures, but if he had failed, he should be judged as one who failed "while daring greatly." Indeed, the quotation argued for the inevitability of failure: "there is no effort without error and shortcoming." In other words, the quotation as used by Nixon asked us to judge him for striving "to do the deeds." But such a claim was ironic. The Watergate cover-up was an act that "dared greatly"; the "deeds" he strove to "do" in authorizing the break into Daniel Ellsberg's psychiatrist's office and approving payments to the Watergate burglars were not noble, but criminal. The House Committee on the Judiciary had judged him by Roosevelt's criteria and found that, "as a man in the arena, he had failed."[110]

Nixon's farewell was unsatisfactory, in part because he could not meet the country's needs in this moment of transition. He could not argue that he had kept the oath of office. At the same time, by disclaiming responsibility for the acts precipitating his resignation, he sacrificed the right to claim responsibility for the legacy of peace.

CONCLUSION

All presidents who complete their terms of office have an opportunity to deliver a farewell address. If they avail themselves of it, they can, through skillful use of language, address history to influence how their presidencies are judged and to define the meaning of the system of government of which the presidency is a part. Their opportunity is an illustration of *kairos*, the ancient concept developed by the Greek sophists to delineate the special moment of opportunity in which one can make the fitting gesture.[111] The moment is that of transition. Their lines of argument must deal with criteria for evaluating the presidency, with the accomplishments of a given administration, and with a legacy, usually involving warnings, addressed to the future. Style and content, however, must be fused if the legacy is to be successfully bequeathed. The ideas that compose the legacy must be in a form that is memorable and vivid and consistent with the discourse and policies that have characterized an administration. When these conditions are met, a satisfying and significant farewell emerges that can bequeath an enduring legacy to the nation.

In their farewells, presidents not only attempt to shape history's assessments of their terms in office, but also try to foster national appreciation of the presidency as an institution and support for principles that will strengthen the system of government as a whole. For a brief period at the end of their tenure, presidents have the opportunity to speak from an exalted position as leader and prophet to bequeath a new understanding of the government and its principles.

In the rhetoric of farewells, the links between the various presidential genres are perhaps most clearly seen. First, farewells are akin to inaugural addresses and impeachment rhetoric: inaugurals involve investiture; impeachment rhetoric involves failed or successful attempts at divestiture; farewell rhetoric involves self-divestiture. Second, farewells are related to inaugurals and to State of the Union addresses: all three attempt to influence coming legislative programs, inaugurals and farewells by creating a view of the country and its future, State of the Union addresses by setting a legislative agenda and making specific recommendations. And there are other, less obvious relationships: like inaugurals and national eulogies, farewells ask audiences to contemplate, not to act; like vetoes, farewells can attempt to halt future legislation by warning of its dangers; like war rhetoric, farewells ask audiences to grant the president unusual powers, although in this case, the powers of prophet rather than commander in chief; like pardoning rhetoric, farewells can successfully bequeath a legacy only if the president speaks in the role of the president; like State of the Union and inaugural addresses, farewells include public meditations on national values and identity.

THIRTEEN

Conclusion

As we noted in chapter 1, *Presidents Creating the Presidency* is different from its predecessor, *Deeds Done in Words*, structurally and conceptually. What have we gained by these changes? As reflected in its title, this book's structure emphasizes the ways in which presidential power varies with presidential functions and expands or contracts in relation to the other branches of government.

Whereas our original structure was chronological, beginning with the inaugural addresses of the president and ascendant vice president and moving to the State of the Union Address, this book's structure highlights the relative control of the president over the deeds called for by the words of the message. In *Presidents Creating the Presidency*, the opening chapters concern those genres in which the president acts unilaterally—in the inaugural, in ascending to the presidency following a death or resignation, in responding to crises or disasters with national eulogies, and in issuing pardons. Put differently, in these genres, the president engages in the creation of meaning unconstrained by the requirements, demands, or prerogatives of the other two branches of government. In each, the president has wide latitude to define the situation.

The next chapters concern those genres that take exception, invite the cooperation of the legislative branch, or assert the right of the executive to act in domains in which the Constitution gives another branch specific powers. Whereas State of the Union addresses propose, Congress disposes. The veto and de facto item veto explicitly respond to the rhetoric of Congress as embodied in legislation, and war rhetoric either invites congressional action in the form of a declaration of war or justifies presidential action in its absence.

The two chapters on forestalling impeachment and impeachment discourse illustrate moments when Congress, which can define what is an impeachable offense, has greater control over the rhetorical situation than does the president. Farewell addresses, which emerge at the end of presidencies and symbolize moments of continuity and change, are another genre of divestiture. At such moments, as in inaugurals, pardons, and national eulogies, presidents are free from the constraints of the other branches, yet these addresses reflect the struggles among the coequal branches and identify potential dangers threatening that relationship as well as the future of the nation.

This organizational structure focuses attention on variations in presidential power, on the relationship of presidential power to the performance of specific rhetorical functions, on the interdependence of and interplay among the branches of government, and on the conditions that foster the expansion or contraction of executive power. In our view, rhetoric is a key part of the ways in which presidents exercise power, expand executive power, and establish precedents for its use by their successors.

The altered order makes sense of the two genres introduced in this book: the national eulogy and the signing statement as de facto item veto. Although it is a comparatively recent genre, the functions of the national eulogy are forecast in the epideictic rhetoric of the inaugural address and the healing rhetoric of the pardon. Two changes in the relationship between the public and the president opened the door for the emergence of this type of rhetoric: the advent of mass broadcasting made it possible for presidents to express the grief of the nation, and the expansive promises made in personally delivered campaign messages expanded the public's expectations of the office.

Focusing on the ways in which presidents use rhetorical genres to define the relationship among the branches of government invites a focus on the second of the genres newly treated in this book. The de facto item veto is a strong assertion of presidential power in the presence of what the president casts as encroachment or constitutional overreaching by the legislative branch. The president's assertion of broad legislative and judicial power in the de facto item veto is simply the extension of the long-standing presidential assertion of a right to interpret the Constitution and to act at the intersection of the powers conferred by the Constitution, particularly in times of national crisis.

Because our earlier study concentrated on genres set in place either in the Constitution or in practice by George Washington, it overlooked these types of rhetorical action. In light of their centrality to the process of constructing what we know as the modern presidency, we regard that as a serious oversight. Bill Clinton helped resurrect his presidency with his national eulogy on the bombing of the Alfred P. Murrah Federal Building in Oklahoma City. Understanding George W. Bush's unique use of the de facto item veto helps make sense of the ways in which he managed to assert the primacy of the executive branch and to take exception to legislation without using the formal means designated by the Constitution. Saying that Bush failed to veto any legislation in the first six years of his presidency without a subsequent chapter explaining his alternative use of the de facto item veto would misrepresent the ways in which presidential rhetoric functioned during his time in office.

This is not another book on what has been called the imperial presidency. Instead, it describes the process by which presidents use constitutionally authorized types of discourse and their offspring to expand the executive's portion of the "shared" powers that reside at the interstices of the Constitution. Here we ask what we have learned about when and how presidents rebalance these shared powers in their favor.

The lines of argument that expand presidential powers are most likely to occur initially in those constitutionally validated genres in which the president has unilateral power—pardons and veto messages—as illustrated by Jefferson's challenge to the constitutionality of legislation by pardoning those convicted under the Sedition Act and by Andrew Jackson's assertion of the presidential right to veto on grounds of constitutionality and to speak as the voice of the whole people. In each of these instances, presidents asserted their right to act on their interpretation of the Constitution. Once that line of argument had been established in genres characterized by wide executive latitude, it was available for use in a genre unspecified by the Constitution: the de facto item veto.

From Lincoln to Wilson to Franklin Roosevelt to George W. Bush, these expansions of executive power have predictably occurred in times of perceived crisis. When institutional redress occurs, as it did in the time of Polk and Lincoln, it tends to take place after the crisis has passed. By then, of course, the executive branch has established a right to use that power in times of crisis and has created a precedent on which subsequent presidents can draw. Similarly, once an individual president is vested as commander in chief by war rhetoric, that president's claim to that expanded power is likely to be made across the other genres as well. (So, for example, it is in part in his role as commander in chief that Abraham Lincoln asserted the right to promulgate the Emancipation Proclamation.)

Presidential powers often expand with the tacit acceptance of Congress and are, in turn, legitimized by the courts. By appropriating funds to support large-scale intervention in a land war in Vietnam, for example, Congress, in effect, ceded its war powers to the president, a view that was affirmed by the courts. When Congress pushed back with the War Powers Resolution of 1973, presidents marshaled a rhetoric that complied with the resolution while asserting that compliance was voluntary. Recall that presidents can meet the reporting requirements of the War Powers Resolution with letters saying that their statement is "consistent with" requirements created by Congress. What is important about this language is what it does not say. Congress requires the president to comply, a rhetoric presidents reject. Their alternative language dilutes congressional power to "require." It also tacitly retains the right not to report in some future instance if a president finds it objectionable.

In the past decade and a half, we have also rethought our original focus on the single speech or message. In its stead, we focus here on the rhetorical act to illuminate generic dynamics. Across the chapters, we have suggested that generic functions can be performed through a variety of acts that revolve around the major addresses that first attracted our interest; a president's earlier comments, for example, may preview what will emerge as a fully formed statement. Seeing generic elements coming together across time as rhetorical acts enables us to trace their development and to recognize that genres meld into one another in predictable and institutionally useful ways. As a result, we can trace the ways in which the inaugural emerges out of campaign rhetoric or the ways in which a national eulogy grounds deliberative discourse that can, in turn, warrant military action. We can also examine the links between proclamations of pardon and the discourse in which presidents defend and explain their decisions. These linkages call attention to the ways in which presidents capitalize on their roles to increase their rhetorical and executive power.

Focusing on the rhetorical act also emphasizes the sense that, once invested in the office, the president is never not the president. So, for example, as we saw in chapter 1, Grant's sniveling notation that he had "been the object of abuse and slander scarcely ever equalled in political history" undercut his reinvestiture as president in his second inaugural, in part because rhetoric appropriate in a campaign becomes inappropriate in the voice of a president. Similarly, as George W. Bush came to recognize, the language of a Texas sheriff (saying "bring 'em on" or "wanted dead or alive") is not suitable language for the commander in chief. That role requires a rhetoric that says that the nation's military might is being mobilized in service of the highest ideals and against an imminent threat. As a nation, we enter war reluctantly. "Wanted dead or alive" reduces the magnitude of the cause to a desire to capture or kill a single person; "bring 'em on" bespeaks bravado, not bravery.

The third element focal to this book is "timing." Activist presidents are aggressive rhetorically; they have a sense of timing, of how to use the occasion or even how to create "the moment." They call special sessions of Congress, as Lincoln did after the first shots of the Civil war were fired. In their hands, timing is a strategic resource. Lincoln, for example, specified that that special session of Congress would be held on July 4.

When a moment calls for rhetoric and none is forthcoming, the president runs the risk that the audience's thirst for words will go unslaked or be satisfied by others, whose stature will be enhanced as a result. In the early hours after the September 11 attacks, for example, George W. Bush's faltering response rendered more important the role of network news anchors who, in the absence of appropriate presidential rhetoric, asserted the nation's resolve, defined the tragedy, characterized the loss, and reassured the viewing public.

We began our earlier study by asking how an institution as unprecedented as the United States presidency has survived the vicissitudes of history and accommodated the rhetorical choices of chief executives as different in talent and temperament as Abraham Lincoln and Jimmy Carter. That focus is central here as well. Our exposition is grounded in the constitutive power of presidential rhetorical genres and in the flexibility permitted them by the Constitution. Their constitutive power and their flexibility enable them to meet at least three vital institutional needs. First, they provide presidents with a symbolic repertoire through which to reassert the fundamental continuity of the presidency while making changes as circumstances require. Second, in and through these genres, presidents produce individualized discourse as they simultaneously reaffirm their place in the unbroken succession of leaders that forms the presidency. Third, those presidents who are less rhetorically sensitive or adept have an incentive to follow precedent; at the same time, these forms offer eloquent presidents the latitude both to satisfy and to transcend audience expectations.

The constitutive power of these genres creates a distinct identity for the presidency as an institution while setting rhetorical boundaries for its occupants. At the same time, the functions performed by these genres ensure that, whatever the level of rhetorical sophistication of those who hold the office, they will be seen as, and as acting as, the president. Finally, the checks and balances among the branches of government invite rhetorical forms that legitimize the presidency while they reaffirm the coordinate powers of all three branches. This function guarantees that, under ordinary conditions as well as in times of crisis, the branches of government will engage in cooperative, mutually reinforcing forms of discourse. However, these genres perform additional institutional functions.

If they are to endure, institutions must find ways to induct new leaders into office, to sustain them in that role, and to facilitate the transitions that mark the end of their tenure. In the case of the U.S. presidency, inaugural addresses seek investiture; State of the Union addresses, veto messages, and war, pardoning, and self-defense rhetoric define and fulfill their essential functions and, by so doing, sustain the presidency as an institution; and the farewell address marks the symbolic end of a president's term of office.

All institutions experience changes in leadership and confront diverse challenges, yet institutions are not identical. The U.S. presidency, for example, is an entity distinct from the British monarchy or the Roman Catholic papacy. The recurrence of recognizable forms of discourse is one important factor distinguishing one institution from another and distinguishing each institution from the personalities or idiosyncrasies of its individual leaders. U.S. presidents issue inaugural addresses, State of the Union addresses, and veto messages, for example, whereas popes issue encyclicals, bulls, and decretals. In comparing the U.S. president's State of the Union address and the British monarch's Speech from the Throne, one apprehends not merely the differences between President George W. Bush speaking the words of a speechwriter to Congress and Queen Elizabeth II pronouncing the words of prime minister Margaret Thatcher before Parliament, but also the differences between the two nations' institutional roles and relationships.

Throughout this book, the constitutive power of presidential rhetorical genres has been noted. In the inaugural, the president is invested with the office in part by speaking presidentially; national eulogies succeed when the country grants the speaking president the power to perform the priestly role; pardoning rhetoric constitutes the president as the final voice in determining what kind of federal justice best serves the public good; veto messages constitute the president in a legislative role; de facto item vetoes strongly assert presidential prerogatives and in the process create them; war rhetoric seeks to legitimize the president's assumption of the role of commander in chief; the very act of speaking presidentially in self-defense against impeachment reminds

the audience that the presumption of office resides in the speaking president. These words are deeds; in their speaking, the presidency is constituted and reconstituted.

The recurrence of recognizable forms of discourse in and of itself
gives the presidency a sense of continuity and stability greater than
that provided by the rhetoric of any single occupant. A mediocre inaugural still invites investiture. Even as the citizens hear such an address,
they can take comfort from the assurance it offers that the presidency is
rhetorically stronger than the discourse of any given president.

The Constitution gives the executive various "powers" (a word we
borrow here from article 2, section 2). The genres that embody these
powers can be distinguished by their functions and by the means necessary to fulfill them. Broadly, the genres described in this book can be
distinguished by such functions as the invitation to investiture of the
inaugural; the exhortation and invitation to investiture of war rhetoric; the bequeathal and divestiture of the farewell; the assessment and
recommendation of the State of the Union address; the interdiction of
legislation and appeal for reconsideration in the veto message; the assertion of the right to take exception to legislation without vetoing it;
the forgiveness of wrongdoing in pardoning rhetoric; the healing and
reconstitution of the wounded nation in the national eulogy; and the
self-exculpation in rhetoric forestalling impeachment and defending
against it. Each sustains the institution; each also enables presidents to
respond to special and changing circumstances.

Inaugural addresses maintain the stability of the presidency insofar as each praises or blames, affirms traditional principles, heightens
what is known and believed, uses elegant language, and focuses on the
nation's eternal present while reconstituting "the people" who witness this ritual and invest this speaker with the presidency. Inaugurals
adapt to changing circumstances by drawing alternative strains from
the past, by featuring different values and principles, and by reconstituting "the people" in diverse roles. The speeches of ascendant vice
presidents reaffirm continuity at moments of unexpected and threatening change.

Pardoning rhetoric reaffirms the president as the symbolic head of
state who acts in the public interest to preserve the public good. Pardoning also enables the president to correct judicial errors that result
from the passions stirred by specific events.

National eulogies reconstitute the citizenry after the national fabric
has been torn by tragedy. This epideictic form mourns those lost to the

tragedy while affirming national resolve and attesting to the resilience of the country and its ideals.

In delivering a farewell address, a president sustains the office by attempting to bequeath a legacy to the nation. Because the legacy is a product of that individual president and of the events of that presidency, it is grounded in historical particulars and uniquely reflects the persona of the individual president.

State of the Union addresses reaffirm continuity by displaying the president as symbolic head of state, by responding to the discourse of past presidents, and by creating and sustaining a national identity. But even as they address enduring national questions, the agendas they offer vary with the period in which they are presented and the specific circumstances in which presidents find themselves.

Veto messages affirm continuity and constancy insofar as they interdict legislation through refutation in a dispassionate document that employs the language of conservation of the government as an institution. By permitting presidents to develop lines of argument and evidence appropriate to the particular case, these messages enable presidents to express their individual beliefs and to adapt to the specifics of legislation they oppose.

The de facto item veto asserts the president's power and obligation to defend the Constitution and the executive powers stipulated or implied by it. It is simultaneously a form of intra- and interbranch communication in which the president defines the limits of legislative authority.

War rhetoric reaffirms the president's role as the nation's defender and its commander in chief. Each assertion of such executive powers sustains or enlarges the latitude for presidential action while responding to external events.

Presidential self-defense rhetoric is part of a dialogue about the limits of executive powers and the nature of the executive's obligations. In the process of considering impeachment, the elected representatives of the people ask whether the president has violated the oath of office; at the same time, presidential rhetoric protects the office from congressional or judicial encroachment as debate emerges about how executive powers are to be understood and interpreted under the particular circumstances of a historical moment.

The functions of each genre remain constant, but the rhetorical means through which they can be performed are variable. The genius of the founders resided in creating a framework that empowered presidents to exercise or not exercise their rhetorical options as circumstances and their temperaments warranted. Through time, presidents tried out lines of argument and developed new rhetorical forms; those conventionalized through use were added to the options available to a president contemplating invitations to investiture, pardoning, vetoing, reporting and recommending, responding to the threat of impeachment, seeking legitimation for assumption of the role of commander in chief, or bidding farewell. Injudicious choices disappeared as live options. Over time, the presidency developed a corpus of time-tested genres signaling the boundaries and characteristics of the rhetoric through which key presidential functions are performed. Those who followed these formulas issued competent but sometimes clichéd presidential discourse. Great presidents enlarged the range of rhetorical possibilities by performing these functions while transcending the formulas.

A generic perspective points out those symbolic similarities among presidencies that contribute to the institution's continuity and identity. It also offers a base for highlighting the ways in which presidencies differ and for identifying unique contributions to the history and identity of the institution. An individual presidency—that of William Howard Taft rather than John F. Kennedy, for example—gains some of its character from the ways in which a given president chooses to exercise or not to exercise the generic options. As noted, war rhetoric and veto messages are particularly sensitive indicators of a president's rhetorical activism. Rhetorical sensitivity and sophistication are at work in the ways in which individual presidents choose to exploit the generic possibilities. Franklin Roosevelt, Kennedy, Nixon, and Reagan were responsive to generic constraints and expectations in ways that Carter and Ford were not. Some presidents excelled in some genres and were wanting in others.

In those unusually artful instances in which presidents both satisfy and transcend the requirements of a genre at a given moment, one sees the rhetorical genius of a president such as Lincoln. Although some believe that presidential eloquence cannot break through the partisanship of recent times, presidents of dissimilar temperament and ideology have done what the nation required when a national tragedy threatened our collective identity. Reagan responded eloquently to the explosion of the space shuttle *Challenger*. Clinton did the same after the Oklahoma City bombing. In both instances, the nation came together under presidential rhetorical leadership. It did the same when George W. Bush finally found the right words after September 11 to make sense of the nation's loss and articulate its resolve in his speeches at the National Cathedral and to the assembled Congress.

Presidents negotiate the institutional shoals of continuity and change in part by judicious use of the past. As noted, presidents constantly claim to be drawing principles for the present from the past. Accordingly, rehearsing the past and forecasting future action are central to inaugural addresses, State of the Union addresses, and farewell addresses. The past is present even in disclaimers, as when Woodrow Wilson asserted in his 1917 inaugural, "This is not the time for retrospect." Yet the past is not a given. The Franklin Roosevelt whom Ronald Reagan invoked was not the Roosevelt invoked by John F. Kennedy. Reliance on the past as a sanction for the present implies continuity; reinterpreting the past enables presidents to adjust its lessons to changing circumstances and purposes.

The recurrence of certain presidential functions invites a rhetoric of stability and continuity. At the same time, the flexibility offered to presidents by these genres ensures adaptability. For example, the president can decide whether, when, and in what medium to issue discourse and what rhetorical strategies to employ in accomplishing an end. The Constitution mandates no presidential discourse other than reporting from time to time on the state of the Union and recommending necessary and expedient legislation. Felt needs reinforced by tradition have paired the inaugural address with the oath of office. At any time, in any circumstance, a president can issue or withhold special messages, pardons, and invitations to declare war or authorize military action. When confronted with congressional action, a president can elect to respond with a veto, a de facto item veto, or a defense against impeachment, or to remain silent. A president can opt to forgo a national eulogy or formal farewell. In their use of these basic genres, presidents signal the continuity of the presidency; in their varying patterns of use, they show their individual dispositions and the adaptations through which presidents can respond to altered circumstances.

A president can choose when to issue discourse, as illustrated by the considerable variation in presidential use of the veto, of the pardoning power, and of the power to invite a declaration of war or legislation supporting more limited military action. For example, a president can exploit the latitude available by issuing a written and an oral State of the Union address, as many modern presidents have done; by orally delivering or issuing in written form a series of messages on major issues, as did Nixon; or by issuing a State of the Union and a State of the World message, as did Nixon and Carter.

Presidents have also adapted these genres through emphasis on some particular generic elements over others. For example, Washington's second inaugural underscored the role of the audience as witnesses and the address as an extension of the oath of office. Adaptation of generic elements to special circumstances has also produced variation. For example, the vice presidents who have ascended to the presidency upon the death of a president have acknowledged the transfer of power and eulogized their predecessors. Only when political conditions, personal credibility, and the state of the nation made it appropriate have these inaugurals included a legislative forecast.

In the ways in which they recast the past, use various genres more or less aggressively, and stress some generic elements over others, presidents distinguish one presidency from another. One genre in particular enables presidents to place an individual imprint on the office. In the farewell address, the personal voices of the presidents speak most clearly. In this genre, the individual president summarizes the unique meaning of a particular presidency and relates it to the past and future of the presidency. The distinctive stylistic voice and the person of the president speak through this final rhetorical act. In the moment of transition from president to citizen, one glimpses how this particular president wishes to be seen in the eyes of history.

The founders protected the country from miscreants and rhetorical bumblers by enabling Congress and the Supreme Court to act as checks on presidential discourse. At some time or another, each is empowered to ask whether the president is discharging appropriately the executive powers specified in the Constitution. Presidents test the limits of their power rhetorically and are called to task by the rhetoric of the other branches. The checks and balances of our system not only control the distribution of power among the branches, but also legitimize each branch in performing its functions. Regardless of its author, for example, the State of the Union address ensures that Congress acknowledges the president's legislative prerogatives; the veto message ensures that Congress attends to presidential objections to a legislative initiative. What makes the de facto item veto of particular interest to us is the difficulty Congress and the courts have in checking its assertions.

In this book, we have explored how genres enable discourse to accommodate the institutional need for stability and change. Even when they engage in their most controversial and unsettling acts, the president and Congress do so in forms whose identity bespeaks continuity. A pardon, even that of Richard Nixon by Gerald Ford, is a form made familiar by past presidential usage. For this reason, even in the most troubling circumstances, such as the ascent of an unelected vice president to the presidency following the resignation of the incumbent or a congressional vote in support of articles of impeachment, politicians, the press, and the public turn to familiar discursive forms to assure the country and themselves that "the system works." In 1974, the long national nightmare was over, not simply because Gerald Ford pronounced those words or because Richard Nixon was no longer president, but because in Ford's speech, the citizenry heard the clearly recognizable rhetoric inviting investiture that characterizes an inaugural address. The beginning of the end was also signaled generically: the public experienced a smooth and orderly transition because Nixon's final speech from the Oval Office took the familiar form of the farewell. After Clinton's impeachment in the House and the failure of the Senate to convict, it was clear that the system worked because Clinton acted chastened by the process, yet remained the president and continued to exercise presidential power in recognizable genres. In a moment of national trauma, then, these genres—the congressional rhetoric of impeachment and the presidential rhetoric of self-defense, farewell, and investiture—were taken as signs that the system still was working.

Our probe of the intersection between the presidency, rhetorical genres, and governance closes on a reassuring note. Functional, flexible genres insulate the institution of the presidency from an Andrew Johnson even as they sustain the initiatives of an Andrew Jackson or an Abraham Lincoln; they enable it to accommodate a Calvin Coolidge as well as a Franklin Roosevelt or a Woodrow Wilson. In sum, the institution of the presidency derives part of its coherence and its ability to survive from the constitutive power of its functional, flexible rhetorical genres. These forms of address enable individual presidents to adapt to changing circumstances without undermining institutional stability, allow presidents to speak both as individuals and as voices of an institution, and enable the less skillful to perform basic institutional functions while not impeding the great from eloquently transcending those formulas.

Appendix: Other Rhetorical Forms

The obligations of the presidency constitute a flexible mandate entailing certain kinds of rhetoric. Article 2, section 1 of the Constitution vests the executive power entirely in the president. The ceremonial forms of discourse required of a head of state grow out of this power. Article 2, section 2, says that the president "shall receive Ambassadors and other public Ministers." As national host, the president welcomes foreign leaders, offers toasts at state dinners, issues communiqués after such meetings, and sends the nation's condolences to other countries upon the deaths of prominent citizens or national leaders. Acting as the executive, the president speaks for the nation to other sovereign states. In *U.S. v. Curtiss-Wright Export Corporation*,[1] the Supreme Court recognized this special presidential role:

> In this vast external realm, with its important, complicated, delicate and manifold problems, the President alone has the power to speak or listen as a representative of the nation. He makes treaties with the advice and consent of the Senate; but he alone negotiates. Into that field of the negotiation the Senate cannot intrude; and Congress itself is powerless to invade it.

The Supreme Court finding that the president has powers equal to those of other world leaders entails latitude for action in foreign affairs. In the *Curtiss-Wright* decision, the court wrote that

> the powers to declare and wage war, to conclude peace, to make treaties, to maintain diplomatic relations with other sovereignties, if they had never been mentioned in the Constitution, would have vested in the federal government as necessary concomitants of nationality.... As a member of the family of nations, the right and power of the United States in that field are equal to the right and power of the other members of the international family. Otherwise, the United States is not completely sovereign.

In other words, no other individual is vested with the right or the power to speak for the country.[2] The president's powers to negotiate, but not ratify, treaties and to make executive agreements are by-products of this power.

An executive agreement is an understanding reached between heads of state. The president's constitutional authority in foreign affairs and as commander in chief authorizes such agreements, which are made without Senate ratification. Although executive agreements usually deal with matters less portentous than those contained in treaties, modern presidents increasingly have substituted executive agreements for treaties in cases in which Senate ratification of a treaty appeared unlikely.

The flexible mandate of the executive was affirmed when the Supreme Court declared that the clause of the Constitution requiring the president to "take care that the laws are faithfully executed" includes not only acts of Congress and treaties, but also those "rights, duties, and obligations growing out of the Constitution itself . . . and all the protections implied by the nature of the government under the Constitution."[3] The "take care" clause is "a comprehensive description of the duty of the executive to watch with vigilance over all the public interests."[4] In article 2, section 1, which specifies the oath the president must take to be invested with the office, the "take care" clause is linked to fundamental presidential obligations.

Although article 1 gives all legislative powers to Congress, Congress and the courts have delegated some legislative responsibilities to the president. These responsibilities take the rhetorical form of presidential proclamations, executive orders, agency regulations, and White House supervision of the rule-making process.

Proclamations create entities such as Law Day and National Transportation Day. Presidents can also proclaim on more substantive matters. When France and Britain went to war in 1793, George Washington issued a proclamation of neutrality, declaring that it was U.S. policy to maintain friendship with both nations. The proclamation threatened all citizens who contravened "that disposition" with prosecution. Similarly, in February 1904, Theodore Roosevelt proclaimed the country's neutrality in the Russo-Japanese war. The systematic check on presidential abuse of this power is court review. For example, when Carter's proclamation 4744 in 1980 imposed a fee on imported oil, a district court held that he had exceeded his inherent and statutory power and had acted beyond congressional intent.

Executive orders include any rule or regulation the president or his subordinate agencies issue in order to interpret or implement a law or treaty. Some executive orders are procedural; others have general applicability as law. Executive orders become law when they proceed from constitutionally specified powers of the president or represent the exercise of powers specifically given the president by Congress. For example, John Kennedy established the Peace Corps through executive order. Executive orders do not supersede statutes or counter existing legislation. In 1943, arguing from his powers as president and commander in chief, Franklin Roosevelt seized shipbuilding and coal companies; subsequently, Congress authorized the actions he had taken. In recent times, Congress has delegated discretionary powers to the executive by statute. These discretionary powers have increased the presidential use of executive orders. An executive order is not valid unless it is published in the *Federal Register.*

A final category of presidential discourse has been created by statute or by court decisions. This discourse arose from a realization that some responsibilities, such as budget and economic messages, need to be performed routinely by the president.

The Budget and Accounting Act of 1921 requires that in January of each legislative session, the president send an annual budget message to Congress. Usually it is sent in written form to be read to each chamber by its clerk. The budget message places responsibility for initiating a financial plan for government on the executive. Legislative bodies begin their consideration of financial matters only after the budget message, with its detailed fiscal recommendations, has been laid before them. The executive can use the budget message to arouse public support for certain programs.

The Employment Act of 1946 requires that the president submit an economic report to Congress each January. The report treats employment trends, production, purchasing power, economic indicators, and recommendations to Congress on maintaining or improving economic activity. The economic report is prepared by the president's Council of Economic Advisors. A joint congressional committee of seven members from each house studies the message and makes recommendations for its implementation.

Notes

1. Michael J. Lax, ed., *The Inaugural Addresses of the Presidents of the United States, 1789–1985* (Atlantic City, NJ: American Inheritance Press, 1985), 4.
2. James D. Richardson, ed., *A Compilation of the Messages and Papers of the Presidents, 1789–1908*, 11 vols. (Washington, DC: Bureau of National Literature and Art, 1909), 4:22–23.
3. For discussion, see Wilfred E. Binkley, *The Man in the White House: His Powers and Duties* (New York: Harper and Row, 1964), 225–26.
4. James Polk, "Fourth Annual Message, December 5, 1848."
5. "[T]he Foreign Assistance Act of 1974 capped the number of American military personnel in South Vietnam at 4,000 within six months. The Lebanon Emergency Assistance Act of 1983 required the president to get Congress's approval for any substantial increase in the number or role of armed forces in Lebanon." Adam Cohen, "Congress, the Constitution and War: The Limits on Presidential Power," *New York Times*, January 29, 2007, A22.
6. James Madison, The Federalist, no. 49, in James Madison, Alexander Hamilton, and John Jay, *The Federalist Papers*, ed. Isaac Kramnick (New York: Penguin Books, 1987), 313.
7. U.S. Constitution, art. 1, sec. 8.
8. 5 U.S. (1 Cranch) 137 (1803).
9. *Worcester v. Georgia*, 31 U.S. 515 (1832).
10. James E. Pollard, *The Presidents and the Press* (New York: Macmillan, 1958), vii; cited in Seymour H. Fersh, *The View from the White House: A Study of Presidential State of the Union Messages* (Washington, DC: Public Affairs Press, 1961), 6.
11. For an alternative view, see Jeffrey Tulis, "Deliberation between Institutions," in *Debating Deliberative Democracy*, ed. James S. Fishkin and Peter Laslett (Malden, MA: Blackwell, 2003), 200–211.
12. For reasons of space and because they are the products of historical change and modern technology, the press conference, the fireside chat, and direct popular appeals to the citizenry lie outside our purview. Unless it is a constitutionally mandated form of address, we ignore discourse that speaks only to a specific occasion or situation. Accordingly, we do not consider executive orders, executive agreements, and most proclamations and special messages to Congress. We have also chosen to exclude discourse mandated by law in

the modern period, such as budget and economic messages. For information about this rhetoric, see the appendix. In addition, our focus on genres that typify the institution of the presidency strikes from our agenda messages of undisputed historical import, such as Jackson's Nullification Proclamation and Lincoln's Emancipation Proclamation. It sidesteps such fine rhetorical moments as John F. Kennedy's "Ich bin ein Berliner," Lyndon Johnson's "We shall overcome," and Ronald Reagan's 1984 speech commemorating the Normandy invasion. We recognize that our focus will preclude analysis of such masterpieces of presidential address as Abraham Lincoln's speech at Gettysburg. We do not dispute either the rhetorical value or the historical importance of these speeches. Because our goal is understanding the presidency as an institution, we focus on those recurrent public rhetorical acts that speak in some important ways to the identity and character of the presidency.

13. See Michael C. McGee, "In Search of 'The People': A Rhetorical Alternative," *Quarterly Journal of Speech* 61 (October 1975): 235–49.

14. Lincoln's redefinition of the people is central to James Arnt Aune's analysis, published as "Lincoln and the American Sublime," *Communication Reports* 1 (Winter 1988): 14–19. That the address may be read differently is demonstrated in the same issue of that journal in analyses by Ronald C. Carpenter, "In Not-So-Trivial Pursuit of Rhetorical Wedgies: An Historical Approach to Lincoln's Second Inaugural Address," 20–25; and by Martha Solomon, "'With Firmness in the Right': The Creation of Moral Hegemony in Lincoln's Second Inaugural," 32–37. See also Glen E. Thurow, *Abraham Lincoln and American Political Religion* (Albany: State University of New York Press, 1977).

15. Murray Edelman, *Constructing the Political Spectacle* (Chicago: University of Chicago Press, 1988), 104.

16. Fred I. Greenstein, "In Search of a Modern Presidency," in *Leadership in the Modern Presidency*, ed. Fred I. Greenstein (Cambridge, MA: Harvard University Press, 1988), 351.

17. David Zarefsky, "The Presidency Has Always Been a Place for Rhetorical Leadership," in *The Presidency and Rhetorical Leadership*, ed. Leroy G. Dorsey (College Station: Texas A&M University Press, 2002), 24.

18. Aristotle described three overlapping and interrelated genres of discourse. Deliberative rhetoric created the rules that allowed people to live together in a community; it concerned future policy, pivoted on the issue of expediency, occurred in legislative assemblies, and, owing to the rough-and-tumble of debate, was cast in low to middle style. Forensic rhetoric dealt with rule breakers; it focused on defining past behavior, pivoted on the issue of justice, occurred in the law courts, proceeded through accusation and defense, and, because its arguments were grounded in laws, developed deductively, usually in middle style. Epideictic rhetoric was ceremonial or ritualistic; it reenacted and reaffirmed the unity of the community, developed through

praise and blame, focused on evaluations in the present, occurred on special occasions, tended to employ strategies of amplification, and was cast in high style. It sought not a judgment about the past or the future, but appreciation of its enactment by the audience. Aristotle, *On Rhetoric: A Theory of Civic Discourse*, trans. George A. Kennedy (New York: Oxford University Press, 1991), 1358b7–37, 1368a27–32, 1413b3–5, 1414a7–18.

19. Alternative generic frameworks include analysis of the presidency by the characterological types of its occupant, a perspective developed by James David Barber, who writes of "regularities, habitual ways of handling similar situations" in *Politics by Humans: Research on American Leadership* (Durham, NC: Duke University Press, 1988), 25. This perspective was first developed in his *Presidential Character: Predicting Performance in the White House* (Englewood Cliffs, NJ: Prentice-Hall, 1972). In a similar move, James MacGregor Burns identified various styles of presidential leadership in *The Power to Lead* (New York: Simon and Schuster, 1984).

Jeffrey Tulis compares and contrasts the early presidency with the modern one, which he argues is "buffeted by two 'constitutions,'" the original Constitution and "a second constitution, which puts a premium on active and continuous presidential leadership of popular opinion, is buttressed by several extra-Constitutional factors such as the mass media and the proliferation of primaries as a mode of presidential selection." *The Rhetorical Presidency* (Princeton, NJ: Princeton University Press, 1987), 17–18.

In contrast to the Wilsonian leader described by Tulis, Philip Abbott has described various roles a president might play in using rhetoric to exercise leadership, such as republican hero (Lincoln), political theorist (Andrew Jackson), and manager (i.e., a policy-making leader whose authority is legitimized by election and by constant dialogue with the nation in speeches). See Philip Abbott, "Do Presidents Talk Too Much? The Rhetorical Presidency and Its Alternative," *Presidential Studies Quarterly* 18 (Spring 1988): 347–62.

In *Verbal Style and the Presidency: A Computer-Based Analysis* (Orlando, FL: Academic Press, 1984), Roderick P. Hart presents his research on qualities of presidential character that contribute to credibility as manifested in language. Subsequently, in *The Sound of Leadership: Presidential Communication in the Modern Age* (Chicago: University of Chicago Press, 1987), Hart studies patterns of presidential utterance in the modern presidency. We note Theodore Lowi's categorization of annual messages as initially constitutive, then distributive, and subsequently regulative and redistributive, in "Four Systems of Policy, Politics and Choice," *Public Administration Review* 32 (July–August 1972): 298–310.

In developing a communication model adapted to the presidency, Robert E. Denton, Jr., identifies four orientations or styles of presidential power: constitutional, administrative, expedient, and charismatic. "A Communication Model of Presidential Power," *Presidential Studies Quarterly* 18 (Summer 1988): 523–39.

20. Adena Rosmarin, *The Power of Genre* (Minneapolis: University of Minnesota Press, 1985), 25.

21. Karlyn Kohrs Campbell and Kathleen Hall Jamieson, "Form and Genre in Rhetorical Criticism: An Introduction," in *Form and Genre: Shaping Rhetorical Action* (Falls Church, VA: Speech Communication Association, 1978), 21.

22. Roderick P. Hart, *The Political Pulpit* (West Lafayette, IN: Purdue University Press, 1977); *The Political Pulpit Revisited*, ed. Roderick P. Hart and John L. Pauley II (West Lafayette, IN: Purdue University Press, 2005).

23. Garry Wills, "At Ease, Mr. President," *New York Times*, January 27, 2007, A16, http://www.nexis.com/ (accessed July 2, 2007).

24. One of the most extreme examples of the misunderstanding of generic criticism can be found in Thomas Conley's "The Linnaean Blues: Thoughts on the Genre Approach," in *Form, Genre, and the Study of Political Discourse*, ed. Herbert W. Simons and Aram A. Aghazarian (Columbia: University of South Carolina Press, 1986), 59–78. As the title of his essay indicates, Conley does not realize that one must distinguish between biology and rhetoric when it comes to systems of classification. Indeed, he explicitly compares generic criticism to Linnaeus's work (60–62). But perhaps the saddest aspect of Conley's misunderstanding is that he seems unconcerned with criticism as a means of providing insight into rhetorical works and preoccupied with some unspecified set of theoretical rules about the nature of criticism.

25. This point of view is argued persuasively by Adena Rosmarin in *The Power of Genre*, 1–22.

26. Paul Hernadi, *Beyond Genre: New Directions in Literary Classification* (Ithaca, NY: Cornell University Press, 1972), 2.

27. Hernadi, 4. Scientific taxonomies are somewhat less rigid than this comment suggests.

28. As an illustration, see Harold Zyskind, "A Rhetorical Analysis of the Gettysburg Address," *Journal of General Education* 4 (April 1950): 202–12.

29. Conley berates generic critics as a group, and the two of us specifically, for "assimilating criticism to a quasi-scientific model" (68). He seems not to recognize the tentative and manifold character of the truths we describe here and elsewhere.

30. *The Philosophy of Rhetoric*, ed. Lloyd F. Bitzer (Carbondale: Southern Illinois University Press, 1963), 1.

31. The terms "ghostwriter" and "speechwriter" are used interchangeably, although ghostwriters are sometimes designated as those whose activity is concealed, while the activities of speechwriters are known and acknowledged. See William Safire, *The New Language of Politics: An Anecdotal Dictionary of Catchwords, Slogans, and Political Usage* (New York: Random House, 1968), 414–15.

32. William N. Brigance, "Ghostwriting before Franklin D. Roosevelt and the Radio," *Today's Speech* 4 (September 1956): 10–11; Lois Einhorn, "The Ghosts Unmasked: A Review of Literature on Ghostwriting," *Communication Quarterly* 30 (Winter 1981): 42.

33. Robert Gunderson, "Political Phrasemakers in Perspective," *Southern Speech Journal* 27 (Fall 1960): 23; Victor H. Paltsits, ed., *Washington's Farewell Address* (1935; reprint, New York: Arno, 1971).

34. Gunderson, 23.

35. Richardson, 2:640–56.

36. Gunderson, 23.

37. Claude M. Fuess, "Ghosts in the White House," *American Heritage* 10 (December 1958): 47.

38. Raymond Moley, *The First New Deal* (New York: Harcourt, Brace, and World, 1960), 115.

39. Eugene D. Fleming, "Ghosts in the Closet," *Cosmopolitan* 147 (August 1959): 70.

40. Dom Bonafede, "Report: Speechwriters Play Strategic Role in Conveying, Shaping Nixon's Policies," *National Journal* 4 (1972): 314.

41. In asking Hamilton to revise his draft of the farewell, Washington wrote, "Even if you should think it best to throw the whole into a different form, let me request, notwithstanding, ... that the whole may appear in plain stile; and be handed to the public in an honest, unaffected, simple garb." John C. Fitzpatrick, ed., *The Writings of George Washington*, 39 vols. (Washington, DC: Government Printing Office, n.d.), 35:48–49.

42. K. H. Jamieson, *Eloquence in an Electronic Age* (New York: Oxford University Press, 1988).

43. James Fallows, "The Passionless Presidency," *Atlantic* 243 (May 1979): 43.

44. Hart, *Verbal Style*, esp. 278–79.

45. In explaining a generic approach to rhetorical analysis, Harold Zyskind contrasts it with two other approaches. The biographer seeks to understand a speaker's life by studying a speech as evidence, while the geneticist seeks to understand a speech by using the speaker's life as evidence. By contrast, the rhetorical critic seeks "to discover [the speech's] meaning and power, as it stands, since he views [it] ... as an artistic creation designed for some end" (203).

46. William Safire, *Before the Fall: An Inside View of the Pre-Watergate White House* (New York: Belmont Towers Books, 1975), 100; William H. Honen, "The Men behind Nixon's Speeches," *New York Times Magazine* (January 19, 1969): 20–21, 63, 65–67, 73, 75.

47. John J. Casserly, *The Ford White House* (Boulder: Colorado Associated University Press, 1977), 58, 77.

48. Fallows, 43.

49. The source of this pun (Carter walked down Pennsylvania Avenue) is William Safire's "Pedestrian Inaugural," *New York Times*, January 24, 1977, 23C, in which he also wrote, "The keynote of the Carter Presidency turned out to be a themeless pudding, devoid of uplift or insight, defensive in outlook and timorous in its reach, straining five times to sell its 'new spirit' slogan in the absence of a message."

50. Woodrow Wilson, *Congressional Government* (1883; reprint, New York: Meridian Books, 1956), 209.

51. We disapprove of male pronouns used as if they were generic or universal when empirical research has shown that audiences read and hear such pronouns as referring exclusively to males. We have decided, however, not to insert [*sic*] each time such language is used, in part because such usage occurs frequently, and in part because we believe that our readers will recognize such exclusionary language when it appears.

52. *Public Papers of the Presidents of the United States: Lyndon B. Johnson, 1968–1969,* 2 vols. (Washington, DC: Government Printing Office, 1968), 1:483.

53. Karlyn Kohrs Campbell and Kathleen Hall Jamieson, *Deeds Done in Words: Presidential Rhetoric and the Genres of Governance* (Chicago: University of Chicago Press, 1990).

54. Theodore Otto Windt, *Presidents and Protestors: Political Rhetoric in the 1960s* (Tuscaloosa and London: University of Alabama Press, 1990), 106–135. See Karlyn Kohrs Campbell, *The Rhetorical Act* (Belmont, CA: Wadsworth, 1982) for initial efforts to approach rhetorical action in these terms.

55. Kathleen Hall Jamieson and Karlyn Kohrs Campbell, "Rhetorical Hybrids: Fusions of Generic Elements," *Quarterly Journal of Speech* 68 (1982): 146–157.

56. William Shakespeare, *Julius Caesar,* ed. Arthur Humphreys (New York: Oxford University Press, 1984), 206.

57. R. Shep Melnick, "The Courts, Jurisprudence, and the Executive Branch," in *The Executive Branch,* ed. Joel Aberbach and Mark Peterson (New York: Oxford University Press, 2005), 454.

58. The language of the Court in *United States v. Curtiss-Wright Export Corp.,* 299 U.S. 304 (1936), explicitly ties presidential power to rhetoric when it says, "In this vast external realm [of foreign policy], with its important, complicated, delicate and manifold problems, the President alone has the power to speak or listen as a representative of the nation."

59. Richard Neustadt, *Presidential Power: The Politics of Leadership* (New York: Wiley, 1960), 33.

60. 343 U.S. 579 (1952).

61. Binkley, 142.

62. Woodrow Wilson, *Constitutional Government in the United States* (New York: Columbia University Press, 1908), 74.

63. Andrew Rudalevige, "The Executive Branch and the Legislative Process," in *The Executive Branch,* 428.

64. Joel Aberbach and Mark Peterson, "Control and Accountability: Dilemmas of the Executive Branch," in *The Executive Branch,* 527.

65. Rudalevige, 438.

CHAPTER 2: INAUGURAL ADDRESSES

1. Arthur M. Schlesinger, Jr., "Introduction," in *The Chief Executive: Inaugural Addresses of the Presidents of the United States from George Washington to Lyndon B. Johnson* (New York: Crown Publishers, 1965), vi, vii. Presidential discourse is generally not of high literary quality. In announcing that Thomas

Jefferson's autobiographical writings and public papers would be included in the Library of America series, Daniel Aaron, president of the selection committee, commented that the works of only a few other presidents—Lincoln, Grant, Wilson, and both Roosevelts—were likely to be included. The criteria for selection were literary, not political, and, as Aaron said, "Some could write well, others were wooden." Herbert Mitgang, "Jefferson's Prose Joins Library of America Series," *New York Times*, May 28, 1984, 15Y.

2. The name of this kind of discourse comes from the Greek term *epideixis*, meaning "display," suggesting the link between this kind of discourse and the proper, even elegant, performance of a ritual. See Aristotle, *Rhetoric*, trans. W. Rhys Roberts (New York: Modern Library, 1954), 1358b12–13, 18–20; 1367b37–38; 1368a27; 1414a17–18.

3. John W. O'Malley, *Praise and Blame in Renaissance Rome: Rhetoric, Doctrine, and Reform in the Sacred Orators of the Papal Court, c. 1450–1521* (Durham, NC: Duke University Press, 1979), 40.

4. O'Malley, 63.

5. Harry Caplan, *Rhetorica ad Herennium* (Cambridge, MA: Harvard University Press, 1954), 173n.

6. Edwin Black, "Gettysburg and Silence," *Quarterly Journal of Speech* 80 (1994): 29.

7. James L. Hoban, Jr., "Rhetorical Rituals of Rebirth," *Quarterly Journal of Speech* 66 (October 1980): 282–83. Investiture necessitates participation in a formal ceremony in which a duly constituted authority, before appropriate witnesses, confers the right to play a certain role or to take a certain position. The ceremony usually involves a demonstration by the candidate for investiture of her or his suitability for such elevation.

8. Karlyn Kohrs Campbell and Kathleen Hall Jamieson, "Form and Genre in Rhetorical Criticism: An Introduction," in *Form and Genre: Shaping Rhetorical Action*, ed. Karlyn Kohrs Campbell and Kathleen Hall Jamieson (Falls Church, VA: Speech Communication Association, 1978), 9–32.

9. For other examples of such speeches, see *Presidential Winners and Losers: Words of Victory and Concession*, ed. John R. Vile (Washington, DC: Congressional Quarterly Press, 2002).

10. November 3, 1992, transcribed from tape.

11. *Public Papers of the Presidents of the United States: William J. Clinton, 1993*, 2 vols. (Washington, DC: Government Printing Office, 1994), 1:2.

12. This unification is almost exclusively of male citizens. In the world of inaugural addresses, women rarely exist. In 1985, for example, Reagan referred to "working men and women," but even such an indirect, casual reference is aberrant.

13. Michael J. Lax, ed., *The Inaugural Addresses of the Presidents of the United States, 1789–1985* (Atlantic City, NJ: American Inheritance Press, 1985), 4. All citations from inaugurals through 1985 are from this work; page references are given hereafter in parentheses in the text.

14. Dumas Malone notes that Jefferson did not capitalize these key terms and turn them into party names. *Jefferson the President: First Term, 1801–1805* (Boston: Little, Brown, 1970), 20. For a detailed analysis of this address, see Stephen Howard Browne, *Jefferson's Call for Nationhood* (College Station: Texas A&M University Press, 2003).

15. See, for example, James Buchanan's 1857 address, which followed an election held during the conflict between pro- and antislavery forces in "bloody Kansas" (68–71); Rutherford Hayes's 1877 address (82–85); Grover Cleveland's 1885 and 1893 addresses (91–93, 100–102); Benjamin Harrison's address in 1889 (94–99); and Richard Nixon's 1969 address (170–72).

16. *Public Papers*, 1993, 1:2.

17. *Public Papers of the Presidents of the United States: George W. Bush, 2001*, 2 vols. (Washington, DC: Government Printing Office, 2003), 1:1.

18. See Denise M. Bostdorff, "George W. Bush's Post-September 11 Rhetoric of Covenant Renewal: Upholding the Faith of the Greatest Generation," *Quarterly Journal of Speech* 89 (November 2003): 293–319.

19. *Public Papers*, 2001, 1:1.

20. George H. W. Bush, "Transcript of Bush's Inaugural Address: 'Nation Stands Ready to Push On,'" *New York Times*, January 21, 1989, 10Y.

21. "Inaugural Address, March 4th, 1841," *The American Presidency Project*, http://www.presidency.ucsb.edu/ws/index.php?pid=25813 (accessed August 9, 2006).

22. Inaugurals frequently praised include Washington's first, Jefferson's first, Lincoln's first and second, Franklin Roosevelt's first, and Kennedy's. Some add Theodore Roosevelt's first, Wilson's first, and Franklin Roosevelt's second (Schlesinger, "Introduction," vii). For an analysis of Franklin Roosevelt's first, see Davis W. Houck, *FDR and Fear Itself: The First Inaugural Address* (College Park: Texas A&M University Press, 2002).

23. See Glen E. Thurow, *Abraham Lincoln and American Political Religion* (Albany: State University of New York Press, 1976), esp. 98–104.

24. Other inaugurals contain admonitions, e.g., Eisenhower's in 1957 (162–63), Truman's (154–57), and Harding's (128–32).

25. The extent to which the founders, including George Washington, were identified with proslavery positions is illustrated in a speech by John C. Calhoun in the Senate on March 4, 1850: "Nor can the Union be saved by invoking the name of the illustrious Southerner whose mortal remains repose on the western bank of the Potomac. He was one of us—a slave-holder and a planter. We have studied his history, and find nothing in it to justify submission to wrong." A. Craig Baird, ed., *American Public Addresses, 1740–1952* (New York: McGraw-Hill, 1956), 83.

26. See John Niven, *Martin Van Buren: The Romantic Age of American Politics* (New York: Oxford University Press, 1983).

27. *Public Papers*, 1993, 1:2.

28. *Public Papers*, 2001, 1:1.

29. *Public Papers*, 2001, 1:3.

30. Bert E. Bradley, "Jefferson and Reagan: The Rhetoric of Two Inaugurals," *Southern Speech Communication Journal* 48 (Winter 1983): 119–36; Gregg Phifer, "Two Inaugurals: A Second Look," *Southern Speech Communication Journal* 48 (Summer 1983): 378–85.

31. *Public Papers of the Presidents of the United States: William J. Clinton, 1997*, 2 vols. (Washington, DC: Government Printing Office, 1998–1999), 1:45.

32. "Inaugural Address, January 20th, 2005," *The American Presidency Project*, http://www.presidency.ucsb.edu/ws/index.php?pid=58745 (accessed June 14, 2006).

33. James D. Richardson, ed., *A Compilation of the Messages and Papers of the Presidents, 1789–1908*, 11 vols. (Washington, DC: National Bureau of Literature and Art, 1909), 4:5.

34. Michael Waldman, *POTUS Speaks: Finding the Words that Defined the Clinton Presidency* (New York: Simon and Schuster, 2000), 27.

35. The problems created by a transition from a president to a political protégé are also illustrated in the inaugurals of Martin Van Buren and George H. W. Bush.

36. *Public Papers*, 1993, 1:1.

37. "Inaugural Address, January 20th, 2005."

38. In his analysis of Richard Nixon's first inaugural, Robert L. Scott calls attention to Nixon's excessive use of the pronoun "I." Such personal references not only violate the presidential persona intrinsic to the address, but also tend to preclude the joint action through which the president and the people covenant together. See "Rhetoric That Postures: An Intrinsic Reading of Richard M. Nixon's Inaugural Address," *Western Speech* 34 (Winter 1970): 47, n. 1.

39. Roderick P. Hart's computerized analysis of 380 modern presidential speeches generated an 8.01 level of self-reference (all first-person pronouns were counted). By contrast, the nine inaugurals in this sample generated a 1.12 level of self-reference. The levels refer to the number of self-references in the middle-most 500 words of the speeches sampled. See *Verbal Style*, 273, 279.

40. The Reverend George St. John, headmaster of Choate, the preparatory school in Wallingford, CT, attended by Kennedy, used to say to his students: "Ask not what your school can do for you; ask what you can do for your school." Walter Scott, "Walter Scott's Personality Parade," *Parade* (December 15, 1968): 2.

41. For a sense of the nation's willingness to consider a powerful, even dictatorial, executive at the time this speech was given, see Jonathan Alter, *The Defining Moment: FDR's Hundred Days and the Triumph of Hope* (New York: Simon and Schuster, 2006).

42. Marcus Cunliffe, *American Presidents and the Presidency* (New York: American Heritage Press, 1968), 149, 152, 154–55, 158, 163, 172.

43. Grant's lack of humility in confronting the future "without fear" and his failure to ask for God's help were remarked by his contemporaries. Lloyd Paul Stryker, *Andrew Johnson: A Study in Courage* (New York: Macmillan, 1929), 346.

44. *Public Papers, 1993*, 1:2.

45. Richardson, 7:6.

46. Mircea Eliade, *Patterns in Comparative Religion*, trans. Rosemary Sheed (Cleveland: World, 1970), 392.

47. "Inaugural Address, January 20th, 2005."

48. Schlesinger, "Introduction," vii.

49. Leah Ceccarelli's "Polysemy: Multiple Meanings in Rhetorical Criticism," *Quarterly Journal of Speech* 84 (1998): 395–415, includes an analysis of differential coverage in newspapers in response to Lincoln's second inaugural.

50. Edward P. J. Corbett, "Analysis of the Style of John F. Kennedy's Inaugural Address," in *Classical Rhetoric for the Modern Student*, 2nd ed., ed. Edward Corbett (New York: Oxford University Press, 1971), 554–65; Sam Meyer, "The John F. Kennedy Inauguration Speech: Function and Importance of Its 'Address System,'" *Rhetoric Society Quarterly* 12 (Fall 1982): 239–50.

51. Chaim Perelman and Lucie Olbrechts-Tyteca, *The New Rhetoric: A Treatise on Argumentation*, trans. John Wilkinson and Purcell Weaver (Notre Dame, IN: University of Notre Dame Press, 1969), 49–51. The seven states that had seceded prior to Lincoln's inauguration already had formed a government and elected Jefferson Davis as its president.

52. Richardson, 5:626–39. Late in his analysis, Buchanan said, "But may I be permitted solemnly to invoke my countrymen to pause and deliberate before they determine to destroy this, the grandest temple which has ever been dedicated to human freedom since the world began?" (636–37).

53. Garry Wills, *The Kennedy Imprisonment: A Meditation on Power* (New York: Pocket Books, 1982), 312.

CHAPTER 3: SPECIAL INAUGURAL ADDRESSES

1. Thomas Doherty, "Assassination and Funeral of John F. Kennedy," *The Museum of Broadcast Communications*, http://www.museum.tv/archives/etv/K/htmlK/kennedyjf/kennedyjf.htm (accessed June 15, 2006).

2. "Address before a Joint Session of the Congress, November 27th, 1963," *Public Papers of the Presidents of the United States: Lyndon B. Johnson, 1964*, 2 vols. (Washington, DC: Government Printing Office, 1965), 1:8–10. Subsequent page references to this source are given in parentheses in the text. The Thanksgiving Day address delivered to the public just one day later is structured similarly: "Transcript of President Johnson's Thanksgiving Day Address to the Nation Urging 'New Dedication,'" *New York Times*, November 29, 1963, 20, http://proquest.com/ (accessed August 9, 2006). The rhetoric that emerged from Johnson over this period illustrates the concept of the rhetorical act. On November 23, 1963, he proclaimed a national day

of mourning for President Kennedy. On November 25, the day of President Kennedy's funeral, he issued an executive order closing government departments and agencies and a message to the members of the armed forces, which included elements of a national eulogy, and he made remarks to state governors after the funeral that began with elements of a national eulogy. On November 26, he delivered remarks on the Alliance for Progress to representatives of the countries of Latin America and made a statement urging that President Kennedy's Thanksgiving Day proclamation be read in U.S. churches on Thanksgiving Day as a memorial to him. These speeches were followed by the address before a joint session of Congress on November 27 and the President's Thanksgiving Day Address to the Nation on November 28. The last two speeches were fully developed national eulogies.

3. Theodore Sorenson, Kennedy's chief speechwriter, was also the chief speechwriter for this address.

4. James D. Richardson, ed., *A Compilation of the Messages and Papers of the Presidents, 1789–1908*, 11 vols. (Washington, DC: Bureau of National Literature and Art, 1909), 6:305. Hans L. Trefousse adds that "for several weeks after his inauguration, the new president took particular care not to commit himself to any specific program": *Andrew Johnson: A Biography* (New York: W. W. Norton, 1989), 197.

5. Richardson, 6:305.

6. Richardson, 6:305.

7. Richardson, 6:306. Trefousse, however, describes the speech as "a short, dignified address" (194).

8. Franklin Moore, ed., *Speeches of Andrew Johnson* (1865; reprint, New York: Burt Franklin, 1970), 457–60; Trefousse, 188–90.

9. Robert W. Winston, *Andrew Johnson: Plebian and Patriot* (1928; reprint, New York: AMS Press, 1970), 262–66; Thomas Lately, *The First President Johnson* (New York: William Morrow, 1968), 293–300. There is also some evidence of rhetorical skill. For example, the speeches he delivered in the Senate on December 18–19, 1860, and on February 5–6, March 2, and July 23, 1861, were highly regarded. Trefousse cites evidence that after the first, Johnson "was lionized and his words circulated by the thousands" (131). Of the second, he writes, "This speech, too, caused a sensation," and notes that many observers credited it with turning the tide against secession in Tennessee (136). Noel B. Gerson also cites evidence of Johnson's successful speechmaking in *The Trial of Andrew Johnson* (New York: Thomas Nelson, 1977), 27–30, 38–39, 51. The most detailed study of Andrew Johnson's speechmaking is Gregg Phifer's analysis of speeches delivered during his "swing around the circle" before the 1866 election, found in "Andrew Johnson Takes a Trip," "Andrew Johnson Argues a Case," "Andrew Johnson Delivers His Argument," and "Andrew Johnson Loses His Battle," *Tennessee Historical Quarterly* 11 (1952):3–22, 148–70, 212–34, 291–328. Phifer acknowledges historians' harsh judgments of this rhetoric and challenges them: "The President's speeches were not crude and coarse unless the spectacle of a man

fighting for what he believes in the only way he knows how deserves such adjectives.... Perhaps the fairest evaluation of the effects of the swing around the circle is that Johnson failed to achieve a political miracle" (318–19). He also points out that article 10, based on these speeches, was the least popular of the articles of impeachment, as it received only 88 affirmative votes in the House, 20 fewer than any other article, with 44 nays and 57 not voting (322). Phifer's study is a very balanced assessment of Johnson's strengths as an oral persuader and his limitations as one who knew how to fight but not how to conciliate.

10. *Public Papers of the Presidents of the United States: Harry S. Truman, 1945* (Washington, DC: Government Printing Office, 1961), 1.

11. *Public Papers, 1945*, 2.

12. *Public Papers, 1945*, 4.

13. Richardson, 4:37; the speech is at 36–39. Richardson labels Tyler's speech an inaugural address, and it is sometimes included in anthologies of presidential inaugural addresses.

14. Richardson, 5:64.

15. Richardson, 10:417–56. Roosevelt sought investiture in his first speech to Congress, an annual message, on December 3, 1901, the first occasion on which the representatives of the people were assembled for him to address. "The Inauguration of Theodore Roosevelt," *Harper's Weekly* 45 (1901): 957, reports that, immediately after the death of McKinley, Roosevelt sent forth to the sorrowing nation not only an example of human strength and fortitude, but also the inspiring message that his future policy would be in accord with that of his murdered chief: "I shall take the oath at once in response to your request; and in this hour of deep and terrible national bereavement I wish to state that it shall be my aim to continue absolutely unbroken the policy of President McKinley for the peace and prosperity of our beloved country." The authors called this "the inaugural address of the twenty-sixth President of the United States." Roosevelt's first proclamation is found in *Harper's Weekly* 45 (1901): 982.

16. Richardson, 10:418.

17. Richardson, 10:418.

18. Richardson, 10:419.

19. Richardson, 10:420–21.

20. Because McKinley was killed by an anarchist; because the country had recently faced recession, the Homestead and Pullman strikes, the Haymarket riot, and the march of Coxey's army; and because fear of social unrest was widespread, the need to assure the people that the presidency would survive the assassin's assault preempted the need to invite the people to ratify Roosevelt's assumption of the office. Only a president already invested with the authority of the office could offer convincing assurances about the institution. These tendencies were enhanced because the speech was also an annual message.

21. "After shaking hands with perhaps 100 correspondents [Coolidge] made his first speech as President. He said: 'Gentlemen: There isn't a thing I can say at the present time about policies of the Administration. There will not be anything until after the final interment of the late President. I am glad of the opportunity to greet you and shake hands with you. The executive offices will always be open, so far as is possible, to give your readers what may be given to them. A good many of you I know personally. This is your Government. You can exercise a great and helpful influence over the Administration and I know you will give the Administration that necessary cooperation.'" *New York Times*, August 5, 1923, 1.

22. *New York Times*, September 27, 1923, 1.

23. Fred L. Israel, ed., *The State of the Union Messages of the Presidents, 1790–1966*, 3 vols. (New York: Chelsea House, 1967), 3:2642.

24. *New York Times*, December 7, 1923, 1.

25. In 1926, the scandals of the Harding administration became a matter of public knowledge with the trial of his attorney general, Henry Daugherty, who was charged with conspiracy to defraud the government. In late 1923, Coolidge probably had some inkling of these potential problems, which would have made it vital for him to distance himself from some of the policies of his predecessor.

26. *Public Papers of the Presidents of the United States: Gerald R. Ford III*, 1974 (Washington, DC: Government Printing Office, 1975), 1.

27. A personal note intruded when Ford said, "I am indebted to no man, and only to one woman—my dear wife—as I begin this very difficult job."

CHAPTER 4: NATIONAL EULOGIES

1. Chicago Historical Society and the Trustees of Northwestern University, *The Great Chicago Fire and the Web of Memory*, www.chicagohs.org/fire/rescue/military.html (accessed May 18, 2006).

2. There are two versions of this telegram. A copy of the telegram is laid out on a desk in what used to be the governor's office as part of an exhibit on the 1906 earthquake at the State Capitol Museum in Sacramento, according to a report by Ruth Skewis for the *Sacramento Bee*: "Sacramento's Exhibit on the S.F. 1906 Earthquake," *RootsWeb*, March 26, 2006, http://archiver.rootsweb.com/th/read/CASANFRA/2006-03/1143418723 (accessed May 18, 2006). In *The Letters of Theodore Roosevelt*, the date is the same, but the text reads: "Telegram: It was difficult at first to credit the news of the calamity that had befallen San Francisco. I feel the greatest concern and sympathy for you and the people not only of San Francisco but of California in this terrible disaster. You will let me know if there is anything the National Government can do." A note reports that "the War Department sent troops, food, and bedding; the Navy Department ordered a Pacific squadron with medical supplies to West Coast ports. Roosevelt himself directed that the United

States Mint at San Francisco be used as a depository for private contribu-tions, ... and sent a special message to Congress recommending appropria-tions to rebuild the damaged government buildings." Elting E. Morison, ed., *The Letters of Theodore Roosevelt*, 8 vols. (Cambridge, MA: Harvard University Press), 5:213. On April 22, Roosevelt sent a letter to Mabel Thorp Boardman, chair of the National Relief Board of the American Red Cross, urging her to "send out an expert auditor to San Francisco to check the expenditures and to keep account of not only the money but of the supplies. ... I do not intend that any red tape shall interfere with at once succoring the San Fran-cisco people in their dire need; but we have to remember that when once the emergency is over there will be plenty of fools and plenty of knaves to make accusations against us, and plenty of good people who will believe them, and it is necessary that at as early a date as possible we shall have things in such shape as to enable us to make a clear statement of what we have done." (Morison, 5:216).

3. Skewis, 2006. See California State Parks, "1906 Earthquake Centennial Project" http://www.parks.ca.gov/?page_id=24204 (accessed July 24, 2006).

4. For an analysis of the role of presidential rhetoric in creating a sense of na-tional identity, see Vanessa B. Beasley, *You, the People: American National Iden-tity in Presidential Rhetoric* (College Station: Texas A&M University Press, 2004).

5. On April 23, 1983, Reagan delivered a radio address to the nation on the death of federal diplomatic and military personnel in Beirut. The address concerns the deaths of sixteen Americans who died in a terrorist bombing of the U.S. Embassy, which included some marines. He also made remarks at a ceremony on the same date honoring the victims of the bombing. See "Radio Address to the Nation on the Death of Federal Diplomatic and Military Per-sonnel in Beirut, Lebanon, April 23rd, 1983," *The American Presidency Project*, http://www.presidency.ucsb.edu/ws/index.php?pid=41228&st=&st1= (ac-cessed July 24, 2006); "Remarks at a Ceremony Honoring the Victims of the Bombing of the United States Embassy in Beirut, Lebanon, April 23rd, 1983," *The American Presidency Project*, http://www.presidency.ucsb.edu/ws/index.php?pid=41230&st=&st1= (accessed July 24, 2006). On November 4, 1983, he delivered remarks to military personnel at Cherry Point, North Carolina, not to the nation, on U.S. casualties in Lebanon and Grenada. See "Remarks to Military Personnel at Cherry Point, North Carolina, on the United States Casualties in Lebanon and Grenada, November 4th, 1983," *The American Presidency Project*, http://www.presidency.ucsb.edu/ws/index.php?pid=40720&st=&st1= (accessed July 24, 2006).

6. See Richard Johnston, Michael G. Hagen, and Kathleen Hall Jamieson, *The 2000 Presidential Election and the Foundations of Party Politics* (New York: Cam-bridge University Press, 2004).

7. *Public Papers of the Presidents of the United States: William J. Clinton, 1995*, 2 vols. (Washington, DC: Government Printing Office, 1996), 1:547. See also

"Finding His Voice—Oklahoma City Bombing," *Frontline*, http://www.pbs
.org/wgbh/pages/frontline/shows/clinton/chapters/4.html#2 (accessed
July 24, 2006).

8. *Public Papers of the Presidents of the United States: William J. Clinton, 1996*, 2 vols.
(Washington, DC: Government Printing Office, 1997–1998), 1:86.

9. For a detailed discussion of the links between the Greek *epitaphios* and the
speeches delivered at Gettysburg, see Garry Wills, *Lincoln at Gettysburg: The
Words that Remade America* (New York: Simon and Schuster, 1992), 41–62.
See also Nicole Loraux, *The Invention of Athens: The Funeral Oration in the Classical City*, trans. Alan Sheridan (Cambridge, MA: Harvard University Press,
1986).

10. *Public Papers of the Presidents of the United States: Ronald Reagan, 1986*, 2 vols.
(Washington, DC: Government Printing Office, 1988–1989), 1:94–95.

11. *Public Papers, 1986*, 1:94–5.

12. *Public Papers, 1986*, 1:95.

13. *Public Papers, 1986*, 1:95.

14. *Public Papers, 1986*, 1:95.

15. "Address to the Nation on the Loss of Space Shuttle *Columbia*, February 1st,
2003," *The American Presidency Project*, http://www.presidency.ucsb.edu/ws/
index.php?pid=181&st=&st1= (accessed July 12, 2006).

16. "Address to the Nation, February 1st, 2003."

17. *Public Papers, 1995*, 1:574.

18. *Public Papers, 1995*, 1:574.

19. *Public Papers of the Presidents of the United States: George W. Bush, 2001*, 2 vols.
(Washington, DC: Government Printing Office, 2003), 2:1108.

20. Presidents can assume the role of national priest in other discourse, as President Kennedy did in his June 11, 1963, televised address to the nation, "Civil
Rights: A Moral Issue."

21. *Public Papers, 1995*, 1:552.

22. *Public Papers, 1995*, 1:573.

23. *Public Papers, 1995*, 1:573.

24. *Public Papers, 1995*, 1:573.

25. "Address to the Nation, February 1st 2003."

26. See Carolyn Marvin and David W. Ingle, *Blood Sacrifice and the Nation: Myth,
Ritual and the American Flag* (Cambridge and New York: Cambridge University Press, 1999).

27. *Public Papers, 2001*, 2:1143.

28. *Public Papers, 1995*, 1:573.

29. *Public Papers, 2001*, 2:1108.

30. *Public Papers, 1986*, 1:118.

31. Sean O'Keefe, "Columbia Space Shuttle Disaster, 1:00 P.M.," transcript,
NBC News Special Report, National Broadcasting Company, Inc., February 1,
2003, http://www.nexis.com/ (accessed July 14, 2006).

32. *Public Papers, 1995*, 1:552.

33. *Public Papers, 2001*, 2:1108.

34. *Public Papers*, 2001, 2:1108.

35. *Public Papers*, 2001, 2:1108.

36. *Public Papers*, 2001, 2:1109.

37. *Public Papers*, 2001, 2:1108.

38. *Public Papers*, 2001, 2:1108.

39. *Public Papers*, 2001, 2:1098.

40. Peter Jennings, "Planes Crash into World Trade Center," transcript, ABC *News Special Report*, American Broadcasting Companies, Inc., September 11, 2001, http://www.nexis.com/ (accessed July 17, 2006).

41. Frank Bruni, *Ambling into History: The Unlikely Odyssey of George W. Bush* (New York: Harper Collins Publishers, 2002), 255.

42. *Public Papers*, 2001, 2:1098. These words echo his father's statement in response to the Iraqi invasion of Kuwait.

43. *Public Papers*, 2001, 2:1098–99.

44. *Public Papers*, 2001, 2:1100.

45. *Public Papers*, 2001, 2:1100.

46. *Public Papers*, 2001, 2:1108.

47. *Public Papers*, 2001, 2:1108–09.

48. *Public Papers*, 2001, 2:1108–09.

49. *Public Papers*, 2001, 2:1108–09.

50. *Public Papers*, 2001, 2:1108.

51. *Public Papers*, 2001, 2:1108.

52. *Public Papers*, 2001, 2:1108.

53. Ian Christopher McCaleb, "Bush tours ground zero in lower Manhattan," *CNN.com*, September 14, 2001, http://archives.cnn.com/2001/US/09/14/bush.terrorism/ (accessed December 5, 2006).

54. For a detailed report on the crafting of this speech, including strong concerns for the elements we have described as a national eulogy, see D. T. Max, "The Making of the Speech," *New York Times*, October 7, 2001, sec. 6, p.32.

55. *Public Papers*, 2001, 2:1140.

56. *Public Papers*, 2001, 2:1140–42.

57. *Public Papers*, 2001, 2:1140–42.

58. *Public Papers*, 2001, 2:1141–42.

59. See John M. Murphy, "Our Mission and Our Moment: George W. Bush and September 11th," *Rhetoric & Public Affairs* 6 (2003): 607–32; Denise M. Bostdorff, "George W. Bush's Post–September 11 Rhetoric of Covenant Renewal: Upholding the Faith of the Greatest Generation," *Quarterly Journal of Speech* 89 (2003): 293–319.

60. "Urgent—Weather Message," *National Weather Service*, New Orleans, LA, August 28, 2005, 10:11 A.M. Also available in U.S. Department of Commerce, "Service Assessment: Hurricane Katrina, August 23–31 2005," June 2006, http://www.nws.noaa.gov/om/assessments/pdfs/Katrina.pdf (accessed July 18, 2006).

61. "Remarks on the Relief Efforts for Hurricane Katrina, August 31st, 2005," *The American Presidency Project*, http://www.presidency.ucsb.edu/ws/index.php?pid=73780&st=&st1= (accessed July 18, 2006).

62. "Waiting for a Leader," *New York Times*, late ed., September 1, 2005, A22, http://www.nexis.com/ (accessed July 20, 2006).

63. Laura Rozen, "Extremely Disappointing Speech," *War and Piece*, http://www.warandpiece.com/blogdirs/002450.html (accessed July 20, 2006).

64. "Remarks on the Aftermath of Hurricane Katrina in Mobile, Alabama, September 2nd, 2006," *The American Presidency Project*, http://www.presidency.ucsb.edu/ws/index.php?pid=64973&st=&st1= (accessed July 13, 2006).

65. "Remarks on Hurricane Katrina Recovery Efforts in Kenner, Louisiana, September 2nd, 2005," *The American Presidency Project*, http://www.presidency.ucsb.edu/ws/index.php?pid=73850&st=&st1= (accessed July 13, 2006).

66. Judy Keen and Richard Benedetto, "A Compassionate Bush Was Absent Right After Katrina," *USA Today*, September 9, 2005, 2A.

67. "Proclamation 7925—National Day of Prayer and Remembrance for the Victims of Hurricane Katrina, September 8th, 2005," *The American Presidency Project*, http://www.presidency.ucsb.edu/ws/index.php?pid=62209&st=&st1= (accessed July 20, 2006).

68. George W. Bush, "President George W. Bush Exclusive Interview," interview by Diane Sawyer, transcript, *Good Morning America*, American Broadcasting Companies, Inc., September 1, 2005, http://www.nexis.com/ (accessed July 13, 2006).

69. "Address to the Nation on Hurricane Katrina Recovery from New Orleans, Louisiana, September 15th, 2005," *The American Presidency Project*, http://www.presidency.ucsb.edu/ws/index.php?pid=58798&st=&st1= (accessed July 20, 2006).

70. "Address, September 15th, 2005."

71. "Address, September 15th, 2005."

72. "Address, September 15th, 2005."

73. "Remarks, September 2nd, 2005."

74. "Address, September 15th, 2005."

75. "Address, September 15th, 2005."

76. "Address, September 15th, 2005."

77. "Bush Katrina Ratings Fall After Speech," *Rasmussen Reports*, September 18, 2005, http://www.rasmussenreports.com/2005/Katrina_September%2018.htm (accessed July 21, 2006).

78. "Bush Approval Rating at 40 Percent," *CNN.com*, September 19, 2005, http://www.cnn.com/2005/POLITICS/09/19/bush.poll/ (accessed July 21, 2006).

79. SurveyUSA polling data from September 2005 to May 2006 document Bush's generally declining approval ratings: in September 2005, approval 41%, disapproval 57%; in May 2006, approval 33%, disapproval 64%.

Obviously, these polls have been significantly affected by events in the Iraq war. "50 State Monthly Tracking," *SurveyUSA*, http://www.surveyusa.com/50StateTracking.html (accessed May 23, 2006).

CHAPTER 5: PARDONING RHETORIC

1. "61-Proclamation 4311, September 8th, 1974," *The American Presidency Project*, http://www.presidency.ucsb.edu/ws/?pid=4696.

2. Before the Nixon pardon, except after the Civil War, the administration of the presidential pardoning power had never excited great public dissatisfaction or questioning. Philip B. Kurland, *Watergate and the Constitution* (Chicago: University of Chicago Press, 1978), 142. See also Jonathan Truman Dorris, *Pardon and Amnesty under Lincoln and Johnson: The Restoration of the Confederates to Their Rights and Privileges, 1861–1898* (Chapel Hill: University of North Carolina Press, 1953).

3. William F. Duker, "The President's Power to Pardon: A Constitutional History," *William and Mary Law Review* 18 (Spring 1977): 476–97.

4. Jacob E. Cooke, ed., *The Federalist* (Cleveland: Meridian Books, 1961), 501.

5. *The Federalist*, 502.

6. *The Federalist*, 502.

7. *The Federalist*, 500–501.

8. *Ex parte Garland* (1867); cited in Henry Steele Commager, *Documents in American History*, 5th ed., 2 vols. (New York: F. S. Crofts, 1948), 2:27.

9. The precedent is from the pardoning powers of the monarch, of whom William Blackstone writes that "the great operation of his sceptre is mercy," and that he "has in his power to extend mercy, wherever he thinks it is deserved." *Commentaries on the Laws of England*, 4 vols. (1765–69; reprint, Chicago: University of Chicago Press, 1979), 4:389, 390.

10. William H. Humbert, *The Pardoning Power of the President* (Washington, DC: American Council on Public Affairs, 1941).

11. *Hoffa v. Saxbe*, 378 F. Supp. 1221 (D.D.C. 1974); cited in Patrick R. Cowlishaw, "Presidential Pardon," *Stanford Law Review* 28 (November 1975): 154–55.

12. 378 F. Supp. 1221. The court also reaffirmed the right of a prisoner to reject a substituted sentence (Cowlishaw, 155).

13. *Ex parte Perovich*, 9 Fed. Rep. (2d) 124 (1925).

14. *Biddle v. Perovich*, 274 U.S. 480 (1927).

15. Jonathan Elliot, ed., *The Debates in the Several State Conventions on the Adoption of the Federal Constitution*, 4:201–6; cited in *The Annals of America*, vol. 3, 1784–1796, ed. Mortimer Adler (Chicago: Encyclopedia Britannica, 1968), 302.

16. "The Objections of the Hon. George Mason to the Proposed Foederal [sic] Constitution," in *Pamphlets on the Constitution of the United States* (Brooklyn, NY: n.p., 1888), 75.

17. 17 Wall. (U.S.) 191.

18. James D. Richardson, ed., *A Compilation of the Messages and Papers of the Presidents, 1789–1908*, 11 vols. (Washington, DC: Bureau of National Literature and Art, 1909), 1:181.

19. Laszlo Versenyi, *Socratic Humanism* (New Haven, CT: Yale University Press, 1963), 42. *Kairos* (timeliness) is linked to *to prepon* (propriety). See John Poulakos, "Toward a Sophistic Definition of Rhetoric," *Philosophy and Rhetoric* 16 (February 1983): 35–48; Michael Carter, "Stasis and Kairos: Principles of Social Construction in Classical Rhetoric," *Rhetoric Review* 7 (Fall 1988): 97–112.

20. Richardson, 7:235.

21. Richardson, 1:559–60.

22. Richardson, 6:189.

23. Dorris, 32–33.

24. Richardson, 6:213, 233.

25. Richardson, 6:310.

26. Richardson, 1:181, 304.

27. Richardson, 1:425, 512.

28. Richardson, 1:425, 514.

29. Richardson, 6:697.

30. Richardson, 6:697.

31. "78-Proclamation 4313, September 16th, 1974," *The American Presidency Project*, http://www.presidency.ucsb.edu/ws/?pid=4714.

32. *Public Papers of the Presidents of the United States: Gerald R. Ford III, 1974* (Washington, DC: Government Printing Office, 1975), 137.

33. Throughout U.S. history, clemency has been granted by presidents to individuals in eight forms and to classes of individuals in two forms. Included among them are the full pardon, pardon to term served and to restore civil rights, pardon just to restore civil rights, conditional pardon, amnesty, amnesty on condition, reprieve, commutation, commutation on condition, and remission of fines and forfeitures. See Christopher Joyner, "Rethinking the President's Power of Executive Pardon," *Federal Probation* 43 (March 1979): 18.

34. Humbert, 125, 127, 131, 136–37.

35. *Public Papers*, 1974, 673.

36. *Public Papers of the Presidents of the United States: Ronald Reagan, 1981* (Washington, DC: Government Printing Office, 1982), 358, 359.

37. *Public Papers*, 1974, 784.

38. In *Ex parte Garland*, the court found that "a pardon reaches both the punishment prescribed for the offense and the guilt of the offender; and when the pardon is full, it releases the punishment and blots out of existence the guilt, so that in the eye of the law the offender is as innocent as if he had never committed the offense."

39. Richardson, 1:184.

40. Richardson, 1:303.

41. Richardson, 1:425.

42. Richardson, 1:514.

43. Richardson, 1:559.

44. Richardson, 6:310.

45. *Public Papers*, 1974, 137.

46. Robert K. Murray, *The Harding Era: Warren G. Harding and His Administration* (Minneapolis: University of Minnesota Press, 1969), 66.

47. Murray, 169.

48. David Johnston, "The Pardons; Bush Pardons 6 in Iran Affair, Aborting a Weinberger Trial; Prosecutor Assails 'Cover-up,'" *New York Times*, late ed., December 25, 1992, A1, http://www.nexis.com/ (accessed August 11, 2006).

49. "The Pardons: Text of President Bush's Statement on the Pardon of Weinberger and Others," *New York Times*, late ed., December 25, 1992, A22, http://www.nexis.com/ (accessed August 10, 2006); Proclamation 6518, 57 *Federal Register* 62, 145 (1992).

50. House Committee on the Judiciary, *Presidential Pardon Power: Hearing before the Subcommittee on the Constitution*, 107th Cong., 1st sess., 2001, 42, http://commdocs.house.gov/committees/judiciary/hju71180.000/hju71180_of.htm (accessed June 20, 2006).

51. *Presidential Pardon Power*, 44.

52. *Presidential Pardon Power*, 54.

53. *Presidential Pardon Power*, 56.

54. *Presidential Pardon Power*, 68.

55. "Bush Issues Pardons, But To A Relative Few," *New York Times*, December, 22, 2006, A31, http://www.nytimes.com (accessed December 22, 2006).

56. "The President's Statement," *New York Times*, July 3, 2007, A15.

57. Adam Liptak, "Commutation Doesn't Rise to Status of a Pardon," *New York Times*, July 3, 2007, A15.

58. Adam Liptak, "Bush Rationale on Libby Stirs Legal Debate," *New York Times*, July 4, 2007, A13.

59. *Public Papers*, 1974, 101–4; subsequent page references to Ford's remarks are given in parentheses in the text. Nixon's resignation before impeachment by the House of Representatives made it possible for Ford to pardon him for what were impeachable offenses.

60. Gerald R. Ford, *A Time to Heal: The Autobiography of Gerald R. Ford* (New York: Harper and Row/Reader's Digest, 1979), 179.

61. The suspicion that there had been an agreement between Ford and Nixon prompted an unprecedented appearance by an incumbent president before the Subcommittee on Criminal Justice of the House Committee on the Judiciary, which called hearings beginning on September 24, 1974, to investigate the reasons for the pardon. In those hearings, Ford reiterated that there had been no deal. House Committee on the Judiciary, *Pardon of Richard M. Nixon and Related Matters: Hearings before the Subcommittee on Criminal Justice*, 93d Cong., 2d sess., September 24, October 1 and 17, 1974.

62. *New York Times*, August 29, 1974, 1.

63. *Public Papers*, 1974, 136–37.

64. *Public Papers*, 1974, 784.

65. *Public Papers*, 1974, 137.

66. Gerald terHorst, *Gerald Ford and the Future of the Presidency* (New York: Joseph Okpaku Publishing, 1974), 236.

67. *Public Papers*, 1974, 153.

68. terHorst, 236.

69. Ford, *A Time to Heal*, 178–79.

70. *Public Papers of the Presidents of the United States: Richard Nixon, 1974* (Washington, DC: Government Printing Office, 1975), 397.

71. Harry Truman, a president Ford deeply admired, kept a copy of the full quotation in a leather portfolio on his desk: "I do the very best I know how—the very best I can; and I mean to keep doing so to the end. If the end brings me out all right, what is said against me won't amount to anything. If the end brings me out wrong, ten angels swearing I was right won't make any difference." Samuel I. Rosenman and Dorothy Rosenman, *Presidential Style: Some Giants and a Pygmy in the White House* (New York: Harper and Row, 1976), 444. Conceivably Ford and his speechwriters had forgotten Nixon's use of the quotation and chose it because of this association.

72. *Public Papers*, 1974, 153.

73. Ford, *A Time to Heal*, 164, 171, 179. However, in his press conference of September 16, he said, "The acceptance of a pardon, I think, can be construed by many, if not all, as an admission of guilt." *Public Papers*, 1974, 147.

74. In *A Time to Heal*, Ford indicates that he and his advisers recognized the omission of such a statement during preparations for the pardon. Initially, Ford's staff solicited a statement of "true contrition" (165) and had discussed making confession of guilt a condition of pardon (179). Nixon's acceptance went through a series of drafts, and the statement Nixon issued was seen as "a good deal less than a full confession" (172), although Ford's staff prevented it from being watered down still further by his former press secretary, Ronald Ziegler (173).

75. The courts eventually nullified the agreement and held that the Nixon tapes and records belonged to the American people.

76. *Pardon of Richard M. Nixon*, 26.

77. William Howard Taft, *Our Chief Magistrate and His Powers*, 123; cited in Humbert, 129.

78. *Pardon of Richard M. Nixon*, 25; Gude's remarks are on page 2, McKinney's on page 14.

79. "Impeachment Inquiry," in *Presidency, 1974* (Washington, DC: Congressional Quarterly, 1975), 36. In *Watergate and the Constitution*, Philip B. Kurland lays out the arguments that might be made against the validity of Ford's pardon of Nixon. Among them is that it was premature to award a pardon because it preceded the filing of any charges of criminality or even of conviction. A more powerful argument is that it failed to conform to the regulations of the

Department of Justice establishing the office and duties of the Watergate special prosecutor and held by the Supreme Court to be binding on the president in *United States v. Nixon* (Kurland, 143–50). However, Ford's pardon of Nixon was judged by special prosecutor Leon Jaworski to be so clearly constitutional "as not to admit to doubt." *The Right and the Power: The Prosecution of Watergate* (New York: Reader's Digest Press, 1976), 299; cited in Mark J. Rozell, "The Presidential Pardon Power: A Bibliographic Essay," *Journal of Law and Politics* 5 (1989): 461.

80. *Public Papers*, 1974, 153.

81. *Public Papers*, 1974, 606.

82. Ford, *A Time to Heal*, 179.

CHAPTER 6: STATE OF THE UNION ADDRESSES

1. This address was called the annual message until 1945, when the title "State of the Union Message" came into use. "State of the State of the Union Talk," *New York Times*, January 28, 1986, 8Y.

2. Fred L. Israel, ed., *The State of the Union Messages of the Presidents, 1790–1966*, 3 vols. (New York: Chelsea House, 1967), 1:xvii. Subsequent page references to this source are given in parentheses in the text. Illness prevented Wilson from delivering his last two addresses orally. The Republican presidents who followed him delivered oral messages intermittently: Harding presented his two addresses orally, Coolidge did so once, and Hoover never.

3. Charles A. Beard, *American Government and Politics*, 7th ed. (New York: Macmillan, 1935), 185.

4. Woodrow Wilson, *The President of the United States* (New York: Harper, 1916), 53–54.

5. See Seymour H. Fersh, *The View from the White House: A Study of Presidential State of the Union Messages* (Washington, DC: Public Affairs Press, 1961).

6. Theodore Roosevelt's addresses best exemplify the lengthy compendia, but Truman followed that precedent generally, and Eisenhower did so in 1953. Focused messages began early. In 1794, for example, Washington devoted nearly all of his annual message to a report on the Whiskey Rebellion. Moreover, in 1887, Cleveland devoted his entire message to the tariff and in 1897 confined himself to foreign trade and financial problems. McKinley also focused his messages, primarily on the Spanish-American War and its aftermath.

7. Jackson not only made specific recommendations, but also used his messages to seek public support for his policies. Polk followed that example, recommending specific measures and appealing for popular support. Lincoln also used the annual message to appeal to the public, discussing administrative proposals in detail, and in 1862, he violated tradition by proposing a specific constitutional amendment providing for the compensated emancipation of slaves.

8. John Adams, Jefferson, Madison, Monroe, and John Quincy Adams generally followed Washington's precedent, only enumerating areas needing congressional attention. On occasion, specific recommendations appeared, such as Jefferson's 1801 proposal that all excise taxes be repealed. John Quincy Adams's 1826 address describes the accepted view of the function of these messages and illustrates their relationship to one another: "Of the subjects recommended to Congress at their last session, some were then definitely acted upon. Others, left unfinished, but partly matured, will recur to your attention without needing a renewal of notice from me. The purpose of this communication will be to present to your [Congress's] view the general aspect of our public affairs at this moment and the measures which have been taken to carry into effect the intentions of the Legislature as signified by the laws then and heretofore enacted" (Israel, 1:250). Tyler, Taylor, Pierce, Buchanan, Grant, Hayes, Benjamin Harrison, Taft, Harding, Coolidge, and Hoover by and large followed the practice of presenting only a very general program, with a report on executive implementation.

9. The structural problems that result from the latter type of message are evident in many addresses. In his eighth message, for example, Theodore Roosevelt discussed finances, corporations, protection for workers, courts, forests, inland waterways, national parks, denatured alcohol, pure food, the Indian service, the secret service, postal savings banks, parcel post, the educational census, public health, the redistribution of government bureaus, the government printing office, soldiers' homes, statehood for New Mexico and Arizona, interstate fisheries, Latin American republics, the Panama Canal, ocean mail liners, Hawaii, the Philippines, Puerto Rico, Cuba, the Japanese Exposition, the Army, the national guard, and the Navy. Presidents who proceed in this fashion make little pretense that their messages are coherently organized. They do not preview their central claims or summarize them in a concluding statement. For example, Roosevelt began his eighth message by abruptly launching into the topic of finance: "The financial standing of the nation at the present time is excellent . . ." (Israel, 2:2296). Without benefit of transition, he lurched from finance to a discussion of corporations: "There have been no new taxes and no increases of taxes; on the contrary, some taxes have been taken off; there has been a reduction of taxation. As regards the great corporations engaged in interstate business, and especially the railroads . . ." (Israel, 2:2297). Once he finished his last topic, the Navy, Roosevelt abruptly concluded his message: "The Board of Visitors should be appointed in January, and each member should be required to give at least six days service, only from one to three days to be performed during June week, which is the least desirable time for the board to be at Annapolis so far as benefiting the Navy by their observations is concerned" (Israel, 2:2336). By contrast, orally delivered messages contain prefatory materials in their introductions and summary gestures of goodwill in their conclusions. Messages organized as laundry lists resemble the memo; orally

delivered messages are structured as unified wholes, the speech. In the modern period, presidents have frequently delivered a shorter address orally and a longer address in writing.

10. See, in particular, Mary E. Stuckey, *Defining Americans: The Presidency and National Identity* (Lawrence: University Press of Kansas, 2004).

11. *Writings of Thomas Jefferson*, 20 vols. (Washington, DC: Thomas Jefferson Memorial Society, 1904), 19:24–25.

12. *Public Papers of the Presidents of the United States: William J. Clinton, 1995*, 2 vols. (Washington, DC: Government Printing Office, 1996), 1:77.

13. *Public Papers of the Presidents of the United States: George W. Bush, 2002*, 2 vols. (Washington, DC: Government Printing Office, 2004–2005), 1:132.

14. "Address before a Joint Session of the Congress on the State of the Union, January 28th, 2003," *The American Presidency Project*, http://www.presidency.ucsb.edu/ws/index.php?pid=29645 (accessed June 13, 2006).

15. W. S. Myers, ed., *State Papers of Herbert Hoover*, 3 vols. (1934), 2:383; cited in Arthur B. Tourtellot, *Presidents and the Presidency* (New York: Doubleday, 1964), 62. That view was echoed most recently by President Reagan in his 1988 address to the Republican National Convention.

16. "Address before a Joint Session of the Congress on the State of the Union, January 20th, 2004," *The American Presidency Project*, http://www.presidency.ucsb.edu/ws/index.php?pid=29646 (accessed June 13, 2006).

17. *Public Papers of the Presidents of the United States: William J. Clinton, 1996*, 2 vols. (Washington, DC: Government Printing Office, 1997–1998), 1:79.

18. *Public Papers of the Presidents of the United States: William J. Clinton, 1997*, 2 vols. (Washington, DC: Government Printing Office, 1998–1999), 1:109.

19. "Address before a Joint Session of the Congress on the State of the Union, February 2nd, 2005," *The American Presidency Project*, http://www.presidency.ucsb.edu/ws/index.php?pid=58746 (accessed June 13, 2006).

20. President's Radio Address, January 20, 2007, http://www.whitehouse.gov/news/releases/2007/01/20070120.html.

21. *New York Times*, February 18, 2007, A16; Sheryl Gay Stolberg, "Bush, in Talk-Show Manner, Promotes His Health Plan," *New York Times*, February 22, 2007, http://www.nytimes.com/2007/02/22/washington/22bush.html?ex=1173416400&en=ffa12469a9361a73&ei=5070 (accessed March 7, 2007).

22. In the world of the State of the Union address, women scarcely exist. Through 1966, they are mentioned in only three addresses: once in relation to polygamy, by Grant (Israel, 2:1316); several times in Theodore Roosevelt's fifth annual message in regard to factory laws to prevent the abuse of women workers, including recognition that some 5 million women were then engaged in gainful occupations ("Fifth Annual Message, December 5th, 1905," *The American Presidency Project*, http://www.presidency.ucsb.edu/ws/print.php?pid=29546); and once in relation to suffrage, by Wilson (Israel, 3:2590). More recently, they have been alluded to indirectly in Ronald Reagan's statements opposing abortion.

23. *Public Papers of the Presidents of the United States: John F. Kennedy, 1963* (Washington, DC: Government Printing Office, 1964), 468–71.

24. *Public Papers,* 1997, 1:116.

25. Many addresses contain similar comments; e.g., Andrew Jackson's (Israel, 1:335), Franklin Roosevelt's (Israel, 3:2812, 2831, 2860), and Lyndon Johnson's (*Public Papers of the Presidents of the United States: Lyndon B. Johnson, 1967* [Washington, DC: Government Printing Office, 1975] 1:9). Abraham Lincoln's comment in 1862 that "the dogmas of the quiet past are inadequate to the stormy present. . . . [W]e must think anew and act anew" (Israel, 2:1084) stands in sharp contrast to these views.

26. Theodore Lowi, "Four Systems of Policy, Politics, and Choice," *Public Administration Review* 32 (July–August 1972): 298–310.

27. *Public Papers,* 2002, 1:133.

28. "Address before a Joint Session of the Congress on the State of the Union, February 2nd, 2005."

29. The treaty of purchase was signed on May 2, but dated April 30, 1803; Jefferson's third annual message was delivered on October 17, 1803; the Senate ratified the treaty on October 20, 1803; and the Spanish gave up physical possession of the territory on November 30, 1803, three weeks before its cession by the French to the United States.

30. *The Writings of Thomas Jefferson,* 5:542. Similarly, when Lincoln suspended habeas corpus, blockaded rebel ports, and called out the state militias in April 1861 during a congressional recess, he later explained his actions and asked Congress to ratify them. Congress did, using language that clearly asserted its powers to act under similar conditions. The acts were approved "as if they had been issued and done under the previous express authority and direction of the Congress": 12 U.S. Stat. 326 (August 6, 1861). In his July 4, 1861, message, Lincoln indicated that necessity justified his right to act. For example, he hesitated to establish military courts to administer justice in the contesting states, he said, "not because I had any doubt that the end proposed—the collection of the debts—was just and right in itself, but because I have been unwilling to go beyond the pressure of necessity in the unusual exercise of power" (Israel, 2:1060).

These examples present presidents as those who can determine whether the safety of the country warrants expansion of what are normally construed to be their constitutional powers. The definition of the president as one who has extraordinary powers in extraordinary circumstances was reinforced when, through executive order, Franklin Roosevelt interned Japanese residents, many of them native-born citizens, in "relocation centers" during World War II, and the Supreme Court upheld the constitutionality of that act. However, when Truman argued that he had seized the steel mills in his role as commander in chief prosecuting the Korean war, his actions were struck down. The Supreme Court reasoned that the president had wide latitude to use instruments of national force "against the outside world for the security of our society," but had no "such indulgence" in "a lawful economic struggle between industry and labor." *Youngstown Co. v. Sawyer,* 343 U.S. 579, 645 (1952).

31. *Supplement to the Messages and Papers of the Presidents, Woodrow Wilson, March 4, 1913 to March 4, 1917* (Washington, DC: Bureau of National Literature, 1917), 7871. Biographer Arthur S. Link describes this as a "vivid assertion of leadership" and emphasizes the symbolic significance of Wilson's decision in *Wilson: The New Freedom* (Princeton, NJ: Princeton University Press, 1956), 152–53.

32. Irwin Ross, *The Loneliest Campaign: The Truman Victory of 1948* (New York: New American Library, 1968), 55–56.

33. The tone of direct address harks back to *ars dictamen,* a written form with the qualities usually associated with oral discourse (Israel, 2:1289).

34. Even in written messages, earlier presidents addressed themselves directly to the public. In 1874, for example, Grant wrote, "I invite the attention, not of Congress, but of the people of the United States, to the causes and effects of these unhappy questions" (Israel, 2:1289).

35. Fersh, 104–5. In 1945, ill once again, he sent a long written document to Congress and repeated parts of it in a radio address in the evening.

36. Dwight D. Eisenhower, *Mandate for Change* (New York: Doubleday, 1963), 286.

37. Cited in Lynn Rosellini, "On the State of the State of the Union," *New York Times,* January 12, 1982, 12Y.

38. Cited in Rosellini, 12Y.

39. Fersh (133) notes a link between effective use of the State of the Union address and the standing of presidents in the eyes of history, on the basis of a poll of historians reported by Arthur M. Schlesinger in *Paths to the Present* (New York: Macmillan, 1949), 96.

40. The following analysis owes much to Darin Patrick McAtee, "Crisis in Epideixis: Ronald Reagan's State of the Union Addresses as Epideictic Successes and Deliberative Failures," honors thesis, University of Kansas, 1988.

41. Ronald Reagan, "State of the Union," *New York Times,* January 28, 1987, 6Y.

42. A lack of legislative specifics in the 1982 address was noted by Walter Isaacson in "States of the Union," *Time* (February 8, 1982): 16. House minority leader Robert Michel noted that the speech did not address the nation's economic problems in the midst of a recession: Hedrick Smith, "Reagan's Gamble to Retain the Upper Hand in an Election Year," *New York Times,* January 27, 1982, 17. A similar lack in the 1983 address was noted by Walter Isaacson in "Mending and Bending," *Time* (February 7, 1983): 13. William Safire described the speech as "themeless pudding" and "a series of banalities": "Reagan's White Flag," *New York Times,* January 27, 1983, 23Y. Failure to detail how the deficit might be reduced in 1984 was noted by Elizabeth Drew, "A Political Journal," *New Yorker* (February 20, 1984): 119; as were the absence of foreign and domestic policy proposals in "State of the Nation III," *Nation* (February 4, 1984): 113; and in Steven Weisman, "Tune in Tonight," *New York Times,* January 29, 1984, 1. The same claims are made in

regard to the 1985 address by Marci MacDonald, "A Militant Birthday Message," *Maclean's* (February 18, 1985): 28; and by Morton Kondracke, "More Than Blind Luck," *Newsweek* (February 18, 1985): 22, who noted that the shift in emphasis was a deviation from the historical pattern and an abandonment of the constitutional enjoinder regarding policy. Reagan's 1986 speech, commented Bernard Weinraub, "offered few specific legislative proposals": "Reagan's Message Appeals for Unity to Curb Spending," *New York Times*, February 5, 1986, 1. His views were echoed in "Heroes Cited, Facts Slighted," *New Republic* (February 24, 1986): 7; in "State of the Union: Playing Chicken," *National Review* (February 28, 1986): 17; and in William Safire, "The Speech That Failed," *New York Times*, February 7, 1986, 17. In 1987, Rep. James Leach (R-IA) was quoted as saying, "the tenor was absolutely right, but the substance was lacking": Linda Greenhouse, "Reagan's Address Provokes a Highly Partisan Reaction," *New York Times*, January 28, 1987, 17. Those comments are supported in part by the analysis of Matthew C. Moen, "The Political Agenda of Ronald Reagan: A Content Analysis of the State of the Union Messages," *Presidential Studies Quarterly* 19 (Fall 1988): 775–85, who also notes that over time the messages became shorter and the proportion of nonsubstantive materials in them increased.

43. George H. W. Bush followed a similar strategy in his first budget message in 1989; in a politically astute move, he espoused ends applauded by the Democratic majorities in both houses, but left to them the difficult choices about how such goals were to be met in a time of fiscal limitation.

44. For example, Reagan delivered no State of the Union address in 1981. Instead, in his first policy speech to the American people, on February 5, he described the nation's economic problems and their causes and suggested the economic goals he would pursue. This speech was followed on February 18 with a speech to Congress that presented his programmatic solutions, which received strong public support and were passed by Congress. This pattern was also followed in speeches seeking funding to support the Contras in Nicaragua and the Duarte government in El Salvador, e.g., in the speech delivered before a special joint session of Congress on April 27, 1983, which was unsuccessful, and the speeches to the nation on May 9, 1984, on aid for El Salvador and on March 16, 1986, seeking support for the Nicaraguan Contras.

45. For instance, the 1983 message alluded to a 92-page legislative proposal, to be submitted to Congress early in the next month, that was a revised version of Reagan's "new federalism" initiative. Robert Pear, "Bill on 'New Federalism' to Merge 27 Programs," *New York Times*, January 26, 1983, 13Y.

46. See, e.g., Fred Barnes, "Nap-Master Ronnie: Conservatism's Lost Opportunities," and Andrew Sullivan, "Mr. Average, The President We Deserved," *New Republic* (January 9 and 16, 1989): 18, 20.

47. Reagan's 1983 message, which ran approximately thirty-eight minutes, was criticized for its length in commentary on a special edition of ABC's "This Week with David Brinkley" following the delivery of the president's speech and the Democratic response.

48. This adaptation to television is of great importance because the State of the Union address is becoming the primary vehicle through which presidential priorities are expressed. That tendency is enhanced because the speech is routinely constructed well in advance and, hence, is less responsive to events, and because it is delivered at the beginning of the calendar year and the legislative year and as far from the November elections as possible. See Moen, 776-77.

49. Lyndon Johnson's first address in 1964, which declared "war on poverty," illustrates an emphasis on legislative action and setting specific priorities. In 1971, Richard Nixon set the agenda by outlining six goals that would guide future legislation in an address that received high praise. In 1980, Jimmy Carter delivered an address that focused almost entirely on foreign policy, following the taking of American hostages in Iran and the Soviet invasion of Afghanistan. By contrast, in 1973, Nixon made no oral address to Congress, but sent a series of five written messages on economic affairs, natural resources, human resources, community development, and defense and foreign policy to Congress on different dates; each was summarized on radio.

50. Fersh, 47. See David Zarefsky, "Lincoln's 1862 Annual Message: A Paradigm of Rhetorical Leadership," *Rhetoric & Public Affairs* 2 (Spring 2000): 5-14. The analysis demonstrates the ways in which Lincoln's rhetoric enacted leadership through prudential judgment.

51. Fersh, 95.

52. James MacGregor Burns describes Franklin Roosevelt's annual messages as "essentially sermons rather than statements of policy. Like a preacher, he wanted and expected his sermons to serve as practical guides to the people." *Roosevelt: The Lion and the Fox* (New York: Harcourt, Brace, 1956), 476. Burns is right to emphasize Roosevelt's adaptation to the public, but Roosevelt also asserted legislative leadership through specific policy recommendations.

53. The State of the Union addresses of John F. Kennedy (Israel, 3:3122-54) are also noteworthy for synthesizing policy recommendations with popular appeals and for being unified, coherent wholes.

54. John Murphy, "Cunning, Rhetoric, and the Presidency of William Jefferson Clinton," in *The Presidency and Rhetorical Leadership*, ed. Leroy Dorsey (College Station: Texas A&M University Press, 2002), 233.

55. "Foreign Affairs: The Grand Bargain," *New York Times*, January 22, 1999, A25, http://www.nexis.com/ (accessed August 9, 2006).

56. Dan Balz, "Claiming the Middle Ground for Democrats," *Washington Post*, January 20, 1999, A1.

CHAPTER 7: VETO MESSAGES

1. In *The Veto Power: Its Origin, Development and Function in the Government of the United States, 1789–1889*, Harvard Historical Monographs, no. 1 (Boston: Ginn and Company, 1890), Edward Campbell Mason cites James Bryce, *The American Commonwealth*, 3 vols. (London and New York: Macmillan, 1888),

112, as saying that by granting the president the veto, the Constitutional Convention made the president "a distinct branch of the legislature, but for negative purposes only." Other sources, cited below, also treat the veto as a legislative power. Jong R. Lee suggests that the research value of analyzing veto messages is that they tend to reveal motivations and rationales for veto actions. See "Presidential Vetoes from Washington to Nixon," *Journal of Politics* 37 (May 1975): 544. In addition, "the veto's utility to the president did and does lie at least partly with his ability to use it as a mode of appealing directly to (and on behalf of) the people." Robert J. Spitzer, *The Presidential Veto: Touchstone of the American Presidency* (Albany: State University of New York Press, 1988), 1.

2. Roderick P. Hart, *The Sound of Leadership: Presidential Communication in the Modern Age* (Chicago: University of Chicago Press, 1987), 51–54.

3. Nixon may have feared that "an anti-Nixon youth rebellion erupting as soon as he vetoed the bill would have even worse political repercussions on his 1972 chances than giving the vote to the potential 11.5 million extra-young voters." Roland Evans, Jr., and Robert D. Novak, *Nixon in the White House* (New York: Random House, 1971), 131.

4. William Howard Taft, *The Presidency* (New York: Charles Scribner's Sons, 1916), 24.

5. Taft, *The Presidency*, 24. Details of the process, which began in December 1893, are found in Edward Stanwood, *A History of the Presidency*, rev. ed., 2 vols. (1928; reprint, Clifton, NJ: Augustus M. Kelley, 1975), 1:523–25. On August 14, 1848, James Polk signed a bill but chose the unusual tactic of sending a message explaining why he had not vetoed it, expressing "the reasons which have constrained me not to withhold my signature from the bill to establish a government over Oregon, even though the two territories of New Mexico and California are to be left for the present without government." James D. Richardson, ed., *A Compilation of the Messages and Papers of the Presidents, 1789–1908*, 11 vols. (Washington, DC: Bureau of National Literature and Art, 1909), 4:607.

6. The means by which presidents throughout our history have succeeded in circumventing parts of statutes are described in Spitzer, 138–40.

7. Richardson, 11:895–926.

8. The pocket, or suspensory, veto is described in article 1, section 7: "If any bill shall not be returned by the President within ten days (Sundays excepted) after it shall have been presented to him, the same shall be a law, in like manner as if he had signed it, unless the Congress by their adjournment prevent its return, in which case it shall not be a law." Disagreements over the meaning of this provision have provoked clashes between the president and Congress, with subsequent involvement of the courts. See *Pocket Veto Case*, 279 U.S. 644 (1929); *Kennedy v. Sampson*, 511 F.2d 430 (D.D.C. 1974); and *Barnes v. Carmen*, 582 F. Supp. 163 (D.D.C. 1984). A discussion of recent court challenges to the pocket veto is found in Spitzer, 112–15. Pocket vetoes made up 42.3 percent of all vetoes cast through 1981: Erwin C. Hargrove and Michael

Nelson, *Presidents, Politics, and Policy* (Baltimore: Johns Hopkins University Press, 1984), 208. Presidents from Madison through Andrew Johnson issued explanatory messages for pocket vetoes in virtually all cases. That practice stopped with Grant, but resumed in 1934, when Franklin Roosevelt issued a formal statement that, henceforth, written messages would accompany his pocket vetoes. Out of 447 pocket vetoes between 1934 and 1953, only four lacked accompanying messages: Clement E. Vose, "The Memorandum Pocket Veto," *Journal of Politics* 26 (May 1964): 397–405. Since 1963, virtually all pocket vetoes have been accompanied by messages: Spitzer, 115–16.

9. On rare occasions, veto messages have been incorporated into other presidential discourse; e.g., Andrew Jackson's last veto of a bill for internal improvements is found in his final annual message of 1834. In some instances, they are incorporated into special messages; e.g., Theodore Roosevelt's January 15, 1909, veto of the James River dam proposal. Richardson, 11:1309–15.

10. Marion Miller, ed., *Great Debates in American History*, 14 vols. (New York: Current Literature Publishing Company, 1913), 1:296. See 286–98 for a general discussion of the veto power. Two-thirds of a quorum, rather than two-thirds of all members, is acceptable for a successful veto override. See *Missouri Pacific Railway Co. v. Kansas*, 248 U.S. 276 (1919).

11. "Presidential Vetoes," *Office of the Clerk, U.S. House of Representatives*, http://clerk.house.gov/histHigh/Congressional_History/vetoes.html (accessed June 21, 2006).

12. Pocket vetoes have been ruled unchallengeable (*Pocket Veto Case*, 279 U.S. 655 [1929]), meaning that they cannot be overridden; Congress must pass a new measure in its next session.

13. Richardson, 1:124.

14. Richardson, 1:212.

15. Andrew Rudalevige, "The Executive Branch and the Legislative Process," in *The Executive Branch*, ed. Joel D. Aberbach and Mark A. Peterson (New York: Oxford University Press, 2005), 421.

16. Scott C. James, "The Evolution of the Presidency: Between the Promise and the Fear," in *The Executive Branch*, 11.

17. Richardson, 4:68. In this respect, Tyler echoed the views of William Henry Harrison, who had stated in his inaugural address, "I consider the veto power … solely as a conservative power." *The Inaugural Addresses of the Presidents of the United States, 1789–1985*, ed. Michael J. Lax (Atlantic City, NJ: American Inheritance Press, 1985), 46.

18. Richardson, 4:662–63.

19. Richardson, 4:663.

20. Richardson, 4:663.

21. Richardson, 4:664–65.

22. Richardson, 4:666.

23. Richardson, 4:667.

24. Richardson, 4:69.
25. Richardson, 5:247. Pierce objected to the provision in the bill requiring the federal government to provide the equivalent of 10 million acres of land for this charitable purpose.
26. Richardson, 5:247–48.
27. Richardson, 8:437.
28. *Senate Journal*, 23d Congress, 1st sess., 65.
29. Fred L. Israel, ed., *The State of the Union Messages of the Presidents, 1790–1966*, 3 vols. (New York: Chelsea House, 1967), 1:772.
30. Richardson, 4:11.
31. Richardson, 4:375.
32. *Public Papers of the Presidents of the United States: Herbert Hoover, 1930* (Washington, DC: Government Printing Office, 1976), 205.
33. *Public Papers, 1930*, 213.
34. Roger Matuz, *The Presidents Fact Book: A Comprehensive Handbook to the Achievements, Events, People, Triumphs, and Tragedies of Every President from George Washington to George W. Bush*, ed. Bill Harris (NY: Black Dog, 2004), 542.
35. *Public Papers of the Presidents of the United States: Harry S. Truman, 1947* (Washington, DC: Government Printing Office, 1963), 298.
36. *Public Papers, 1947*, 306.
37. David McCullough, *Truman* (New York: Simon and Schuster, 1992), 696.
38. "First Kennedy-Nixon Presidential Debate, September 26th, 1960," *The American Presidency Project*, http://www.presidency.ucsb.edu/showdebate.php?debateid=1 (accessed June 20, 2006).
39. *Public Papers of the Presidents of the United States: William J. Clinton, 1994*, 2 vols. (Washington, DC: Government Printing Office, 1995–1996), 1:131.
40. The Supreme Court supported this argument when, in *La Abra Mining Co. v. U.S.*, 175 U.S. 423 (1899), it held that "undoubtedly the President when approving bills may be said to participate in the enactment of laws, which the Constitution requires him to execute."
41. Aristotle, *Rhetoric*, trans. W. Rhys Roberts (New York: Modern Library, 1954), 1358b21–25.
42. Richard A. Watson's study of the 169 vetoes cast in the years 1933–1981 found that 111 (65.7%) were based on "unwise public policy" and 33 (19.5%) claimed the act was "fiscally unsound." "Reasons Presidents Veto Legislation," paper delivered at the American Political Science Association Convention, 1988; cited in Martha Joynt Kumar, "News Notes," *Presidential Studies Quarterly* 18 (Winter 1988): 212.
43. In a letter to James Madison of December 20, 1787, Thomas Jefferson expressed reservations about the judicial dimension of the executive veto: "I like the negative given to the Executive with a third of either house, though I should have liked it better had the Judiciary been associated for that purpose, or invested with a similar and separate power." *The Papers of Thomas*

Jefferson, ed. Julian Boyd, 31 vols. (Princeton, NJ: Princeton University Press, 1955), 12:439–42; cited in *Selected Readings in American History*, ed. John A. DeNovo, 2 vols. (New York: Charles Scribner's Sons, 1969), 1:126.

44. Mason, 32, 129–39.

45. Jacob E. Cooke, ed., *The Federalist* (Cleveland: Meridian Books, 1961), 495.

46. Three of the first six presidents cast no vetoes.

47. Marquis James, *The Life of Andrew Jackson* (Indianapolis: Bobbs-Merrill, 1938), 525–27.

48. In an appendix (105–77) to *The Executive Veto* (London: Oceana Publications, 1988), Chester James Antieau reproduces what he describes as "the most significant and/or interesting veto messages delivered by American Presidents from the beginning of the Nation. ... chosen to highlight either the philosophies of the Presidents (e.g., Presidents Madison and Kennedy) or the reasoning of the Chief Executives who could not accept the judgments of Congress in coping with major issues of American history" (103). The selection is historical, not rhetorical, but omits some messages of historic import, such as Truman's veto of the Taft-Hartley Act and Nixon's veto of the War Powers Resolution.

49. Jackson not only used the veto more frequently than his predecessors, but also focused on policy concerns in his veto messages; in addition, he "freed himself from the constraints of Madisonian strict construction." Patricia Lee Sykes, "The President as Legislator: A 'Superepresenator,'" *Presidential Studies Quarterly* 19 (Spring 1989): 305. See also Richard A. Watson, "Origins and Early Development of the Veto Power," *Presidential Studies Quarterly* 17 (Spring 1987): 408–9.

50. Richardson, 2:582.

51. Miller, 13:88.

52. Just how controversial early use of the veto power was became evident in 1848, when the Whigs campaigned against the extensive use of the veto by Jackson, Tyler, and Polk. Their candidate, Zachary Taylor, pledged that if he were elected, he would reserve the veto for those instances in which legislation clearly violated the Constitution or was a blatant encroachment on executive prerogatives. Neither Taylor nor his philosophically kindred successor, Millard Fillmore, ever exercised that power in any form.

In order to justify its use, later presidents emphasized the veto's limited power. In a veto message of February 17, 1855, for example, Franklin Pierce wrote that the president's participation in the formal business of legislation is limited to the single duty, in a certain contingency, of demanding for a bill a particular form of vote prescribed by the Constitution before it can become a law. He is not invested with power to defeat legislation by an absolute veto, but only to restrain it, and is charged with the duty, in case he disapproves a measure, of invoking a second and a more deliberate and solemn consideration of it on the part of Congress (Richardson, 5:308).

53. Richardson, 5:307; see also Stanwood, 2:319–30.

54. Richardson, 1:555–57.

55. Richardson, 2:576–91.

56. Richardson, 1:584–85.

57. Stanwood's analysis of the enlarged legislative power of the executive, developed through the veto power, recognizes this relationship (2:330–31). Truman, for example, viewed the veto message as "an opportunity to set forth clearly and in detail ... the policies of his administration." Herman Finer, *The Presidency* (Chicago: University of Chicago Press, 1960), 75.

58. Patricia Lee Sykes has coined the term "superepresenator" to describe this role (Sykes, 301–15).

59. Richardson, 1:557.

60. *Public Papers of the Presidents of the United States: Harry S. Truman, 1946* (Washington, DC: Government Printing Office, 1947), 289.

61. Because the president must obtain the votes of only one-third of a quorum of a single chamber to defeat an override attempt, as ruled in *North Pacific Railway Co. v. Kansas*, 248 U.S. 276 (1919), the veto message need not be as conciliatory as a State of the Union address.

62. Douglas Jehl, "Clinton Promises to Veto Measure on Police Funding," *New York Times*, late ed., February 12, 1995, sec. 1, p. 6, http://www.nexis.com/ (accessed August 10, 2006).

63. *Public Papers of the Presidents of the United States: William J. Clinton, 1995*, 2 vols. (Washington, DC: Government Printing Office, 1996), 2:1743.

64. Henry Steele Commager, ed., *Documents of American History*, 7th ed., 2 vols. (New York: Appleton-Century-Crofts, 1963), 2:63.

65. Miller, 9:55.

66. Richardson, 6:413. Of this message, Hans L. Trefousse writes, "Using drafts prepared by Seward, [Gideon] Welles, James Doolittle, Edgar Cowan, and others, but deliberately rejecting Seward's more conciliatory formulations, the president strongly put his own stamp on the final draft." *Andrew Johnson: A Biography* (New York: W. W. Norton, 1989), 242. Of the March 27, 1866, veto of the Civil Rights Act, Trefousse writes, "The veto message was again based on drafts of friendly advisers like Seward, Welles, and Henry Stanbery. ... Once more rejecting Seward's more moderate versions in favor of his own racist views, the president took no precautions to mollify Congress" (246). See also John H. Cox and La Wanda Cox, "Andrew Johnson and His Ghost Writers: An Analysis of the Freedmen's Bureau and Civil Rights Veto Messages," *Mississippi Valley Historical Review* 48 (December 1961): 460–79.

67. Miller, 7:196.

68. Miller, 9:52.

69. *Public Papers of the Presidents of the United States: Jimmy Carter, 1977*, 2 vols. (Washington, DC: Government Printing Office, 1978), 2:1972; *Public Papers of the Presidents of the United States: Jimmy Carter, 1980–1981*, 3 vols. (Washington, DC: Government Printing Office, 1981), 1:5.

70. Analyses of presidential use of the veto reveal that this power is most likely to be used when an executive of one party faces a legislature dominated by the other. See Lee, 526–40; Hargrove and Nelson, 209. A later study of vetoes from Eisenhower to the present found no important differences between the vetoes of Democratic and Republican presidents, but concluded that "the categories of and reasons for presidential vetoes are remarkably similar from president to president." Albert Ringelstein, "Presidential Vetoes: Motivations and Classifications," *Congress and the Presidency* 12 (Spring 1985): 52–53; cited in Spitzer, 77.

71. *Public Papers,* 1996, 1:567.

72. *Public Papers of the Presidents of the United States: William J. Clinton,* 1998, 2 vols. (Washington, DC: Government Printing Office, 1999–2000), 2:1292.

73. Use of the veto power tends to bring an issue to public attention, and the veto message, particularly as part of the struggle between the executive and the legislature, becomes an appeal to the people (Spitzer, 64, 69).

74. In the modern period, "the average annual number of vetoes (both regular and pocket) has ranged from Lyndon Johnson's low of 2.6 to 25.2 during the tenure of Gerald Ford"; moreover, Congress attempted to override 87.5 percent of Richard Nixon's vetoes, but no override was attempted during the John F. Kennedy and Lyndon Johnson administrations. David W. Rhode and Dennis M. Simon, "Presidential Vetoes and Congressional Response," *American Journal of Political Science* 29 (1985): 401.

75. Woodrow Wilson, "The Reconstruction of the Southern States," *Atlantic Monthly* 87 (January 1901): 2–11; cited in *Reconstruction in the South,* ed. Edwin C. Rozwenc (Boston: D. C. Heath, 1952), 9.

76. Richardson, 3:7. More recent analysts of the election results have concluded that Jackson's reading was in error.

77. As in other rhetorical discourse, the lines of argument found in veto messages are affected by the audience to which they are directed. The primary audience for both the State of the Union address and the veto message is Congress, although increasingly both address the public simultaneously. In some extraordinary cases, presidents have taken their objections to the citizenry directly. For example, Harry Truman presented a veto message to Congress arguing against the Taft-Hartley Act: *Public Papers,* 1947, 288–97. However, he also made a separate radio address to the people (298–301). Eisenhower followed a similar pattern when he delivered a radio message on the agriculture bill of 1958 after presenting a veto message to Congress: *Public Papers of the Presidents of the United States: Dwight D. Eisenhower,* 1958 (Washington, DC: Government Printing Office, 1959), 255–56. However, as specified by the Constitution, the purpose of the veto message is shaped by its primary audience, Congress.

78. *INS v. Chadha,* 51 USLW 4907, June 23, 1983. See Harold M. Barger, *The Impossible Presidency* (Glenview, IL: Scott Foresman, 1984), 137–38.

79. In "Why the Legislative Veto Isn't Dead," *Presidential Studies Quarterly* 16 (Summer 1986): 491–502, Daniel Paul Franklin describes options with

similar effects, including political compromise, that are available to Congress. Franklin also provides various definitions of the "legislative veto" (491–92).

80. Data collected by the U.S. Senate Library, as cited by Steven V. Roberts, "Key to Strategy: The Pocket Veto," *New York Times*, September 18, 1986, 12Y.

81. William M. Goldsmith, ed., *The Growth of Presidential Power*, 3 vols. (New York: Confucian Press, 1980), 3:271.

82. Theodore Roosevelt, *An Autobiography* (New York: Charles Scribner's Sons, 1913), 389.

83. Theodore Roosevelt, *The New Nationalism* (New York: Outlook, 1910), 21.

84. John G. Nicolay and John Hay, *Works of Abraham Lincoln*, 10 vols. (New York: C. S. Hammond, 1894), 10:65–68.

85. Richard M. Pious, "Legislative Leadership," in *The American Presidency*, ed. David C. Kozak and Kenneth M. Ciboski (Chicago: Nelson-Hall, 1975), 276.

86. Richardson, 2:483–93.

87. Carlton Jackson, *Presidential Vetoes, 1792–1945* (Athens: University of Georgia Press, 1967), 15.

88. Richardson, 2:484.

89. Goldsmith, 1:335.

90. When ranked by veto use, Reagan stands fifteenth. In 1982–1987, he averaged only 8.9 vetoes per year (Spitzer, 75).

91. Woodrow Wilson, *Congressional Government* (1885; reprint, New York: Meridian Books, 1956), 53, 173.

92. 22 U.S. Stat. 214 (1882).

93. Richardson, 9:445.

94. Richardson, 8:785.

95. Richardson, 10:824.

96. *Congressional Record* 52, 63d Cong., 3d sess. (January 28, 1915), 12:2481–82. Subsequent page references to this source are given in parentheses in the text.

CHAPTER 8: THE SIGNING STATEMENT AS DE FACTO ITEM VETO

1. The de facto item veto should not be confused with the line item veto, which was struck down by the Supreme Court in the 1990s. For another rhetorical perspective on signing statements, see David S. Birdsell, "George W. Bush's Signing Statements: The Assault on Deliberation," *Rhetoric & Public Affairs* 10 (2007): 335–60.

2. *Public Papers of the Presidents of the United States: William J. Clinton, 1996*, 2 vols. (Washington, DC: Government Printing Office, 1997–1998), 2:1071.

3. *Public Papers of the Presidents of the United States: George H. W. Bush, 1989*, 2 vols. (Washington, DC: Government Printing Office, 1990), 2:1298.

4. T. J. Halstead, "Presidential Signing Statements: Constitutional and Institutional Implications," September 20, 2006, Congressional Research

Service Report for Congress, Received through the CRS Web, Summary, 1, http://www.fas.org/sgp/crs/natsec/RL33667.pdf (accessed December 15, 2006).

5. Walter Dellinger, "Memorandum to Bernard N. Nussbaum: Counsel to the President," *Ark. L. Rev.* 48 (1995): 333. This memorandum is dated November 3, 1993.

6. Christopher N. May, "Presidential Defiance of 'Unconstitutional' Laws: Reviving the Royal Prerogative," *Hastings Const. L. Q.* 21 (1993–1994): 932.

7. May, 937.

8. Jonathan Elliot, ed., *The Debates in the Several State Conventions on the Adoption of the Federal Constitution*, 2nd ed. (1836): 446, quoted in Dellinger, 336.

9. "To Mrs. Adams, Sept 11, 1804," in *The Writings of Thomas Jefferson*, ed. H. A. Washington, 9 vols. (New York: John C. Riker, 1857), 4:561. Consistent with this notion, James Buchanan was advised by his attorneys general that the president "was not bound by a law that unconstitutionally encroached on his powers" (Dellinger, 336).

10. James D. Richardson, ed., *A Compilation of the Messages and Papers of the Presidents, 1789–1908*, 11 vols. (Washington, DC: Bureau of National Literature and Art, 1909), 2:582.

11. 17 U.S. (4 Wheat.) 316 (1819).

12. Arthur M. Schlesinger, Jr., *The Imperial Presidency* (Boston: Houghton Mifflin Co, 1973), 83–84. The notion of a constitutionally based "executive privilege" encapsulates the claim by the president of the right to withhold access to conversations with and materials prepared for the executive. The process of asserting this power was a central element in efforts to forestall the impeachment of Richard Nixon. When President Nixon's attorney, James St. Clair, was asked by Justice Thurgood Marshall, in the case involving disclosure of the Watergate tapes, whether the issue of executive privilege was being "submit[ted] to this Court for decision," he responded that the submission was for "guidance and judgment with respect to the law." St. Clair then tacitly asserted the president's right to deny access to some of the contents of the audiotapes made of Oval Office conversations. Reiterating a point he had made a moment earlier, he added, "The President, on the other hand, has his obligations under the Constitution." Philip B. Kurland and Gerhard Casper, eds., "*United States v. Nixon* (1974)," *Landmark Briefs and Arguments of the Supreme Court of the United States: Constitutional Law* (Arlington, VA: University Publications of America, 1975), 79:872. That exchange raised the possibility that if he was required to submit the tapes, President Nixon would refuse. Instead, shortly after the ruling, his office indicated that he would do as the Court required. Such instances inform the understanding that the president, the Congress, the courts, and the public have of presidential and Court prerogatives.

13. See the War Powers Resolution of 1973 (Public Law 93–148, 93d Cong., H.J. Res. 542, November 7, 1973) and Congressional Research Service,

"War Powers Resolution: Presidential Compliance," February 14, 2006, *University of North Texas Libraries,* http://digital.library.unt.edu/govdocs/crs/permalink/meta-crs-8452.1.

14. The justification that Lincoln used in suspending habeas corpus and in issuing the Emancipation Proclamation provides the closest historical parallel to George W. Bush's argument that in times of national crisis the president, by invoking his war powers, can take exception to accepted practice.

15. Roy P. Basler, ed., *The Collected Works of Abraham Lincoln,* 8 vols. (New Brunswick, NJ: Rutgers University Press, 1953), 4:430–31.

16. Basler, 4:429.

17. Basler, 6:29.

18. Basler, 4:268.

19. Richardson, 2:483.

20. Richardson, 4:159.

21. Louis Fisher, *Constitutional Conflicts between Congress and the President* (Lawrence: University Press of Kansas, 1997), 128.

22. Basler, 5:328–331.

23. Arthur S. Link, ed., *The Papers of Woodrow Wilson,* 69 vols. (Princeton, NJ: Princeton University Press, 1992), 66:89.

24. Richardson, 17:8871–72.

25. Richardson, 17:8871–72.

26. *Public Papers of the Presidents of the United States: George H. W. Bush, 1991,* 2 vols. (Washington, DC: Government Printing Office, 1992), 2:1046.

27. *Public Papers of the Presidents of the United States: Harry S. Truman, 1950* (Washington, DC: Government Printing Office, 1965), 616.

28. *Public Papers of the Presidents of the United States: Jimmy Carter, 1979,* 2 vols. (Washington, DC: Government Printing Office, 1980), 2:1432.

29. *Public Papers of the Presidents of the United States: Ronald Reagan, 1982,* 2 vols. (Washington, DC: Government Printing Office, 1983), 2:1072.

30. *Public Papers, 1989,* 2:1613.

31. *Public Papers of the Presidents of the United States: Dwight D. Eisenhower, 1959* (Washington, DC: Government Printing Office, 1960), 549.

32. "Statement on Signing of the Department of Defense, Emergency Supplemental Appropriations to Address Hurricanes in the Gulf of Mexico, and Pandemic Influenza Act, 2006, December 30th, 2005," *The American Presidency Project,* http://www.presidency.ucsb.edu/ws/index.php?pid=65259&st=&st1= (accessed June 26, 2006).

33. Other statements by George W. Bush draw on a broader rationale for nondisclosure. "The executive branch shall construe provisions in the Act that purport to mandate or regulate submission of information to the Congress in a manner consistent with the President's constitutional authority to withhold information that could impair foreign relations, national security, the deliberative processes of the Executive, or the performance of the Executive's constitutional duties." "Statement on Signing the Departments of

Labor, Health and Human Services, and Education, and Related Agencies Appropriations Act, 2006, December 30th, 2006," *The American Presidency Project*, http://www.presidency.ucsb.edu/ws/index.php?pid=65260 &st=& st1= (accessed June 26, 2006). Importantly, under this broader construction, neither the public nor Congress can reasonably tell whether information is being withheld and, if so, what is being withheld and why.

34. *Public Papers, 1991*, 2:1349.

35. *Public Papers, 1996*, 1:434.

36. *Public Papers of the Presidents of the United States: George H. W. Bush, 1990*, 2 vols. (Washington, DC: Government Printing Office, 1991), 2:1558. *Precatory* is defined as "expressing entreaty or supplication" (*Oxford English Dictionary*).

37. *Public Papers, 1996*, 1:434.

38. Despite their shared technical language, the statements of Clinton and George W. Bush are actually more different than similar. Clinton and Reagan, as we shall argue in a moment, engaged in a rhetoric of persuasion that explained and gave reasons for the conclusion that the president had the right to take exception. In Clinton's statement on the Cuban Liberty and Democratic Solidarity Act, for example, the sentences before the one quoted above say "Consistent with the Constitution, I interpret the Act as not derogating the President's authority to conduct foreign policy. A number of provisions [and he then lists the sections] could be read to state the foreign policy of the United States, or would direct that particular diplomatic initiatives or other courses of action to be taken with respect to foreign countries or governments" (*Public Papers*, 1996, 1:434). Here Clinton is explaining what he finds problematic about the legislation.

39. *Public Papers, 1982*, 2:1072.

40. "Statement on Signing the Science, State, Justice, Commerce, and Related Agencies Appropriations Act, 2006, November 22nd, 2005," *The American Presidency Project*, http://www.presidency.ucsb.edu/ws/index.php?pid =73754&st=&st1= (accessed July 7, 2006).

41. *Public Papers, 1982*, 2:1072.

42. "Statement, November 22nd, 2005."

43. *Public Papers, 1982*, 2:1072.

44. *Public Papers, 1982*, 2:1072.

45. *Public Papers, 1982*, 2:1072.

46. "Statement, December 30, 2006."

47. "Message to the House of Representatives Returning Without Approval the 'Stem Cell Research Enhancement Act of 2005,' July 19th, 2006," *The American Presidency Project*, http://www.presidency.ucsb.edu/ws/index.php ?pid=351&st=&st1= (accessed August 2, 2006).

48. 478 U.S. 714, 719fn. 1(1986); cited in Halstead, "Presidential Signing Statements."

49. Halstead, "Presidential Signing Statements."

50. "Address by Attorney General Edwin Meese III," National Press Club, Washington, D.C., February 25, 1986; quoted in Marc N. Garber and Kurt

A. Wimmer, "Presidential Signing Statements as Interpretations of Legislative Intent: An Executive Aggrandizement of Power," *Harvard Journal on Legislation* 24 (1987): 367. See also Steven G. Calabresi and Daniel Lev, "The Legal Significance of Signing Statements," *The Forum*, vol. 4, issue 2, article 8, pp. 1–9, http://bepress.com/forum/vol4/iss2/art8 (accessed February 1, 2007).

51. *Public Papers of the Presidents of the United States: Ronald Reagan, 1986*, 2 vols. (Washington, DC: Government Printing Office, 1988–1989), 2:1522–24.

52. Robert Pear, "President Signs Landmark Bill on Immigration," *New York Times*, November 7, 1986, A12, http://www.nexis.com/ (accessed July 20, 2006).

53. "Remarks Following a Meeting with Senators John McCain and John Warner, December 15th, 2005," *The American Presidency Project*, http://www.presidency.ucsb.edu/ws/index.php?pid=65221 &st=&st1= (accessed June 26, 2006).

54. Josh White, "President Relents, Backs Torture Ban," *Washington Post*, December 16, 2005, A1, http://www.nexis.com/ (accessed July 20, 2006).

55. Deb Riechmann, e-mail correspondence, July 28, 2005.

56. "Remarks, December 15th, 2005."

57. "Statement, December 30th, 2005."

58. "Remarks, December 15th, 2005."

59. "Remarks, December 15th, 2005."

60. "Statement, December 30th, 2005." A report of the U.S. Government Accountability Office released in June 2007 concluded that "in 6 out of 19 cases it studied, the [George W. Bush] administration did not follow the law as written after President Bush expressed reservations about some legislative directives." Carl Hulse, "Lawmakers to Investigate Bush on Laws and Intent," *New York Times*, June 20, 2007, A16. See "Presidential Signing Statements Accompanying the Fiscal Year 2006 Appropriations Acts," United States Government Accountability Office, June 18, 2007.

61. The theory of the "unitary executive branch" relies on the vesting clause of article 2, "The executive Power shall be vested in a President," along with the take care clause, "[The President] shall take care that the laws be faithfully executed," to argue that the Constitution creates a hierarchical, unified executive under the direct control of the president. The theory also argues for strict limits to the power of Congress to remove executive agencies or offices from direct presidential control.

62. "Statement, December 30th, 2005."

63. "Statement, December 30th, 2005."

64. Charlie Savage, "Bush Could Bypass New Torture Ban," *Boston Globe*, January 4, 2006, A1, http://www.nexis.com/ (accessed July 20, 2006).

65. "Remarks on Signing the USA PATRIOT Improvement and Reauthorization Act of 2005, March 9th, 2006," *The American Presidency Project*, http://www.presidency.ucsb.edu/ws/index.php?pid=65325&st= &st1= (accessed June 26, 2006).

66. Charlie Savage, "Bush Shuns Patriot Act; In Addendum to Law, He Says Oversight Rules Are Not Binding," *Boston Globe*, March 24, 2006, A1, http://www.nexis.com/ (accessed July 20, 2006).

67. "Statement, March 9th, 2006."

68. John Warner and John McCain, "Senator John W. Warner, R-VA. and Senator John McCain, R-AZ. Statement on Presidential Signing Detainee Provision," *U.S. Senator John McCain* [online], press release, January 4, 2006, http://mccain.senate.gov/press_office/view_article.cfm?ID=105 (accessed August 2, 2006).

69. Lawrence Tribe, on *Justice Talking*, National Public Radio, November 17, 2006, Annenberg Public Policy Center, aired the week of December 4, 2006.

70. Kathleen Day, "Whistle-Stop Campaigns: Some Firms are Trying to Limit Protection of Workers Who Expose Wrongdoing," *Washington Post*, April 23, 2006, F01, http://www.nexis.com/ (accessed July 20, 2006).

71. *Ameron, Inc. v. United States Army Corps of Engineers*, 809 F.2d 979 (3d Cir. 1986), cert. dismissed, 488 U.S. 918 (1988); *Lear Siegler, Inc. v. Lehman*, 842 F.2d 1102 (9th Cir. 1988); *Parola v. Weinberger*, 848 F.2d 956 (9th Cir. 1988).

72. David Kmiec, personal communication, July 17, 2006.

73. American Bar Association, "Task Force on Presidential Signing Statements and the Separation of Powers Doctrine," August 2006, http://www.abanet.org/op/signingstatements/aba_final_signing_statements_recommendation-report_7-24-06.pdf (accessed August 1, 2006), 25.

74. Charlie Savage, "Specter Considers Suit over Bush Law Challenge," *Boston Globe*, June 28, 2006, A1, http://www.nexis.com/ (accessed August 1, 2006).

75. Douglas W. Kmiec, *The Attorney General's Lawyer: Inside the Meese Justice Department* (New York: Praeger Publishers, 1992), 54.

76. Senate Committee on the Judiciary, *Hearing before the Senate Judiciary Committee on the Use of Presidential Signing Statements*, 109th Cong., 2d sess., 2006, http://judiciary.senate.gov/testimony.cfm?id=1969&wit_id=5482 (accessed August 2, 2006).

CHAPTER 9: WAR RHETORIC

1. See, e.g., Clarence A. Berndahl, *War Powers of the Executive in the United States* (Urbana: University of Illinois Press, 1921); Thomas F. Eagleton, *War and Presidential Power: A Chronicle of Congressional Surrender* (New York: Liveright, 1974); Jacob K. Javits, *Who Makes War: The President versus Congress* (New York: William Morrow, 1973); Edward Keynes, *Undeclared War: Twilight Zone of Constitutional Power* (University Park: Pennsylvania State University Press, 1982); Merlo J. Pusey, *The Way We Go to War* (Boston: Houghton Mifflin, 1969); Ann Van Wynen Thomas and A. J. Thomas, Jr., *The War-Making Powers of the President* (Dallas, TX: SMU Press, 1982). We shall not retrace the history of executive war powers here nor attempt to define just what

powers the president may rightfully exercise without explicit congressional authorization.

2. Keynes, 175.

3. See, for example, Kathleen J. Turner, *Lyndon Johnson's Dual War: Vietnam and the Press* (Chicago: University of Chicago Press, 1985); Bob Woodward, *State of Denial* (New York: Simon and Schuster, 2006).

4. See "President Outlines Strategy for Victory in Iraq," November 30, 2005, *The White House*, http://www.whitehouse.gov/news/releases/2005/11/20051130-2.html (accessed December 13, 2006); "President Discusses War on Terror and Rebuilding Iraq," December 7, 2005, *The White House*, http://www.whitehouse.gov/news/releases/2005/12/20051207-1.html (accessed December 13, 2006); "President Discusses War on Terror and Upcoming Iraqi Elections," December 12, 2005, *The White House*, http://www.whitehouse.gov/news/releases/2005/12/20051212-4.html (accessed December 13, 2006); "President Discusses Iraqi Elections, Victory in the War on Terror," December 14, 2005, *The White House*, http://www.whitehouse.gov/news/releases/2005/12/20051214-1.html (accessed December 13, 2006).

5. See "President Discusses Creation of Military Commissions to Try Suspected Terrorists," September 6, 2006, *The White House*, http://www.whitehouse.gov/news/releases/2006/09/20060906-3.html (accessed December 13, 2006); "President Bush Discusses Progress in the Global War on Terror," September 7, 2006, *The White House*, http://www.whitehouse.gov/news/releases/2006/09/20060907-2.html (accessed December 13, 2006). For a more detailed analysis of the use of the term "war on terror," see Robert L. Ivie, *Democracy and America's War on Terror* (Tuscaloosa: University of Alabama Press, 2006).

6. Public Law 93-148, 93d Cong., H.J. Res. 542, November 7, 1973, sec. 2. (a).

7. Thomas and Thomas, 1; Charles Funderburk, *Presidents and Politics: The Limits of Power* (Belmont, CA: Wadsworth, 1982), 243; Richard F. Haynes, *The Awesome Power: Harry S. Truman as Commander in Chief* (Baton Rouge: Louisiana State University Press, 1973), 6. Louis Fisher wrote, "Presidents, with neither statutory authority nor a declaration of war, have used force abroad on many occasions, ostensibly to protect life and property. ... [justifying] their actions on the basis of executive responsibilities they find inherent in the Constitution. Expeditions of this nature number around two hundred although if the total were to include actions that merely represent a show of force (such as deploying a battleship off a coast), it would be larger." *The Constitution between Friends: Congress, the President, and the Law* (New York: St. Martin's Press, 1978), 226. In a note, Fisher cites J. Terry Emerson, "War Powers Legislation," *West Virginia Law Review* 74 (1972): 53, and Emerson's "Constitutional Authority of the President to Use Armed Forces in Defense of American Lives, Liberty, and Property," reprinted in *Congressional Record* 121, 94th Cong., 1st sess. (May 6, 1975): P13205; James Grafton Rogers, *World Policing and the Constitution: An Inquiry into the Powers of the President*

and Congress (Boston: World Peace Foundation, 1945); *Background Informa-tion on the Use of United States Armed Forces in Foreign Countries,* prepared for the House Committee on Foreign Affairs, 91st Cong., 2d sess. (Washington, DC: Committee Printing, 1970), 50–57; and R. Ernest Dupuy and William H. Baumer, *The Little Wars of the United States* (New York: Hawthorn Books, 1968).

8. In contrast to other constitutionally enumerated executive powers, desig-nation as commander in chief "is unique among the clauses outlining the powers and duties of the President in that it confers an office rather than a mere function . . . [implying] that whatever powers and duties are necessar-ily associated with the exercise of supreme military command belong to the President by constitutional prescription and cannot be constitutionally di-minished or controlled by statute." Joseph E. Kallenbach, *The American Chief Executive* (New York: Harper and Row, 1966), 526.

9. Jacob E. Cooke, ed., *The Federalist* (Cleveland: Meridian Books, 1961), 148. Executive power is implied in provisions governing the sovereignty of the states: "Article 1, Sec. 10 provides that no state may, without consent of Congress, 'engage in war unless actually invaded, or in such imminent dan-ger as will not admit of delay.' One can reasonably contend that at least this much power must be vested in the President to protect the United States as a whole." Abraham D. Sofaer, *War, Foreign Affairs, and Constitutional Power* (Cambridge, MA: Ballinger, 1976), 4.

10. 67 U.S. (2 Black) 635, 668 (1863); cited in W. Taylor Reveley III, *The War Powers of the President and Congress: Who Holds the Arrows and Olive Branch* (Charlottesville: University of Virginia Press, 1981), 140.

11. Jonathan Elliot, ed., *The Debates in the Several State Conventions on the Adoption of the Federal Constitution,* 5 vols. (Philadelphia: Lippincott, 1866, 1876, 1891), 2:528, cited in Reveley, 102.

12. *The Papers of Thomas Jefferson,* ed. Julian Boyd, 31 vols. (Princeton, NJ: Princ-eton University Press, 1958), 15:397; cited in Reveley, 106.

13. John Mabry Mathews argues that the president "may prevent a declaration of war by Congress by declining to recommend or approve it." *The Conduct of American Foreign Relations* (New York: Century, 1922), 307–8, cited in Charles C. Tansill, "The President and the Initiation of Hostilities: The Precedents of the Mexican and Spanish-American Wars," in *The President's War Powers: From the Federalists to Reagan,* ed. Demetrios Caraley (New York: Academy of Political Science, 1984), 76.

14. Robert McElroy, *Grover Cleveland: The Man and the Statesman; An Authorized Bi-ography,* 2 vols. (New York: Harper and Brothers, 1923), 2:249–50; cited in Fisher, 214.

15. Christopher H. Pyle and Richard M. Pious, *The President, Congress, and the Constitution* (New York: Free Press, 1984), 325.

16. James D. Richardson, ed., *A Compilation of the Messages and Papers of the Presi-dents, 1789–1908,* 11 vols. (Washington, DC: Bureau of National Literature

and Art, 1909), 1:504–5. Robert L. Ivie, in "The Metaphor of Force in Prowar Discourse: The Case of 1812," *Quarterly Journal of Speech* 68 (August 1982): 240–53, illustrates the power of metaphor in war rhetoric, particularly calls to arms based on images of savagery.

17. "Address by the President of the United States," *Congressional Record* 55, 65th Cong., 1st sess. (April 2, 1917): S102–3.

18. Richardson, 10:53–54.

19. Richardson, 10:55.

20. Richardson, 10:73.

21. Reveley, 125.

22. Thomas and Thomas, 88–89.

23. *Public Papers of the Presidents of the United States: George H. W. Bush, 1991*, 2 vols. (Washington, DC: Government Printing Office, 1992), 1:43.

24. Richardson, 1:500. Madison's narrative extends from page 500 to page 502, interspersed with argumentative comments.

25. Richardson, 4:442; Polk's narrative covers two pages, 438–39, and is followed by argumentative claims.

26. Richardson, 6:23. Lincoln's narrative in his July 4, 1861, special session message illustrates the link between narrative and threat (Richardson, 6:20–22).

27. The narrative about the U.S.S. *Maine* in McKinley's earlier speech is in Richardson, 10:53–55. The narrative in this speech begins with the Cuban revolution in February 1895 and includes past analyses of Cuban-American relations by presidents Jackson and Van Buren (Richardson, 10:57–63). A very different narrative of events leading to this war is found in Stephen Kinzer, *Overthrow: America's Century of Regime Change from Hawaii to Iraq* (New York: Times Books/Henry Holt, 2006), 31–55.

28. Richardson, 10:64.

29. Richardson, 10:831.

30. Capp, 151–52; this argument is part of the narrative, which begins in the second paragraph, on page 151, and continues through most of page 153. In Kathleen M. German's "The Declaration of War in World War I: An Instrument for Socio-Political Enactment," *Central States Speech Journal* 36 (Spring/ Summer 1985): 105–13, the declarations of each of the major belligerent nations (Germany, France, Russia, Britain, United States) are analyzed for evincing a posture of self-defense; use of condensation symbols; use of tradition or the past causing the future, appeals to the supernatural, and calls for individual sacrifice to preserve the nation.

31. "Special Message to the Congress, July 15, 1958," *Public Papers of the Presidents of the United States: Dwight D. Eisenhower, 1958* (Washington, DC: Government Printing Office, 1959), 552.

32. *Public Papers of the Presidents of the United States: Lyndon B. Johnson, 1965*, 2 vols. (Washington, DC: Government Printing Office, 1966), 1:469. Johnson's televised address to the nation on April 28, 1965, was little more than an

announcement that troops had been sent; no narrative was included (1:461). His televised statement of April 30, 1965, began with two paragraphs of narrative, followed by a suggestion that outsiders had infiltrated the rebel camp and a chronicle of efforts by the Organization of American States to resolve the situation (1:465–66). His televised address to the nation on May 2 attempted to justify the U.S. intervention; much of it was narrative, which began, "To understand, I think it is necessary to begin with the events of 8 or 9 days ago," and ended with the report of a cable from Ambassador Bennett urging an immediate landing (1:469–70). What followed was largely argument, interspersed with reports of developing events. The speech illustrates not only the use of narrative, but also the fifth characteristic of war rhetoric, the strategic use of misrepresentation, particularly claims that the Dominican revolution had been taken over by Communists, which could not be substantiated.

33. Richardson, 1:500, 503, 504.

34. Richardson, 4:440, 441, 442–43.

35. *New York Times,* June 29, 1950, 10.

36. *Public Papers,* 1991, 1:42–43.

37. *Public Papers of the Presidents of the United States: William J. Clinton,* 1995, 2 vols. (Washington, DC: Government Printing Office, 1996), 2:1785.

38. "Address to the Nation on Iraq, March 17th, 2003," *The American Presidency Project,* http://www.presidency.ucsb.edu/ws/index.php?pid=63713 &st=&st1= (accessed June 16, 2006).

39. Richardson, 1:502, 504–5.

40. Richardson, 4:439, 442.

41. Capp, 153.

42. Glenn D. Paige, *The Korean Decision, June 24–30, 1950* (New York: Free Press, 1968), 189.

43. *Public Papers,* 1965, 1:461.

44. *Public Papers,* 1965, 1:465.

45. "Address to the Nation on Iraq, March 19th, 2003," *The American Presidency Project,* http://www.presidency.ucsb.edu/ws/index.php?pid=63368&st =&st1= (accessed June 16, 2006).

46. "138-Address to Congress Requesting a Declaration of War with Japan, December 8th, 1941," *The American Presidency Project,* http://www.presidency .ucsb.edu/ws/index.php?pid=16053&st=&st1= (accessed June 19, 2006).

47. "138-Address, December 8th, 1941."

48. Herman G. Stelzner, "'War Message,' December 8, 1941: An Approach to Language," *Communication Monographs* 33 (1966): 419–437.

49. There are many similarities between presidential war rhetoric as described here and the crisis rhetoric of John F. Kennedy and Richard Nixon described by Theodore Windt in "The Presidency and Speeches on International Crises: Repeating the Rhetorical Past," *Speaker and Gavel* 2, no. 1 (1973): 6–14. In those cases in which a crisis involves U.S. military intervention, rhetorical

similarities result from the processes we have described. In other instances in which external events compel a presidential response, as when a Korean airliner was shot down by the Soviet Union in 1983 with some U.S. passengers on board, presidential efforts to avoid military action, as illustrated by Reagan's speech in response to this incident, generate epideictic rhetoric exhorting the nation to support current foreign policy initiatives. See Bonnie Dow, "The Function of Epideictic and Deliberative Strategies in Presidential Crisis Rhetoric," *Western Journal of Speech Communication* 53 (Summer 1989): 294–310. See also Marilyn J. Young and Michael K. Launer, "KAL007 and the Superpowers: An International Argument," *Quarterly Journal of Speech* 74 (August 1988): 271–95. This case illustrates the unfolding of a rhetorical act through a series of statements and speeches by the president and cabinet members between September 1 and 6.

50. Richardson, 4:389.

51. Richardson, 1:512.

52. Richardson, 4:470.

53. *Public Papers of the Presidents of the United States: Lyndon B. Johnson, 1966,* 2 vols. (Washington, DC: Government Printing Office, 1967), 1:517–18.

54. *Public Papers of the Presidents of the United States: Richard Nixon, 1969* (Washington, DC: Government Printing Office, 1970), 909.

55. *Public Papers of the Presidents of the United States: Richard Nixon, 1970* (Washington, DC: Government Printing Office, 1971), 410.

56. *Public Papers,* 1995, 2:1787.

57. Samuel I. Rosenman, ed., *Public Papers and Addresses of Franklin D. Roosevelt* (New York: Random House, 1938–1950), 6:407; cited in Ruhl J. Bartlett, ed., *The Record of American Diplomacy* (New York: Alfred A. Knopf, 1950), 578.

58. James MacGregor Burns, *Roosevelt: The Lion and the Fox, 1882–1940,* 2 vols. (New York: Harcourt Brace Jovanovich, 1956), 1:318.

59. Samuel I. Rosenman, *Working with Roosevelt* (New York: Harper and Brothers, 1952), 167; cited in Waldo Braden, "Roosevelt's Wartime Fireside Chats," in *The President and National Security,* ed. Gordon R. Hoxie (New York: Center for the Study of the Presidency, 1984), 135.

60. Braden, 140. In particular, see Roosevelt's State of the Union message, "The Four Freedoms," of January 6, 1941.

61. Richardson, 10:67.

62. Richard M. Pious, *The American Presidency* (New York: Basic Books, 1979), 51–52.

63. Keynes, 159.

64. Abbot Smith, "Who Declares War? Madison in 1812," in *The President's War Powers,* 29–46; see 40, 45.

65. The annexation of Texas led to a break in diplomatic relations with Mexico, which had never formally recognized Texas's independence, and created a United States–Mexico boundary dispute. The historic southern border of Texas had been the Nueces River, the border recognized by the Mexican

government, while the United States recognized the Rio Grande, the border claimed by Texas based on the treaties Santa Anna was forced to sign after his capture. See "The Annexation of Texas," U.S. *Department of State*, http://www.state.gov/r/pa/ho/time/dwe/16341.htm (accessed December 7, 2006). Polk is quoting from his earlier annual message.

66. Richardson, 4:440. See also Sîan Owen-Cruise, "James Polk's Mexican War Rhetoric," unpublished M.A. thesis, University of Minnesota, 1989. Polk is citing a report from General Zachary Taylor.

67. Pyle and Pious, 321–22.

68. Richardson, 6:23.

69. *Durand v. Hollins*, 4 Blatchf. 451, 454 (1860); cited in Fisher, 227.

70. Arthur M. Schlesinger, Jr., *The Imperial Presidency* (Boston: Houghton Mifflin Co, 1973), 89.

71. *Public Papers*, 1958, 549; see also 550–51, 553.

72. *Public Papers*, 1970, 406.

73. Paige, 189. In subsequent hearings, Secretary of Defense Louis Johnson was even more explicit, saying, "We have joined the United Nations, which had certain commitments contained in its Charter, and this was a direct violation of that Charter" (Paige, 177). However, when Congress passed the United Nations Participation Act in 1945, it carefully restricted the president's authority to negotiate agreements under which American troops might be assigned to peacekeeping tasks around the world (Eagleton, 67). This case is complicated because World War II did not formally end until April 1952, when the Japanese peace treaty took effect, so Truman was initiating military operations under operative wartime statutes (Keynes, 111).

74. John T. Rourke and Russell Farnen, "War, Presidents, and the Constitution," *Presidential Studies Quarterly* 18 (Summer 1988): 514. Again, members of Congress did not envision the treaty as self-triggering, but believed that a commitment of U.S. combat forces would be contingent on congressional approval (Eagleton, 89–90). The Gulf of Tonkin Resolution, however, referred to U.S. obligations under SEATO.

75. Reveley, 149.

76. Gerald R. Ford, "Address at the University of Kentucky," April 11, 1977, in Senate Committee on Foreign Relations, *Hearings on a Review of the Operation and Effectiveness of the War Powers Resolution*, 95th Cong., 1st sess. (1977), 327, 328–330. On April 30, 1975, North Vietnamese troops accepted the surrender of Saigon.

77. Schlesinger, *Imperial Presidency*, 308.

78. The role that this dilemma played in Whig votes in the Mexican War is described by Frederick Merk, *Manifest Destiny and Mission in American History: A Reinterpretation* (Westport, CT: Greenwood Press, 1963), 93–95. For background, see Ronald Hatzenbuehler and Robert Ivie, *Congress Declares War: Rhetoric, Leadership, and Partisanship in the Early Republic* (Kent, OH: Kent State University Press, 1983).

79. *Public Papers*, 1965, 1:494, 498; cited in Reveley, 155.

80. "Between August 1964 and November 1969 Congress enacted the Gulf of Tonkin Resolution and at least 23 other laws that authorized the conduct of military operations in South Vietnam" (Keynes, 117), including defense appropriations acts that the State Department in 1966 argued were endorsements of the administration's actions (Eagleton, 124). *Fleming v. Mohawk Wrecking and Lumber Co.*, 331 U.S. (1) (1947), supports the view that a congressional appropriation may supply the needed ratification of presidential action taken under the presidential war powers (Thomas and Thomas, 162 n. 210). However, the courts have not always interpreted appropriations bills as approval of executive action. For example, *Ex parte Endo*, 323 U.S. 283 (1944), denied that an appropriation act ratified all the activities encompassed by the appropriation, and in *Mitchell v. Laird*, Judge Wyzanski wrote, "A Congressman wholly opposed to the war's commencement and continuation might vote for the military appropriations and for the draft measures because he was unwilling to abandon without support men already fighting. An honorable, decent, compassionate act of aiding those already in peril is no proof of consent to the actions that placed and continued them in that dangerous posture." 488 F.2d 611, 615 (D.C. Cir. 1973); cited in Keynes, 137.

81. Public Law 93-148, sec. 3.

82. Public Law 93-148, sec. 4. (a).

83. Public Law 93-148, sec. 5 and 6.

84. Gerald Ford, *A Time to Heal* (New York: Harper and Row, 1979), 275–76.

85. Ford, 280–81.

86. Ford, 280.

87. Ford, 281.

88. *Public Papers of the Presidents of the United States: Gerald R. Ford III*, 1975, 2 vols. (Washington, DC: Government Printing Office, 1977), 1:670.

89. *Public Papers of the Presidents of the United States: Ronald Reagan*, 1982, 2 vols. (Washington, DC: Government Printing Office, 1983), 2:1238.

90. *Public Papers of the Presidents of the United States: Ronald Reagan*, 1983, 2 vols. (Washington, DC: Government Printing Office, 1984–1985), 2:1521. For a careful and detailed review of the use of terrorism as a justification for military action, see Carol K. Winkler, *In the Name of Terrorism: Presidents on Political Violence in the Post–World War II Era* (Albany: State University of New York Press, 2006). See Martin J. Medhurst, Robert L. Ivie, Philip Wander, and Robert L. Scott, *Cold War Rhetoric: Strategy, Metaphor, and Ideology* (New York: Greenwood, 1990), for an analysis of cold war rhetoric.

91. *Public Papers of the Presidents of the United States: George H. W. Bush*, 1989, 2 vols. (Washington, DC: Government Printing Office, 1990), 2:1722–23.

92. *Public Papers*, 1991, 1:40.

93. *Public Papers of the Presidents of the United States: George W. Bush*, 2002, 2 vols. (Washington, DC: Government Printing Office, 2004–2005), 2:1814.

94. Elizabeth Bumiller, "With a Few Humble Words, Bush Silences His Texas Swagger," *New York Times*, late ed., May 27, 2006, A11, http://www .nexis.com/ (accessed August 10, 2006). For the "bring 'em on" quote, see "President Bush Names Randall Tobias to Be Global AIDS Coordinator," July 2, 2003, *The White House*, http://www.whitehouse.gov/news/ releases/2003/07/20030702-3.html (accessed August 17, 2006). In video and audio recordings, President Bush said "bring 'em on." Transcripts reflect him as saying "bring them on." (Video and audio recordings, as well as the transcript, are available at the White House Web site.) For the "dead or alive" quote, see *Public Papers of the Presidents of the United States: George W. Bush, 2001*, 2 vols. (Washington, DC: Government Printing Office, 2003), 2:1120.

95. For a sustained argument about the undesirable long-range effects of strategic deception in U.S. foreign policy, see Eric Alterman, *When Presidents Lie: A History of Official Deception and Its Consequences* (New York: Viking, 2004). The examples include Franklin Roosevelt's misrepresentation of decisions at Yalta, Kennedy's misrepresentation of negotiations to end the Cuban missile crisis, Lyndon Johnson's misrepresentation of the incidents in the Gulf of Tonkin, Reagan's misrepresentation of the Iran-Contra relationship, and Bush's misrepresentations that led to the invasion of Iraq.

96. Kenneth Burke writes, "Even if any given terminology is a reflection of reality, by its very nature as a terminology it must be a selection of reality; and to this extent it must function also as a deflection of reality." *Language as Symbolic Action* (Berkeley: University of California Press, 1966), 45.

97. *Martin v. Mott*, 25 U.S. (12 Wheat.) 19, 30–31 (1827).

98. Berndahl, 80.

99. *Letters and Other Writings of James Madison*, 4 vols. (Philadelphia: J. B. Lippincott, 1865), 2:140–41, cited in Abbot Smith, in *The President's War Powers*, 34.

100. Berndahl, 80. They were referring primarily to the so-called XYZ correspondence.

101. Samuel Eliot Morison, "Dissent in the War of 1812," in *Dissent in Three American Wars* (Cambridge, MA: Harvard University Press, 1970), 3, 5.

102. Frederick Merk, "Dissent in the Mexican War," in *Dissent in Three American Wars*, 35–63. Merk also argues that dissent was effective in influencing the terms of the treaty that ended the war.

103. Merk, 40.

104. *Congressional Globe*, 30th Cong., 1st sess. January 3, 1848, 95.

105. Frank Freidel, "Dissent in the Spanish-American War and the Philippine Insurrection," in *Dissent in Three American Wars*, 93; see 92–93, n. 25, for sources of testimony at hearings and courts-martial.

106. Capp, 157.

107. Javits, 203; cited in Thomas and Thomas, 17.

108. "When You See a Rattlesnake Poised to Strike, You Do Not Wait Until He Has Struck before You Crush Him"—Fireside Chat to the Nation, September

11, 1941, in Rosenman, *Public Papers*, 10:384–92. The address also contains exhortations to unanimity; e.g., "Do not let us be hair-splitters. Let us not ask ourselves whether the Americas should begin to defend themselves after the first attack, or the fifth attack, or the tenth attack, or the twentieth attack. The time for active defense is now" (390).

109. Pusey, 72. See also Javits, 225–26, who points out that the fate of the U-boat is still unknown, and that Roosevelt's use of this incident set a precedent followed by Lyndon Johnson in requesting the Gulf of Tonkin Resolution.

110. "Hearing of the Congressional Human Rights Caucus Committee," *Federal Information Systems Corporation Federal News Service*, October 10, 1990.

111. *Public Papers of the Presidents of the United States: George H. W. Bush, 1990*, 2 vols. (Washington, DC: Government Printing Office, 1991), 2:1482.

112. *Public Papers, 1990*, 2:1512.

113. John R. MacArthur, *Second Front: Censorship and Propaganda in the Gulf War* (New York: Hill and Wang, 1992), 57–60.

114. For more details on the role of the press in this period, see Kathleen Hall Jamieson and Paul Waldman, *The Press Effect: Politicians, Journalists, and the Stories that Shape the Political World* (New York: Oxford University Press, 2003), 15–20.

115. Michael Duffy and James Carney, with reporting by Massimo Calabresi, Matthew Cooper, and Adam Zagorin/Washington, John F. Dickerson with Bush in Africa, J. F. O. McAllister/London and Andrew Purvis/Vienna, "A Question of Trust," *Time*, July 21, 2003, 22ff., http://www.nexis.com/ (accessed August 10, 2006).

116. Seymour Hersh, "Up in The Air: Where Is the Iraq War Headed Next?" *New Yorker*, December 5, 2005, 44, http://www.nexis.com/ (accessed August 10, 2006).

117. *Public Papers of the Presidents of the United States: Lyndon B. Johnson, 1963–1964*, 2 vols. (Washington, DC: Government Printing Office, 1965), 2:927–28. Subsequent page references to this source are given in parentheses in the text. See also "Special Message to the Congress on U.S. Policy in Southeast Asia," August 5, 1964, 2:930–32, which recommends "a Resolution expressing the support of the Congress for all necessary action to protect our armed forces and to assist nations covered by the SEATO Treaty.... The Resolution could well be based upon similar resolutions enacted by the Congress in the past—to meet the threat to Formosa in 1955, to meet the threat to the Middle East in 1957, and to meet the threat in Cuba in 1962."

118. The speech diverges from others of this genre by including only a little narrative material, which is also true of the special message to Congress on August 5. A more extended narrative is found in Johnson's remarks at Syracuse University, August 5, 1964 (*Public Papers, 1963–1964*, 2:928–30). An example of extended narrative is found in Richard Nixon's speech of November 3, 1969, which announces and defends his Vietnamization plan (*Public Papers, 1969*, 901–9).

119. The notion that the power to declare and wage war, conclude peace, make treaties, and maintain diplomatic relations was inherited from the British crown as a condition of sovereignty is found in *U.S. v. Curtiss-Wright Export Corp.*, 299 U.S. 304 (1936). A contrary view, that all executive powers derive from the Constitution, is found in *Reid v. Covert*, 354 U.S. 1, 5–6, 14 (1957).

120. The questionable elements in Johnson's characterization of these events are described in Pusey, 115–47. See also the testimony of Secretary of State Robert S. McNamara in Senate Committee on Foreign Relations, *The Gulf of Tonkin, the 1964 Incidents, Hearing before the Committee on Foreign Relations*, 90th Cong., 2d sess., February 20, 1968 (Washington, DC: Government Printing Office, 1968), 3–56.

121. Eagleton, 100n.

CHAPTER 10: RHETORIC OF SELF-DEFENSE

1. The courts also examine the legislative history of any act.

2. For a discussion of this kind of rhetorical situation, see S. Michael Halloran, "Doing Public Business in Public," in *Form and Genre: Shaping Rhetorical Action*, ed. Karlyn Kohrs Campbell and Kathleen Hall Jamieson (Falls Church, VA: Speech Communication Association, 1978), 118–38.

3. The rhetoric of presidential self-defense, whether before or after formal charges, does not consist of a single text, but illustrates the concept of the rhetorical act; in this case, usually a combination of texts, statements, court briefs, and the like, many of which come not from the president, but from attackers and defenders.

4. C. Vann Woodward, "Introduction," in *Responses of the Presidents to Charges of Misconduct*, ed. C. Vann Woodward (New York: Delacorte, 1974), xii.

5. That controversy was eventually a subject of two Supreme Court decisions. As Edward Keynes points out, however, "With the exception of Chief Justice Roger Taney's opinion in *Ex parte Merryman*, 17 F. Cas. 144 (C.C.D. Md. 1861) (No. 9, 487), the Federal courts sustained President Lincoln's exercise of extra constitutional power. Indeed, in *Ex parte Vallandigham*, 68 U.S. (1 Wall.) 243 (1864), the Court avoided a confrontation with the president by denying its jurisdiction to review or reverse the findings of a military commission. Only after the Civil War had ended, in *Ex parte Milligan*, 71 U.S. (4 Wall.) 2 (1866), did the Supreme Court challenge the president's authority to suspend the privilege to the writ of habeas corpus and to substitute a military commission for a civilian court outside the actual theater of military operations." *Undeclared War: Twilight Zone of Constitutional Power* (University Park: Pennsylvania State University Press, 1982), 173.

6. The most obvious difference among these seven instances of self-defense against impeachment is that six of them are responses by the president speaking as the president and one—Reagan's statement—is by the president speaking as an individual. They share the goal of forestalling impeachment; in Reagan's case, the Tower Commission's findings were an implicit

accusation of presidential mismanagement and suggested the possibility that they might lead to charges of impeachable offenses.

7. A discussion of the nature of the apologia and its rhetorical advantages may be found in Edwin Black, *Rhetorical Criticism; A Study in Method* (1965; reprint, Madison: University of Wisconsin Press, 1978), 151–61.

8. John Henry Cardinal Newman, *Apologia pro Vita Sua*, ed. Charles Frederick Harold (New York: Longmans, Green, 1947).

9. Henry Steele Commager, *Documents of American History*, 7th ed., 2 vols. (New York: Appleton-Century-Crofts, 1963), 2:604.

10. Commager, 2:604.

11. *Weekly Compilation of Presidential Documents* 23, no. 9: 220. Subsequent page references to this source are given in parentheses in the text.

12. When Reagan testified via videotape as a defense witness in the 1990 trial of his former national security adviser, John M. Poindexter, he had difficulty recalling many of the events related to the Iran-Contra affair, and the videotape is a historical record of his failing memory, foreshadowing his disclosure in 1994 that he had Alzheimer's disease. See Robert Johnston, "A Historic Moment if Cheney Testifies Live, as Expected," *New York Times*, February 12, 2007, A16; see also "Reagan Testifies, For Better or Worse," *New York Times*, February 25, 1990, http://select.nytimes.com/search/restricted/article?res=F30615FB34540C768EDDAB0894D8494D81 (accessed April 7, 2007).

13. Note that Reagan's apologia is paradoxical, asking us to forgive him for acts committed in his administration of which he was ignorant.

14. In his statements of May 22, 1973, for example, Nixon said, "Allegations surrounding the Watergate affair have so escalated that I feel a further statement from the President is required at this time." *Public Papers of the Presidents of the United States: Richard Nixon, 1973* (Washington, DC: Government Printing Office, 1974), 547. Later he noted, "As President, I must and do assume responsibility for such actions despite the fact that I at no time approved or had knowledge of them" (551). Nixon phrased the issue precisely in his speech of April 29, 1974: "The basic question at issue today is whether the President personally acted improperly in the Watergate matter." *Public Papers of the Presidents of the United States: Richard Nixon, 1974* (Washington, DC: Government Printing Office, 1975), 391.

15. Abraham Lincoln, "To Erastus Corning and Others, June 12, 1863," in *The Writings of Abraham Lincoln*, 8 vols., ed. Arthur Brooks Lapley (New York: G. P. Putnam's Sons, 1906), 6:311–25. Subsequent page references to this source are given in parentheses in the text.

16. Lincoln, of course, chose the arguments he refuted strategically. For example, he did not respond to the argument that the provision for suspension of habeas corpus was in article 1, section 9, suggesting that the suspensory power belonged to Congress, or that granting the government power to suspend habeas corpus is not equivalent to granting that power to the president.

17. Jacob E. Cooke, ed., *The Federalist* (Cleveland: Meridian Books, 1961), 441.

18. James D. Richardson, ed., *A Compilation of the Messages and Papers of the Presidents, 1789–1908*, 11 vols. (Washington, DC: Bureau of National Literature and Art, 1909), 4:190.

19. Richardson, 3:70.

20. Richardson, 3:92–93.

21. Richardson, 4:190.

22. Richardson, 5:618.

23. Richardson, 3:72.

24. Richardson, 5:621.

25. Richardson, 5:620.

26. Richardson, 5:619.

27. Richardson, 4:190.

28. Richardson, 4:193.

29. Richardson, 3:72.

30. Richardson, 3:86.

31. Richardson, 3:91.

32. Richardson, 5:618, 619.

33. Richardson, 5:618.

34. Richardson, 3:76. Andrew Johnson was similarly angered that those who had passed the Tenure of Office Act, which he considered unconstitutional, should also have the power to judge whether his violation of the act was unconstitutional. Hans L. Trefousse, *Andrew Johnson: A Biography* (New York: W. W. Norton, 1989), 321.

35. Richardson, 4:191.

36. Richardson, 5:617–18.

37. Richardson, 5:615.

38. Richardson, 4:193.

39. Richardson, 3:71–72.

40. *Public Papers*, 1974, 391, and *Public Papers*, 1973, 547.

41. "The President's Main Brief in *United States v. Nixon*," in *United States v. Nixon*, ed. Leon Friedman (New York: Chelsea House, 1974), 337–47. Subsequent page references to this source are given in parentheses in the text.

42. *Public Papers*, 1974, 396.

43. Because members of the House are elected every two years, this argument is an indirect appeal to vote out of office those who are endangering the presidency. Because most congressional efforts to charge a president with misconduct require long gestation, it is likely that the people will have an opportunity to act on this appeal. The president can also claim that in the next election, members of the House and Senate will be repudiated by the people should they act unfairly. The potential force of this view is demonstrated by a comparison of the membership of the Congress elected in 1974, following the resignation of Richard Nixon, with that of the Congress elected in 1972: Republicans lost forty-eight House seats and five Senate seats. That

this concern looms large is reflected in John McCain's statement explaining his vote in favor of the impeachment of Bill Clinton:

> As my colleagues across the aisle have so often reminded me, the country does not want the President removed. And, they ask, are we not, first and foremost, servants of the public will? Even if we believe the President to be guilty of the offenses charged, and even if we believe those offenses rise to the level of impeachment, should we risk the national trauma of forcing his removal against the clearly expressed desire of the vast majority of Americans that he should not be removed even if he is guilty of perjury and obstruction of justice?
>
> I considered that question very carefully, and I arrived at an answer by reversing the proposition. If a clear majority of the American people were to demand the conviction of the President, should I vote for his conviction even if I believed the President to be innocent of the offenses he is charged with? Of course not. Neither, then, should I let public opinion restrain me from voting to convict if I determine the President is guilty. (Senator McCain of Arizona, speaking on the trial of William Jefferson Clinton, President of the United States, *Congressional Record* 145, 106th Cong., 1st sess. [February 12, 1999], S 1473)

44. *Public Papers of the Presidents of the United States: William J. Clinton, 1998,* 2 vols. (Washington, DC: Government Printing Office, 1999–2000), 2:1457.
45. *Public Papers,* 1998, 2:1457.
46. *Public Papers,* 1998, 2:1457.
47. *Public Papers,* 1998, 2:1457.
48. *Public Papers,* 1998, 2:1457.
49. *Public Papers,* 1998, 2:1457.
50. *Public Papers,* 1998, 2:1565.

CHAPTER 11: RHETORIC OF IMPEACHMENT

1. James D. Richardson, ed., *A Compilation of the Messages and Papers of the Presidents, 1789–1908,* 11 vols. (Washington, DC: Bureau of National Literature and Art, 1909), 6:730.
2. Richardson, 6:736.
3. Richardson, 6:747.
4. *Public Papers of the Presidents of the United States: Richard Nixon, 1973* (Washington, DC: Government Printing Office, 1974), 547–55.
5. These announcements were made on August 6, 1974; on that date, House minority leader John J. Rhodes (R-AZ) stated at a news conference that he would vote for article 1, charging the president with obstruction of justice. Washington Post, *The Fall of the President* (New York: Dell, 1974), 196.
6. Whether at Haldeman's instigation or not, a CIA operative entered the residence of arrested burglar James McCord shortly after the Watergate break-in and destroyed documents that might have shown a link between McCord and the CIA. Before leaving as CIA director, Richard Helms or-

dered all existing tapes, as well as transcriptions of telephone and in-person conversations, destroyed, including conversations with Nixon, Haldeman, John Ehrlichman, and other White House officials. *Final Report of the Select Committee on Presidential Campaign Activities,* S. Rep. no. 93-981, 93d Cong., 2d sess. (1974), 1127, 1131–32.

7. John R. Labovitz, *Presidential Impeachment* (New Haven, CT: Yale University Press, 1978), 100.

8. Morris B. Schnapper, ed., *Presidential Impeachment: A Documentary Overview* (Washington, DC: Public Affairs Press, 1974), 95.

9. Jacob E. Cooke, ed., *The Federalist* (Cleveland: Meridian Books, 1961), 440.

10. Many Democratic senators shared their Republican colleagues' distaste for President Clinton's conduct. Dianne Feinstein (D-CA), a member of the Senate Committee on the Judiciary, proposed a censure resolution as an alternative to impeachment before and after the Senate trial. The earlier resolution proposed censure on the grounds that the "president of the United States, deliberately misled and deceived the American people, and people in all branches of the United States government" and that his "conduct in this matter is unacceptable for a president of the United States, does demean the office of the president as well as the president himself, and creates disrespect for laws of the land." A longer, more detailed resolution was offered subsequently. See "The President's Acquittal; Senator Feinstein's Motion on Censure," *New York Times,* February 11, 1999, A8.

11. Philip B. Kurland, *Watergate and the Constitution* (Chicago: University of Chicago Press, 1978), 116–17; Hans L. Trefousse, *Andrew Johnson: A Biography* (New York: W. W. Norton, 1989), 328–29.

12. *Supplement to Congressional Globe, Containing the Proceedings of the Senate Sitting for the Trial of Andrew Johnson, President of the United States, Fortieth Congress, Second Session* (Washington City: F. and J. Rives and George A. Bailey, 1868), 450. Subsequent page references to this source are given in parentheses in the text.

13. William M. Goldsmith, *The Growth of Presidential Power: A Documentary History,* 3 vols. (New York: Chelsea House, 1974), 2:1060.

14. The report makes the distinction between the personal and the presidential that we have treated in terms of the nature of the personal apologia. The majority report said, "In approaching a conclusion, we do not fail to recognize two stand-points from which this case can be viewed—the legal and the political. Viewing it from the former, the case upon the law and the testimony fails. Viewing it from the latter, the case is a success. . . . While we acquit him of impeachable crimes, we pronounce him guilty of many wrongs. . . . Judge him politically, we must condemn him." *The Reports of the Committees of the House of Representatives for the First Session of the Fortieth Congress,* 1867 (Washington, DC: Government Printing Office, 1868), 104–5.

15. Goldsmith, 2:1060.

16. Goldsmith, 2:1061.

17. Johnson made this attack on the grounds that Congress did not represent all states in the Union because of its refusal to seat representatives from the states that had seceded.

18. See the speech by Henry Stanbery, one of Johnson's counsel, *Globe*, 368, 371. See also the majority report of the House Committee on the Judiciary in *Reports of the Committees*, 1867. Charles L. Black, Jr., in *Impeachment: A Handbook* (New Haven, CT: Yale University Press, 1974), discusses the problems involved in determining whether an impeachment trial is a "criminal proceeding" (14–19).

19. For a more detailed discussion of this problem, see the book by Edmund G. Ross (R-KS), who cast the deciding vote in the trial: *History of the Impeachment of Andrew Johnson* (Santa Fe, NM: New Mexican Printing Co., 1896), esp. 132–39.

20. *The Federalist*, 446.

21. *The Federalist*, 446.

22. *The Federalist*, 441. On November 29, 1787, James McHenry of Maryland defended the proposed Constitution to the ratifying convention in his home state with assurances that the Senate would debate in a cool, dispassionate manner. Max Farrand, ed., *The Records of the Federal Convention of 1787*, 3 vols. (New Haven, CT: Yale University Press, 1911), 3:148.

23. *The Great Impeachment and Trial of Andrew Johnson, President of the United States* (Philadelphia: T. B. Peterson and Brothers, 1868), 23.

24. "Chief Justice William Rehnquist, Administering the Oath of Impartiality to Members of the U.S. Senate in the Trial of William Jefferson Clinton, President of the United States," *Congressional Record* 145, 106th Cong., 1st sess. (February 4, 1999): P51229.

25. These events are detailed in J. G. Randall, *The Civil War and Reconstruction*, 2nd ed. (Boston: D. C. Heath, 1961), 601–17; and in Kenneth M. Stampp, *The Era of Reconstruction, 1865–1877* (New York: Vintage, 1967), 146–52.

26. *Congressional Globe*, vol. 39, pt. 2:525.

27. Raoul Berger, *Impeachment: The Constitutional Problem* (Cambridge, MA: Harvard University Press, 1973), 274. After the trial, Evarts was confirmed as Johnson's attorney general.

28. The language of the debates in the House was even less restrained. See David Miller DeWitt, *The Impeachment and Trial of Andrew Johnson* (Madison: State Historical Society of Wisconsin, 1967), 363–64. It is noteworthy that in calling Johnson "a common scold," the managers reflect pervasively negative attitudes toward the speech of women.

29. Manager Benjamin F. Butler (R-MA) attempted to use this statement as the basis for challenging Nelson to a duel.

30. Ross, *History of the Impeachment of Andrew Johnson*.

31. Cited in Eric McKitrick, *Andrew Johnson and Reconstruction* (Chicago: University of Chicago Press, 1960), 487 n. 2.

32. *The Trial of Andrew Johnson*, 3 vols. (Washington, DC: Government Printing Office, 1868), 3:30. For other factors affecting the outcome of the trial, see Trefousse, 328–31.

33. See, particularly, Jackson Harrell, B. L. Ware, and Wilmer A. Linkugel, "Failure of Apology in American Politics: Nixon on Watergate," *Communication Monographs* 42 (November 1975): 245–61; and Barry Brummett, "Presidential Substance: The Address of August 15, 1973," *Western Speech Communication* 39 (Fall 1975): 249–59. Comment on some of the administrative processes that led to rhetorical choices is found in Dennis S. Gouran, "The Watergate Cover-Up: Its Dynamics and Its Implications," *Communication Monographs* 43 (August 1976): 176–86.

34. David R. Mayhew, *Congress: The Electoral Connection* (New Haven, CT: Yale University Press, 1974), 106.

35. House Committee on the Judiciary, *Debate on Articles of Impeachment: Hearings of the Committee on the Judiciary, House of Representatives*, 93d Congress, 2d sess., pursuant to H. Res. 803, July 24, 25, 26, 27, 29, and 30, 1974 (Washington, DC: Government Printing Office, 1974), 12. Subsequent page references to this source are given in parentheses in the text.

36. "Sides" here does not refer to parties, but to those who would later vote for and against at least one article of impeachment.

37. Northrop Frye, *The Well-Tempered Critic* (Bloomington: Indiana University Press, 1963), 44–46.

38. Before these events, Charles Black argued that "radio, television, and cameras have no more place in this solemn business than they have in any other trial, and for the same reasons" (19), but his analysis fails to take into account the role of electronic media in legitimating the decision reached in a public proceeding.

39. For reports on the poor newspaper and television coverage of Watergate, see Barry Sussman, *The Great Cover-up: Nixon and the Scandal of Watergate* (New York: Signet, 1974), 134–35; and Timothy Crouse, *The Boys on the Bus: Riding with the Campaign Press Corps* (New York: Random House, 1972), 295–99. Crouse reports a Gallup poll taken around the time of the 1972 election, in which 48% of the American public had never heard of the Watergate affair (295).

40. Frye, 44.

41. Alan F. Westin, "The Case for America," in *United States v. Nixon: The President before the Supreme Court*, ed. Leon Friedman (New York: Chelsea House, 1974), xii.

42. For a timeline of the events leading up to and though the Clinton impeachment trial, see "A Clinton Timeline," *CBS News*, January 12, 2001, http://www.cbsnews.com/stories/2001/01/08/politics/printable262484.shtml (accessed August 16, 2006); and "The President's Acquittal; The Senate Trial: In the End, An Acquittal," *New York Times*, February 13, 1999, A11, http://www.nexis.com/ (accessed August 16, 2006).

43. *Clinton v. Jones*, 520 U.S. 681 (1997).

44. *Public Papers of the Presidents of the United States: William J. Clinton, 1998*, 2 vols. (Washington, DC: Government Printing Office, 1999–2000), 1:111.

45. *Public Papers, 1998*, 2:1457.

46. "The Starr Report: Full Text of Findings Sent to Congress—Part One of Thirteen," *New York Times*, late ed., September 12, 1998, B1, http://www.nexis.com/ (accessed August 10, 2006).

47. "The President's Trial; Article II: Obstruction of Justice," *New York Times*, January 22, 1999, A21, http://www.nexis.com/ (accessed August 10, 2006).

48. "The President's Trial: Weight of History Is 'on All of Us,' Senate Is Told by One of Its Own," *New York Times*, late ed., January 22, 1999, A19, http://www.nexis.com/ (accessed August 10, 2006).

49. "The President's Trial."

50. "The President's Trial."

51. "The President's Trial."

52. "The President's Trial."

53. That likelihood is strengthened by his farewell address, which was a polemic against his enemies; see "The President's Address," *New York Times*, March 4, 1869, 8. The efforts of his counsel to prevent him from responding to the charges against him in interviews or speeches are described in Trefousse, 318–21. Howard P. Nash, Jr., comments, "The trial would all but certainly have ended differently if Johnson, under the tutelage of his counsel, had not conducted himself with the greatest circumspection while it lasted. This surprising behavior almost surely prevented his conviction, . . . for if he had acted in his usual manner in straitened circumstances, it is difficult to doubt that at least one more senator would have voted guilty on some count, particularly as even the Republicans who voted to acquit him detested him personally." *Andrew Johnson: Congress and Reconstruction* (Rutherford, NJ: Fairleigh Dickinson University Press, 1972), 153.

54. S. Michael Halloran, "Doing Public Business in Public," in *Form and Genre: Shaping Rhetorical Action*, ed. K. K. Campbell and K. H. Jamieson (Falls Church, VA: Speech Communication Association, 1978), 119.

55. Halloran, 121.

CHAPTER 12: FAREWELL ADDRESSES

1. Burton Ira Kaufman, ed., *Washington's Farewell Address: The View from the Twentieth Century* (Chicago: Quadrangle, 1969).

2. *Public Papers of the Presidents of the United States: William J. Clinton, 2000–2001*, 3 vols. (Washington, DC: Government Printing Office, 2001–2002), 3:2953.

3. Fred L. Israel, ed., *The State of the Union Messages of the Presidents, 1790–1966*, 3 vols. (New York: Chelsea House, 1967), 3:2994. This quote is taken from Truman's farewell address to Congress.

4. Jean Zaun DeWitt, "The Rhetoric of Induction at the French Academy," *Quarterly Journal of Speech* 69 (November 1983): 413–22.

5. *Public Papers of the Presidents of the United States: Gerald R. Ford III, 1976–1977*, 3 vols. (Washington, DC: Government Printing Office, 1977), 3:2916–26.

6. *Public Papers of the Presidents of the United States: Lyndon B. Johnson, 1968–1969*, 2 vols. (Washington, DC: Government Printing Office, 1969), 2:1263–70.

7. "Radio Address to the Nation," *Public Papers of the Presidents of the United States: Harry S. Truman, 1952–1953* (Washington, DC: Government Printing Office, 1953), 1197–1202; Israel, 3:2993–3010.

8. *Public Papers, 1968–1969*, 2:1350–56. Reagan followed Lyndon Johnson's precedent in addressing leave-taking rhetoric to many groups: "As he enters his final weeks in office, President Reagan has been giving a series of farewell speeches and interviews that amount to his first draft of history, an attempt to defend his record and shape the views of future scholars as they evaluate the events that dominated Washington over the last eight years." Steven V. Roberts, "Some See Smooth Face on History's Rough Draft," *New York Times*, December 29, 1988, 10Y. See also Julie Johnson, "A Grateful Pentagon Says Its Farewell to Reagan," *New York Times*, January 13, 1989, 9Y; and *Weekly Compilation of Presidential Documents* 25, no. 2 (January 12, 1989): 57–58, and (January 16, 1989): 41–45, in addition to his broadcast farewell to the American people.

9. Israel, 2:1318–31.

10. Israel, 1:99.

11. Israel, 1:145–46.

12. Israel, 1:230.

13. Israel, 1:630.

14. Israel, 1:764–72.

15. Israel, 1:850–53.

16. Israel, 2:1511.

17. "The President's Address" [Washington, March 3, 1869], *New York Times*, March 4, 1869, 8. The address is not included in any of the compilations of presidential messages and papers edited by Richardson, although Johnson was still president when it was delivered to the press and did not leave office until noon of the day when it was printed. Some sources state that "it was speeding over the telegraph wires as General Grant was taking the oath in front of the Capitol": George Fort Milton, *The Age of Hate: Andrew Johnson and the Radicals* (New York: Coward-McCann, 1930), 652; Lloyd Paul Stryker, *Andrew Johnson: A Study in Courage* (New York: Macmillan, 1929), 772. However, its dateline and the date of publication in the newspapers document its production during his presidency. Its omission from the official record may be explained by its vituperative character. In the speech, Johnson compares the Reconstruction policies of the radical Republicans to the oppressive acts of the Roman Sylla (presumably Lucius Cornelius Sulla, c. 138–78 B.C.E.) and contends that they were more oppressive of the South than were the

British policies that led to the American Revolution. Hans L. Trefousse writes, "The address was not well received. It was a display of 'bad temper,' commented the *New York Times* [March 4, 1869]. But it was the *New York Herald* [March 4, 1869] that made the most telling observation. 'These parting words of the retiring President might have done very well at some political gathering in Tennessee . . . ,' it wrote. 'But as they stand they smell of chagrin, distrust, ill nature, and bad blood.'" *Andrew Johnson: A Biography* (New York: W. W. Norton, 1989), 352.

18. "Statement at Plains, Georgia, January 22, 1981," *Vital Speeches* 47, no. 9 (February 15, 1981): 260–61.

19. "Remarks on Departure from the White House, August 9, 1974," *Public Papers of the Presidents of the United States: Richard Nixon, 1974* (Washington, DC: Government Printing Office, 1974), 630–32.

20. Farewell Address to the Nation, *Weekly Compilation of Presidential Documents,* 25, no. 2 (January 11, 1989): 56.

21. Recognizing that if they appear to covet the office or its power, their legacies will not be accepted, some presidents have offered special guarantees of impartiality. They aver, as did Ford and Washington, that they look forward to a return to civilian life. They pledge their support to their successors, as did Truman, Johnson, Eisenhower, Nixon, and Carter. Or, with Jackson, they suggest that theirs is the legacy of dying men. Before long, Jackson said, he would pass "beyond the reach of human events and cease to feel the vicissitudes of human affairs": James D. Richardson, ed., *A Compilation of the Messages and Papers of the Presidents, 1789–1908,* 11 vols. (Washington, DC: Bureau of National Literature and Art, 1909), 1:308. This extraordinary warrant was necessary because the legacy embodied in Jackson's farewell had assumed a highly partisan form in his battle over the Bank of the United States. Jackson had to strip his call for recognition of constitutional limits of its partisanship, a move he made by claiming that this was the legacy of a man near death.

22. Samuel R. Driver, *A Critical and Exegetical Commentary on Deuteronomy* (Edinburgh: T. and T. Clark, 1902), 347. The form of the farewell in Deuteronomy was drawn, in turn, from an earlier form, that of ancient treaties defining obligations of suzerain and vassal, which was adapted analogically to the relationship between Israel and Yahweh. What began in Deuteronomy becomes a regular covenanting formulary that recurs in "farewell speeches or speeches made when laying down an office, by men who have taken a definite task of leadership in Israel," such as Joshua (Josh. 23:1–24:28), Samuel (1 Sam. 12), and David (1 Chron. 22 and 29). Gerhard Von Rad, *Deuteronomy: A Commentary* (Philadelphia: Westminster Press, 1966), 22–23.

23. Martin Buber writes that Moses's "personal task was based on the same man receiving the will of God and directing its execution; it is one of the firmest foundations of his work that 'religion' and 'politics' are inseparable." *Moses: The Revelation and the Covenant* (New York: Harper and Brothers, 1946), 199. In Buber's view, Moses was a prophet, but in a special sense, not reflected

in the lives of those who followed him, because he was "that undivided entire person who receives the message and as such endeavors to establish the message in life" (200).

24. *Public Papers, 1968–1969*, 2:1270.

25. *Public Papers, 1976–1977*, 3:2918.

26. *Public Papers, 1976–1977*, 3:2920.

27. *Public Papers of the Presidents of the United States: George H. W. Bush, 1992–1993*, 2 vols. (Washington, DC: Government Printing Office, 1993), 2:2158.

28. *Public Papers, 1992–1993*, 2:2189.

29. *Public Papers, 1992–1993*, 2:2191.

30. *Public Papers, 1992–1993*, 2:2191.

31. *Public Papers, 1992–1993*, 2:2192.

32. *Public Papers, 1992–1993*, 2:2194.

33. *Public Papers, 1992–1993*, 2:2229–30.

34. *Public Papers, 2000–2001*, 3:2952.

35. *Public Papers, 2000–2001*, 3:2953.

36. *Public Papers, 2000–2001*, 3:2953.

37. *Public Papers, 2000–2001*, 3:2953.

38. *Public Papers 2000–2001*, 3:2952.

39. Lyndon Johnson, too, included a detailed legislative agenda in his final annual message because of his desire to ensure the continuation of Great Society programs. However, the inclusion of this agenda interferes with the speech's function as a farewell.

40. Andrew Johnson's extraordinary address vividly illustrates this aim. He characterized his farewell as "a few parting words in vindication of an official course so ceaselessly assailed and aspersed by political leaders, to whose plans and wishes my policy to restore the Union has been obnoxious" ("The President's Address" [Washington, March 3, 1869], 8). Defense of his actions and attacks on the radical Republicans who opposed him overwhelm all other farewell functions. David Warren Bowen, in *Andrew Johnson and the Negro* (Knoxville: University of Tennessee Press, 1989), points out that the address was part of a consistent effort to shape perceptions of the conflict between the president and Congress: "Johnson never changed his basic argument. ... His official address to the people upon leaving office, largely a self-serving defense of his policies, is a perfect example of this fetish-like incantation. The word 'constitution' is repeated no fewer than forty-two times. ... [In its] eleven pages with over 5,000 words, terms referring to the black race—Negro, black, freedmen, or any equivalent—are never used. It was as if four million people had simply ceased to exist and the only real problem between the president and his enemies concerned the Constitution. This perception was no accident; it was the way Johnson consciously defined the situation in his own mind as well as in public statements" (140–41).

41. Farewell Address (January 11, 1989), 56.

42. *Public Papers, 1976–1977*, 3:2926.

43. Richardson, 3:308.

44. Richardson, 1:224.

45. "Remarks, August 9, 1974," 629.

46. *Public Papers of the Presidents of the United States: Dwight D. Eisenhower, 1960–1961* (Washington, DC: Government Printing Office, 1961), 1040.

47. Noel B. Gerson, *The Trial of Andrew Johnson* (New York: Thomas Nelson, 1977), 28–30, 38–39. The most famous were delivered December 18–19, 1860, February 5–6 and July 27, 1861, and January 31, 1862 (Trefousse, 130–31, 135–36, 144–45, 151).

48. Farewell Address (January 11, 1989), 56.

49. *Public Papers, 1952–1953, 1197.*

50. *Public Papers, 1952–1953, 1197.*

51. *Public Papers, 1952–1953, 1197.*

52. *Public Papers, 1952–1953, 1198.*

53. *Public Papers, 1952–1953, 1198.*

54. *Public Papers, 1952–1953, 1198–99.*

55. *Public Papers, 1952–1953, 1202.*

56. *Public Papers, 1952–1953, 1202.*

57. *Public Papers, 1952–1953, 1198.*

58. *Public Papers, 1952–1953, 1200.*

59. *Public Papers, 1952–1953, 1200.*

60. Richardson, 3:301.

61. Richardson, 3:295.

62. Richardson, 3:307.

63. Richardson, 3:304.

64. Dante Alighieri, *La Divina Commedia: Inferno,* "II Canto di Ulisse," bk. 26, 11. 90–142.

65. Several works discuss its composition. See Horace Binney, *An Inquiry into the Formation of Washington's Farewell Address* (Philadelphia: Parry and Macmillan, 1859); and James Thomas Flexner, *George Washington: Anguish and Farewell, 1793–99* (Boston: Little, Brown, 1969), 292–307.

66. Richardson, 1:216.

67. Richardson, 1:222–23.

68. Richardson, 1:217, 218.

69. Richardson, 1:221.

70. Richardson, 1:224.

71. Richardson, 1:215.

72. Richardson, 1:215.

73. Richardson, 1:215.

74. Richardson, 1:218.

75. Richardson, 1:219.

76. Richardson, 1:220.

77. Richardson, 1:219.

78. Richardson, 1:218.

79. Richardson, 1:218.

80. *Public Papers of the Presidents of the United States: Ronald Reagan, 1988–1989*, 2 vols. (Washington, DC: Government Printing Office, 1991), 2:1722.

81. *Public Papers, 1960–1961*, 1039.

82. *Public Papers, 1960–1961*, 1037.

83. *Public Papers, 1960–1961*, 1038.

84. "State of the Union Address, January 9, 1958," *Public Papers of the Presidents of the United States: Dwight D. Eisenhower, 1958* (Washington, DC: Government Printing Office, 1959), 7–9; "Special Message to Congress on Reorganization of the Defense Establishment, April 3, 1958," *Public Papers, 1958*, 274–90.

85. See also "Special Message, April 3, 1958"; "Statement by the President on the Defense Reorganization Bill, May 28, 1958"; "Statement by the President on the Defense Reorganization Bill, July 23, 1958"; and "Statement on Signing Department of Defense Reorganization Act, August 6, 1958," *Public Papers, 1958*, 274–90, 439–43, 564, 597.

86. *Public Papers, 1960–1961*, 1039–40.

87. *Public Papers, 1960–1961*, 1040. Two books add significantly to an understanding of Eisenhower as a rhetor: Martin J. Medhurst, *Dwight D. Eisenhower: Strategic Communicator* (Westport, CT: Greenwood, 1993), and Ira Chernus, *General Eisenhower: Ideology and Discourse* (East Lansing: Michigan State University Press, 2002).

88. *Public Papers, 1960–61*, 1045.

89. "Transcript of President Johnson's Thanksgiving Day Address to the Nation urging 'New Dedication,'" *New York Times*, November 29, 1963.

90. Ronald Reagan, *A Life in Letters* (New York: Simon and Schuster 2003), 833.

91. Andrew Johnson's farewell is a special case. That his angry self-defense failed to bequeath a legacy is evidenced by its omission from Richardson's compilations and by contemporary commentary identifying it as a vindictive, partisan polemic.

92. *Public Papers of the Presidents of the United States: Jimmy Carter, 1980–1981*, 3 vols. (Washington, DC: Government Printing Office, 1981), 3:2891.

93. *Public Papers, 1980–1981*, 3:2893.

94. *Vital Speeches*, 260.

95. *Vital Speeches*, 261.

96. *Vital Speeches*, 261.

97. *Public Papers, 1980–1981*, 3:2890.

98. *Public Papers, 1980–1981*, 3:2891.

99. *Public Papers, 1980–1981*, 3:2892.

100. *Public Papers, 1980–1981*, 3:2891. It is noteworthy that Carter failed to mention what was clearly a singular achievement of his presidency, the signing of the Camp David accords between Egypt and Israel.

101. See *Conversations with Carter*, ed. Don Richardson (Boulder and London: Lynn Rienner, 1998), 252, 256.

102. *Public Papers, 1974*, 627.

103. *Public Papers*, 1974, 627.

104. *Public Papers*, 1974, 627.

105. *Public Papers*, 1974, 627–28.

106. *Public Papers*, 1974, 629.

107. *Public Papers*, 1974, 629.

108. *Public Papers*, 1974, 628. Earlier, he said, "I have concluded that because of the Watergate matter, I *might* not have the support of the Congress that I would consider necessary . . ." (627; emphasis added).

109. *Public Papers*, 1974, 629.

110. House Committee on the Judiciary, *Debate on Articles of Impeachment: Hearings of the Committee on the Judiciary, House of Representatives*, 93d Congress, 2d session, pursuant to H. Res. 803, July 24, 25, 26, 27, 29, and 30, 1974 (Washington, DC: Government Printing Office, 1974). See particularly the opening statements of Jack Brooks (D-TX), M. Caldwell Butler (R-VA), and John Seiberling (D-OH), which explicitly discuss the importance of politicians judging the behavior of another politician.

111. See chap. 5, n. 19.

APPENDIX

1. 299 U.S. 304 (1936).

2. On rare occasions, Congress can speak with a single voice. *In Myers v. the United States*, 327 U.S. 349, 353 (1958), the Supreme Court permitted the attorney general to attack a congressional statute that circumscribed the president's removal power and permitted Senator George Wharton Pepper of Pennsylvania to rebut on behalf of Congress.

3. *In re Neagle*, 135 U.S. 1. 64 (1890).

4. *Field v. People*, 2 Scan. 79 (Ill. 1839).

Index

Made in the USA
Lexington, KY
11 March 2015